T0329632

A WAR ON GLOBAL POVERTY

A War on Global Poverty

THE LOST PROMISE OF REDISTRIBUTION AND THE RISE OF MICROCREDIT

Joanne Meyerowitz

PRINCETON UNIVERSITY PRESS

PRINCETON & OXFORD

Copyright © 2021 by Princeton University Press

Princeton University Press is committed to the protection of copyright and the intellectual property our authors entrust to us. Copyright promotes the progress and integrity of knowledge. Thank you for supporting free speech and the global exchange of ideas by purchasing an authorized edition of this book. If you wish to reproduce or distribute any part of it in any form, please obtain permission.

Requests for permission to reproduce material from this work should be sent to permissions@press.princeton.edu

Published by Princeton University Press
41 William Street, Princeton, New Jersey 08540
6 Oxford Street, Woodstock, Oxfordshire OX20 1TR

press.princeton.edu

All Rights Reserved
ISBN 978-0-691-20633-2
ISBN (e-book) 978-0-691-21997-4

British Library Cataloging-in-Publication Data is available

Editorial: Eric Crahan, Priya Nelson and Thalia Leaf
Production Editorial: Jenny Wolkowicki
Jacket design: Layla Mac Rory
Production: Danielle Amatucci
Publicity: Kate Hensley and Kathryn Stevens
Copyeditor: Maia Vaswani

Jacket art: Weavings by Dharamshi Maheshwari of Gujarat Rann of Kutch, Ningad Harijan Village. Photo, travelib prime / Alamy Stock Photo

This book has been composed in Miller Text

Printed on acid-free paper. ∞

Printed in the United States of America

10 9 8 7 6 5 4 3 2 1

For Pat Swope

CONTENTS

List of Abbreviations · ix

Introduction: From Modernization
to Microcredit   1

PART I   A WAR ON GLOBAL POVERTY

CHAPTER 1   The Trouble with Foreign Aid   15

            "Assaulted by Waves from Left and Right"   18

            The Challenge of World Poverty   29

            Rejecting Trickle Down   36

            Redistribution?   42

CHAPTER 2   Redistribution: South and North   53

            A New International Economic Order?   56

            *"To Satisfy, as a Matter of Urgency,
            the Basic Needs"*   66

            Jimmy Carter's Hunger   78

            An International Tax   85

PART II   HOW WOMEN BECAME
            THE DESERVING POOR

CHAPTER 3   Developing Women   97

            Making Women Modern   99

            The Percy Amendment   108

*"Was This Yet Another Experiment in
Neocolonialism?"*   116

Worldwide WID   123

The Mainstream Appeal   129

CHAPTER 4   Private Developments   140

Beyond Charity   144

Private WID   149

Poor Women as Entrepreneurs   153

The Reaganomics of Global Poverty   160

WID, WAD, GAD   170

PART III   THE MICROCREDIT MOMENT

CHAPTER 5   Macro Debt and Microcredit   183

Dangerous Debt   184

Promising Credit   193

The Grameen Model   200

Empowering Women?   208

EPILOGUE   The Development of Poverty   221

Acknowledgments · 231
Notes · 235
Index · 293

ABBREVIATIONS

ACVFA Advisory Committee on Voluntary Foreign Aid

BRAC Bangladesh Rural Advancement Committee

CD community development

CGAP Consultative Group to Assist the Poorest

CWID Coalition for Women in International Development

DAWN Development Alternatives with Women for a New Era

DGAP Development Group for Alternative Policies

ECLA Economic Commission for Latin America

G-77 Group of 77

GAD gender and development

GNP gross national product

IBRD International Bank for Reconstruction and Development

IDA International Development Association

IFAD International Fund for Agricultural Development

ILO International Labour Organization

IMF International Monetary Fund

IPS Institute for Policy Studies

NCNW National Council of Negro Women

NGO nongovernmental organization

NIEO New International Economic Order

ODC Overseas Development Council

OECD Organisation for Economic
Co-operation and Development

OEF Overseas Education Fund

OPEC Organization of the Petroleum Exporting Countries

PISCES Program for Investment in the Small
Capital Enterprise Sector

RIO Reshaping the International Order

SEWA Self-Employed Women's Association

SODEPAX Joint Committee on Society, Development and Peace

TVA Tennessee Valley Authority

UN United Nations

UNCTAD United Nations Conference on Trade and Development

UNDP United Nations Development Programme

UNEP United Nations Environment Programme

UNICEF United Nations Children's Emergency Fund

USAID United States Agency for International Development

WAD women and development

WCC World Council of Churches

WEP World Employment Programme

WID women in development

WWB Women's World Banking

From Modernization to Microcredit

A poverty curtain has descended right across the face of our world, dividing it materially and philosophically into two different worlds, two separate planets, two unequal humanities—one embarrassingly rich and the other desperately poor.

—MAHBUB UL HAQ, *THE POVERTY CURTAIN*

IN 1976, Michael Harrington traveled to India, Kenya, and Tanzania to witness global poverty. A prolific author with a prophetic bent, Harrington had risen to fame in 1962 with *The Other America*, a book that stunned readers with its searing exposé of poverty in the United States. The book caught the attention of President Kennedy and inspired policy makers in Washington, who invited Harrington to consult on President Johnson's War on Poverty. *The Other America* eventually sold more than a million copies and made Harrington, as the *Village Voice* pronounced, a "vital voice of conscience" on the American stage.[1] Fifteen years later, in 1977, Harrington promoted a different war on poverty. In a new book, *The Vast Majority: A Journey to the World's Poor,* he recounted his travels abroad and brought a global scale to his voice of conscience. "In the nineteen hundred seventies," he wrote, "the government and the people of the United States are turning their backs on the wretched of the earth." Poverty "in the globe's South" had left "great masses of people . . . on the margin of human existence."[2]

With *The Vast Majority*, Harrington joined an impressive array of public figures—including Pope Paul VI, Swedish economist Gunnar Myrdal, and Tanzanian president Julius K. Nyerere—who had turned to "the challenge of world poverty" and asked Americans to address "the widening gap" between the world's rich and the world's poor.[3] In the 1970s United States, a growing concern with global poverty deflected attention from a failing war on domestic poverty and an unpopular war in Vietnam. High-school students went on antipoverty fundraising walkathons, the World Bank called for an end to "absolute poverty," and Congress passed a "New Directions" mandate that aimed to nudge foreign assistance away from Cold War geopolitics and toward aid for the poor.

This book recounts the checkered history of US involvement in the campaigns against global poverty of the 1970s and 1980s. It focuses especially on the attempts in the 1970s to place antipoverty efforts at the center of international development, and on the reformulation of those efforts in the more conservative 1980s. Over the course of two decades, development experts, policy makers, and international officials shifted their vision of economic assistance from the modernization projects funded in the 1960s to the microcredit programs that won acclaim in the 1980s. They moved away from large-scale industrial and infrastructure projects aimed at national economic growth and toward small-scale antipoverty projects aimed at individual enterprise.

Over the same period, they redirected their antipoverty efforts away from men and toward women. As programs and policies shifted from the macro level of the nation to the micro level of the individual, development advocates paid increasing attention to women's everyday economic activities. They gradually turned to women as the economic actors who could lift families and villages out of poverty. In the 1970s, while US conservatives branded impoverished women, especially Black women, within the United States as welfare cheats and irresponsible mothers, development advocates positioned impoverished women overseas as the deserving poor.[4] In the 1980s, as faith in the market impinged on faith in the state, they reimagined poor women as the entrepreneurs who would borrow money, build their businesses, repay their debts, and leave poverty behind.

—————

The campaigns against global poverty belong in a longer history that includes centuries of plans and programs to change economic conditions in the poorer parts of the world. In the twentieth century, these economic interventions came to be called "development." Economists described wealthier industrialized nations as "developed" and poorer nonindustrial nations as "underdeveloped," "less developed," and "developing." They constructed theories and models to develop the undeveloped, and if they had influence, they persuaded policy makers to put their ideas into practice.[5] The programs that ensued consisted of a complicated mix of national self-interest, political power, international rivalry, transnational collaboration, technocratic faith, humanitarian ideals, and social justice commitments. In the United States, experts and policy makers expressed hopes that economic development in Africa, Asia, and Latin America would improve the living conditions of the poor and also expand markets for investment and trade, stabilize friendly regimes, and prevent communist revolution.

In the 1950s and 1960s, development experts had put their faith in multiple versions of "modernization." They promoted schemes that supplied technology, built industry, and constructed infrastructure to boost the productivity of poorer nations, and they experimented with crops and farming techniques to increase the output of foodstuffs. They encouraged civic participation at the village level and insisted on population control to reduce the number of people who taxed the world's resources. The US government played a central role in devising and implementing these plans. But in the late 1960s and early 1970s modernization in its various guises came under fire, tainted by failures, corruption, coercive practices, and environmental damage, and by its close alignment with US power, corporate interests, authoritarian regimes, and Cold War military interventions.

Historians have written excellent accounts of the rise and fall of the US-sponsored modernization programs of the 1950s and 1960s.[6]

But what happened next? Development did not crash to a halt, and it did not leap from modernization to the austere free-market policies of the 1980s. In the 1970s, development experts reframed their work as antipoverty programs. They moved to the left, pushed by social democrats in Europe, socialists in the global South, and religious idealists, all of whom denounced poverty as evil and pointed to the inequities that kept nations and peoples impoverished. With a critical version of economics, they rejected "trickle-down" theories that positioned national economic growth as the primary measure of success, and they called for a redistribution that would benefit the world's poor.

It might seem surprising to point to the Left in the 1970s. In 1976, the author Tom Wolfe characterized the 1970s as the "'me' decade," with a self-absorbed populace retreating en masse from social change, and for a while the phrase stuck.[7] More recently, historians have described the decade as years of rightward turn.[8] With hindsight, it might seem clear that billowing debt in the global South, Augusto Pinochet's coup in Chile, Margaret Thatcher's ascent to power in the United Kingdom, and the growing clout of the Christian Right in the United States portended the coming conservative era. But in the 1970s, those trends and events, significant as they were, had not quashed the quest for change that fueled left and liberal attempts to address inequality. The radical ethos of the 1960s reached into the 1970s, with the spirit of social movements informing at least some facets of law and policy.[9] On the international scene especially, socialism, anticolonialism, economic redistribution, antipoverty, racial justice, and gender equity all had legs in the 1970s, and sometimes they entered and walked the halls of power.

That quest for change included calls to restructure international trade, to meet the basic needs of all the world's citizens by the year 2000, and to levy global taxes to pay for a transfer of resources from the rich to the poor. It also came with a new twist in the politics of gender. In the 1950s and 1960s, development experts had shown minimal interest in women, except as excessive breeders who needed to curtail their reproduction or uneducated mothers who needed help in rearing their children. They offered technical advice, vocational training, and jobs primarily to men. Over the course of the 1970s, they revised their views. An international "women in development" movement called for gender equity and saw impoverished women as potential earners. Its supporters pushed for programs to give women income-earning work beyond the piecemeal craft sales that some development plans already promoted. They asked for a fundamental reconsideration of who and what development entailed.

In the 1970s, the left-leaning development advocates had widespread impact, including on US policy. In the US government, liberals searched for politically palatable ways to win support for foreign aid. They wanted to disarm their critics on both the left and right, and they hoped that the moral inflection of the antipoverty cause would have greater public appeal than the technocratic monotone of modernization. In the Foreign Assistance Act of 1973, they codified their new approach with a legislative mandate to reorient foreign aid toward the poor and an amendment that required the inclusion of women.[10] But in the US government, the liberals who fought for foreign aid faced constraints, and sometimes also their own half-hearted commitment. International and domestic politics, the stagnating economy, and conservative opposition diluted and washed out the more ambitious antipoverty proposals. International development was (and is) a tangled thicket of politics, economics, morality, justice, and condescending benevolence.

In 1980, with the election of Ronald Reagan, US antipoverty advocates tamped down their expectations, but did not relinquish them entirely. Some resisted the cooler political climate; others accommodated to it. For the most part, they retreated from their more radical calls for structural change in the international economy and large-scale transfer of resources from the wealthier to the poorer nations. They looked for funds to implement small-scale projects in cities and villages, and they ramped up their interest in women. Microcredit—with its tiny loans to the poor for building business enterprise—seemed to offer an antipoverty approach tailored for wide appeal and custom fit for the limited prospects of the era.

Microcredit came to prominence in the same years that an international debt crisis devastated the economies of dozens of poorer nations. The notion that loans to poor people would alleviate poverty rose, in other words, just when loans to poorer nations dragged them down toward bankruptcy. But in some ways the proffered solutions for nations resembled those for individuals. The World Bank and the International Monetary Fund instituted structural adjustment policies that extended loans to indebted nations only if they promised policy changes that would introduce free-market ideals and cut government spending. In a similar vein, microcredit provided loans to the poor in return for market-based activities and fiscal discipline in investing, borrowing, and saving.

With the rising interest in the smallest enterprises, and in conjunction with the global women's movement, development experts devised microcredit programs that extended loans to indigent women. Women, they claimed, saved money, cared for their children, and repaid their loans, while men wasted their income on alcohol, tobacco, and prostitutes. Women, they now suggested, were better investments than men.

This book looks primarily at development advocates—economists, other social scientists, policy makers, officials, and activists who worked in government, international institutions, foundations, universities, nongovernmental organizations (NGOs), and think tanks—and asks how they attempted to address global inequality. It picks up the story of development at the moment when most histories leave off, and tracks the transnational circulation of ideas and their impact in the United States.[11] It does not focus on US development policy in a particular region of the world or offer in-depth assessments of specific development projects. Rather, it follows the trends in development thought that found their way into US policy and economic assistance programs and shows us a neglected genealogy that extended, and then withdrew, the promise of global redistribution.

In the 1970s and 1980s, the United States did not start the war on global poverty or take the lead in fighting it. One aim of this book is to place US programs and policies in international context; that is, to study the United States and at the same time decenter it. In the 1950s and 1960s, US economists and policy makers had played a critical part in constructing development programs. The American economist Walt Rostow, to give the most obvious example, had an outsized role in theorizing modernization. But from the start, development was an international project with a global network of experts who devised, circulated, and debated competing theories and models.[12] In the 1970s, the United States was still a superpower with major sway in international affairs, but it was no longer in the vanguard, if it ever had been, of the transnational conversations on development. In some respects the US campaigns against global poverty borrowed from US domestic policy, most notably from Johnson's War on Poverty.[13] But in the 1970s and 1980s the United States imported ideas and programs as much as it exported them.[14]

The chapters that follow point to a number of informal ambassadors or "influencers" who came from outside the United States and had unusual clout within it. In our social-media-saturated culture today, "influencers" are public figures who promote products. In this book, the "influencers" (a term used now, but not then) are public figures who promoted policy. Barbara Ward, a British author, and Mahbub ul Haq, a Pakistani economist, shaped the campaign against global poverty. Ester Boserup, a Danish economist, played a formative role in launching the international "women in development" movement, and Ela Bhatt, an Indian activist, advanced programs for self-employed women in the informal economy. Muhammad Yunus, a Bangladeshi economist, made microcredit a worldwide phenomenon. All of them, and others as well, knew how to sell their ideas in the United States. They developed connections with people in power; they influenced institutions, including, among others, the United Nations (UN), the US government, the World Bank, and the Ford Foundation; and they created networks of development experts who joined them in their efforts. Within the United States, they helped shape policy and made the multiple sources (and geographic range) of development thinking harder to ignore.[15]

More generally, this is a history of how left-leaning economists, postcolonial leaders, and feminists, all renegades of sorts, protested inequities in development programs. Some of them worked with government agencies, international organizations, and foundations, and some established their own NGOs. Many of them worked with research institutions outside the United States—the Institute of Development Studies at the University of Sussex, the Dag Hammarskjöld Foundation, and the International Labour Organization, for example—and incubated development plans that had an impact on US policy. In the 1970s, those who had entered established institutions introduced what the Hammarskjöld Foundation labeled "another development," an alternative approach that attempted to move beyond colonial hierarchies and Cold War rivalries.[16] They foregrounded the issues of poverty, public services, fair trade, redistribution, and equity rather than economic growth, and they moved toward the human metrics of life expectancy, literacy, and health, to replace, supersede, or at least accompany the economism of gross national product (GNP), per capita income, population statistics, and agricultural yield. They tried, with some success, to institute change. But from the start they also encountered resistance and saw their bolder ideas for redistribution and equity ignored, underfunded, coopted, and reshaped.

The advocates of "another development" included (and demanded inclusion of) experts from the global South. The paired words "developed" and "developing" or "traditional" and "modern" had replaced the racialized language of "savage" and "civilized" or "Christian" and "heathen." In general, in the late twentieth century, development experts across the political spectrum avoided discussions of race. But the race-blind vocabulary of economics could not hide the obvious: most of the "developing" nations were inhabited by people of color and most of the "developed" nations were majority White.[17] "Another development" embraced an inclusive, cosmopolitan vision and had some success in fostering it. Over the course of the 1970s and 1980s, the center of gravity in international development circles shifted subtly but perceptibly from North to South. International conferences and commissions, once dominated by Americans and Europeans, responded to demands for inclusion from those who came from poorer nations, and economists and officials from the global South formed their own organizations and think tanks. Nonetheless, those involved in the expanded networks sustained the faith that "developed" was inherently better than "developing," and even with global participation, they maintained the technocratic hierarchies in which educated professionals could figure out what was best for the far-flung cities and villages that they hoped to change.

In some ways, the new generation of development experts added layers onto, rather than replacing, older programs and policies. (In the field of development, it seems, nothing is wholly new.) They built on earlier programs aimed, for example, at rural productivity, women's labor, and credit for farmers, and they reiterated and reanimated earlier demands for inclusion from the global South.[18] But in the 1970s, they also challenged what had become the conventional wisdom in their professional circles. Their repeated repudiation of trickle-down economics, their collective retreat from Cold War rhetoric, their insistent turn to development for the most impoverished, their specific plans to end the worst of poverty within a generation, and the high priority they came to place on increasing women's income marked departures from the past. Equally important, they understood themselves as game changers who hoped to rewrite the rules of development for a new era.

The results were decidedly mixed. In the United States, the attention to global poverty inspired some projects that helped the poor, including poor women, and others that floundered. By the end of the 1980s, US development officials were seeking greater collaboration with experts and organizations from the global South, but they retained their commitment to US national interests. They cooperated selectively with those who knew how to court them, and they molded their programs to fit the changing political parameters of Washington as well as those of the wider world. Along the way, a global redistribution—the transfer of resources from the wealthy to the poor—was lost, and so was the goal of ending poverty by the turn of the century.

———

This book is divided into three parts. It begins with two chapters on the war on global poverty in the 1970s. The next two chapters show how women became the deserving poor, and the final chapter and the epilogue provide a history of the early microcredit movement. The three parts could be read independently, but taken together they relate a more complex history. The war on global poverty provides critical context for understanding why development experts turned their attention to women as "income generators" in the 1970s, and the rise of microcredit in the 1980s allows us to see how the growing interest in women's economic activities sustained the war on global poverty in a more conservative time. Some parts of the book will be more familiar to historians of development, and others more familiar to historians of global feminism or scholars of microcredit. The chapters are written, I hope, so that readers without background in these fields will gain some fundamental understanding of their history, and readers steeped in any or all of the fields will also learn something new in every chapter and see interconnections they had not seen before.

Chapter 1, "The Trouble with Foreign Aid," shows how and why development economists rejected an earlier generation of development plans, especially the trickle-down economics that presumed national economic growth would benefit the poor. As critics discredited foreign aid, a global antipoverty movement, inspired in part by religious ideals and left-leaning activism, made its way into US legislation and World Bank policies. In the government and the Bank, calls for redistribution came conjoined with an ongoing faith in economic growth and market-based solutions.

Chapter 2, "Redistribution: South and North," turns to the late 1970s and proposals that aimed to redress inequities in the global economy. The New International Economic Order (NIEO), a UN declaration written and backed by leaders of the global South, asked for fundamental changes in the patterns of trade that subordinated the poorer nations. The NIEO won support from the US Left but not from the US government or the World Bank, both of which came to advocate programs to meet the "basic needs" of the world's poorest. At the end of the 1970s, some influential development experts proposed a global tax to fund the transfer of resources that the NIEO and basic needs programs would have required. But a global tax was an aspirational gambit in the late 1970s, and even less likely in the 1980s.

In their early articulations, the war on global poverty, the NIEO, and the basic needs approach had almost nothing to say about women. In response, an international "women in development" (WID) movement pushed economists and policy makers to consider women seriously in their plans to address the poor. Chapter 3, "Developing Women," traces the WID movement in the 1970s, including the Percy amendment that committed the US government to integrating women into its foreign aid programs. In the United States, the women who supported the WID movement ranged politically from Republican to Marxist. With the rise of a global feminist movement, they all wanted equity for women, but they disagreed, sometimes forcefully, on what development and equity meant. In the US government, the Ford Foundation, and international organizations, they won clout by building on the concerns—productivity, poverty, and population control—of mainstream development experts.

Chapter 4, "Private Developments," follows the privatization of development and the rising interest in women. In the 1970s and 1980s, a number of US-based international charities and private organizations moved from short-term disaster relief to longer-term programs that aimed to alleviate poverty. The US government funded NGOs to undertake such antipoverty development. With the urging of the WID movement and with a new interest in the poorest workers in the informal economy, more of those projects focused on women. The "NGOization" of development took off in the 1970s and continued after the election of Ronald Reagan in 1980. The chapter uses one NGO, the Overseas Education Fund, to show how private organizations refashioned their women's projects as "business development" to align with the policies of the Reagan administration. But not all NGOs steered to the right. A more radical WID movement flourished outside the government, especially in the global South.

Microcredit combined the concerns with women and poverty, and promised a new approach to those who were disillusioned with state-led planning, large-scale public projects, and top-down modernization schemes. Chapter 5, "Macro Debt and Microcredit," asks how credit came to the forefront of development plans in the 1980s, the very years when the overextension of credit was creating a global crisis in debt. Microcredit seemed to avoid the problems with funding that stymied other antipoverty schemes. Its calls for self-empowerment appealed to a wide swath—left and right—of the political spectrum, and it democratized finance by offering loans to the poor people whom conventional banks routinely excluded. But it backed away from redistribution. Through tiny loans to women, it professed a faith in capital investment, even at the smallest scale, as the route to prosperity, and at the same time it deepened surveillance through fiscal discipline at the micro level of everyday life.

The epilogue, "The Development of Poverty," moves to the later career of microcredit and suggests how the war on global poverty of the 1970s and 1980s has shaped—and limited—the parameters of antipoverty programs and women's "empowerment" in more recent years.

———————

A note on terminology: I have avoided the value-laden terms "developed" and "developing" to characterize nations, and I have also eschewed "third world," which is rarely employed today. Instead, I use other imperfect terms: "poorer nations," "global South," and sometimes "postcolonial" to refer to the nations—mostly in Africa, Asia, and Latin America—that received foreign aid, and "wealthier nations" and "global North" to refer to noncommunist donor countries, mostly western European nations and the United States, Canada, Australia, and Japan. These terms are still, unfortunately, homogenizing, as are references to poor, indigent, impoverished, or destitute people. "Poor people" are not an ethnic group or unified class; they do not share customs, traditions, community, or politics. And "poorer" nations too, of course, had and have significant variations among them and within them. The use of "poorer" and "wealthier" nations tends to erase the enduring poverty within the wealthier nations and the entrenched elites within the poorer ones. "Poorer," "wealthier," "global South," and "global North" are convenient terms in use today, but like their earlier counterparts they carry their own problematic connotations and fail to capture the heterogeneous complexity of the world in which we live. I ask my readers to keep these caveats in mind as they read this book.

PART I

A War on Global Poverty

—————◆—————

What matters today, the issue which blocks the horizon, is the need for a redistribution of wealth.

—FRANTZ FANON, *THE WRETCHED OF THE EARTH*

CHAPTER ONE

The Trouble with Foreign Aid

IN HIS 1961 inaugural address, President John F. Kennedy called attention to the world's poor. "To those people in the huts and villages of half the globe struggling to break the bonds of mass misery," he promised "our best efforts to help them help themselves . . . not because the communists may be doing it, not because we seek their votes, but because it is right."[1] In his first year in office, Kennedy established the Peace Corps to send American volunteers overseas, the Alliance for Progress to promote economic growth in Latin America, and the United States Agency for International Development (USAID) to provide economic assistance to the poorer nations of the world. Over the course of a decade, the new agencies pursued a variety of "modernization" approaches. They built dams, power plants, and highways, dispersed high-yield seeds in what came to be called the "green revolution" in food production, and encouraged villagers overseas to participate as active citizens in "community development" plans. None of these modernization schemes was new in the 1960s, but taken together they pointed to a pervasive optimism that the United States could export infrastructure, technical expertise, and democratic processes and thereby develop the "underdeveloped" nations of the world.

Within a few years the optimism had vanished. In late 1961, the UN, inspired by Kennedy, had pronounced the 1960s the "development decade." In 1966, George D. Woods, president of the World Bank, worried that it would instead "recede into history as a decade of disappointment."[2] In the second half of the 1960s, development programs were under attack and on the decline. Large-scale infrastructure projects had created some monuments to modernity, but they had, by all accounts, failed to make a serious dent in global inequities. The high-yield seeds of the "green revolution" had benefited larger landowners who could afford irrigation and fertilizer, and displaced landless and small-holding farmers. Community development programs, too, had reinforced the local hierarchies in which powerful landlords exploited peasants. Development projects had increased the debt and impinged on the sovereignty of postcolonial states, and they had diverted funds to authoritarian leaders at the expense of the poor.[3] In Kennedy's "huts and villages," and in cities as well, poverty remained unquestionably rampant.

The corrosive disappointment reached beyond the limits of specific programs. By the early 1970s, scholars had repudiated modernization theories, which had provided the intellectual underpinnings of Kennedy's foreign aid. They disputed the notion that the United States stood at the apex of development, providing a universal model for modernizing the world. They argued against the theorists who imagined that infrastructure or capital-intensive industry could jump-start the economies of poorer nations into self-sustained growth, they pointed to the environmental damage caused by unquestioned faith in technology, and they exposed the ways that economic development involved manipulation, coercion, and upheaval.[4]

For the American public, too, optimism sank. With its bombings, napalm, massacres, and daily death tolls, the war in Vietnam deflated the fantasy of US benevolence overseas. Economic assistance seemed to drag the United States into international muddles, buttress repugnant armed interventions, and bolster repressive regimes. And when the domestic war on poverty sputtered and when inflation rose and the trade deficit grew, fewer claimed that the US economy stood as the yardstick for prosperity in the rest of the world. Money spent on foreign aid, some critics complained, only contributed to "chronic deficits" in the United States. "The

Americans," the *Economist* reported, "bogged down in Vietnam, frustrated in the search for quick solutions, long for . . . disengagement." In this inauspicious climate, support for foreign aid dwindled and the funding for economic development collapsed. In 1963, the US government spent $3.3 billion (in constant dollars, indexed to 1961) on development assistance; ten years later the figure (again in constant dollars) had dropped to $1.8 billion. The United States, which had once given more per capita than any other nation, now ranked twelfth in per capita giving among the sixteen noncommunist nations that contributed substantially to nonmilitary foreign aid.[5]

In the late 1960s and early 1970s, advocates of foreign aid scrambled in response. They conducted studies, held conferences, drafted legislation, and reformulated policies. They were pushed to the left by international protests that cast aid as imperialism and attacked from the right for wasting money overseas. As they wended their way through the rocky terrain, they crafted a new orthodoxy that relied less on Cold War arguments about national security and more on ethical arguments about the injustice of inequality and the immorality of deprivation. In the early 1970s, they vented their frustrations with the failures of modernization and embraced a growing global antipoverty movement.

In a striking reorientation of development discourse, they turned their attention to projects that aimed to benefit "the poorest of the poor." They focused less on building the economies of poorer nations from the top down and more on lifting the poorest people in the poorer nations out of the worst of poverty. Most crucially, they rejected trickle-down economics. They disputed the prevalent models in which national economic metrics indicated on-the-ground progress in the fight against global poverty. Economic growth, they conceded, might not help the poor. If developing the nation did not reach the neediest, then development programs would have to shift their scale to the local level.

Soon the US government, the World Bank, and others joined the campaigns against global poverty. In Congress, government agencies, and international institutions, various officials repeated the repudiation of trickle-down economics and expressed a growing interest in targeting poverty directly. But in the mainstream institutions the promise of redistribution could go only so far. In new development programs, officials would not agree to any significant commitment to reallocation of resources. Instead they focused on redirecting development programs to address the labor and technologies of the rural poor. They continued to promote a "politics of productivity," less at the national level and more at the village level, less in industry and more in agriculture.[6] Still, they helped promote the new consensus, repeated again and again in the collaborative networks of development economists and policy makers: trickle-down economics had failed. They placed their faith instead in small-scale local projects that addressed the poor.

"Assaulted by Waves from Left and Right"

In 1966, when George Woods despairingly warned that development could devolve into disappointment, he hoped to reverse the decline. A year later, at an informal weekend meeting in England, he hatched a plan with a small and clubby group of like-minded foreign aid advocates. Organized by Barbara Ward, a prominent British author and popular economist, and William Clark, the head of Britain's Overseas Development Institute, the group turned to the Marshall Plan of the late 1940s for their inspiration. Earlier (and later) foreign aid advocates had frequently invoked the Marshall Plan as an ideal and a model. They remembered how the United States had contributed billions of dollars to rebuild the war-torn nations of Europe, and they wanted the United States and Europe to make similar commitments to the poorer nations of the world. They knew, of course, that industrial nations decimated by war were not the same as agricultural nations that exported natural resources and imported manufactured goods. Economic recovery was not economic development. Nonetheless, they used the Marshall Plan as an evocative touchstone to imagine another massive infusion of funds. As Clark remembered it, "all of us . . . had been touched enormously by the Marshall Plan, and our enthusiasm for something similar was really one of the prime things in our approach." The weekend confab proposed a commission, similar to the one in 1947 that had drafted the details of the European recovery plan. Shortly after, at a speech in Stockholm, Woods made the proposal public with a call for an international committee of recognized experts—a "grand assize"—that would investigate and report on the past and future of development aid.[7]

The following year, when Robert S. McNamara replaced Woods as World Bank president, he took up the baton. He invited Lester B. Pearson, former Canadian prime minister and Nobel Prize winner, to head the Commission on International Development. In 1969, the commission released its report, *Partners in Development.* "The widening gap between the developed and developing countries," it stated in its opening sentence, "has become the central issue of our time." The report acknowledged that "the climate surrounding foreign aid programs is heavy with disillusion and distrust," and it called, as others had earlier, for a renewed commitment to economic assistance to poorer nations. Donors, it claimed, had expected "too much too soon" from their contributions. Now they needed to give again and give more. The report hoped to reinvigorate the optimistic vision of a world made better through foreign aid.[8]

From the 1950s on, those who endorsed US foreign aid had made three key arguments—political, economic, and humanitarian—in its favor.[9] The political argument claimed that poverty overseas undermined US security. In this view, people in poorer nations were discontented and potentially violent. But with generous economic aid the United States could win friends, calm the restless poor, stabilize the regimes of allies, and thereby reduce threats to US political interests. More specifically, advocates for economic assistance saw it as a key way to court postcolonial nations and prevent them from turning to communism. At its crudest, the political argument saw foreign aid as a tool for Cold War hegemony. In 1962, for example, Kennedy bluntly told an audience, foreign aid "is a method by which the United States maintains a position of influence and control around the world." The Pearson report, though, took a decidedly softer approach. "Cooperation for development," it conceded, could "establish or strengthen a friendly political relationship." But it warned against using aid for "short-term political advantage."[10]

The economic argument posited that "underdeveloped" economies impeded the expansion of markets, food supplies, trade, and investment. Foreign assistance, it claimed, would bring poorer nations further into the global economy and thereby advance economic growth by creating goods, consumers, and investment opportunities for wealthier nations as well as poorer ones. On an ideological level, the economic argument reflected an abiding belief that expanding capitalism would benefit everyone. On a grubbier plane, it appealed to those who hoped to profit from the business of aid to impoverished nations. The US policy known as "tying" bound recipient nations to spend economic assistance funds on American products and services, thus guaranteeing that substantial sums redounded to US contractors, shippers, farmers, and manufacturers. Here the Pearson report supported "enlightened and constructive self-interest" but backed away from any appeal to naked gain. With a win-win vision of capitalism, it found that all nations could benefit from the "fullest possible utilization of all the world's resources" and supported "the general increase in international trade which would follow international development." But it stated outright that "development will not normally create, nor should it be expected to create, immediate economic windfalls for a donor country." It recommended gradual change in "a sequence of steps leading to progressive untying."[11]

The humanitarian argument depicted poverty as a wrong, an evil, and a source of human misery, and presented foreign assistance as a moral route to ending it. This argument appeared frequently in the public speeches of politicians, the popular writings of development experts, and the funding appeals of charities. It sometimes served as a rhetorical veneer for self-serving policies, but it also reflected conviction. As Didier Fassin has written recently, humanitarianism, even at its most sincere, veers toward a condescending paternalism, "always directed from above to below, from the more powerful to the weaker, the more fragile, the more vulnerable." But it can also lean in the direction of social justice, solidarity, and redistribution in the face of inequities.[12] Even hard-core realists, who saw economic aid primarily as a way to advance US interests, responded on occasion to various moral claims. The Pearson report, too, placed its bet in the humanitarian corner. In answer to the question "why aid?" its "simplest answer" was "the moral one." It echoed Kennedy's inaugural address in posing foreign aid as "right": "It is only right for those who have to share with those who have not." The report spoke of "world community," "international cooperation," and mutual obligation, and asked wealthier nations to refuse "to tolerate the extreme and shameful disparity in standards of life."[13]

The Pearson report advanced a long list of recommendations, including more international trade with better terms for developing nations, more private foreign investment, and support for debt relief, population control, and international organizations. But it focused at heart on increasing foreign aid with greater commitments from wealthier nations. It insisted that foreign aid had already contributed to economic progress in the poorer nations, and it made a politic call, as one reporter stated, for "more, more, more." Pearson himself told a journalist that he saw the report in part as "a Methodist sermon" directed especially at the United States, which had placed foreign aid low on its list of priorities. He had deliberately stacked the commission with government officials, businessmen, and economists from the wealthier nations. Only two of the eight commissioners came from nations that received foreign assistance, and none came from Africa or Asia. At their first meeting, Pearson told his fellow commissioners that he had selected them in a "conscious choice to preserve the [commission's] credibility in donor countries."[14]

For the most part, US pundits admired the report but considered it unsurprising. Its calls for change echoed what others had said earlier. An editorial in the *Washington Post* noted that the report adopted a tone intended to "stimulate," not to "offend or discourage." One reviewer found that the report had "little in the way of serious analytical content." Instead, it aimed, a different reviewer claimed, to "reassure donor countries that they did not participate in vain." As a British commentator wrote, the report attempted to reach "hard-bitten, basically conservative, politicians and senior civil servants . . . of the West and . . . disillusioned aid administrators." To keep it palatable to its intended readers, the report subsumed its occasional mentions of significant change—on, say, restructuring land ownership—deep within the text "as one buries worm powders in chocolates for dogs."[15]

Despite (or maybe because of) its inoffensive flavor, the Pearson report had little immediate impact in the United States. Among its dispirited allies was the British author Barbara Ward, who had played an unusually central role in US economic assistance since the 1950s. An Oxford University graduate, Ward established her reputation first in the United Kingdom as an author, an editor of the *Economist*, and a BBC radio personality, and then won international acclaim for her freelance writing on foreign affairs. In the 1950s, she lived mostly in Ghana, where her husband, Robert G. A. Jackson, a UN official, worked as an economic advisor on the construction of the Volta River dam. She also established a part-time home in the United States. In the late 1950s and through most of the 1960s, with funding from the Carnegie Foundation, she spent winters and springs in Cambridge, Massachusetts, as a visiting lecturer at Harvard. She was already known in US academic circles, with honorary degrees from Smith College in 1949 and Harvard in 1957. A liberal anticommunist and devout Catholic, Ward's writings and speeches positioned her as a social democratic, moralist advocate of economic assistance. By the 1960s, she was hobnobbing regularly with policy makers, UN leaders, and Vatican officials.[16]

In popular books, magazine articles, and newspaper opinion pieces, Ward pushed insistently for greater commitment to foreign aid. She made the humanitarian case for aid and conjoined it neatly with arguments that appealed to national self-interest. In her 1962 best seller, *The Rich Nations and the Poor Nations*, she popularized the modernization theory in which poorer nations needed "a 'big push' to get the economy off the launching-pad and into orbit." The phrase "big push" came from a 1943 article by economist Paul Rosenstein-Rodan, but Ward gave it the space-age twist.[17] Like others, she exhorted the wealthier nations to contribute to foreign aid in the same way that the United States had spent billions of dollars, via the Marshall Plan, in a big push to rebuild the decimated nations of postwar Western Europe.

Ward was a smart popularizer with a penchant for stylish rhetorical flourish, and she was also a charmer who knew how to influence men in power. She personally advised an array of public officials, including presidential candidate and UN ambassador Adlai Stevenson, UN secretary-general U Thant, Presidents Kennedy and Johnson, and World Bank presidents Woods and McNamara. Johnson claimed that *The Rich Nations and the Poor Nations* inspired him. "I read it," he said, "like I do the Bible." Johnson's wife Lady Bird recalled that "Lyndon listened" to Ward, "something he doesn't always do, especially to women."[18] Ward drafted speeches for Johnson as well as for Stevenson, Woods, and Vice President Hubert Humphrey. In fact, it was Ward who drafted Woods's lyrical speech that called for the "grand assize," which led to the Pearson commission. She also wrote parts of the Pearson report's introduction and worked on Pearson's speech announcing its release.[19]

By the end of the 1960s, Ward had taken a position as the Albert Schweitzer Professor of International Economic Development at Columbia University. The Economics Department rejected the appointment, which the state of New York funded, because, as one professor put it, Ward was "not really a scholar doing original research." But Ward won the chair anyway when Columbia's School of Business agreed to host her.[20] From that perch she organized a major conference to publicize the Pearson report and grapple with its findings. Ward sensed rebellion in the air. In 1969, she had attended an "eye-opener" conference and told a colleague afterwards that she had seen the "radicalization of Latin America" and connected it to "American student disgust." Startled by the protests of a younger generation, she kept her eyes peeled. Before she sent out invitations to her conference, she consulted with left-leaning development economists at the Institute of Development Studies at the University of Sussex and asked them to help her find participants beyond the "old hands and predictable results." She ended up with a broad mix of "'everybody' in the field," including "younger 'out of the box' thinkers" as well as top officials, renowned scholars, and behind-the-scenes movers and shakers.[21] And in so doing, she managed to organize a major international (and not just regional) development conference that included significant numbers of economists from the global South.

With funds from the Ford Foundation, the World Bank, and others, the Columbia Conference on International Economic Development met for a full week in February 1970. The event turned into a lengthy critique of foreign aid as usual and the Pearson report that supported it. For the first few days, more than one hundred specialists from thirty-nine nations, mostly academics, convened in Williamsburg, Virginia, and then for the weekend several dozen

FIGURE 1.1. The British author and popular economist Barbara Ward (right)
with Lady Bird Johnson at a reception on the White House lawn, 1965.
Ward was an ardent and influential advocate of antipoverty foreign aid.
(Francis Miller/The LIFE Picture Collection/Getty Images)

additional economists, policy makers, and administrators joined
them at Columbia University.[22] Instead of the expected "tedium
of international conferences," the days in Williamsburg were, one
participant claimed, "exciting" with "lively controversy," and the

follow-up at Columbia revealed "a positive chasm" that separated "the traditional liberal approach to development and aid" from "the radicalism of the new generation of academics."[23]

Toward the end of the conference, a few of the participants met in a hotel room and crafted, at Ward's suggestion, a document known as the Columbia Declaration, and most of the conference attendees signed it. The declaration acknowledged "a deep sense of frustration in the developing countries" and painted "a more pessimistic picture" of trade, development, and aid. It claimed that the Pearson report's recommendations, tailored to appeal to public opinion in the wealthier nations, "fall short of what is required." It asked for "massive increases" in aid, especially to the poorest nations, aiming for "a minimum average per capita income of $400" by the year 2000 and a "focus on the living standards of the bottom quarter of each country's population." The declaration also contested trade policies—tariffs, for example—that benefited wealthier nations and harmed poorer ones, and pushed for changes, including "income distribution" and "land and tax reforms," within developing nations. But the short declaration only hinted at policy; more definitively, it voiced dissent.[24]

The conference and the declaration marked a turning point in international development discourse. As one participant noted, "One could almost see the shifting of ideas taking place at the conference." More radical voices expressed impatience with the timidity of the Pearson report, the inequities in the distribution of wealth, and the postcolonial hierarchies that development programs had failed to address. Between the weekend in 1967 when he had hosted the informal meeting that led to the Pearson report and the drafting of the Columbia Declaration in 1970, William Clark had changed jobs from head of Britain's Overseas Development Institute to Robert McNamara's right-hand man at the World Bank. When the Pearson report came out, he remembered, he thought it was "very good"; in retrospect, though, he saw it as "the last shout of the traditional values." Walt Rostow, a chief intellectual architect of Kennedy's modernization programs, had a somewhat similar take. He spoke at the Columbia conference but did not sign the declaration. In a later recounting, he positioned the declaration as part of a "revolt against the perceived inadequacies of development doctrines." "A good many analysts and commentators," he wrote, found the Pearson report "too modest and conventional."[25]

In its critique of the Pearson report, the Columbia conference reflected a gnawing unease with the practice of foreign aid. As the *Washington Post* noted, it also highlighted "the increasing political sensitivities of the poor world." For the most part, participants from the global South endorsed more economic assistance, but they also "warned that their government[s] would tolerate less advice and less interference." According to the reporter, an expert from the South stated directly, "We'll take the cash; you keep the advice."[26] But at least a few radicals favored refusing aid entirely. Samir Amin, an Egyptian Marxist economist, captured the critique when he stated that foreign aid supported "the present structures of inequality." Amin signed the Columbia Declaration, but he also posed a deeper challenge to the liberal commitment to capitalism. If the global economy was already stacked against the poorer nations, then encouraging their integration into existing markets— through aid and trade—only maintained the dominance of wealthier nations. "There is not the shadow of a doubt," Amin wrote, that aid, in this case to Africa, "was intended to maintain political, state, and economic structures inherited from colonial days."[27]

Leftists around the globe joined Amin in condemning foreign assistance as imperialism in new clothes. Where the Pearson report suggested that poverty persisted because the poorer nations had been "left behind by the technological revolution," leftists argued instead that poverty endured because the rich nations still exploited the poor ones.[28] The British radical Teresa Hayter published a book with the stark title *Aid as Imperialism*. Aid, she wrote, was "a concession by the imperialist powers to enable them to continue their exploitation of the semi-colonial countries." In Latin America and elsewhere, leftist scholars developed dependency theory, which pointed to the ongoing economic systems that kept poorer nations subordinated to wealthier ones. By extracting raw materials and paying little for them, by exploiting labor overseas, and by charging high prices for exported manufactured goods, the predatory capitalism of the developed nations created, preserved, and profited from "underdevelopment" in the global South. In this view, foreign aid perpetuated dependency: wealthier nations dispensed grants and loans that maintained their economic advantage in the global hierarchy, and they sustained local support by protecting authoritarian governments and the private interests of global South elites.[29]

In the United States, leftist scholars and activists adopted dependency theory and lambasted foreign aid for its bolstering of rapacious capitalism, and also for its role in Vietnam and other hot spots, where it provided cover and support for US military action. In 1969, Harry Magdoff, a Marxist economist, spelled out the argument in *The Age of Imperialism: The Economics of U.S. Foreign Policy*. For Magdoff, foreign aid aimed to preserve and expand US access to raw materials, markets, and investment, and it boosted US business and finance through tied exports, shipping charges, agricultural products sent overseas, and protections for private foreign investment. Aid kept poorer nations as "dependencies of the system" and served in the end "as a means of controlling and dominating the imperialist network." In the midst of a vibrant antiwar movement, Magdoff described the US intervention in Vietnam as a cog in the wheel of US economic imperialism. The book sold more than a hundred thousand copies.[30]

As a sign of the contentious times, just three days after the Columbia conference ended, around a hundred "hecklers" attended the 1970 International Development Conference at the posh Mayflower Hotel in Washington, DC. The protesters, mostly young, included college students, returned Peace Corps volunteers, and activists from Washington's leftist Institute for Policy Studies. The confrontation began in the opening session when a young man shouted "imperialist!" at Barbara Ward just after she finished her keynote address. According to one account, Ward, in schoolmarm dudgeon, "grabbed him by his jacket, shook him, and lectured him severely." Foreign aid, the protesters claimed, had utterly failed. It "had enriched the elite," "drain[ed] resources from the developing nations," and "open[ed] them for exploitation by U.S. international corporations."[31] At a stand in the hotel lobby, the protesters sold a sixty-two-page pamphlet, *International Dependency in the 1970's: How America Underdevelops the World*, that condemned US imperialism, corporate capitalism, and foreign aid.[32]

Not to be outdone, critics on the political right leveled their own assault. Conservative politicians had long decried foreign aid as

liberal internationalism that created unnecessary foreign entangle-
ments, wasted money, and fostered dangerous government expansion. By the early 1970s, they had a wider range of arguments and
a longer list of backers. The political scientist Samuel Huntington, for example, was neither an isolationist nor an opponent of
big government. He endorsed foreign aid for immediate needs,
such as famine relief, but otherwise rejected what he construed as
"the rhetoric and sentimentality" of foreign aid advocates. He was
not convinced that foreign aid enhanced the economies of poorer
nations, but even if it did, he supported it only when and where the
United States had "special political, economic, or security interests."
US funds, he argued, needed to serve the US government's foreign
policy goals.[33]

In the 1970s, Peter T. Bauer, a British economist, played the
leading intellectual role in elaborating the conservative arguments.
In essays and books, he repeatedly attacked the mainstream foreign
aid advocates, and various US politicians used his work as scholarly ballast for their floating opposition to aid.[34] In a 1972 *Wall
Street Journal* opinion piece, Bauer summarized his views: Foreign
aid led to inefficient planned economies, it supported repressive
policies and exported "unsuitable . . . models" (including "uneco-
nomic heavy industries and national airlines," "Western-type universities," and "Western-style trade unions"), it interfered with the
flow of private capital, it encouraged and sustained "torpor" and
"fatalism" among its recipients, and it funded "wasteful show projects."[35] Bauer tended to blame the poor for their own impoverishment. For Bauer, the primary cause of poverty was not colonialism
and its legacies, predacious capitalism, or even technological lag. A
nation's domestic social conditions—"abilities and attitudes, mores
and institutions"—were "major determinants of economic performance and thus of material progress." Private foreign investment,
he claimed, could stimulate modernization of markets, skills, and
mindsets, but economic assistance would not.[36]

By the early 1970s, then, foreign aid was under siege, "assaulted,"
as one commentator wrote, "by waves from left and right."[37] In
Congress, liberal and conservative critics collaborated in unusual
cooperation to oppose President Nixon's foreign aid proposals. Nixon hoped to shift more development aid to international

institutions, such as the World Bank, and his requests to Congress were, by any standard, modest. Because of their growing fury at the war in Southeast Asia, though, liberals, who usually supported foreign aid, joined conservatives to vote against Nixon's proposed economic assistance programs. One reporter called the consensus "a rarely seen coalition of Congressional doves, Southern Democrats, and conservative Republicans," and another labeled it "a coalition of disenchanted liberals and fiscal conservatives."[38] C. Fred Bergsten, an economic adviser in the Nixon administration, recalled later that "the invasion of Cambodia in late April 1970 had . . . poisoned the foreign affairs climate in Congress."[39]

Meanwhile, journalists uncovered damning evidence of incompetence and corruption in US-funded development projects. In one Latin American highway project, poor planning and "lax supervision" had led to "numerous land slides and full washouts." "Laborers' food money" from the project went into the pocket of an employee of Brown & Root Overseas Inc., a Halliburton subsidiary, who used the funds for "construction of a $16,000 house, his wedding, a stereo, office equipment, table silver and building tools." More alarming still was the account of "millions wasted" in Vietnam. Investigative journalist Jack Anderson wrote: "A federal audit of our economic aid program in South Vietnam uncovered so much bickering, blundering and boondoggling that the Nixon Administration classified it before the ink was dry." Anderson had a copy of the "suppressed report," which found that "more than $38 million was wasted" on bureaucracy and failed programs. The misappropriation included USAID funds funneled to Operation Phoenix, a CIA counterinsurgency program that tortured and killed alleged members and sympathizers of the Viet Cong. Economic assistance had reached a new low.[40]

The Challenge of World Poverty

While the critics hammered foreign aid, a campaign against global poverty won a host of new supporters. From the mid-1960s on, the US press gave increasing publicity to the starkest of poverty in Asia and Africa. In 1964, when President Johnson announced a "war on poverty" within the United States, American newspapers reported on famines in India, Indonesia, and Somalia. In seeming response, a roster of public figures endorsed a war on global (as well as domestic) poverty. The eighty-five-year-old photographer Edward Steichen, famous for his Family of Man exhibit, planned a new "exhibit on poverty as it exists all over the world," and evangelist Billy Graham called for extending the US war on poverty across the globe. Pope Paul VI, preparing for a trip to India, asked "all Christians to help the suffering of the poor," and then donated his "three-tiered gold and silver tiara . . . encrusted with diamonds, sapphires, and rubies" to the poor of the world. At his Nobel Prize lecture in Oslo, civil rights leader Martin Luther King Jr. proclaimed, "The time has come for an all-out world war against poverty." "The rich nations," he insisted, "must use their vast resources of wealth to develop the underdeveloped, school the unschooled, and feed the unfed."[41] These public calls to end world poverty responded implicitly to the horrific reports of starvation, and they carefully sidestepped the problems with foreign aid. They appealed to morality, charity, justice, and compassion. They elevated poverty not as a problem within nations but as a global concern.

Over the course of the late 1960s, Johnson's war on domestic poverty succumbed to infighting, backlash, and retrenchment, but a transatlantic global antipoverty movement took on a new life. At the international level, Catholic and Protestant churches pushed beyond traditions of mission and charity, and tried to position themselves as moral leaders in a war on global poverty. Here, too, Barbara Ward organized and advised. In 1964, she began to work with a group of liberal European and American Catholics who wanted the Vatican to take a leading role in antipoverty efforts. The group included Americans James Norris, a layman, and Joseph Gremillion, a priest, both of whom worked with the charity Catholic Relief Services. Ward wrote their foundational document, "An Ecumenical Concern for World Poverty," which proposed that the Vatican create a "secretariat to coordinate action in the attack on world poverty." In November 1964, at a global gathering of bishops, Norris presented the proposal for a "world-wide attack on poverty." (Norris spoke to the Ecumenical Council because Pope Paul VI himself insisted that a woman—that is, Ward—should not.) After more than two years of behind-the-scenes maneuvers, in early 1967 the Vatican established the new secretariat, the Commission for Justice and Peace, with Gremillion as secretary and Ward and Norris as members.[42]

Two months later the Pope issued an encyclical, *Populorum Progressio* (On the development of peoples), that endorsed the campaign against global poverty. "The superfluous goods of wealthier nations," he wrote, "ought to be placed at the disposal of poorer nations." He asked "world leaders to set aside part of their military expenditures for a world fund to relieve the needs of impoverished peoples." The document maintained the Catholic Church's longstanding opposition to communism, but it also criticized unbridled capitalism and subordinated the principle of free trade to "the demands of social justice." The *Washington Post* called the encyclical a "jolt to [Catholic] conservatives," and the *Wall Street Journal* described it, with some hyperbole, as "warmed-over Marxism."[43]

At the same time, the World Council of Churches (WCC), the international body for Protestants, also addressed global poverty as a critical issue. In 1958, the WCC had urged wealthier nations to devote 1 percent of their national income to the poorer nations of the world, and in 1960, the UN had endorsed the proposal.[44] But it was not until its 1966 World Conference on Church and Society, held in Geneva, that the WCC took up the issue of development at length. In a substantial section of the meeting devoted to "economic development in a world perspective," it recommended increased foreign aid and suggested "the possibilities of instituting a system of international taxation for world development." In 1968, at its international assembly held in Uppsala, the section on "world economic and social development" once again called for more aid and international taxation, but it also expressed the spreading concern that the development decade had become the "decade of disillusionment." The section now referred to "the struggle against world poverty" as well as the "promotion of development." It called on wealthier nations to "shed all tendencies to exploit economically or to dominate the poorer . . . economies," and it suggested that "Christians should promote social policies" that "redress the balance between the poor and the rich rather than merely make the rich richer." Barbara Ward, the leading light of the global antipoverty movement, lectured as an invited guest at both WCC conferences.

She spoke of the gap between rich and poor nations and asked the Christians of wealthier nations "to put the world's miseries above the upward drift of our ample domestic comforts" and "above the world's vast expenditure on a sterile defence."[45]

Shortly after the 1968 conference, the WCC and the Catholic Church formalized an unprecedented collaboration: the Joint Committee on Society, Development and Peace, a social justice group whose first priority was ending global poverty. Along with the Vatican and WCC, the Ford Foundation provided substantial funds to launch the new initiative. Under the leadership of a liberal American Jesuit, George Dunne, the Joint Committee, known as SODEPAX, held conferences around the globe and disseminated an antipoverty message. It also published pointed critiques of foreign aid.[46]

For a few years, SODEPAX tried to translate the vocabulary of aid and development into antipoverty social justice terms. Charles Elliott, an Anglican priest and economist on the SODEPAX staff, noted that some wanted to "challenge the whole concept of aid" to acknowledge that "transfers of . . . resources are not aid but simply redistribution in the way that a progressive taxation system is redistribution." The "concept of aid," he said, was "inadequate and antique," even if "inevitable" in mainstream development circles.[47] On the Catholic side, the leftist Peruvian priest Gustavo Gutiérrez questioned development itself. He presented his founding (and now classic) essay on liberation theology at a 1969 SODEPAX conference in Switzerland. He asked his audience to replace the language of "development" with the language of "liberation." Economic development, he wrote, supported the interests of the powerful, but liberation addressed the hopes of the oppressed. He labeled poverty "an evil" and called on his listeners to "protest" it, to "discover ways of abolishing it," and to act "in solidarity with the poor."[48]

Soon, though, SODEPAX ran afoul of Vatican insiders who saw it as competition for their own independent efforts. It was also too outspoken and too far to the left to please the Catholic bureaucracy. In one of its conference reports, SODEPAX called "most of the existing power relationships . . . morally unjustifiable and economically oppressive." As a newspaper report noted, SODEPAX critiqued racist South Africa and "the systematic use of torture in

Brazil, Greece, Vietnam, Haiti, and Zanzibar," and thereby "upset the Vatican diplomats."[49] A 1971 Ford Foundation report confirmed that SODEPAX encountered "resistance from more conservative elements in the church." The Vatican "required a thorough review of its activities," and in 1972 hobbled it by cutting its budget by almost 80 percent and forbade it from seeking additional outside funds. SODEPAX limped along until 1980.[50]

Elsewhere, though, antipoverty efforts continued to surge. In Britain, a number of new organizations sprang up at the end of the 1960s. Many of them appealed to a younger generation schooled in the social protests of the 1960s. They responded especially to reports of dire conditions in former British colonies, including famine in India and starvation in the Biafran War in Nigeria. In 1968, one such group, including workers from the charities Oxfam and Christian Aid, issued the Haslemere Declaration, denouncing global poverty and calling for justice instead of charity. The next year it organized a conference in London on "Poverty as Violence." Another group called itself the New Abolitionists and lobbied Parliament to increase foreign aid. It took its name from a speech by the ubiquitous Barbara Ward, in which she called for "new abolitionists" to fight "the slavery of poverty-stricken stagnation." And in 1969, some recent Oxford graduates, involved with Oxfam and Christian Aid, formed Third World First and promised to give 1 percent of their earnings to the cause. Around a thousand Oxford undergraduates joined them in the pledge to tax their own incomes. The group founded a magazine, the *Internationalist*, later renamed the *New Internationalist*, which had a circulation of sixteen thousand by the mid-1970s. For these activists and others, poverty came to play the part that heathenism had played for earlier missionaries: it was the thing to get rid of.[51]

By 1970, when the Swedish economist Gunnar Myrdal published *The Challenge of World Poverty: A World Anti-Poverty Program in Outline*, he recognized that a movement of sorts had already taken off, and he hoped to spur it on. Myrdal had addressed questions of world equity since at least the late 1950s, when he proposed expanding the welfare state into a "welfare world." With *The Challenge of World Poverty*, he adapted his call to the emerging antipoverty discourse.[52] The book supplemented his three-volume *Asian Drama:*

An Inquiry into the Poverty of Nations, published in 1968. *Asian Drama* addressed "experts, officials, and professional politicians," but *The Challenge of World Poverty* aimed to reach "interested persons among the general public" with a "message as direct and simple as possible." Myrdal saw that "the international problems of the poverty in underdeveloped countries and the poverty problems in the United States" had "surfaced to popular consciousness," but he also worried that the attention to world poverty, like Johnson's War on Poverty, had "lost momentum." He hoped to accelerate it again. He reiterated the "moral imperative" of "solidarity with people in distress."[53]

Myrdal pushed further than the Pearson report in insisting on the moral argument and in criticizing existing foreign aid practices. He blasted the United States for its diminishing contributions to foreign aid, its use of aid to further military goals, and its self-serving "tying" policy that forced recipient nations to spend their aid money on US exports. He wanted to move the American conscience. "The moral reason for aid," he wrote, "has to be separated and cleansed from all the spurious reasons of national interest." Along with the WCC, he suggested an international system of taxation. Myrdal already had clout with American liberals because of his pivotal 1944 book *An American Dilemma* on US race relations. He was, as a *New York Times* reviewer put it, someone "whose opinions must command the utmost attention."[54]

But others also captured the public eye. In the United States and elsewhere, everyday activism publicized the antipoverty groundswell. After youth staged antipoverty walkathons in Europe and Canada, the movement spread to the United States. The American Freedom from Hunger Foundation, an affiliate of the UN's Food and Agriculture Organization, organized the US events. In 1968, the first such fundraisers took place in Fargo, North Dakota, and Madison, Wisconsin, and then spread nationwide over the following years. By 1972, hundreds of thousands of walkers, mainly youth, had participated in "International Walk for Development" or "March against Hunger" days in the United States. In more than 150 American cities (and many more worldwide), hikers had raised more than $11 million from sponsors who pledged to donate for every mile walked.[55] One reporter read the walks as a sign "that

FIGURE 1.2. A "March against Hunger" in New York City in 1970. The American Freedom from Hunger Foundation sponsored walkathons to raise funds to combat global poverty. (Fred Morgan/*New York Daily News*)

youth are turning their attention from the war in Vietnam to helping the poor here and abroad."[56] The fight against hunger and
poverty captured imaginations, it seems, in ways that foreign aid
could not.

Rejecting Trickle Down

It was in this context that development experts increasingly
insisted that foreign aid needed to have a direct impact on the poor.
As Richard Jolly, one of the drafters of the Columbia Declaration,
wrote, "Ending world poverty must be the long-run target." Earlier
modernization theorists had often cast national economic growth
as the sine qua non of development. They had assumed that economic growth would eventually reach the poor—but, as the critics
noted, it had not. In an open revolt against trickle-down economics, development experts of the early 1970s rejected GNP and per
capita income as the metrics of development. In an influential lecture in 1969 (later published as an article), the British economist
Dudley Seers, director of the Institute of Development Studies at
the University of Sussex, asked, "What Are We Trying to Measure?"
The critical questions, he wrote, are: "What has been happening to
poverty? What has been happening to unemployment? What has
been happening to inequality?" It was no longer sufficient to argue
that national economic growth or greater dollar commitments to
foreign aid served as a measure of progress. It was also not enough
to point to higher agricultural yields or local participation in community development programs. An increasingly vocal group of
development experts now wanted assurance that the transfer of
resources had economic benefits for the poor.[57]

Through much of the 1960s, US scholars had played a leading
role in constructing and implementing various versions of modernization theory, but all along they had joined transnational conversations.[58] On specific projects, in the UN, at the World Bank,
and at international conferences, US advocates of development
met and worked with colleagues from other nations. At the end
of the decade, with modernization theory under siege, US intellectual leadership receded. As the ground shifted in the late 1960s
and early 1970s, US development economists joined a global

antipoverty movement, but they could not dominate it. When Dudley Seers rejected trickle-down economics, for example, he drew on British and Indian economists who had defined a "poverty line" more than on US development experts.[59]

In the first years of the 1970s, Seers and his Sussex colleagues Richard Jolly and Hans Singer worked with the International Labour Organization (ILO), headquartered in Geneva, on a major project that rejected the trickle-down model. Inaugurated in 1969, the World Employment Programme (WEP) turned its attention to questions of poverty with a focus on unemployment and underemployment in the global South. It was inspired, the head of its research branch remembered, "by the realization that economic growth in and of itself did not necessarily lead to an improvement in the living standards of the great majority of the population."[60] The early WEP studies brought together new transnational teams of development experts and publicized the growing concern that development aid had not sufficiently addressed inadequate incomes, inequality, and the distribution of wealth. The first study—on Colombia—found, for example, that "the poorest sections of the population have gained little, if anything, from the growth . . . of the economy." The WEP came to view "employment-oriented strategies . . . as the principal means of eliminating mass poverty in developing countries."[61]

The concern with global poverty spread quickly to other development specialists. In 1972, a UN pamphlet, *Attack on World Poverty and Unemployment*, noted that "finding solutions to the problems of mass poverty" had "come into vogue." It reported the recommendations of the UN's Committee for Development Planning, which called for "radical poverty-reduction programmes" that could increase the productivity and incomes "of the poorest groups." In the same year, the Ford Foundation conducted an internal review of its own funding of economic development programs. The Foundation spent tens of millions annually on programs in "less developed countries." The internal report called for continuing the programs but with "somewhat broader objectives." Under the first such objective, it stated, "the greatest concern should be with the neediest."[62] And the Overseas Development Council (ODC), a private think tank in Washington, DC, founded in 1969 and funded by the Ford and Rockefeller Foundations, began to argue for development from the bottom up. Its president, James P. Grant, a former administrator at USAID, had attended the Columbia conference on the Pearson report and signed the Columbia Declaration. He saw the ODC as a leading exponent of "growth with trickle-up," as opposed to trickle-down, economics.[63]

In the early 1970s, development economists published new research that showed how earlier programs and policies had failed to alleviate poverty. Albert Fishlow, for example, measured growing inequality in Brazil. Despite a decade of rapid economic growth, income inequality had increased. The government policies that favored investment and private capital accumulation would not, he claimed, lead to a redistribution of income. "Brazilian poverty," he wrote, "is directly linked to low levels of productivity, particularly rural." He called for new policies that directed resources to the poor. In a similar vein, two other economists, Irma Adelman and Cynthia Taft Morris, found that economic growth had enriched the elites in developing nations. "Our findings," they wrote, "strongly suggest that there is no automatic, or even likely, trickling down of the benefits of economic growth to the poorest segments of the population in low-income countries." They, too, called for programs that addressed the rural poor.[64]

By 1973, the new antipoverty, anti-trickle-down approach had reached the US Congress. In April, fifteen members of the House Foreign Relations Committee—fourteen Democrats and one Republican—sent President Nixon a letter in which they pushed for reforms in the foreign aid program. They hoped to move US economic assistance away from large-scale, top-down construction projects and toward programs that reached and involved the poor. "Hunger, malnutrition, disease, ignorance, and poverty continue to plague the majority of the human race," they wrote. They asked for US foreign aid to focus on the "basic sectors where progress can affect the welfare of many." Over the next few weeks, they held a series of breakfast meetings, including one with Barbara Ward, to plan new legislation. Led by Donald M. Fraser, a Democrat from Minnesota, and Clement J. Zablocki, a Democrat from Wisconsin, they worked closely with officials at USAID and staff from the ODC. They drafted amendments to Nixon's foreign aid authorization legislation and introduced them in Congress at the end of May.[65]

The amendments called for $1 billion, which was the same amount that Nixon had requested for nonmilitary foreign aid, but they "redirected" the funds "to focus on the most acute problems of the poorest nations." The funds would go to "rural development, food and nutrition, population growth and health, education and human resources development." Twenty-six of the forty members of the House Foreign Relations Committee cosponsored the amendments. In a joint statement issued to the press, they said that the money would support projects that "most directly benefit the poorest majority of the people."[66] The amended bill nudged the center of gravity in US foreign aid from capital-intensive to labor-intensive projects, from economic growth to poverty alleviation, and from the poverty of nations to the poverty of people within them. It came to be called the "New Directions" mandate.

The ODC steered the bill to and through Congress. James Grant, the ODC president, helped plan the legislation, and other ODC staff members outlined and drafted it. Before the press conference announcing the bill, Grant advised Fraser to "avoid any impression that this is an anti-Administration move." He told Fraser to frame the bill as building on Nixon's preference for more selectively targeted aid.[67] The ODC also chose several of the witnesses who testified at congressional hearings and then wrote their testimony. In his own testimony before the House Committee on Foreign Affairs, Grant claimed that the proposed legislation was "possibly the most far-reaching and important" foreign aid initiative "since the launching of the Marshall Plan 25 years ago." He rejected GNP as a measure of success and instead advocated for meeting "minimum human needs." He wanted "social justice" along with economic growth. "Ten years ago," he said, "we wanted growth." Now he pushed for a "focus on the human problems of the poor in the developing countries."[68]

Other supporters of the bill outlined what was emerging as a new liberal orthodoxy. From early in the process, Edgar Owens, a USAID official and coauthor of the book *Development Reconsidered*, advised Fraser in constructing the New Directions approach. He submitted a written statement for the House hearings titled

"The New Look in Development." The "new look," he said, involved creating "conditions of access . . . for the multitude of small producers who now lack them." Owens called for participation by the poor and a focus on "small producer economics." He disputed the notion that developing nations should "follow the pattern of western industrialization." Instead, he endorsed labor-intensive plans that increased employment, especially for small farmers and small entrepreneurs. In the Senate hearings, Reverend Theodore M. Hesburgh, president of the University of Notre Dame and also chair of the board of directors of the ODC, made similar statements. He asked Congress to join the scholars who now opposed "the old, growth-only, capital-intensive model" and supported "a better . . . labor-intensive model . . . that seeks to give first priority to the needs of the poorest majority."[69]

Supporters of the proposed legislation hoped to separate their concerns about poverty from the superpower rivalries and military interventions that had tainted foreign aid. In the age of détente, they placed less emphasis on the Cold War. They adopted what one 1973 report called the "widely held view that . . . the cold war is passing into history."[70] The prognosis was premature, but it allowed the bill's proponents to place more stress on humanitarian goals and appeal to their colleagues and constituents who recoiled from the debacle in Vietnam. Nonetheless, they still framed their testimony, at least in part, in terms of national interest. Various supporters made familiar arguments about security and economics. Hesburgh insisted that the new legislation not only addressed "the essence of morality" but also "hard-headed self-interest." He warned that poverty could harm the United States through unrest, instability, and retaliation by the resentful poor. And Edgar Owens stated that "events in developing countries" would shape US "prospects for trade, travel, [and] investment." "Small producer economics," he found, could "deter revolution."[71]

In its committee report, the House Foreign Affairs Committee was particularly pointed. It reassured Congress that foreign assistance would not hurt the US balance of payments. It projected that all of the money spent on economic assistance would return to the United States in the form of products and services purchased by developing nations and in repayment of and interest on foreign aid loans. The authors of the Pearson report, Gunnar Myrdal, and the representatives of poorer nations, among others, had campaigned for untying aid, but their arguments had limited purchase in Congress, which had an inherent commitment to advancing US strategic and economic interests. By emphasizing its benefits to the United States, supporters of the bill hoped to stave off their long-standing opponents who complained of the "billions of dollars . . . wasted in Foreign Aid."[72]

As the bill worked its way through Congress, provisions were dropped and added, but the legislation survived with its focus on poverty intact. When Nixon signed it into law in December 1973, it called for less emphasis on "large-scale capital transfers" and more on "critical problems . . . which affect the lives of the majority of the people in the developing countries." And it gave "highest priority to undertakings . . . which directly improve the lives of the poorest." Nixon disliked USAID. He found its personnel incompetent and hoped to dismantle it. But with the New Directions legislation, USAID officials saved their agency by promising to revamp it.[73]

In mid-1974, the USAID administrator Daniel Parker sent instructions to all mission offices, guiding his staff on how to address the new legislation. "Bear in mind," he wrote, "that A.I.D. must more than ever before reach out to the growing number of people living at or beyond this level of absolute poverty." The focus would be on the rural poor. The "'trickle down' strategy of concentrating on large farmers," he claimed, "almost never succeeds." He called, among other things, for "employment-creating forms of agriculture," "off-farm employment," and "the development of market towns and small scale relatively labor-intensive industrial and commercial enterprises related to agriculture and rural life." He promised that the Washington office of USAID would "provide top budget and manpower priority to projects which will both raise output and bring tangible benefits to small farmers and other elements of the rural poor."[74] For the rest of the decade, USAID avoided large-scale infrastructure projects and funded more small-scale projects that focused on "the poorest, usually rural, majorities in the developing countries." By the end of the 1970s, more than half of USAID disbursements came from its "agricultural, rural development, and nutrition category" and almost three-quarters

of "the proposed projects named the poor as intended beneficiaries." The geography of aid also shifted, with a greater percentage
of funds going to African nations.[75]

Redistribution?

While USAID reorganized in response to the new legislation,
development experts increasingly argued that donor governments
should channel more of their contributions through multilateral (or
international) institutions. Bilateral aid—or aid that went directly
from one nation to another—led to tension, conflict, and rancor
between donor and recipient nations. In the global South, bilateral aid from the United States was particularly suspect, sullied by
support for repressive regimes, promotion of US business interests,
and the use of economic assistance in military efforts. "The United
States," a Ford Foundation report stated, "has become a more
prominent and mistrusted target of third world critics than the former colonial powers."[76] Nixon (and Johnson earlier) expressed a
preference for shifting aid from bilateral to multilateral funding, in
part as a way to launder the funds and forestall recriminations from
poorer nations that resented US hegemony. The Pearson report and
the Columbia Declaration also endorsed multilateral aid. With its
measured moderation, the Pearson report found multilateral aid
allowed for better coordination and distribution of aid and countered the "tones of charity or interventionism which have at times
embittered the aid process in the past."[77]

For the nations of the global South, the UN held promise as a
multilateral institution. The superpowers ran the UN's Security
Council, but they could not control its General Assembly, which
operated on a one-nation-one-vote basis. As more and more
new postcolonial nations joined the UN, the balance of voting
power shifted. In 1964, the representatives of seventy-seven self-
proclaimed "developing countries" formed a coalition, the Group
of 77 (or G-77), to advocate as a bloc within the UN for their economic interests. At their first meeting, held in Algiers in 1967, they
crafted a charter calling for better terms of trade, increased levels of economic assistance, and the untying of aid. They hoped to
push the United Nations Conference on Trade and Development

(UNCTAD), established in 1964, from the "stage of deliberation to the plane of practical action."[78]

For the US government, though, multilateral aid via the World Bank held more advantages. It avoided the appearance of national self-interest that tainted bilateral aid, and it also maintained a significant measure of US control. Member nations contributed to the Bank and an international board governed it, but the United States dominated from the start. The United States, which made the largest capital contributions to the Bank, had the largest voting share in the Bank's governing board. The United States chose the Bank's presidents, who were always US citizens, and the Bank's headquarters were (and are) in Washington, DC. In addition, in the 1970s Congress routinely tried to shape the Bank's policies by threatening to withhold US contributions. As Robert McNamara remembered, "the US treated the Bank as though it were a US institution."[79]

In the early 1970s, the World Bank took up the antipoverty mantle and became its most forceful advocate within mainstream development circles. The International Bank for Reconstruction and Development (IBRD), as the World Bank is officially known, had not entirely ignored poverty in its first twenty-five years. Founded in 1944, it shifted the bulk of its loans early on from rebuilding the nations of Europe to promoting the economic development of poorer nations. And in 1960 it established a subsidiary, the International Development Association (IDA), specifically to provide loans to the poorest nations on concessional terms. The "soft" IDA loans had low or no interest rates, prolonged years of repayment, and longer grace periods before any payments were due. But through the 1960s, the IBRD and the IDA envisioned development primarily as infrastructure and national economic output. They provided loans and technical advice to recipient nations with the expectation that the funded projects would foster economic growth, and they defined poverty as a political, social, or distributional issue that fell mostly outside the Bank's purview.[80]

In 1968, when Robert McNamara came in as World Bank president, he transformed the institution. William Clark, the director of the Bank's Information and Public Affairs Department, remembered that when McNamara initially joined the Bank, he was "shocked" to learn that it did not "help the poorest." Within six

months, McNamara had convinced the Bank's board of governors
to let him double the Bank's lending over the course of the next
five years. While expanding its operations and staff, he turned the
Bank toward poverty alleviation with a passion that distinguished
him from earlier presidents and from most members of his staff.[81]
At the Columbia conference in 1970, McNamara announced that
the Bank would now focus on "social" as well as economic development, with special emphasis on policies that reached the most
impoverished people of the poorer nations. He imagined that the
new approach would attract the support of socially conscious youth.
"If development . . . aims squarely at an end of grinding poverty
and gross injustice," he said, "I believe it has a constituency waiting
for it among the emerging generation of young adults."[82]

In the fall of 1973, while Congress fine-tuned the New Directions legislation, McNamara formally outlined the Bank's antipoverty strategy. At his speech to the Bank's annual board of governors'
meeting, held that year in Nairobi, he defined "absolute poverty" as
"a condition of life so degraded by disease, illiteracy, malnutrition,
and squalor as to deny its victims human necessities." Absolute
poverty was not mere deprivation. It was the barest of bare life, in
which "brains have been damaged," "bodies stunted," and "vitality
sapped," and economic growth had not substantially diminished it.
McNamara proposed to lend $22 billion over five years with "far
greater emphasis on policies and projects . . . to attack the problems
of absolute poverty." He hoped "to redefine the objectives and measurement of development." Progress in the war on poverty could not
be gauged "with a single measuring rod" of GNP. McNamara called
for new measurements and, more crucially, for significant aid that
reached "the absolute poor." They "were not merely a tiny minority
of unfortunates," he said, but "roughly 40% of the nearly two billion
individuals living in the developing nations." Like the New Directions mandate, the Bank's new strategy focused on the rural poor.
It aimed to make small farmers more productive through access to
credit, irrigation, education, and health services.[83]

Before he came to the World Bank, McNamara had little experience with development or finance. He had served as the president
of Ford Motor Company and as secretary of defense under Kennedy

and Johnson. By the time he left the Johnson administration to assume the presidency of the World Bank, he had earned international infamy for his central role in escalating US warfare in Vietnam. Antiwar protesters roundly vilified him as a war criminal— "the butcher of Vietnam"—and routinely shouted him down in public. As he moved the Bank toward its war on global poverty, some commentators suggested that he had become a "do-gooder" to atone for "the black deeds of Vietnam." His friends "scoffed" at the suggestion, and he himself rejected it as "absurd."[84]

Whatever his motives, McNamara was a Kennedy-era liberal and attuned to trends in liberal thought. In the late 1960s, he may have inched a bit to the left, pushed by increasing skepticism about the war in Vietnam and by the radicalism, social conscience, and protests of a younger generation. His own son had become radicalized while a student at Stanford University, and moved to Chile to support Salvador Allende's socialist government in the first years of the 1970s. According to McNamara's biographer, the 1970 Columbia conference was "a turning point" for him. He heard "the Young Turks critical of the aid establishment." He took notes and "barraged the younger men with questions," including, "How would you reach the poor directly?"[85] More generally, McNamara's approach to aid reflected the changing politics of development economics, with its 1970s rejection of 1960s trickle-down modernization.

In his own accounts, McNamara pointed to other factors. Barbara Ward, he said, "influenced me more than anyone in my life." McNamara had heard Ward speak in the early 1960s at Robert and Ethel Kennedy's home, and he met her again as World Bank president through her friend William Clark. He was "very impressed by the lucidity of her writing and thought and also impressed by the breadth of her vision and her feeling for the people involved." Ward was, he remembered, "an important outside influence," an economic popularizer who had his ear, "just like President Kennedy turning to John Galbraith." McNamara consulted with her often, sent her drafts of his speeches, and took inspiration from her religiously inflected antipoverty message.[86]

An inside influence was Mahbub ul Haq, a Pakistani economist, who was more of a provocateur. Before he came to the World

Bank, Haq had studied at the Government College in Lahore, Cambridge University, and Yale University, and then worked as the chief economist in Pakistan's National Planning Commission. There he publicly renounced the trickle-down model in a 1968 speech that sent, he wrote, "shock waves within Pakistan." His country's touted economic growth had benefited the twenty-two wealthiest families and left most of the population in poverty. "It was quite clear," he remembered, "that even though we had increased the national income, we hadn't changed the lives of people."[87] In 1970, Haq helped draft the Columbia Declaration, and then took up a position at the World Bank, where he represented the left end of its political spectrum. His "first encounters with McNamara" were, he recalled, "extremely unhappy ones." McNamara was unpersuaded by what he saw as Haq's "belligerent questioning of growth." But by 1972, McNamara was won over, "convinced that growth was not trickling down."[88] Haq became the director of the Bank's Policy Planning and Program Review Department and in that position served as "McNamara's unofficial poverty activist." As one of his colleagues recalled, Haq was the person who wrote McNamara's 1973 speech that launched the Bank's antipoverty campaign, and as McNamara himself remembered, Haq was "absolutely invaluable to me."[89]

Some of the senior economists, who had worked at the Bank for years, resented and resisted the change in approach. Amid the grumbling, McNamara hired a new team, with Hollis Chenery, a Harvard professor and former USAID administrator, as his chief economist. Chenery recounted the self-questioning of the staff: "Why were we lending so much to electric power where there was very little relation to income distribution and why not more to poor farmers?" Once the Bank moved into the antipoverty lane, Chenery and his colleagues debated "how rapidly we could move in the direction of supporting small farmers and shifting toward poverty-focused agricultural programs."[90]

In 1973, in collaboration with development economists at the Institute of Development Studies at the University of Sussex, the Bank's research staff set out to articulate a strategy for its antipoverty approach. They commissioned a set of papers on the "state of the art" in the field, and discussed and refined them at two conferences—one, ironically, at the Rockefeller Foundation's luxe conference center in Bellagio, Italy, and the other in down-to-earth Sussex. The result was *Redistribution with Growth*, a volume that provided the intellectual framework for the Bank's antipoverty projects in the mid-1970s. Chenery wrote the book's introduction and opened with the now-expected renunciation of trickle-down theories. "It is now clear," he wrote, "that more than a decade of rapid growth in underdeveloped countries has been of little or no benefit to perhaps a third of their population."[91]

Redistribution with Growth asked for a "redirection of development strategy." The new direction focused, as McNamara had suggested, on "increasing the productivity of the small farmer and self-employed" and also on "more labor-intensive products and processes" in urban areas. Chenery and his coauthors rejected the trickle-down approaches, but they still insisted on "growth as an objective." Their strategy of "redistribution with growth" built on and borrowed from the concept of "redistribution from growth," which underpinned the ILO's 1972 study of employment in Kenya.[92] They called for "redistribution of the benefits of growth," but they refrained from asking for any significant redistribution of existing wealth.[93] They asked simply that more of the funds from future growth go to enhancing the skills, access to assets, and productive capacities of poorer farmers and self-employed workers. In that way, they simultaneously acknowledged the need for redistribution and deferred it to a later date.

McNamara considered *Redistribution with Growth* the "most fundamental economic research" conducted during his tenure. But it was a relatively tame book. It endorsed mainstream economists' usual quest for development via productive capacity. Furthermore, it mostly avoided suggestions that addressed the international economic structures that gave the advantage to wealthier nations; instead, it asked poorer nations to "reorient" their own internal policies. In the book's chapter on "international dimensions," Richard Jolly hoped in the long run for "deliberate policies" that addressed international inequality, but he resigned himself to the realities of working in the halls of power. He concluded that "such talk still appears idealistic or nonsensical." The "international agencies" could "play only a modest role," he conceded, "particularly on

FIGURE 1.3. Robert S. McNamara (facing camera, far right), president of the World Bank, with farmers in West Bengal, India, 1976. In the 1970s, McNamara positioned the Bank as an antipoverty institution. (Keystone/Getty Images)

issues where direct interests of the larger and richer countries may be threatened."[94]

At the same time that USAID redirected its projects toward the rural, small scale, and impoverished, the World Bank did much the same. In the mid-1970s, the Bank increased what it called "poverty lending," most of which went to "small-farmer projects." In the fiscal year 1974 alone, the Bank approved fifty-six such "new-style" projects, which aimed to increase the income of the rural poor.[95] From the Nairobi speech in 1973 to the end of 1975, the Bank had doubled the funds spent on agriculture, with more than $1 billion annually committed to rural development programs.[96]

The Bank insisted that its poverty lending would not and could not come at the expense of economic growth. It steered clear of "aggressive redistribution" as well as "welfare spending" and public works employment programs.[97] In its initial poverty lending, it also avoided projects for landless laborers and the urban poor, which Bank officials deemed less "feasible operational objectives."[98] The ultimate goal, as one study found, was to "make subsistence or near-subsistence farmers into commercial ones."[99] The underlying logic reflected a faith in the market economy as the solution to poverty. In a policy paper on rural development, the Bank identified its strategy as concerned "with the modernization and monetization of rural society, and with its transition from traditional isolation to integration with the national economy." In this view, poverty resulted from exclusion from the market, not from exploitation or subordination within it.[100]

In the US government and the World Bank, the antipoverty advocates presented their programs as "new directions" and "new style," but the focus on the rural poor was not exactly new. In fact, it sounded suspiciously similar to the 1950s and 1960s "community development" (or CD) programs that operated at the local level. Those who studied and advocated the 1970s programs acknowledged the similarities, but distinguished the new variant from the old. In Edgar Owens's view, CD had its roots in charity and lacked "economic and business discipline." The "new look," he said, promoted structural change, such as "re-arranging the credit structure" to give smaller farmers their fair share. Another advocate of the new approach claimed, likewise, that CD "focused on public goods and welfare more than production," with "little attention to the economic basis of rural uplift." In general, advocates of the new approach kept CD's rhetoric on popular participation and technical assistance but placed lesser emphasis on the Cold War courtship of peasants and on instilling democratic processes from the bottom up. They expressed more concern with the productivity of small farmers and income for the poor. They returned repeatedly to issues of economic distribution. As one 1980s commentator described it, the CD programs of the 1950s and 1960s stressed "energizing rural communities for self-help" while the 1970s programs sought "greater equity in the distribution of the gains from economic growth."[101]

—————

But like the older CD programs, the new antipoverty development strategy did not end the trouble with foreign aid. The new programs entered the scene at a moment of economic shock. In October 1973, one month after McNamara announced the World Bank's antipoverty strategy and while members of Congress were negotiating the New Directions amendments, the Arab oil-producing nations placed an embargo on their oil exports, and the price of oil quadrupled. Within the United States, the oil crisis came conjoined with runaway inflation, high rates of unemployment, and new trade deficits. The combination of rising prices and stagnant economic growth—dubbed "stagflation"—further eroded the US commitment to sending tax dollars abroad rather than spending them at home. In the 1970s, US expenditure on development assistance (measured in constant dollars) never came close to the Kennedy-era level of funding.[102]

The antipoverty approach also failed to appease the critics of foreign aid. On the left, protesters continued to position foreign aid as an imperialist gambit. They criticized US economic assistance as a boon for authoritarian regimes, wealthy elites, multinational corporations, and US military endeavors.[103] On the right, conservatives still depicted foreign aid as unproductive handouts.[104] At the same time, the new programs won a tepid reception in the global South, where leaders turned increasingly to the rhetoric of self-reliance. Not surprisingly, officials in recipient nations resented programs that aimed to intervene in their internal policies of distribution and income.[105]

Meanwhile, in the poorest nations, the spike in oil prices led to economic crisis. Grain prices escalated, too, when the United States sold millions of dollars of stockpiled grain to the Soviet Union, reducing world reserves. In 1973 and 1974, Bangladesh and the African Sahel, the region just south of the Sahara, collapsed into famine. With floods, drought, and the rising price of oil-based fertilizers, food production dropped, and with the higher cost of imported grain, thousands died of starvation or succumbed to cholera, diphtheria, malaria, meningitis, and other diseases, while others held on, undernourished, to the barest of existence. At the very moment when development experts launched the new antipoverty programs, the famines provided evidence that the direst poverty perdured.

And at USAID, the World Bank, and elsewhere, the rural development programs ran into obstacles from the start. The new programs focused on rural productivity, and in search of success, they retreated from the kinds of programs that reached the poorest people who did not have access to their own farmland. USAID and the World Bank also backed away from land reform, which would have involved politically fraught attempts to give land to the landless.[106] Moreover, the rush to spend funds on new rural development programs created a bureaucratic morass in USAID and the World Bank, with recalcitrant staff bogged down with too many small-scale projects to plan, implement, and assess. It was, it turns out, easier to administer a handful of huge projects than dozens of tiny ones.[107] A recent overview of the World Bank's antipoverty projects in the 1970s found "corruption and the diversion of resources from intended beneficiaries," projects that "forced peasants off their land," and others that "generally failed to meet their goals." In an internal assessment of its McNamara-era agricultural projects, the Bank rated almost half "unsatisfactory" in reaching its own economic benchmarks.[108]

But the new approach did make a difference, if not in diminishing poverty then in the conception of development. As the political scientist Martha Finnemore has argued, it "*internationalized* responsibility for the world's poor," transforming poverty into a global problem and not just the domestic concern of each individual nation.[109] Development experts rejected modernization theories that relied on national economic growth as the key measure of success, and they turned away from large-scale infrastructure projects, at least in part. They disputed the assumption that prosperity would drop with gravitational pull from the wealthy to the poor. In so doing, they elevated and legitimated calls for equity and redistribution, even among economists who preferred the technocratic language of graphs and equations.

As usual, Barbara Ward, still "the darling of the international development set," had her finger on the pulse of change.[110] She publicized the emerging view with her signature style. "Growth and success in the economy," she wrote in 1974, "have been measured in tons of steel and kilowatt hours of energy, of cattle on the hoof and grain deliveries." But such measures no longer sufficed. Ward pointed to impoverished people "in rundown rural hovels, on squatter settlements in the big cities," and insisted on a strategy that addressed the "needs of these masses at the bottom of the human pyramid." There was, she said, "a new awareness of the critical role of employment and income distribution" in "the theory and practice of development."[111] She thus outlined concisely the early 1970s changes in development circles.

Over the next few years, liberal development experts tried to push the new awareness further. They replaced the early 1970s strategy of "redistribution with growth" with a late 1970s movement for "basic needs." But as they did so, they confronted a challenge from leaders of the global South, who asked for structural changes in a global market that served the interests of the North. In what came to be called the "North-South dialogue," policy makers and others engaged in an ideological tug of war over who could and should dictate the premises of economic development, poverty alleviation, and the distribution of wealth.

CHAPTER TWO

Redistribution

SOUTH AND NORTH

IN 1977, when Michael Harrington published *The Vast Majority: A Journey to the World's Poor,* he hoped to pique the emotions of his American readers. He wrote the book, he said, "to persuade a decent people to turn toward the wretched of the earth and to cooperate with them in the work of justice."[1] Like Barbara Ward, Harrington used moral arguments to move the conscience of his readers, and, like Ward, he drew on the language of human suffering. ("The wretched of the earth," borrowed from Frantz Fanon, is just one example.) He described poverty as "a global system of injustice that warps or destroys the minds and bodies of hundreds of millions of human beings." But unlike Ward, Harrington did not have a history of involvement in international development circles, and he refused to position himself as an expert on global poverty. With a dose of humility, he called himself a "tourist of degradation." He recounted his brief trips to India, Kenya, Tanzania, and Mexico, and after a short time abroad, he questioned his own "wheedling, jesuitical conscience; a sloppy, sentimental, pathetic . . . hypocritical conscience." He wanted "to change the world." But he was "dog-tired," he said, "of empathy, especially empathy at an impotent, passive, Northern distance."[2]

Harrington also differed from Ward in his politics. Both were anticommunists with deep roots in the Catholic Church, but Harrington was a lapsed Catholic, an atheist, and a leading American

[53]

socialist. He borrowed from Marxist dependency theory to explain world poverty. Capital from the North had subordinated the global South through "unfavorable terms of trade and the outflow of profit and fees to the advanced economies." Accumulating debt had left a "Third World . . . short of cash," and US corporations roamed the world in search of "underpaid labor." Harrington conveyed his outrage at the disparities in wealth exploited by profit-seeking globetrotters, and also expressed distaste for American consumers who wasted money on pointless possessions. "Standing," he wrote, "in the detritus of a poverty-stricken market place in Nairobi, where the workers live in cardboard shacks and make carved napkin rings for the tables of San Francisco, I realized that capital would go to the moon if it thought there was cheap labor there."[3]

Harrington, though, was not content with a critical outsider stance. He was, as a review in the *Nation* noted, "a man who attempts to influence the mainstream." He considered the wholesale rejection of capitalism insupportable, impractical, and doomed to failure. Like Ward, he called for more foreign aid and a US commitment to ending global poverty. Harrington trod lightly on the liberals who worked within the development establishment. He said that Robert McNamara was "doing a decent job" as president of the World Bank. He "reject[ed] the basic capitalist structures and assumptions of the bank itself," and he saw McNamara as "a technocrat, not a comrade." Still, he appreciated McNamara's "moral intensity" and "commitment." McNamara, he wrote, was quintessentially American, expressing "decent feelings within a framework of action that is basically conservative."[4]

The Vast Majority was just a blip in Harrington's long career as an author and activist, but at the time of its publication, it won attention and acclaim. The *New York Times* praised its "perceptive reportage and passionate social analysis," and the National Book Award judges selected it as a finalist for their 1978 prize in contemporary thought.[5] Much of the book's appeal came from Harrington's soul-searching ambivalence, which refracted the uneasy alliances in global antipoverty circles. Harrington was caught, the *Nation*'s reviewer wrote, "between his liberal and radical commitments." He supported the liberal foreign aid advocates who argued that the US government should make a greater commitment to reducing poverty outside the nation's boundaries, and he also listened to more radical voices from the global South. With *The Vast Majority*, he captured an international conversation in which the tensions between North and South—and between liberals and leftists—were palpable.

In the late 1970s, US foreign aid was in decline, but, as Harrington's book suggests, global antipoverty efforts were on the public agenda. Development experts had rejected the trickle-down versions of modernization in the early 1970s; in the second half of the decade they rerouted their antipoverty efforts in two distinct directions. Leaders of the global South and their leftist allies looked to the New International Economic Order, a UN declaration approved in 1974. Written and supported by leaders from the South, the NIEO demanded structural changes in the global economy, especially in the inequitable terms of trade that favored wealthier nations. It imagined an economic playing field that could redistribute wealth, narrow the "widening gap" between the rich nations and the poor ones, and lift the poorer nations out of poverty. At the same time that the NIEO addressed the poverty of nations, economists and policy makers in the ILO, the World Bank, the US government, and elsewhere turned to the grassroots poor. They reformulated the early 1970s "New Directions" and "new style" mandates into late 1970s programs that aimed to fulfill "basic needs." They called for a global movement—across nations and within them—to supply the funds and services required to meet the minimum needs of the poorest people in the poorest lands.

The two approaches were not mutually exclusive. They both called for redistribution that would send funds from North to South, but they adopted different methods and different vocabularies. In addition to changing the terms of trade, the NIEO asked for "transfer of resources" from northern to southern nations as a matter of justice and reparation. The NIEO envisioned global poverty as a product and extension of colonial exploitation. The transfer of capital and technology could help right a history of wrongs. In contrast, the basic needs programs called for "aid," closer to charity than to restitution, that funneled assistance directly to programs for the poor. It positioned the poor as neglected people left behind in a modernizing world. It was both ambitious in its aim to eradicate the worst of poverty and acquiescent when it backed away from structural changes in the global economy. Together, the two approaches—one aimed at poor nations, the other at poor people—provided the substance of Harrington's ambivalence, and on a larger scale they structured the "North-South" debates on development of the late 1970s.

A New International Economic Order?

In April and May 1974, the UN General Assembly met in a special session and approved the Declaration on the Establishment of a New International Economic Order. With the NIEO, the nations of the global South, working in alliance, flexed their muscles and pushed back against the hegemony of the North. They called for an end to their economic subordination. "The developing world," the Declaration announced, "has become a powerful factor that makes its influence felt in all fields of international activity." The NIEO insisted on respect for national sovereignty and "participation on the basis of equality of all countries in the solving of world economic problems." It included nations' rights to "regulation . . . of the activities of transnational corporations" and "effective control over their natural resources and economic activities," and it asked to free "assistance to developing countries" from "any political or military conditions."[6]

At the most general level, the NIEO highlighted the shifting balance of power within the UN. It served notice, as one newspaper put it, "that the rich nations could no longer make all the rules and interpret them without involving the poor."[7] More specifically, the NIEO aimed to revise the patterns of trade that maintained the economic disparities between the North and South. Its program of action asked for higher prices for raw materials exported from the global South and better access to the markets of the North. And along with "collective self-reliance" and cooperation among the nations of the South, it called for redistribution between the poorer and wealthier nations, including emergency aid, the renegotiation of debt, and the transfer of financial resources, technology, and skills.[8]

The NIEO could not have come as a total surprise. For at least twenty-five years, the emerging "Third World" had been pushing, with minimal success, for changes in the global economic system. In 1949, at a conference of the UN's new Economic Commission for Latin America (ECLA), the Argentine economist Raúl Prebisch presented a groundbreaking paper that delineated the unequal exchange between the industrialized nations and the nations that exported raw materials. The wealth gap had widened, he argued, because prices paid for imported manufactured goods had risen while prices earned from exported commodities had dropped. The poorer nations at the "periphery" of the economic system remained subordinate to the wealthier nations at the "center." At ECLA, which Prebisch led for more than a decade, he called for international reforms to promote industrialization and lift commodity prices in Latin America.[9] In 1955, at a major conference in Bandung, Indonesia, the representatives of twenty-nine Asian and African nations, most of them recently independent, issued their own manifesto. They stressed self-determination, racial equality, and an end to violations of their national sovereignty, and they also noted economic inequities.[10] In the years following, their calls for political independence came conjoined with growing demands for an end to economic exploitation.

Within the UN, as the number of postcolonial members rose, a fragile coalition exercised its growing clout. In 1962, at Prebisch's urging, the UN General Assembly voted to establish the United Nations Conference on Trade and Development, which held its first session in 1964. Under the leadership of Prebisch, UNCTAD pointed to the systemic ways in which the global market disadvantaged the South. At the end of UNCTAD's first session, the nations of the South formed the Group of 77 within the UN, and tried to push UNCTAD to move from words to action. But by the early 1970s the G-77, which now included almost one hundred nations, had to acknowledge that little had changed. In fact, with crop failures, rising prices, and the accumulation of debt, the economic situation in many poorer nations had worsened.[11]

In 1974, the NIEO pulled the economic issues out of the confines of ECLA and UNCTAD and into the UN as a whole. Along with its demands for national sovereignty and economic self-determination, the NIEO linked poverty in the global South to the self-serving economic system created and sustained by the wealthier nations.

Changing the rules of economic engagement, the NIEO claimed, would redistribute wealth. Some of the most avid supporters of the NIEO represented socialist nations, and the leftist influence shaped the Declaration's economic critique. But supporters of the NIEO covered a wide political swath. They included Ferdinand Marcos, the right-wing dictator of the Philippines, and the monarchical Shah of Iran, as well as charismatic socialists, such as Julius Nyerere in Tanzania and Michael Manley in Jamaica. The NIEO was "third worldist" more than socialist; it expressed the collective will of postcolonial leaders. It did not reject either development or capitalism. It aimed to give more power to nations of the global South via a "trade union of the poor," and its version of collective bargaining did not repudiate international trade or private investment.[12] Instead, it asked for faster economic development through reforms at the highest level of international collaboration. It encouraged industries in the South and pushed for more equitable integration into global markets.

Nonetheless, for US policy makers, the NIEO was unwelcome. Just one year earlier, in 1973, the Arab nations of the Organization of the Petroleum Exporting Countries (OPEC) had imposed their oil embargo on nations, including the United States, that supported Israel in the 1973 Arab-Israeli War, and they had also restricted oil production, dramatically escalating prices on the international market. OPEC's actions demonstrated how much impact commodity-producing nations, working in concert, could have on the world economy. It suggested a future in which cooperation in the global South could wrest concessions from the global North. And it thereby inspired the poorer nations and alarmed the wealthier ones.

Within the United States, the preeminent Cold War paranoia— that the postcolonial nations would turn to communism—had diminished, at least temporarily, but now another threat seemed to have replaced it. The economist C. Fred Bergsten, who had served in the Nixon administration until 1971 and later served in the Carter administration, spelled out the perceived dangers in 1973. "The major threat to the United States from the Third World," he wrote, "is likely to be economic." OPEC might serve as the model for additional consortia that could place embargos on or raise the prices of other raw materials, such as copper, coffee, rubber, and tin. Poorer nations might nationalize US investments, they might repudiate their debts, and they might flood the United States with cheap manufactured imports, undermining US industry.[13]

For US officials, the NIEO's declaration of economic independence suggested that the dangerous future had arrived. At the time of its adoption, the US ambassador to the UN, John Scali, complained that the NIEO had "too many objectional features."[14] Among them were the provisions that endorsed collective actions of commodity exporters, à la OPEC, and the nationalization of natural resources without a guarantee of compensation to foreign investors. "In this house," Scali warned, "the steamroller is not the vehicle for solving vital, complex problems."[15]

In the months that followed, various other policy makers and policy followers voiced their irritation. The most extended diatribe came from Daniel Patrick Moynihan, who in early 1975 had just completed a stint as ambassador to India. In an influential article in *Commentary*, published in March of that year, Moynihan positioned the NIEO as a new incarnation of anti-American redistributionist socialism, in which the poorer nations made "threatening" claims on US wealth. He asked the United States to reject appeasement, move "into opposition," and defend the virtues of market economies, liberal trade policy, and multinational corporations. In the Ford administration, free market ideologues, including Secretary of the Treasury William Simon and economic advisor L. William Seidman, agreed. They blasted the NIEO as "socialist" interference with "the principles of free markets and free enterprise." Predictably, the *Wall Street Journal*, too, voted in favor of "market economics." Progress in the global South, it claimed, came "largely through the offices of . . . multinational corporations."[16]

Secretary of State Henry Kissinger shared the negative assessments of the NIEO but found Moynihan's approach too openly pugnacious. He adopted a manipulative approach instead. He hoped to defuse the NIEO with mollifying speeches and minor concessions. In a 1975 conversation, he told President Ford, "I don't want a New Economic Order," but he stated, too, that he did not "want to confront." He argued for less ideological defensiveness and more obfuscation. "I want to fuzz the ground," he said. He rejected open promotion of free market ideals; he saw "no reason to talk theory when we can in a practical way just screw up the negotiations."[17] In much-publicized speeches, Kissinger put on a conciliatory face with rhetoric that cloaked his oppositional stance. He stressed mutual interests, cooperation, and interdependence of North and South, and he promised food aid and negotiations on the price of individual commodities. Meanwhile, he conceded behind the scenes that he hoped to drive a wedge between the oil-producing and non-oil-producing nations of the global South. "Obviously we can't accept the new economic order," he stated, "but I would like to pull its teeth and divide those countries up."[18]

In the development establishment, liberals had a less cynical response. At the World Bank, Robert McNamara expressed initial interest in working with the UN to further at least some of the NIEO's goals. Shortly after the UN approved the NIEO, he had a meeting with Kurt Waldheim, the UN secretary-general, to see how the World Bank might help. The NIEO's call for transfer of resources aligned neatly with McNamara's push for more funds for multilateral foreign aid. McNamara also wanted the wealthier nations to increase their imports from the global South. As one historian has noted, the NIEO appealed to "McNamara's reformist sympathies." But his sympathies had their limits. McNamara saw the NIEO as political, and therefore outside the Bank's economic purview, and he opposed its calls for debt relief. Ultimately he had little incentive to engage directly with it. If implemented in full, the NIEO could reduce the Bank's central position in the global economy and give greater power to the governments of the South, many of which McNamara distrusted. He continued his push for antipoverty programs, but not via the NIEO.[19]

The liberal Overseas Development Council engaged more concertedly with the NIEO but refrained from outright support for it. ODC president James Grant acknowledged the need for "equity," with "greater sharing in decision making and the benefits of growth," and he called for "fuller understanding" in the North "of the nature of the aspirations of the developing countries."[20] By early 1975, he was, one observer noted, "working on State to soften their position on [the New] International Economic Order."[21] With funds from the Carnegie Endowment for International Peace, the

ODC held dinner seminars for policy makers in Washington, urging a less oppositional stance, and with grants from the Ford and Rockefeller Foundations, it produced a series of pamphlets on the NIEO.[22] As a Ford Foundation report stated, the ODC, like McNamara's World Bank, took "an essentially reformist approach." In general, it played the role of "upbeat" booster for foreign assistance and repeatedly worked to convince Washington insiders, the media, NGOs, and the general public to commit more funds to development programs.[23] But on the NIEO it focused primarily on ways to sidestep confrontational showdowns.

Instead of embracing the specifics of the NIEO, the ODC pushed, with blandness calibrated to soothe, for North-South negotiation and cooperation. It defended US interests and refrained from criticizing the practices of multinational corporations, but it also granted that the nations of the global South had reason for discontent. It endorsed what it came to call the "mutual gains thesis," an optimistic scenario in which increased trade and investment, stable prices, and the transfer of "surplus capital" from wealthier to poorer nations would benefit all. In 1978, it sponsored a conference on "mutual gains" at Princeton, with twenty-two mainstream development experts. Not surprisingly, the few participants from the global South wondered whether increased trade and investment would actually benefit their nations. They wanted structural changes in the global market to end their economic subordination.[24]

In Europe, social democrats expressed more direct support for the NIEO than did American liberals. In May 1975, the government of the Netherlands sponsored an international symposium on the NIEO, headed by Dutch socialist Jan Pronk, his nation's minister for development cooperation. The Netherlands, Pronk later claimed, was the first government in the North to endorse the NIEO.[25] Around the same time, in Sweden, the Dag Hammarskjöld Foundation also brought together an international group of development experts and then published *What Now? Another Development* on next steps for promoting international equity. It asked the UN to appoint a "Ministerial Committee" to "assure the implementation of the new international economic order," and it called for "an international redistribution of resources" and "the abolition of unequal economic relations."[26] And in Britain, in the fall of 1975, the *New Internationalist*, a left-leaning antipoverty magazine, published a special issue on the NIEO. It positioned the NIEO as the "main hope and rallying point for change towards a more just, and therefore less hungry, less crowded, less violent and less physically degraded world."[27]

In the United States the outright endorsements were fewer and farther between, and they came primarily from the Left. In the summer of 1974, for example, the Institute for Policy Studies, a leftist think tank in Washington, DC, took up the NIEO as one of its key issues. It embraced the NIEO but also critiqued its implicit acceptance of capitalism. The IPS hired Chilean exile Orlando Letelier, an economist and former ambassador to the United States, to head a special division on the NIEO. Letelier worked to forge a global network of activists in support of the NIEO until September, 1976, when Augusto Pinochet's ruthless regime planted the car bomb in Washington that killed him. After his murder, the Transnational Institute, an affiliate of the IPS, issued a pamphlet, *The International Economic Order*, by Letelier and IPS economist Michael Moffitt. The wealthier nations, they said, had answered the South's "claim for a more equitable world order" with responses that "ranged from callous indifference to outright hostility." US policies, they noted correctly, "had not changed significantly."[28]

And Michael Harrington, too, came out in support of the NIEO. He declared himself "in complete sympathy" with its demands. He saw "the distribution of the world's resources" as "intolerably unjust." Like the IPS, Harrington considered the NIEO "too moderate." He appreciated its general sentiment but remained unconvinced that it "would actually have the effect of closing the gap between the rich and the poor." Still, he wrote, "I continue to advocate the moderate program. . . . [T]here is no immediate possibility of a much more radical program." He hoped for "a world government that would allocate the goods and resources of the earth on something like a fair basis." But he dismissed his own "utopianism" and settled for the slow slog of practicality. "One must," he concluded, "be chastened, humbled, prepared to search for the miserable, inadequate increment of change that will help us transform the structure."[29]

But even incremental change had little chance of success. In mid-1975, *Newsweek* had characterized the North-South split as "the world's new Cold War." Over the next two years, skirmishes took place at various international meetings and conferences. Development economists at the University of Sussex urged the nations of the global North to make equitable counterproposals to the NIEO. They wanted serious negotiations on chapter and verse, instead of "suspicion and fear," "stone-walling," and "playing the game of making sympathetic noises."[30] And various economists, policy makers, and pundits came to agree at least on "the need for discussion and dialogue."[31] Talk, though, did not mean action. At the prolonged Conference on International Economic Co-operation, which held sessions in Paris from 1975 to 1977, delegates from "eight industrial countries" and "19 developing countries" convened, as one reporter put it, "in commissions and haggled over paragraphs about food, debts, prices, supplies, grants and guarantees." But the conference, as another analysis described it, "dissolved in total failure" with "literally no constructive results."[32]

The lack of progress in negotiations pointed to some of the thornier underlying issues, including racism and political economy. Although the NIEO did not use the language of race, everyone involved knew that the leaders of the global South were primarily people of color and the leaders of the global North were almost wholly white. The disparities in global wealth and the unequal participation of nations in international decision-making reflected the legacy of colonialism and its enduring racial hierarchies. In his essay "The Politics of the New International Economic Order," C. Clyde Ferguson Jr., an African American lawyer who had served, among other roles, as ambassador to Uganda, noted that "the third world has identified racism as an attribute of the present economic system." "It is," he wrote, "the allegation that the colonialist system and mentality has persisted." There had "been little public discussion of this aspect of the confrontation between the first and the third worlds," but "experienced diplomats" had "often remarked on the obvious presence of racial tensions."[33] Ferguson also addressed the tensions that arose from different approaches to economic regulation. In the North, the United States and West

Germany expressed the most resistance to intervening in the mechanisms of the market. But in many European nations and in much of the global South, statist planning, to varying degrees, trumped the unregulated market as the economic ideal. Supporters of the NIEO saw the US government, with good reason, as particularly oppositional, even obstructionist, and unwilling to tinker with a market that benefited the North.

The North-South dialogue had reached a stalemate. In the United States, those on the right reviled the NIEO, those on the left supported it, and those in the liberal development mainstream hoped to accommodate it piecemeal without swallowing it whole. The US government had made some minor concessions. It had set up a system of preferences that eliminated duties on some goods imported from the poorest nations, but only those goods that did not compete with products made in the United States. On every larger issue, negotiations had stalled. With a sense of despair, Barbara Ward captured the deadlock: "Nothing perhaps in the economic relations between the world's people over the last eighteen months has been more depressing and discouraging than the contrast between the continuous talk about a new economic order, the long official sessions, the tides of rhetoric, the oceans of print on the one hand and on the other, the complete failure of the developed and developing governments to agree on a single major point."[34]

In January 1977 when Jimmy Carter assumed the presidency, he brought renewed hope for something more than inertia. Two months after his inauguration, Carter spoke at the UN of "molding a global economic system which will bring greater prosperity to all the people of all countries." He promised "a positive and open attitude" in negotiations on commodity prices, and he expressed support for "developing countries" to participate more fully in "global economic decision making."[35] The content of his message was not all that different from the conciliatory rhetoric that Kissinger had adopted, but with Carter, a devout Southern Baptist, it rang with righteous sincerity. On the North-South dialogue, Carter followed the lead of the ODC, which pushed for more dialogue and more aid. In May 1977, at the Conference on International Economic Cooperation in Paris, Secretary of State Cyrus Vance announced that

Carter planned to ask Congress for a "substantial increase" in funds for development in the global South.[36]

Liberals and leftists expressed a guarded optimism. In the fall of 1977, Barbara Ward told Robert McNamara that she had heard that Carter was "considering a sort of 'North South' Marshall plan," which, she said, "would be the most hopeful of all possible developments." Michael Harrington also had "some cautious hopes for modest gains."[37] In the global South, too, expectations rose with the Carter administration. When Carter appointed Andrew Young, an African American civil rights activist and member of Congress, as the first Black US ambassador to the UN, he boosted his stock in African nations. And when he invited Julius Nyerere, the socialist president of Tanzania and a leading intellectual of the postcolonial world, to visit the White House in the summer of 1977, he signaled a welcome to a government that avidly supported the NIEO. During his visit, Nyerere gave a speech at Howard University that positioned the NIEO as the solution to global poverty, and after his meetings with Carter, which focused on ending White rule in Rhodesia (now Zimbabwe), he spoke with appreciation of "the genuineness, the determination and the sense of urgency" of the Carter administration. In the spring of 1978, a few days before Carter embarked on state visits to Venezuela, Brazil, Nigeria, and Liberia, the *Washington Post* reported that "the United States finds its Third World standing higher than it's been in years."[38]

From the start, though, Carter did not see the NIEO as his preferred route to fostering North-South harmony or to making the world more just and less impoverished. In early March, 1977, Carter and members of his administration met with congressional leaders to discuss foreign assistance. The administration's "talking points" stated clearly that "aid," not restructuring the economic order, "will be central to our constructive leadership of the North-South dialogue." It was "not in our national interest," they said, "to agree to all the demands of the developing countries." Many of those demands "would damage the world economy." They wanted "to shift the focus from the more irrational proposals" and increase US contributions to development assistance. Later in the year, the Carter administration publicly "pledged American leadership toward a new international economic system based on growth, equity and justice." But the language—"a new international economic system" as opposed to the New International Economic Order—subtly rejected the NIEO. On specific issues, such as stabilizing commodity prices, the administration might negotiate, but it would not accept the broader planks of the NIEO.[39]

By early 1978, the Carter administration had adopted a defensive stance. According to one National Security Council staffer, the other foreign aid donor nations viewed the United States as either "conservative" or "an obstacle to real progress in the North-South Dialogue."[40] The US government, it seemed clear, would not make any leaps toward global redistribution. The Carter administration opposed indexed prices, in which the price of the poorer nations' commodity exports would rise in tandem with the price of their imported manufactured goods. It refused to agree to contribute to a proposed international fund that would help poorer nations diversify and process the commodities they exported. In general, it rejected most of the proposals that came from the global South.[41] In the mid-1970s, the "trade union of the poor" had grabbed the attention of the wealthier nations and won a few concessions, but it could not restructure the international economy or recalibrate the balance of international power.

"To Satisfy, as a Matter of Urgency, the Basic Needs"

The Carter administration turned instead to a different antipoverty approach, known as "basic needs" or "basic human needs." Like the "New Directions" or "new style" programs of the early 1970s, the basic needs approach rejected trickle-down economics and redirected programs to the poorer people within the poorer nations. And like New Directions and earlier community development plans, it called for participation by the poor, sometimes sincerely but often perfunctorily, to indicate that its top-down programs would encourage democracy and refrain from coercing the people it claimed to help. But the basic needs approach differed, at least in stated intent, from earlier international antipoverty initiatives. It aimed to specify and meet the minimum needs of the poor worldwide and thereby eradicate the direst poverty. Its advocates came up with different permutations of what constituted needs, how to configure the minima, and how to determine who needed programs to lift them above the bar. Most agreed, though, that even a bare-bones version of basic needs should target food, clean water, shelter, health care, and primary education for those in "absolute" as opposed to "relative" poverty. The plan was to raise the global floor and ensure that the poorest of the poor had the resources to live above a defined level of sufficiency.

To do so, basic needs advocates continued to call for productivity and employment, but they positioned output and income as means to abolish poverty rather than as ends in themselves. They hoped to shift production away from luxury items for the wealthy and toward goods needed by more of the population, and they aimed to increase the purchasing power of the poor. They also emphasized the distribution and delivery of public services, such as water supply and schools, in a move to democratize the services already enjoyed by the wealthy. In the imagined happy ending, each nation would produce more of the goods it needed, public services would reach all citizens, and even the most indigent people would have the means to purchase what they needed.[42]

In the second half of the 1970s, antipoverty advocates and development experts converged on basic needs as a critical new step in the redistribution of wealth. Unlike many advocates of the NIEO, basic needs supporters often stressed inequality within the poorer nations. They sometimes made an explicit critique of development programs that enriched the wealthy elite of the global South and ignored the impoverished, and thereby placed the burden of redistribution on the poorer nations themselves. Still, the basic needs approach was not just an attempt to distract attention from global redistribution and structural change in the economic order. On the international level, most versions of basic needs also included redistribution among nations, with substantial transfer of funds to institute its programs. The World Bank, for example, estimated that basic needs programs would take twenty years and an additional $20 billion annually in multilateral and bilateral grants and loans to end extreme poverty.[43]

And basic needs demanded new ways of calculating progress. Trade and production figures could not show whether the most impoverished people had benefited. In their rhetoric, if not always in practice, basic needs supporters elevated fighting poverty over economic growth. For that reason, economic growth could not serve as the measure of success; it was instead a potential, but not sufficient, path to ending the direst of poverty, and it was also an expected result of poverty alleviation. Instead, development economists turned to different metrics and eventually constructed new indices that included life expectancy, infant mortality, and literacy.[44]

The ideas that underlay basic needs—poverty lines, minimum needs, and public services—were hardly new. Various advocates found prior articulations in, among other places, nineteenth-century England, mid-twentieth-century India, and welfare states more generally. But it was not until the mid-1970s that basic needs emerged in international development circles as a ubiquitous buzz phrase and explicit antipoverty alternative to trickle-down versions of modernization. An early prod, in the form of a foil, came from environmentalists who predicted global disaster. A 1972 study, *The Limits to Growth*, commissioned by the Club of Rome, an elite think tank centered in Europe, argued that existing patterns of economic development and population growth would outstrip the world's food supplies, exhaust its natural resources, and poison the earth. It made the case, as its title suggests, for "deliberately limiting growth."[45] Basic needs advocates attempted to counter this gloomy scenario by showing how development, now framed as poverty eradication, might take place without ruining the environment.

In the summer of 1974, at a seminar at the Dag Hammarskjöld Foundation, Maurice Strong, director of the United Nations Environment Programme (UNEP), discussed "his plan for an enquiry into the means of satisfying basic human needs without transgressing the outer limits of the biosphere." The UNEP hired Marc Nerfin, a Swiss consultant and former UN staffer, to write a "Feasibility Study," and in the fall it promoted a basic needs approach at a symposium, cosponsored with UNCTAD, in Cocoyoc, Mexico.[46] At the Cocoyoc symposium, Barbara Ward placed herself once again at the center of emerging development trends. In the early 1970s, she had turned her attention to the environment. In 1972, she coauthored *Only One Earth: The Care and Maintenance of a Small Planet*, the book that served as the background report for the UN Conference on the Human Environment, and in the fall of 1974, she chaired the symposium in Cocoyoc, called "Patterns of Resource Use, Environment and Development Strategies." She also drafted the declaration that the thirty-two symposium participants adopted.

With Ward's politic hand, the Cocoyoc Declaration had something for everyone in mid-1970s development circles. For environmentalists, it promoted development that would conserve natural resources and protect the earth, and it criticized the wasteful consumption of the rich. For leftists, it rejected the unregulated market and inequitable terms of trade, and endorsed the NIEO. For liberals, it reworked Ward's campaign for more international funds to address world poverty. But this time it avoided the language of "foreign aid," which offended leaders from the global South with its overtones of political meddling and paternalist handouts, and asked instead for "transfers of resources." And it placed basic needs as its top priority. "Our first concern," it stated, "is to redefine the whole purpose of development. . . . [T]he most important concern of development is the level of satisfaction of basic needs for the poorest sections of the population."[47] The Declaration was translated into five languages and circulated at the UN.

A month or so later, the Dag Hammarskjöld Foundation printed the Cocoyoc Declaration in its journal *Development Dialogue*, and began to elaborate on the basic needs strategy. Marc Nerfin had attended the Cocoyoc conference, and he used its declaration as the springboard for the Foundation's project, cosponsored by the UNEP, to construct "a conceptual framework" and "alternative policies . . . for satisfying basic human needs."[48] The following year, 1975, the project findings were put into print in *What Now? Another Development*, which aimed "to define a global approach to problems" and reform the UN system. In the midst of the North-South impasse, *What Now?* not only endorsed the NIEO but also called to "place the satisfaction of needs—beginning with the eradication of poverty—at the focal point of the development process." "In the Third World," it stated, "concrete programmes are required to satisfy, as a matter of urgency, the basic needs." Like the Cocoyoc Declaration, *What Now?* refused to accept doomsday environmentalism as an excuse for inaction. "Resources are available to satisfy basic needs," it claimed. "The question is primarily one of distributing them more equitably."[49]

At roughly the same time, the ILO selected basic needs as "the single most important idea" of its 1976 World Employment Conference.[50] In 1975, as they planned the conference, staff at the ILO were surprised to learn that the Hammarskjöld Foundation had already worked on the same approach. In January, Appiah Pathmarajah, the special adviser for the ILO conference, wrote in a memo that Nerfin's "outline follows remarkably along the same line that we have proposed." And when *What Now?* arrived in the summer, Pathmarajah greeted it with alarm: "everything we have said in our [draft] . . . already appears in the Nerfin report. . . . [U]nless in our own paper we either acknowledge the Marc Nerfin study or indicate that we are carrying it forward, it would appear that we plagiarized the Dag Hammarskjöld report."[51] As Pathmarajah indicated, the ILO's version of basic needs lined up neatly with the basic needs strategy seen in the Cocoyoc Declaration and the Hammarskjöld Foundation's *What Now?* Its model aimed to lift the poorest 20 percent of the world's population out of poverty within one generation.[52]

At the ILO conference, held in June 1976, the debates highlighted the global divides. On one side, delegates from "a few industrialized market economy countries" and some representatives of employers wanted more emphasis on economic growth and less attention to "structural change and redistribution." For them, the problem of "underdevelopment in the Third World" resulted from problems within the poorer nations. The delegates from the United States, appointed by the Ford administration, were particularly oppositional. At an earlier planning consultation, held at the US Department of Labor in 1975, American participants had already complained to the ILO that "the basic needs development strategy . . . smacks of socialism." After the conference, Louis Emmerij, the annoyed director of the ILO's World Employment Programme, grumbled that the Americans viewed basic needs as "bullshit" that involved "planning," "interfering with free market forces," "collectivisation," and even "violent revolution." As Michael Harrington described it later, the US delegates "were horrified by proposals to interfere with the 'market' mechanism, carefully ignoring the fact that the market has been rigged for four hundred years."[53] On the other side, those from "developing and socialist developed countries" and representatives of workers worried that labor-intensive work for the poor would perpetuate the technological gap between the North and South. For them, the real problem was the "international economy." The two sides also disagreed about—in fact, "the sharpest differences of opinion" arose over—multinational corporations and whether to institute a "legally binding code of conduct" on them. But somehow the delegates managed to agree by acclamation on the basic needs approach. The conference adopted a program of action that began with "the promotion of employment and the satisfaction of the basic needs of each country's population."[54] One of the virtues of a basic needs strategy, it seems, was that it was hard in the end to oppose the eradication of poverty.

Meanwhile, variants of basic needs sprouted in other sites as well. Researchers at the Fundación Bariloche, a think tank in Argentina, rejected the dark Malthusian vision of *The Limits to Growth* by constructing their own global model for how to fulfill "minimum requirements of food, housing and education." They first presented their research at a conference in 1975, and then published it in 1976 as *Catastrophe or New Society? A Latin American World Model.* Poorer nations, they suggested, should not bear the burden of limiting growth. Instead, they claimed, nations could fulfill basic needs by reducing "nonessential consumption," producing "basic goods," optimizing land use, diminishing trade deficits, and improving distribution of "goods and services."[55] And even the Club of Rome, which had sponsored *The Limits to Growth*, retreated from its earlier intimations of environmental disaster. It commissioned Jan Tinbergen, a Nobel Prize–winning Dutch economist, to coordinate a team study on RIO, or "Reshaping the International Order." The end result, published in 1976, pointed to the basic needs approach. Instead of pitting "growth versus environment," the study suggested using "renewable resources" and "giving priority to the satisfaction of the fundamental needs of the whole population, starting with the eradication of poverty."[56]

Soon the World Bank, too, jumped on the basic needs juggernaut and even hoped to steer it. In 1974 and 1975, Bank staff consulted with the UNEP and the ILO during their early discussions of basic needs, and by late 1976 Robert McNamara had started reframing his earlier antipoverty message in the lexicon of basic needs. At his annual speech to the Bank's board of governors that year, McNamara spoke of meeting "basic human needs . . . by the end of the century." Shortly after, he asked his senior staff to consider "a dramatic change in the intellectual leadership role of the Bank," with a proposed goal of "meeting basic human needs or eliminating absolute poverty."[57] Much of the staff, it seems, opposed the reorientation. Basic needs, a reporter wrote, was "highly controversial inside the institution." Staff members complained that basic needs projects were "harder to devise, harder to implement, harder to supervise and harder to evaluate."[58] They created bureaucratic headaches. They also seemed prone to failure and dangerously removed from the Bank's work as a lending institution that had favored economic growth. McNamara called for additional research, and he turned to the Bank's house radicals: Mahbub ul Haq, Paul Streeten, and their allies.

From 1978 to 1981, Haq, Streeten, and their colleagues—Shahid Javed Burki, Norman Hicks, Paul Isenman, and Frances Stewart—produced a series of studies that positioned the basic needs approach as the mission of the Bank. Streeten, who served as the primary researcher, had come to the Bank in 1976 as a senior advisor. He had grown up in Austria and fled to Britain when the Nazis came to power. In his youth he was a socialist activist, and later he studied at Oxford, worked with Gunnar Myrdal, and helped found the Institute for Development Studies at the University of Sussex.[59] Haq was the public voice of the Bank's basic needs approach. He had already established himself within the Bank hierarchy as its vocal antipoverty advocate, and he had adopted the underlying assumptions of basic needs as early as 1971. In a keynote address that year to the Society for International Development, he had called for "developing countries" to "define minimum (or threshold) consumption standards" that might be met "in a manageable period of time, say a decade." He wanted "a minimum bundle of goods and services . . . provided to the common man to eliminate the worst manifestations of poverty."[60]

In the mid-1970s, with tensions over the NIEO, Haq played an especially crucial role. Economists from the global North could no longer monopolize the decision-making positions in international organizations. Haq had a reputation as a relatively moderate advocate for the South. In 1973, he had helped found the Third World Forum, a group of development experts who hoped to represent the views of the global South. As a left-leaning liberal from Pakistan, he became the "Third World spokesman within the Bank" and gave a hint of legitimacy to the Bank's claim to represent the "world." As he recalled, he helped McNamara "when it came . . . to articulating the developing countries' point of view and to putting on pressure for change." A *Washington Post* reporter described him as "an international citizen, one of Washington's truly intriguing people" and "an operator" as well.[61]

Haq's personal views sometimes diverged from the official positions taken by the Bank. To conservatives, inside the Bank and out, he was, he said, a "raving socialist" who refused to stay in line. McNamara had a drawerful of letters demanding Haq's resignation. Within the Bank, Haq generated resentment for his high profile and his willingness to push the boundaries. He created a firestorm when he spoke up publicly in favor of debt forgiveness. As McNamara remembered it, Haq "proposed that all debt to the developing countries be forgiven, which included our debt. My god, there was a revolution at the Bank! You know, here we've got, whatever it was, 11 billion dollars of debt out, and Mahbub is recommending it be forgiven. . . . Oh, Jesus! The Bank erupted!"[62]

But Haq also took heat, as he noted, from radicals of the global South who saw him as an apologist for capitalism, the World Bank, and the United States. Still, he was much in demand among liberal and left advocates of basic needs. In the mid-1970s, he participated in several of the seminars and conferences—at the Hammarskjöld Foundation, at Cocoyoc, and in Jan Tinbergen's RIO group—that established the basic needs approach. Haq's book, *The Poverty Curtain: Choices for the Third World*, published in 1977, gave him even more intellectual capital. The book reprinted a number of his earlier speeches and articles, promoted a basic needs approach, and attempted to explain the demands of the South to readers in the North.[63]

As spelled out by Streeten and Haq, the Bank's authorized approach to basic needs sounded similar to what others had proposed. It aimed for the end of absolute poverty via productivity and public services. Some critics, however, considered the World Bank's version a weaker variant, in part because it came from an

FIGURE 2.1. While working at the World Bank, Mahbub ul Haq, a Pakistani
economist, promoted the "basic needs" approach to eradicating poverty.
(UN Photo by Miguel Jimenez)

institution they already distrusted.[64] The World Bank had a well-
earned reputation for top-down, technocratic approaches to economic development, and it provided generous loans to repressive, authoritarian governments. It had refused to give loans, for
example, to Salvador Allende's socialist government in Chile in the
early 1970s, and then provided them when Augusto Pinochet seized
power and established his brutal dictatorship. When Streeten, Haq,
and others suggested repeatedly that the basic needs strategy was

essentially apolitical—compatible with "a wide variety of political regimes"—they hoped to broaden its appeal, but they simultaneously aroused suspicion on the left. "It is that sort of statement," Guy Standing, a British economist who worked for the ILO, wrote, "that . . . bolsters a politically conservative ideology."[65]

Standing pointed to the limits of the Bank's basic needs approach. He considered its programs "selective, piecemeal interventions . . . little more than palliatives to preserve the socio-economic structure, which in reality has been the fundamental cause of the perceived poverty." He wanted to end "exploitation and domination," not just measure poverty, count calories, and provide bundles of services.[66] Without the NIEO, the World Bank's variant of basic needs adopted humanitarian rhetoric that may have widened its appeal but also signaled its lesser ambitions. It imagined the end of poverty but failed to envision significant redistributions of power or changes in social relations, either within nations or between them. It recognized the failures of earlier modernization programs that had relied on trickle-down economics, and it tried to replace them with labor-intensive production and public services that refrained from threatening the political status quo.

In its early incarnations in the Cocoyoc Declaration and the Hammarskjöld Foundation, the basic needs approach came conjoined with support for the NIEO, and in that form it won support from the global South. Gamani Corea, a Sri Lankan economist and secretary-general of UNCTAD, for example, saw the two approaches as complementary.[67] From early on, African socialist leaders had supported antipoverty programs. In Tanzania, for example, Nyerere, a staunch supporter of the NIEO, pursued plans to redistribute wealth in a concerted attack on his nation's poverty. Economic growth, he said, should serve "the basic needs of food, shelter, health, and education." As historian Vijay Prashad has noted, Nyerere made basic needs "the cornerstone of his theory of development." In the late 1970s, US diplomats in Tanzania were, according to Michael Harrington, "surprisingly sympathetic" to Nyerere and his socialist egalitarian aims, despite the coercive collectivization in the countryside. And the Tanzanian government accepted significant funds from USAID, including a $15 million basic needs grant "to increase the income and welfare of families in rural villages."[68] In Jamaica, Prime Minister Michael Manley, also a socialist and strong NIEO advocate, accepted $15 million in USAID loans for an urban basic needs program. Orlando Patterson, Manley's special advisor, remembered "an unusually strong commitment to the basic needs approach" in 1970s Jamaica.[69]

But supporters of the NIEO balked when basic needs seemed to serve as a substitute for the NIEO rather than a complement to it, and when it appeared as a foreign imposition rather than an internal commitment. The World Bank's focus on antipoverty programs within the poorer nations suggested that it planned to avoid the issue of the global economic order and bypass postcolonial governments with programs and priorities devised in Washington. "The developing countries," the economist Hans Singer wrote, "tend to be deeply suspicious of the tendency of western governments to talk about poverty and human needs. . . . They consider this preference of the West partly as an intervention in their own internal affairs and partly as a device to avoid the discussion of really important questions." Without the NIEO, basic needs could look like a form of "neo-colonialism" that undermined the sovereignty of independent nations, and it could divert attention from the structural inequities that kept some nations poor. Economists from the global South also worried that basic needs—with its focus on labor-intensive productivity—would "discourage industrial development." According to one such critic, Ajit Singh, an Indian economist at the University of Cambridge, basic needs appeared "to the LDCs [Less Developed Countries], rightly or wrongly, to be designed to hamper their industrialization" and thereby eliminate potential competition for goods manufactured in the wealthier nations.[70]

At the 1978 International Development Conference, held in Washington to address the theme of meeting basic human needs, Streeten and Haq promoted their approach and insisted that there was "no conflict between basic human needs and the New International Economic Order." But other participants from the South expressed skepticism. They emphasized repeatedly that meeting basic needs could happen only "within the framework of broad international economic structural reform." It "must not, they warned, serve as a substitute for global economic restructuring." Moreover, it would take "radical internal changes in the developing societies" and an "unprecedented, massive capital infusion" that seemed unlikely in an era of "general retrenchment in the giving of foreign assistance."[71]

They had reason for concern. Who would supply the unprecedented, massive capital infusion? In the early 1960s, the United States had led the way in contributing to overseas development. But over the course of fifteen years, US assistance funds had shriveled in tandem with the disillusionment with foreign aid and the slowdown in the US economy. At its peak, in 1963, the United States had contributed 0.59 percent of its GNP to official development assistance; by 1978 the figure had dropped to 0.23 percent. In 1978 only four of the seventeen Organisation for Economic Cooperation and Development (OECD) donor nations—Sweden, Norway, the Netherlands, and Denmark—met the UN target, adopted in 1970, requesting donor nations to make annual contributions of 0.7 percent of their GNP. The United States hovered in thirteenth place among the seventeen nations. (In unadjusted dollar figures, the US contribution had increased from $3.6 billion in 1963 to $4.8 billion in 1978, but in buying power $4.8 billion in 1978 was the equivalent of roughly $2.25 billion in 1963. Over the course of fifteen years, then, US official development assistance had declined by almost $1.4 billion in 1963 dollars.) Under pressure, the OPEC countries had begun to contribute to development efforts, and the Soviet Union, China, and other socialist nations had their own investments in economic development programs, geared mostly toward bolstering trade, promoting industry, and building infrastructure in the poorer nations.[72] But the World Bank, the ILO, and others hoped that the basic needs message— its hard-to-object-to quest for poverty eradication—would pry open the coffers and leverage additional funds, especially from the United States.[73]

Within the United States, the ODC stepped into the fray to advocate for basic needs policies and the funds to support them. It called on "the rich countries," especially the United States, to increase aid "linked specifically to programs aimed at the most essential needs of the world's poorest billion people." It retreated from the UN's 0.7 percent target, and claimed that if donor nations would contribute just 0.5 percent of GNP and direct it to basic needs in the poorest countries, then "the worst aspects of absolute poverty could be eliminated" by the year 2000.[74] It considered its advocacy of basic needs "rather successful" in, among other places, "the U.S. Congress [and] the World Bank." And it had the ear of Jimmy Carter. Even before he won the presidency, Carter turned to the ODC for advice. During his campaign, he relied on James Grant, the ODC president, for help with speeches and debates. Once in the White House, he consulted frequently with Theodore Hesburgh, the influential Catholic priest who headed the ODC board, and he hired Roger D. Hansen, an ODC staff member, as an adviser on his National Security Council. From the start, the ODC's vision of basic needs shaped Carter's foreign policy.[75]

Jimmy Carter's Hunger

In 1974, the famines in Bangladesh and the Sahel moved the American public in ways that only disasters can. Media coverage, with photos "of skeletal children and desiccated cows," revived support for global charities. Relief agencies, public and private, shifted into high gear, raising funds for the emergency and shipping tons of grain to Asia and Africa.[76] In November 1974, the UN sponsored a World Food Conference in Rome to address the crisis. The resulting declaration stated, "every man, woman and child has the right to be free from hunger and malnutrition."[77] The following year the National Council of Churches established the Coordinating Council for Hunger Concerns, and Protestant, Catholic, and Jewish leaders joined in the Interreligious Task Force on US Food Policy and published the newsletter *Hunger*. By mid-1975, Bread for the World, a Christian organization, had 9,400 dues-paying members, just one year after its national debut. On the left, Frances Moore Lappé and Joseph Collins, who met at the UN's World Food Conference, founded the Institute for Food and Development Policy, known as Food First. Starvation, they argued, was not a result of scarcity but of cost, distribution, and control of resources.[78] By 1978, a student intern at the White House could identify around a hundred US organizations that addressed world hunger. Many of them—The Hunger Project, World Hunger Year, Bread for the World, and Food First, for example—were new groups, formed after the press reports on famine. Meanwhile, scholars also took up hunger as a subject of study. In the volume *World Hunger and Moral Obligation*, philosophers debated ethical duty and tilted sharply toward feeding the poor.[79]

For Jimmy Carter, too, hunger served as a touchstone. During his presidential campaign, he defined "doing what's right" as "caring for the poor, providing food, becoming the bread basket of the world instead of the arms merchant of the world." After he took office, he used hunger, consciously or not, as a rhetorical tool. He repeatedly invoked hunger and disease in conjunction with poverty. In March 1977, when Carter asked Congress to increase both multilateral and bilateral aid, he promoted assistance as a way "to help poor nations overcome the problems of hunger, disease, and illiteracy," and he requested an additional $50 million for the famine-stricken nations of the Sahel. In other speeches as well, Carter spoke of "oppressive hunger and disease and poverty," "alleviation of hunger, poverty, and disease," and "hunger, suffering, poverty, and disease."[80] Hunger and disease had an amplifying effect, upping the urgency and highlighting the humanitarian justification for foreign assistance funds.

From early on, Carter committed his administration to basic needs policies. In his first address to the UN, in March 1977, he promised that the United States would advance "proposals aimed at meeting the basic human needs of the developing world."[81] In the months that followed, Secretary of State Cyrus Vance and other US officials promoted the basic needs approach at the Conference on International Economic Cooperation and the OECD, and the National Security Council began to coordinate a multiagency study that aimed, as one newspaper reported, to position basic needs "as a complement to the Carter Administration's human rights campaign."[82] For Carter, the basic needs approach had appeal. It emphasized the compassionate side of foreign aid and sat comfortably with his religious convictions, which included charity for the poor.

It held wider potential as well. With food as an undeniable need, it could draw from the well of sentiment inspired by the famines. Public opinion polls showed overwhelming support for food and medical supplies sent overseas for emergency relief but less support for other economic aid. A 1974 poll conducted by Louis Harris and Associates, for example, surveyed 1,513 American adults and found that 93 percent supported emergency relief and 79 percent favored foreign "economic aid if sure that it ended up helping the poor," but only 52 percent supported "economic aid for purposes of economic development and technical assistance."[83] In September 1977, Carter appointed a World Hunger Working Group to study potential policies. "I have repeatedly emphasized as a major goal of foreign policy the importance of meeting basic human needs," he said, "in particular, the alleviation of world hunger and malnutrition."[84] The call to feed the hungry gave basic needs a do-good feel that the numbing negotiations on international trade lacked. As a public relations move, basic needs could boost the Carter administration onto the moral high ground.

Carter started off optimistically with hopes of doubling foreign aid and implementing a basic needs strategy. By the end of 1977, his Development Coordination Committee, his Policy Review Committee, and the Brookings Institution had all issued reports supporting the basic needs approach. Taken together, the various documents recommended basic needs as "the primary focus of U.S. development assistance programs" and positioned it as "part of our approach to supporting human rights," which now included "the right to be free from poverty."[85] Beyond the transparent appeal of alleviating poverty, the Policy Review Committee suggested a further reason to endorse the basic needs approach. It could keep "a spotlight on what LDC's [Less Developed Countries] do for themselves and on the economic inequities *within* them." For the Carter administration, basic needs was not a complement to the NIEO. It was a weaker version of basic needs that might deflect attention from the US role in development and from the NIEO's protests against global inequality.[86]

USAID backed the new approach. In a press release, its new administrator, John J. Gilligan, said that he hoped to help "developing countries . . . meet the minimum basic needs . . . and thus virtually eliminate the worst vestiges of absolute poverty" by the year 2000.[87] Gilligan worked to streamline the agency, to decentralize it so that more of the staff worked outside the United States, and to focus it on antipoverty programs. The agency, he said, was "strangled in paperwork" with "too much emphasis on Washington operations . . . and too little in actually delivering goods and services to the poor majority in the developing countries." As one journalist described it, USAID, "heavily influenced by politics," had "failed to save the save the hearts and minds of Southeast Asia from communism." Now Gilligan and his allies aimed "to stick to economic goals and zero in on the lot of the world's poor."[88] In response to the basic needs consensus, USAID launched a number of small-scale projects aimed at poverty alleviation. The projects captured the tenor of the times, addressing ongoing concerns about population growth, with funds for "family planning," and concerns about food, with attention to agricultural production. In the era of "small is beautiful," they focused on the local and on less complicated, less costly "appropriate technology" for rural development.[89]

But reorganizing an agency, resetting its priorities, and initiating small programs in various settings could not possibly meet the larger goal of eradicating the worst of global poverty. Carter's endorsement of basic needs carried a price tag that his call for human rights did not. Basic needs programs required funds. In 1973, liberal members of Congress had pushed through the New Directions mandate, but now the support for foreign assistance had dwindled. Congress posed an obstacle. Members of Congress did not object to basic needs policies per se, but they had ongoing concerns about the foreign aid bureaucracy, its lackluster staff, its spending, and its backscratching contracts with some US firms. The World Bank, too, came under scrutiny for its high salaries, first-class flights, and lavish annual parties. In the government and elsewhere, conservatives still envisioned foreign aid as money wasted on ungrateful "Third World beggars," and they condemned aid to socialist governments.[90] Liberals remembered how foreign aid had supported military operations in Vietnam, and they protested the way it continued to uphold authoritarian regimes. And both conservatives and liberals warned that money intended for the indigent often ended up in the hands of the wealthy elites in the poorer nations.

The troubled US economy added another layer of resistance. In the late 1970s inflation rose and so did the US trade deficit. Imports of oil, steel, and other products surged. Domestic industries wanted protection from overseas competition, and budget-conscious poli-ticians gave priority to domestic spending. In this climate, Carter retreated from his promise to increase foreign aid. The administra-tion decided not to ask Congress for additional funds for develop-ment assistance. Despite earlier intimations of a "grand attack on world poverty," the *Washington Post* reported, the administration had "trimmed its ambitions to its political constraints."[91]

To the Carter administration, the "opposition to foreign aid" in Congress seemed "wholly disproportionate." In response, Carter tried to up the moral ante. In the summer of 1978, he brought reli-gious leaders to the White House on two occasions and asked them to help him persuade Congress to vote for his foreign aid propos-als. He stressed the argument for charity, familiar to his ministe-rial audience, "that we should be responsible for the well-being of those throughout the world less fortunate than we." But Carter was not just a pious paternalist. In the US government, foreign aid was never solely or simply a humanitarian issue. Like his predecessors, he invoked geopolitical rivalries, national security, and economic benefits. With détente on the decline, Carter, an avid Cold Warrior, reminded the religious leaders that "atheistic, communist, totali-tarian governments" in Africa posed "competition," and he warned of "failing in many parts of the world if we dash the hopes of those who look to us for aid, for help, and for understanding." He also pointed to trade in the global South that supplied the "raw materi-als that we can use to keep our own people at work" and provided the markets for US exports "that also keep our people at work."[92]

In discussions with Congress, the economic arguments loomed even larger. There the Carter administration emphasized "the importance of the foreign aid contracts to American business." As a *New York Times* reporter explained, the ongoing policy of "tying" mandated that much of the money spent by USAID "be used for the purchase of American goods and services," with profits accruing across a corporate field, from "agricultural, industrial and transpor-tation equipment manufacturers to fertilizer, chemical and rubber producers." USAID advertised its projects in the *Commerce Daily*, a US newspaper, and American businesses then pursued contracts. The World Bank, too, had multi-million-dollar deals with Ameri-can firms, and American investors also benefited from interest paid on bonds issued by the Bank. Aid for the poor was big business. For this reason, the American Chamber of Commerce supported foreign aid, and some development experts refrained from criticizing the practice of tying because they feared they would lose the support of corporate lobbyists.[93]

A few liberal policy makers, such as Representative Clarence Long, a Maryland Democrat, recoiled from "the argument that foreign aid should be supported because it benefits American business." Reporters, too, occasionally published critical articles that found that "companies and consultants at home, rather than poor people abroad, receive most of AID's economic development funds." But the Carter administration used the argument of domestic gain unabashedly in its attempt to lift the levels of aid. In 1979, the White House Press Office announced that "Foreign aid is domestic aid." While poorer nations spiraled into debt, it touted the economic windfall from their loan repayments, which, it said, "are currently coming in at such a rate that many countries are sending us more in repayments than we are sending them in new assistance." It noted, too, that nations "which receive loans from the MDBs [multilateral development banks] in turn then spend a major percentage of those funds back in the United States." In this way and others, it attempted to reassure Congress and the American public that the United States reaped financial profits from aid to poorer nations.[94]

But even blatantly America-first arguments had limited success. The administration returned to the issue of hunger, which might elicit more support than proposals for foreign aid. In September 1978, at the urging of Congress, Carter signed an executive order to form the Presidential Commission on World Hunger. "This administration," he promised, "will intensify its efforts to meet the world hunger problem." In behind-the-scenes planning, Carter's advisors suggested, and Carter agreed, that the commission should focus less on policy recommendations and more "on building public support." The administration might use the commission to "build up the foreign assistance constituency."[95]

In the commission's final report, issued in March 1980, hunger served as a metonym for poverty. The commission called for making "the elimination of hunger the primary focus" of the US government's "relationships with the developing countries." It positioned food as "the most basic" of human rights and human needs, and it pulled out the usual trinity of justifications—"moral obligation and responsibility," "economic self-interest," and "national security"—for US contributions to "a vigorous attack on the world hunger problem." It repeated the timeline routinely used by advocates of basic needs, and imagined "eliminating at least the very worst aspects of hunger by the year 2000." And it asked the US government to "immediately double the level of US development assistance." Eventually, it said, the United States should reach the UN's target contribution of 0.7 percent of GNP, which was "about three times the current level."[96]

The commission's final report also had surprisingly strong policy recommendations on stabilizing the price of raw materials, reducing barriers to the poorer nations' exports, "'wiping out' the debt currently owed by the poorest developing countries," shifting assistance to grants rather than loans, and establishing "standards of conduct for multinational companies in developing countries." By the summer of 1980, Carter's advisers had reviewed the report and planned to use it in Carter's second term to revive the flagging interest in funding foreign aid, but the second term never came to be.[97]

In any case, by 1980, the Carter administration had mostly given up. In the end, Carter was unable and unwilling to adhere to his own antipoverty agenda. The ODC wrote of "missed opportunities" and rated "the record" on foreign assistance "poor." And Carter administration insiders were increasingly critical. On the National Security Council, Thomas Thornton found that Carter's public campaign for foreign assistance came "too late." Plus, he said, Carter's basic needs approach "was seen as patronizing, if not interventionist, by most of the poorer countries with whom we deal," and it was "ultimately, not a convincing rationale for selling a systematic program of foreign assistance to the American people and Congress." Former National Security Council staffer Roger Hansen also expressed disappointment. He claimed that the administration had tried to co-opt the wealthier nations of the South while "stonewalling on structural reform," and he accused it of "heavy-handedness in introducing the basic needs theme" to the exclusion of global equity. He still hoped, though, that the US government would "refine" the basic needs approach to "overcome present Southern concerns and objections," and "generate the substantial Northern financial commitment which will be required." Meanwhile, the administration gave increased priority to security or military aid, with billions committed especially to Egypt and Israel. And other issues commanded attention. In Carter's last year in office, his foreign policy advisers focused on the US hostages held by the new regime in Iran and the Soviet invasion of Afghanistan.[98]

An International Tax

In the last years of the 1970s, supporters of the NIEO and of basic needs worked to salvage and join the two approaches in yet another attempt to glean something productive from the North-South negotiations. Despite the difference in connotation, the NIEO's "transfer of resources" was not all that different from the liberal mainstream's "foreign assistance." Advocates of both strategies pushed for a redistributive movement of capital from North to South. At a minimum, both generally asked that the wealthier nations meet the UN's unmet target in which donor nations contributed 0.7 percent of their GNP to the economic development of the global South. In the late 1970s they converged on the ideas of "automaticity" and international taxation. An automatic tax provided a potential way to work around the failure of nations, notably the United States, to contribute consistently and unconditionally to global development programs.

The notion of an international tax for global economic development had popped up sporadically since World War II. Among the advocates was Gunnar Myrdal, who briefly mentioned an international tax in his popular 1970 book *The Challenge of World Poverty*.[99] But the notion of automatic payments into an international fund took on a new life in the late 1970s, especially with the rise of the environmental movement. Support came from a roster of big names in development circles, including Barbara Ward, Mahbub ul Haq, Paul Streeten, Jan Tinbergen, James Grant, and Maurice Strong. In 1974, the Cocoyoc Declaration, drafted by Ward, provided an early articulation. It stated that "the uses of international commons should be taxed for the benefit of the poorest strata of the poor countries." A tax on the commons—"for instance, tolls . . . levied from vessels crossing the high seas"—might curb the depletion of resources and pollution of the environment, and it might also serve as "a first step towards the establishment of an international taxation system aimed at providing automatic transfers of resources to development assistance."[100]

The call for automatic payments and international taxes quickly gained traction and began to show up repeatedly in other discussions of development. At the September 1975 UN Special Session, the General Assembly, in support of the NIEO, endorsed automatic (and not just voluntary) contributions to development in the global South. It approved a resolution that asked for substantial growth in "financial resources to developing countries . . . made predictable, continuous and increasingly assured." The following year the Club of Rome's report on RIO elaborated on the theme. Mahbub ul Haq and James Grant coauthored the technical section of the RIO report, "Income Redistribution and the International Financing of Development." They hoped for "increased transfer of resources" between and within nations, and they imagined "an element of automation . . . built into the resource transfer system." It was "still too early," they acknowledged, to win acceptance for "the concept of international taxation of the rich nations for the benefit of the poor nations," but they hoped it could be "introduced gradually over time." They listed additional goods and activities that might eventually be taxed, including, among others, "non-renewable resources," "international pollutants," "transnational enterprises," and "commercial activities arising out of international commons," which now included "ocean beds, outer space, [and] the Antarctic region."[101]

Maurice Strong, the Canadian head of the United Nations Environment Programme, convinced the Brookings Institution to investigate the feasibility of the various proposals. In 1977, with funds from the UNEP and the Rockefeller and Ford Foundations, the Brookings Institution convened a conference at the Rockefeller center in Bellagio, Italy, and the following year published a book, *New Means of Financing International Needs*. The book concluded with several potential taxes that "could be used to finance any agreed upon international programs": a tax on governments based on their gross domestic product, a tax on extraction from the ocean floor, and a tax on international trade and financial transactions.[102]

At the end of the decade, international taxation was an aspiration more than a real possibility. It was a way to rethink the ongoing quest for redistribution from wealthier to poorer nations and a way to appeal to advocates of both the NIEO and the basic needs approach. And, as such, it needed publicity as much as it needed a technical report designed to convince development experts. It finally got its wider airing in the report of the Independent Commission on International Development Issues, commonly known as the Brandt Commission. The commission was the brainchild of Barbara Ward, Mahbub ul Haq, and others, who wanted a more influential and updated version of the 1969 report of the Commission on International Development, led by Lester Pearson. The discussions for the new commission started soon after Carter defeated Ford in the presidential election. "Now that Jimmy Carter has won the presidency," Haq wrote to Ward, "I wonder if we dare raise our hopes again and revive our own intellectual mafia committed to a cooperative change in the world order." He suggested "something like a floating, informal Pearson Commission of 25–30 leading opinion makers of the world who could get the dialogue on the new international order pointed in the right direction." Ward agreed. "The time is ripe," she responded, "for the type of 'Pearson' reconsideration of where we are going." Two months later, Robert McNamara proposed the new commission in a speech in Boston. He called for "a high-level, deliberately unofficial Commission" that could generate independent findings and avoid the wrangling of official or governmental negotiations. It would seek "mutually agreeable solutions" rather "than the continued exchange of proposals and counter-proposals."[103]

The Pearson Commission, which McNamara had also initiated, was not exactly an inspiring model. "Some economists," the *New York Times* reported, were "skeptical," remembering that the Pearson Commission's "massive study of world poverty . . . came to nought." But McNamara wanted "to have another go at it—and also to take a crack at resolving the tensions and conflicts between the industrial countries of the North and the developing countries of the South."[104] McNamara suggested that Willy Brandt, a Nobel

FIGURE 2.2. Julius K. Nyerere, president of Tanzania, and Willy Brandt, former
chancellor of West Germany, 1976. Nyerere was an avid supporter of both the NIEO and
the basic needs approach. In the late 1970s, Brandt chaired the Independent Commission
on International Development Issues. The commission's report, *North-South: A Program
for Survival*, called for an international tax to transfer resources from wealthier to
poorer nations. (picture alliance/Getty Images)

Peace Prize winner and the former chancellor of West Germany,
might chair the new commission, and Brandt eventually signed on.
The commission began its work in December 1977 with an opening
session in Germany.

In some respects, Brandt's commission did resemble Pearson's.
It brought together well-known figures from development circles
and international politics to promote "solutions to the problems
involved in development and in attacking absolute poverty." But
the Brandt Commission also differed from the earlier venture.
Unlike the Pearson Commission, it did not receive financial support from the World Bank. Brandt wanted it "very independent of
[the] World Bank." And McNamara, too, hoped to ensure that it
would not look like an in-house operation. To attract "widespread
Third World support" and contribute "to N-S dialogue," one memo
stated, the Bank would have to "keep a low profile."[105] Around half

of the money for the Brandt Commission came from the Dutch government, the rest from nineteen other nations, which gave money
or paid the costs of hosting commission meetings and delegations,
and also from a handful of private donors and international organizations, funds, and foundations.[106]

And unlike the Pearson Commission, most of the commissioners
came from the global South. The times had changed, and leaders
in the North had learned that they could not hold credible international forums if they failed to include the South. Brandt insisted on
"a majority of Third World commissioners," and refused to agree to
run the commission until he found that leaders of the global South
would not object to it. In a further sign of the times, when Brandt
announced the commission after its first meeting, he said that
"words like 'aid' or 'the rich helping the poor'" were "deliberately
avoided and replaced by the notion of interdependence and mutu-
ality of interest."[107] The NIEO had made its mark, at least in terms
of who participated in mainstream commissions, whose endorsement mattered, and what language the commission adopted.

Nonetheless, Brandt and his colleagues had to overcome suspicions on all sides. In the South, the commission's explicit attention
to "basic needs" and "mutual interests" aroused concerns that it
would refrain from addressing global inequities, and in the North,
the commission had to contend with "growing coolness . . . towards
the South," "foreign aid fatigue" and "more conservative and inward
looking governments."[108] The commission report, *North-South: A
Program for Survival*, tried to disarm the skeptics. Published in
1980, it went for breadth instead of depth, covering a range of top-
ics from poverty and hunger to population growth, disarmament,
trade, energy, finance, and transnational corporations. It gave top
priority to the "needs of the poorest," endorsing the basic needs initiatives that called for "the abolition of hunger" and "the elimination of absolute poverty."[109] And it supported much of the NIEO,
including stabilized commodity prices, the removal of protectionist barriers that restricted exports of manufactured goods from the
poorer nations, a code of conduct for transnational corporations,
debt relief, and better representation of the global South in the governing of the World Bank and International Monetary Fund (IMF).
The report also brought together the NIEO's call for increasing the

transfer of resources and the basic needs demand for more foreign assistance.

And then it went a step further, with what it called "a new approach to development finance." By 1980, the new approach was familiar, at least in the networks of development experts. It included "predictable and long-term" support through "universal taxation." It aimed to meet the UN's existing 0.7 percent target, now applied to all nations and not just the wealthier ones, by 1985, and hoped to reach 1 percent by 2000, and it asked for "more funds" from "'automatic' sources." The list of potential sources mostly repeated the earlier lineup of "international trade, military expenditures or arms exports, and revenues from the 'global commons,' especially sea-bed minerals," and also added "international travel."[110] Altogether, the commission imagined "increased lending," "increased official aid," and "other resource-transfer mechanisms" that added up to the ambitious "sum of the order of $50–60 billion annually by 1985," well above the existing $20 billion per year but well below the $450 billion spent annually on arms. For the next step forward, it asked for "a summit of world leaders" where its proposals could be "thrashed out with candour and boldness."[111]

In 1969, the Pearson report, *Partners in Development*, had also requested substantial increases in foreign assistance, and it had inspired rebellion in development circles. At the 1970 Columbia Conference on International Economic Development, convened to discuss the Pearson report, development experts had turned south and shifted left, and reset the dialogue on development for a decade. The Brandt report reflected the changes and, for the most part, rehashed them. It moved as far to the left as it could go and still appeal to the liberal mainstream of development networks, and it went too far for conservatives. Writing in the *Wall Street Journal*, the right-wing, free-trade, anti-statist economist Melvyn B. Krauss proclaimed the report as "by Social Democrats for Social Democrats." It "closely follows the party line," he wrote, "throughout its 304 pages." He rejected its recommendations for "the most lenient" loans to the poorer nations (they encouraged "economic irresponsibility"), for protecting the rights of migrant workers (it would "increase the cost . . . to prospective employers and thus decrease . . . employment opportunities"), and for regulating transnational corporations (it would raise "the cost of doing business" and "less business" would "be done"). Krauss's gripe provided a taste of the conservative backlash to come.[112]

———

Eventually, in October 1981, world leaders did meet in Cancún, Mexico, for the summit the Brandt Commission had requested. The Mexican president José López Portillo, who supported the NIEO, and the liberal Canadian prime minister Pierre Trudeau cochaired the conference. By then, though, the NIEO had withered on the vine, damaged by its opponents, divisions in the South, and years of stalled negotiations. The OPEC nations still had their wealth, and the state-supported economic growth that had transformed Hong Kong, Singapore, South Korea, and Taiwan had done little for the most impoverished nations in Africa, Asia, and Latin America. Meanwhile, the basic needs approach had fragmented into scattershot small and local projects that might address poverty but could not possibly end it. And the political winds continued to shift, with a cold front moving in from the Right. After 1973 free-market advocates held sway in Augusto Pinochet's Chile, after 1978 in Margaret Thatcher's Britain, and, after the election of Ronald Reagan in 1980, in the United States as well. The war in Afghanistan had reignited tensions between the United States and the Soviet Union, and another hike in the price of oil and rising debt in much of the global South had escalated the sense of a looming economic storm.

Before the conference began, Reagan went on the offensive. In late September, in a speech to the board of governors of the World Bank Group and the IMF, he spoke of "the magic of the marketplace," and reiterated his commitment "to policies of free trade, unrestricted investment, and open capital markets." And in mid-October, a week before the conference convened, in a speech in Philadelphia, he cautioned against "oversimplified and unproductive" approaches, including those of people who "claim massive transfers of wealth somehow miraculously will produce new well-being." Private investment, he said, "is the lifeblood of development."[113] The Philadelphia speech, the *Boston Globe* stated, consisted of "doctrinaire one-liners and homespun homilies about the virtues of free enterprise, the necessity of self-reliance and the need of underdeveloped countries to emulate the methods of American capitalism." On the eve of the summit, newspapers reported, "diplomats from . . . developing countries" took note and "expressed both disappointment and irritation." The conference began in an "air of discord," with low expectations on all sides.[114]

On October 24, "security agents with walkie talkies," Mexican soldiers, and "1,500 foreign delegates and over 2,000 journalists" crowded onto the resort island of Cancún, where they joined the leaders of twenty-two nations—"8 industrialized and 14 developing"—for the International Meeting on Cooperation and Development.[115] The group included Julius Nyerere, Indira Gandhi, Ferdinand Marcos, Margaret Thatcher, and Ronald Reagan, as well as UN secretary-general Kurt Waldheim. The Soviet Union declined to attend, and Fidel Castro, who had hoped to participate, found himself removed from the invitation list at the US government's insistence.

The conference served as a coda of sorts to a decade when the global South and the Left had pushed the mainstream. After a long battle with cancer, Barbara Ward had died in May at the age of sixty-seven, another sign of the end of an era—and the beginning of a new one in which her liberal version of anticommunism had little purchase in the US government. At Cancún, Reagan, his secretary of state Alexander M. Haig Jr., and his treasury secretary Donald T. Regan promoted "trade not aid, economic growth not a redistribution of wealth, and the private market not new major government-to-government involvement." Haig stated directly that "transfer of resources in a wholesale way" was "a conception we reject."[116] Most of the leaders at the summit had wanted to give greater power in international economic negotiations to the UN General Assembly, but the United States, along with Britain and West Germany, insisted "that any deals to remake the world economy take place in the existing global agencies"—that is, in the World Bank, the IMF, and the General Agreement on Tariffs and Trade. These were agencies, a *New York Times* reporter recognized, "that the rich control." After the conference ended, the liberal columnist Carl T. Rowan concluded that "the U.S. is headed by people who are so steeped in 'free enterprise' cliches that they have only disdain for the poor."[117]

In the second half of the 1970s, the NIEO and the basic needs approach had animated a global antipoverty movement and highlighted the need for redressing inequities on the global as well as the national scale. As one scholar wrote, the NIEO had "given rise to an unprecedented debate on the subject of global distributive justice."[118] And basic needs supporters had dared to imagine a world without poverty. The Brandt Commission report, which supported both the NIEO and the basic needs approach, showed how far the mainstream had moved. Mahbub ul Haq saw it as "a tremendous advance in the intellectual journey . . . since the days of the Pearson Commission in 1969." And in 1984, Michael Harrington remembered it with admiration. "It stressed," he said, "the structural solution of transferring capital and technology from north to south, from rich to poor, with the proviso that these be used to help the people rather than dictators of either left or right."[119] But for the next decade and then some, the report and its call for a redistributive international tax were pretty much forgotten.

PART II

How Women Became the Deserving Poor

———◆———

Most of the poor are women. Most of the unemployed are also women. The majority of refugees are women. The majority of the undernourished are also women. The majority of women are not represented in important assemblies where decisions on development are taken.

—KRISHNA AHOOJA-PATEL,
"ANOTHER DEVELOPMENT WITH WOMEN"

CHAPTER THREE

Developing Women

IN 1976, USAID approved an economic development project for sixty villages in Upper Volta (now Burkina Faso). The project statement outlined a plan to provide training and low-interest loans for small projects, such as raising poultry, growing peanuts, and marketing vegetables. Over the next few years, USAID committed more than a million dollars to fund the endeavor. The Upper Volta project fit neatly with the New Directions mandate of the 1973 Foreign Assistance Act and the growing focus on basic needs. It allocated foreign aid to indigent people in an African nation, and it aimed to enhance productivity and nutrition at the local level through small-scale, labor-intensive, rural development. But it departed from the typical USAID project in one significant respect: it focused on women. Titled "Strengthening Women's Roles in Development," it called for "improving rural women's capacity . . . to organize, manage, invest in and carry out social and economic development activities." More specifically, it aimed to give women "the means to engage in production for the cash economy." Women, it promised, "will directly receive the major portion of benefits."[1]

Just a few years earlier, at the start of the 1970s, US development projects rarely mentioned impoverished women at all, and when they did, they understood them primarily as mothers, either as child rearers, who required training in family health and child development, or as child bearers, who needed to limit their reproduction. In the course of the 1970s, though, development experts repositioned women as producers, or, in the lingo of the day, "income generators," and made increasing attempts to pull indigent women's labor out of subsistence and into the market economy. In an emerging "women in development" (WID) movement, they asked to bring women into the kinds of training and technical programs routinely provided to men.

Starting with a small group of advocates, the WID movement took off in the early 1970s. The new approach resulted in part from the women's movement, with its calls for gender equity. But it also built on the campaigns against global poverty, which emphasized productivity at the grass roots in the poorest nations. Like the (mostly male) economists who rejected trickle-down development in the early 1970s and the (mostly male) global South leaders who pushed for the New International Economic Order, the (mostly female) WID advocates initially saw themselves—and were often seen—as rebels within development circles. They encountered resistance from their colleagues, but they gradually institutionalized their movement in UN resolutions, US legislation, and the policies and programs of agencies and foundations. Through research, strategy, and persistence, they inched their way into the everyday discourse of development experts.

From the start, the WID movement was international. In the United States, WID supporters joined a global movement already underway. Under its general rubric, advocates protested the neglect of women in development programs, and they agreed that projects should recognize, include, and increase women's productivity, and not just the unpaid labor women performed as mothers who fed and cared for their families. As one American WID supporter put it, "planners must do more to enhance women's non-mothering productive tasks."[2] Through the 1970s, the WID activists sustained a concern for the material deprivations of women's lives and promoted a faith in the benefits of remunerative labor. They proposed and debated new policies that focused on the economic activities of women.

Within its compass, though, the WID movement fractured. The divisions tended to mirror those in development networks more generally. Tensions emerged between women from the global South and global North, between leftists and liberals, and between academics and practitioners. As WID advocates fought for recognition in development circles, they disputed priorities among themselves. They all protested the subordination of women, encouraged women's income-earning activities, and supported the fulfillment of basic needs, but some saw progress for women and for ending poverty inextricably tied to structural change at local and international scales. Should the WID movement simply include women in existing economic development programs, or did it require deeper transformations of international hierarchies, class relations, and gendered labor?

By the end of the 1970s, the WID movement, in its various forms, had only begun to result in actual income-generating projects. But within the United States, WID supporters had set up shop in the larger agencies, institutions, and foundations. They won their place because they found allies in various settings. But they also tailored their arguments, sometimes strategically, to appeal to mainstream policy makers and development professionals. The move away from large-scale infrastructure projects and toward small-scale antipoverty projects gave WID supporters leverage to bring women to the center of development efforts. They downplayed feminism and argued that women as "income generators" were crucial to productivity, population control, the satisfaction of basic needs, and the alleviation of poverty. In so doing, they hitched their movement to existing development programs and helped foster new policies in which development planners gave women producers a critical role in their projects.

Making Women Modern

In the 1950s and 1960s, the US government (and others) pumped millions of dollars into building dams, irrigation systems, power plants, and roads overseas. These large-scale projects involved men as planners, men as workers, and men as beneficiaries of training in farming, construction, and industrial techniques. Even in "community development" programs aimed at the rural village, most of the modernizers presumed that men were the rightful household heads, primary breadwinners, local leaders, and key project participants. In the heat of the Cold War, they also envisioned impoverished men as prone to revolution and therefore in need of placatory programs that might mollify their discontent. In the rush to modernize, development planners usually treated women as irrelevant or saw them as impediments to change. "Development experts," one historian wrote, "overwhelmingly lumped women in post-colonial societies with the peasantry as repositories of backwardness." And when the experts did include women, they saw them mostly as homemakers and mothers and only rarely as producers.[3]

In the early 1960s, for example, USAID worked with the US Department of Agriculture to publish a series of pamphlets on sanitation aimed at impoverished women overseas. The illustrated series attempted to modernize homemaking by depicting women in poorer nations engaged in hygienic practices. It fit in a longer history—in colonies, on reservations, in impoverished urban neighborhoods and rural hamlets—of training poor women in cleanliness, especially through what one anthropologist has called the "didactic hygiene booklet."[4] The 1960s pamphlets included, among others, "Wash Dishes Right," "How to Wash Your Clothes," and "Prepare and Serve Safe Meals," and they warned against bacteria, dirt, disease, excrement, lice, maggots, mold, pesticides, and rodents. The concern with homemaking acknowledged (and also reinforced) the unpaid care work or reproductive labor that women routinely performed, and it aligned with domestic programs for health and nutrition within various nations. But the US pamphlets also veered from strict adherence to health-related themes. They encouraged women to iron clothes, use placemats and tablecloths, and make "food taste better" and "dishes look more attractive," all seemingly unselfconscious attempts to export American home economics to women in other nations.[5] As one 1970s critic of this approach commented, it taught "flower-arranging and cake-baking . . . even in countries where there are few flowers and no ovens." Flowers and cakes exaggerate the cluelessness of the home economists involved, but they capture the way in which some modernizers attempted to teach midcentury, middle-class ideals of appropriate housewifely behavior to poorer women in the global South.[6]

In some variants of modernization theory, mothers also played a central role in the psychology of child development. If it was too late, as some thought, to change the mind-sets of adults, then mothers, if trained, could mold the minds of malleable children

Remember.....

WASH DISHES RIGHT TO...

- Prevent Disease Germs

- Make Food Taste Better

- Make Dishes Look More Attractive

FIGURE 3.1. From Kathryne Sheehan Hughes, *Wash Dishes Right: An Aid to Extension and Village Workers in Many Countries*, Sanitation Series 4 (1963). In the 1960s, USAID joined with the US Department of Agriculture to produce this pamphlet and others that aimed to teach hygienic homemaking to women of the global South. (Courtesy of USAID, Development Experience Clearinghouse)

into modern subjectivity. The modernization scholar David McClelland, a Harvard psychologist, wrote the most influential account of this approach in his 1961 book *The Achieving Society*. In McClelland's view, a decisive element in national economic growth was "achievement motivation," an individual will to achieve related to independence and entrepreneurial spirit. "Achievement motivation" prevailed, he claimed, in the United States and Europe but not in impoverished nations. McClelland positioned mothers as the critical actors who could shape the personalities of their sons and instill achievement motivation in the next generation of men. In his protofeminist prescription, McClelland called for the emancipation of wives and children from domineering husbands and fathers who squelched the will to achieve in their sons. Mothers should rear their sons with affection and push them to "reasonably high standards of excellence" and self-reliance when they were six to eight years old, which McClelland considered neither too early nor too late to shape core personality. If mothers used these modern child-rearing methods and if fathers refrained from domineering, a nation could accelerate its economic growth, he said, through a new generation of achieving sons.[7]

The lessons for mothers embodied plans to manage populations in service to development. This basic approach gave mothers a role in the biopolitical economy. In Michel Foucault's influential formulation, biopolitics refers to "the administration of bodies and the calculated management of life." It involves "disciplining the body and . . . regulating populations."[8] Government programs and US private agencies used child development theories, including McClelland's, to promote the biopolitics of modernization. They sponsored schools, orphanages, and other programs overseas in attempts to place the next generation on the road to economic growth. These micromodernization projects included training impoverished mothers in the latest Euro-American child-rearing methods. With new methods, mothers, the modernizers hoped, could rear children with new personalities and avoid the perceived problems of German authoritarianism, communist conformism, Asian superstition, and rural fatalism. Mothers, then, were seen as central not only to sanitation, nutrition, health, and homemaking, but also to training children, especially sons, in democracy, freethinking, rationality, and ambition.[9]

In the mid-1960s, development experts shifted their interest in women, in large part, from child rearing to childbearing. "Economic planners and development assistance agencies," one study noted, had turned to women's fertility—"their acquiescence in bearing children"—as a fundamental source of poverty and "a menace to economic progress and security." The population control movement of the 1960s and after differed from the eugenic science of the early twentieth century. Its advocates rarely promoted the breeding of so-called higher quality humans. With neo-Malthusian theories on the limits of resources, they sought instead to reduce the numbers of children overall, but, like eugenicists, they focused their alarm on the children of the poor. On the local level, poor parents, they claimed, bred children they could not afford to rear, and on the global level, elevated birth rates threatened to outstrip the food supply and damage the environment. The best-selling book *The Population Bomb*, published in 1968, spelled out the fears graphically by predicting mass starvation. By 1974, the book had sold two million copies.[10] The heightened concern with childbearing built on concerns with child rearing. The population controllers claimed that if poor mothers had fewer children, they would have the resources for modern child rearing: more time, more energy, and more money to invest in the health and education of each child.

In the mid-1960s, population control programs won the backing of President Johnson. In cooperation with the Ford Foundation, the Population Council, the World Bank, and others, the US government began to funnel money into population programs overseas. In 1967, Congress stipulated that $35 million of the USAID budget go for "family planning," and the annual spending rose from there, surpassing $200 million by 1978. In the mid-1970s, USAID was by far the largest funder in the world of international population control.[11]

But the population control movement was already sinking under its own heavy-handed weight. International family planning programs quantified impoverished women overseas as "targets" for birth control and sterilization, with little concern for their health and well-being. With US foreign assistance funds, the movement actively promoted and paid for dangerous intrauterine devices, exporting birth control methods already condemned at home. It also supported mass sterilizations, funding coercive programs that pressured indigent women and men into limiting or eliminating their fertility. The US government denied involvement in such programs, but it nonetheless continued to underwrite them and thereby to uphold long-standing racist practices that treated poor people of color as excessively fecund and less deserving of quality health care.[12]

Even as funds for population control shot up in the 1970s, critics mounted their opposition. Feminists demanded attention to women's health and status as well as their right to choose (or reject) birth control without pressure or compulsion, and environmental activists complained that the funded programs identified the problem as the high fertility of the poor and not the wasteful consumerism of the rich. Other critics pointed to the racist history of population control and the racist assumptions of some of its new supporters. The Catholic Church opposed contraception entirely, and the "targets" themselves rebelled against coercion. The conflicts erupted at the 1974 UN World Population Conference in Bucharest, which marked a turning point in the movement. "Speaker after speaker," one reporter wrote, "insisted that development aid is more important than family planning."[13] In the late 1970s, too, demographers began to report "an unexpected decline in the rate of world population growth." As one headline put it, the "population bomb" had been "defused."[14] At the same time, the Carter administration backed away from the population control movement. Carter himself took a more pro-natalist stance, and policy planners began to endorse an emerging approach that still called for population decline but embedded it in broader programs for health and education.[15]

As population control lost its luster, a group of development experts shifted the spotlight to a third approach to women. Instead of envisioning women as child rearers or child bearers, the "women in development" movement reimagined indigent women as "income generators." They explicitly avoided treating women solely as mothers. In a 1978 statement to congressional subcommittees, Elsa Chaney, a WID official in USAID, explained, "We are interested in supporting projects and studies which explore *alternative roles to motherhood.*"[16] The WID experts, who were almost all women themselves, showed that impoverished women worked—not only in child rearing, but also in home production, agriculture, local markets, and elsewhere—but their labor rarely appeared in national statistics on production and employment. And the existing modernization programs had, they said, discounted women's labor in their blinkered attempts to accelerate national economic growth. To the early WID supporters, modernizers had rendered women's work invisible, "bypassed" indigent women, and left them behind "in a traditional sector." The WID movement did not call, as some 1970s Marxist-feminists in Europe and the United States did, for wages for housework, but it recognized the range of women's labor and understood it as work. It asked policy makers to redefine their vision of development, and of economics more generally, to include women's labor, paid and unpaid, and to promote women's income-earning activities.[17]

From the start, the WID advocates adopted the keywords of 1970s economic development programs. They spoke the language of technology, training, efficiency, and output. To enhance their productivity, women in rural areas would use "technological improvements to reduce time spent" in the care work of feeding and clothing their children, and they would benefit from "training and technology to improve their efficiency in agricultural work." In the cities, "more paid jobs for women" would not only "raise their status" and "reduce their drudgery," it would at the same time "raise the national output."[18] In this version of progress, early WID advocates portrayed women's income generation as a sign of national economic improvement as well as a marker of modernity and a source of power for women.

By all accounts, Ester Boserup's 1970 book *Woman's Role in Economic Development* helped launch the WID movement. Boserup was a Danish economist with extensive experience in the UN. She had, as one colleague recalled, a "reserved, even austere personality," and she took a no-nonsense, practical approach to economics. She had traveled widely in Asia and Africa, observed the world around her, and refused to rely on others' economic models. In the late 1950s, she and her husband worked with Gunnar Myrdal on his study of development in Asia, but she broke with Myrdal in 1960 when she no longer agreed with his premise of a labor surplus in agriculture. In a long letter, she also disagreed with his neglect of women. "The restrictions on female activities," she told Myrdal, "are . . . of great importance for living standards in the region."[19]

By 1970, Boserup already had clout in international development circles, primarily for her work on population and agriculture. In a controversial book, *The Conditions of Agricultural Growth*, published in 1965, she rejected the neo-Malthusian alarmism of the population control movement. Food production, she claimed, did not set limits on how much population could grow. She reversed the causal chain: when population grew, it did not lead to mass starvation; instead, it exerted the pressure that pushed farmers to more productive agricultural techniques.[20] Because of her prominence, Boserup's new book on women had an immediate impact.

In *Woman's Role in Economic Development*, Boserup held that European and American modernizers—both earlier "colonial administrators" and newer "technical advisers"—were responsible for "the deterioration in the status of women." In Africa and Asia, where women had traditionally engaged in agricultural production and local exchange, foreign assistance had focused on men, providing training, machinery, and wage labor to men only, and thus, she wrote, "enhancing the prestige of men" and "lowering the status of women." Modernization projects then did not just neglect women; they also harmed them.[21] For reasons of equity and to promote economic growth, Boserup called for education, training in agriculture and industry, and wider job opportunities for women.

Boserup suggested a redistribution of aid funds so that development projects addressed women as producers, but she refrained from questioning development itself. She favored enhanced productivity and expansion in the private sector. She construed a transition from "tradition" to "modern" as an ongoing, almost inevitable process, and she argued that excluding women would impede economic growth. "The obvious danger" in modernization, she wrote on the first page of her book, was that "women will be deprived of their productive functions, and the whole process of growth will thereby be retarded."[22] In this early iteration of the WID movement, Boserup attempted to integrate women into existing development schemes, but her focus on employment, productivity, and income matched the concerns of antipoverty advocates in early 1970s development circles and positioned programs for women as key components of the antipoverty efforts.

Boserup did not initiate the growing interest in women's work, but she brought attention to it. Others had already called for more training and better jobs for women in the global South. In 1947, the National Planning Committee of the Indian National Congress recognized the economic contributions of women in the home, agriculture, and industry, and included wage work for women in its development plans. In the 1950s and 1960s, as the decolonization movement accelerated, a number of other postcolonial nations also envisioned women as productive contributors to their national economies. By the late 1950s, the International Labour Organization (ILO), too, had begun to direct more attention to women's labor and income in the global South, and by the late 1960s the UN and its agencies, such as the Economic Commission for Africa, had also evinced a growing interest in women's economic activities. Among foreign assistance donors, Sweden played an early role. In 1964, Inga Thorsson, in Sweden's Ministry of Foreign Affairs, convinced her government to include women in its development programs.[23]

Boserup's book drew on these earlier efforts. She collated statistics and synthesized the existing studies of women's economic roles. She placed them in the context of ongoing development programs and broadcast them to an international audience. The book won positive reviews in scholarly journals and inspired academic interest in women and development. It captured the attention, too, of development practitioners. A year after the book came out, an excerpt from it appeared in the journal *Development Digest*, a publication printed for USAID and sent to US embassies.[24] The book also caught the spirit of the growing feminist movement that had brought renewed attention to equal employment opportunities for women. In short order, Boserup's book became the Bible—the oft-cited foundational text—for the women in development movement.

A series of events in the early 1970s publicized Boserup's book and promoted the WID movement. In 1971, in its strategy for the second development decade, the UN resolved to encourage the "full integration of women in the total development effort," and in 1972 it held an Interregional Meeting of Experts on the Integration of Women in Development, with Boserup as vice-chair and also the author of the background paper that guided the meeting's deliberations. The meeting brought together not only "women" and "development" but also two UN cosponsoring agencies, the Commission on the Status of Women and the Commission on Social Development, that had worked independently in the past.[25] In the same year the Society for International Development, a professional organization for development experts, inaugurated a "women in development" caucus, and early the following year the OECD, the consortium of foreign aid donor nations, held a planning meeting at its headquarters in Paris to discuss its own "project for studying the role of women in development." Meanwhile, the UN began to plan for International Women's Year, to be held in 1975 with a major conference in Mexico City. The UN chose three themes for the conference—equality, peace, and development—with the last theme drawn from Boserup's work. To publicize the development theme, the UN Development Programme asked Boserup to summarize her book in pamphlet form. With her coauthor Christina Liljencrantz, she wrote *Integration of Women in Development: Why, When, How*, which the UN distributed at the conference.[26]

The Percy Amendment

The WID movement took off after 1970, but by the spring of 1973, it had not yet made its way into US government policy. The New Directions bill, which aimed to revise the Foreign Assistance Act, called for programs for the poor but without any mention of women. Still, the proposed legislation opened new possibilities for women's inclusion. When the end goal of a foreign aid project was a functioning airport or dam, women's direct participation seemed less obviously relevant. But when smaller grassroots projects proposed to enhance individual productivity and address the worst of poverty, women, as half the adult population, had a clearer claim. In the fall of 1973, as Congress debated and refined the foreign assistance bill, a group of liberal feminist Washington insiders managed to add an amendment to it that mandated the integration of women into the new development programs.

One meeting in particular launched the WID movement in the US government. In September 1973, the State Department held a "National Foreign Policy Conference" for leaders of NGOs, and it included a short workshop on how the United States might participate in the upcoming UN-sponsored International Women's Year. The State Department invited representatives from various NGOs to attend the conference, including a handful of women from the National Organization for Women. Following the usual format, State Department officials stood at the front of the room and gave presentations. As Irene Tinker, a local political scientist and a founder of the WID caucus in the Society for International

Development, later remembered, the meeting erupted. "Women in these new egalitarian organizations were used to interacting and criticizing; leadership was suspect," she wrote. "Finally, a woman from out of town, rejecting the niceties of the setting, blurted out her complaint, punctuated with four letter words, that State was putting us on, that there would be no time for discussion." Virginia Allan, a deputy assistant secretary of state, had put International Women's Year on the conference agenda, and in response to the protest, she opened the floor for debate and then agreed to continue the meeting the following day to allow more time for discussion. At eight o'clock the next morning, about thirty-five people met at the State Department. As part of the continuing conversation, Irene Tinker spoke about "the detrimental impact of development on women," echoing Boserup's work.[27]

Later that same day, a handful of women, including Virginia Allan, held a private meeting. Among those in attendance was Clara Beyer, a labor economist who had been active in women's labor circles since the late 1910s. Beyer had worked in the US Department of Labor for thirty years and later for USAID as a consultant in the agency's Office of Labor Affairs. In 1973, she was eighty-one years old, still working for the federal government and linking a new generation of liberal feminists to an earlier generation of women reformers who had advocated for working women. At USAID, she had argued for "programs for women . . . along with those for men." But as she later recalled, she would "recommend action that was not followed up." While she tried to nudge the bureaucracy, she closely followed "the integration of women into the development process" in the UN, the ILO, and the OECD. At the private meeting in the State Department, Beyer suggested adding "something about women" to the foreign assistance bill under debate in Congress.[28]

Shortly after the meeting, Mildred Marcy, in charge of women's programs in the United States Information Agency, acted on Beyer's suggestion. She drafted a few sentences, stating that women should be included in US-funded development programs. Marcy's husband was chief of staff of the Senate Foreign Relations Committee, and Marcy used her connections to have her statement placed in the Senate report on the Foreign Assistance Act. A week or so later, as she recalled, she realized that sentences in a report would have no impact at all. Once again she relied on connections. She consulted with her husband about an amendment to the foreign assistance bill. They considered asking Hubert Humphrey, a Democratic senator from Minnesota, to sponsor the amendment. Humphrey was a prominent liberal who had served as vice-president in the Johnson administration. But, as Marcy later recalled, despite "his enthusiasms," Humphrey "didn't have a great reputation for follow-through." Instead, she asked Charles Percy, a liberal Republican senator from Illinois, who had presidential aspirations, to sponsor the amendment.[29]

The Percy amendment stipulated that the foreign aid programs mandated by the 1973 legislation "shall be administered so as to give particular attention to those programs, projects, and activities which tend to integrate women into the national economies of foreign countries, thus improving their status and assisting the total development effort."[30] The phrase "integrate women into the national economies" indicated that women were not to be construed as child rearers or child bearers but as economic actors. "Once this provision becomes law," Beyer wrote to a friend at the ILO, "it will be difficult for men to say, as they so often have said, that women have no priority in the development process."[31]

The Percy amendment cost nothing, and it nodded to women just when International Women's Year preparations had put women's development issues on the national agenda. In the Senate, no one objected. The amendment passed by voice vote within minutes of its introduction. But once the amendment passed in the Senate, it went to the House conference committee, which considered adding it to the House of Representatives' version of the bill. And there it ran into trouble. Members of the committee, which was dominated by Democrats who supported foreign aid, did not, it seems, have serious reservations about the contents or wording of the amendment, which was relatively tame. But they refused to take it seriously, mocking it as "apple pie and motherhood," an empty statement designed to help Percy pander to women voters.[32]

Appalled, the women who had crafted the amendment turned to their networks for support. The National Federation of Business and Professional Women (Virginia Allan was a former president), the League of Women Voters (Mildred Marcy was a long-time leader), the National Council of Jewish Women, and the Young Women's Christian Association all got involved, urging their members to flood Congress with phone calls, letters, and telegrams in support of the Percy amendment. As Irene Tinker recalled, it was "harder to ignore" the old-line established mainstream organizations than what she called "the more strident newer women's groups." Officials in the Young Women's Christian Association also enlisted Arvonne Fraser, a prominent DC liberal feminist and the wife of Representative Donald Fraser, who had cosponsored the New Directions bill and served on the conference committee that had rejected the amendment. She persuaded her husband in person and then wrote individual letters to the other members of the committee, asking them to support the amendment and letting them know that women's groups were watching and waiting. In this hands-on, pressure-group, inside-the-beltway fashion, the Percy amendment made it into the law as part of the Foreign Assistance Act of 1973.[33]

After Nixon signed the act in December 1973, USAID officials began to discuss how they might implement the amendment. In February, Clara Beyer complained to the agency's general counsel that "women's groups within AID and in the private sector" had been shut out of the discussions. Women, she said, had "brought about the passage of the Amendment," and she wanted them involved. The letter, it seems, had its intended effect. The following month the head of USAID, Daniel Parker, appointed a committee, including Beyer and several other women, to draft an "action plan." He asked Nira Hardon Long, an African American lawyer who directed the agency's Office of Equal Opportunity, to lead the effort.[34]

At Long's request, various USAID missions, divisions, and offices sent in lists of their ongoing programs that had an impact on women. The inventory included projects for population control, health, higher education, leadership training, and home economics, but only a few of the kind of employment, productivity, or income-oriented projects that might foster integration into national economies. The major exception was Clara Beyer's work in USAID's Office of Labor Affairs. An early advocate of WID, she had managed to launch two WID-related programs in a collaborative effort with the US Department of Labor. In Latin America, Beyer's Office of Labor Affairs gave funds to promote women's bureaus within national labor ministries, and in Africa it supported an emerging women's program, including vocational training, that the UN's Economic Commission for Africa had launched in 1971.[35] But Beyer's efforts were clearly the exception.

The advocates of WID had to acknowledge that they found limited enthusiasm for the Percy amendment. One USAID staff member wondered how "to persuade the male leaders" in the United States and in the global South "to become more actively involved." Another questioned "the social attitudes" of the field staff. He suggested that the directive sent to the USAID mission offices would have to make it clear that "This is policy, bud!" And indeed the subsequent airgram from the USAID administrator reminded the mission directors that "attention to the role of women" not only made "good sense"; it was also "legally required."[36]

Supporters of the Percy amendment emphasized that WID was already "widely accepted" in UN circles, and they reminded their colleagues that the amendment had "generated a good deal of attention."[37] They had fielded multiple "inquiries on the Percy Amendment from outside AID," including "phone calls, visits, speaking and conference requests, and letters" as well as "applications for funding."[38] To convince the staff in African nations, USAID sent Sarale Owens, a program officer from the United States Information Agency, to visit "embassies and [USAID] missions to enlist their interest in and understanding of the problems of integrating women in development." Senator Percy himself took an active interest in promoting and monitoring the implementation of the amendment. At a congressional hearing, he asked Secretary of State Henry Kissinger to endorse the amendment. In response to Percy's request for his "personal assurance and . . . personal support," Kissinger stated on the record that the Department of State had "instructed the various aid missions that [it] must be pursued assertively" and "it does have our full support."[39]

In September 1974, after reports and deliberations, Daniel Parker signed the policy order "requiring all AID operations to emphasize and support the role of women in development efforts in the poor countries." With Senator Percy in attendance, he announced that USAID would establish a Women in Development section with Nira Long, who had chaired the working group committee, as its first coordinator.[40] Long immediately aligned the WID section with the New Directions mandate and USAID's emphasis on smaller rural projects. Her section, she said, would "concentrate on examining the economic role of women in rural development, in farm production [and] in marketing to see where women's needs may have been overlooked by the development process."[41]

In its first years, the WID section pushed USAID offices to include women in their development projects and sponsored panels and seminars to arouse interest in the Percy amendment. It also gave out small grants, mostly for research and conferences. One of the early grants, to give one example, provided $100,000 to the National Council of Negro Women (NCNW) for workshops on WID. The grant funded orientation and caucus sessions for women of African descent at the International Women's Year conference in Mexico City, paid for a small group's postconference tour of rural development projects in Mississippi, and then provided seminars at Bethune-Cookman College in Florida. The NCNW reported that twenty-three women from abroad participated, along with American women. The project launched the NCNW's new international division, and Dorothy Height, the NCNW's long-time president, remained an avid supporter of USAID's WID program.[42]

In the larger scheme of development aid, the WID section's early grants were tiny. To the dismay of its advocates, the section had little money and minimal clout. Within the agency, Nira Long observed that some staff members saw WID as "merely another faddish program" that would "fade away in time," and others considered "special efforts" on behalf of women unnecessary impositions on the poorer nations.[43] Along with calls for new development programs, the supporters of WID asked USAID to hire more women onto its professional staff, both because they endorsed gender equity and because they assumed that women would do more than men to promote WID programs. To push the bureaucracy, Irene Tinker established the International Center

for Research on Women in 1976, in part as an extragovernmen-
tal watchdog organization "to monitor the implementation of the
Percy Amendment."[44] In the same year, the Overseas Education
Fund, a subdivision of the League of Women Voters, organized the
Coalition for Women in International Development (CWID), an
umbrella group "committed to seeing that U.S. foreign assistance
programs further the economic and social integration of women
in the development of their countries." Within two years, CWID
claimed as members "some 80 national voluntary organizations
and about 50 women leaders." Its members, one study found,
"remind AID administrators of outside support for WID." They
lobbied Congress and pressured the agency through "regular formal visits to top officials" in USAID.[45]

With pressure outside and in, the WID division of USAID gradually grew in size and clout, especially after the Carter administration came into office. The new USAID head, the liberal Democrat
John J. Gilligan, hoped to enhance the WID office.[46] In 1977, he
appointed Arvonne Fraser as the office's new coordinator. Fraser
was a former president of the Women's Equity Action League, a
founder of the National Women's Political Caucus, a US delegate
to the UN International Women's Year conference, and the wife of
Representative Donald Fraser who fought for foreign aid. She was,
for the most part, unprepared for the job. She did not have "overseas experience or even much exposure to development issues," as
one critic noted, but she did have liberal feminist credentials and
government connections.[47] She hired staff—Elsa Chaney, Jane
Jaquette, and Kathleen Staudt—who had relevant academic training and research experience in the field. She and her coworkers
built on the growing interest in WID, and they used their friends
in Congress, including Fraser's husband, to win more resources for
their office. By the end of the decade, the WID division's annual
budget had increased from $300,000 to almost $3 million, and
Congress pushed USAID as a whole to spend another $10 million
of its budget on integrating women into its other projects.[48]

Still, through the 1970s, the women who staffed the WID office
saw themselves as beleaguered, outnumbered, and stymied. The
typical foreign assistance project still involved men working with

FIGURE 3.2. President Jimmy Carter appointed Arvonne Fraser, pictured here, to head
USAID's Office of Women in Development. (Connor Flecks/Alamy Stock Photo)

men, and the WID advocates complained of the time and energy
it took to confront bureaucratic inertia, dismissive comments,
and out-and-out hostility from midlevel USAID staff. Jaquette, a
WID policy analyst from 1979 to 1981, vetted proposals and plans
for their inclusion of women. At meetings, she recalled, she was
"expected to raise my hand and say 'Women' while almost everyone
in the room . . . looked at the ceiling until I was finished." When
asked what they had done to integrate women, the cynics sometimes claimed that every foreign assistance project had an impact
on women. According to Jaquette, foot-dragging bureaucrats could
say that road construction projects met the Percy amendment's
mandate to integrate women "because 'women walk on roads.'"[49]
Chaney, the deputy coordinator of USAID's WID office in the late
1970s, remembered that some bureaucrats met the letter of the
law through "the cut and paste ruse that involved cutting the WID
statement from another project paper and pasting it into the new
one." In 1978, Senator Percy complained to Gilligan, the USAID
head, "I continue to hear that bureaucratic resistance to the concept [of WID] has impeded progress."[50]

"Was This Yet Another Experiment in Neocolonialism?"

Within the US government, the Percy amendment appealed to liberal feminists. It fit within the larger 1970s efforts to integrate women into male-dominated programs, positions, and labor markets. Inside USAID, WID advocates pushed for programs for women and recorded the obstacles they encountered from their mostly male colleagues. But WID supporters were not of one mind. The same fault lines that divided 1970s antipoverty advocates extended through the WID movement. Leftists and third worldists could read the Percy amendment as yet another sign of American imperialism. Once again the United States seemed to assume the authority to dictate change in the rest of the world. From around the globe, the various supporters of WID wanted equity for women, but many of them remained suspicious, often for good reason, of the motives and actions of the US government and the assumptions held by Americans more generally.

From early on, the US WID advocates encountered skepticism from WID supporters in the global South. The very first grant from the WID office of USAID went to sponsor a seminar on WID, held in Mexico City in the week before the 1975 UN International Women's Year conference. Irene Tinker ran the seminar under the auspices of the American Academy for the Advancement of Science, and Ester Boserup, seen as a founding mother and foremost expert of the WID movement, attended. Ninety-eight invited participants from fifty-five nations joined in. As Tinker remembered it, the seminar "avoid[ed] the acrimony that characterized many subsequent meetings on the topic." But a participant had a different recollection. "It was a controversial meeting," she said, "partly because the American women there were not at all—it was so obvious to me—not at all recognizing or listening to the knowledge and the experience of the women from the South."[51]

Other pointed encounters also punctuated the International Women's Year conference. Throughout the conference, both official delegates and informal participants engaged in open confrontations over Zionism, repression in Chile, racism, neocolonialism, and more. Joan Goodin, an alternate representative to the US delegation, came away stunned at "the unbelievably low esteem in which the U.S. is held by developing countries."[52] The conference took place in the year after the G-77 had convinced the UN General Assembly to adopt the New International Economic Order (NIEO). In opposition, the Ford administration instructed US delegates to the International Women's Year conference to reject any moves to support the NIEO. Nonetheless, the official conference World Plan of Action endorsed the NIEO after the Mexican president, Luis Echeverría, and others gave impassioned speeches embracing it. The North-South tensions at the conference coexisted uneasily with the sense of sisterhood that many participants noted.[53]

In this contentious setting, WID was not the most controversial issue at the conference, but it was also not immune from dissent. The differing perspectives came up at a public panel on "women and development assistance," sponsored by the United States to address the Percy amendment. Senator Percy moderated the session, which advertised the amendment that carried his name. But the women on the panel—from Ghana, Nigeria, Korea, and Trinidad—responded by calling for channeling funds through the UN and NGOs rather than from government to government.[54] It was not a bitter exchange, but it was revealing. The women on the panel distrusted government and questioned the politics and priorities of Americans, who often assumed they had not only the funds but also the expertise and authority to take the leadership role.

In 1976, the conflicts flared at a large "Women and Development" conference, sponsored by Wellesley College and funded in part by the WID office of USAID. Of the five hundred plus in attendance, only fifty-five to seventy came from the global South. "Women from developing countries," one USAID observer wrote, "sat in the audience listening to Americans and expatriates discussing the plight of women in their countries." The women from the South saw their homelands as "both under-represented and misrepresented." "There was an element," the observer wrote, "of: 'What gives you the right to study *us*?'" Another USAID participant confessed that she "was overwhelmed by the hostility of third world women to the whole conceptual framework of development

as viewed by the conference organizers." The "third world women,"
she said, disliked the "western model of women's liberation," condemned "all manifestations of capitalism," and favored "national
liberation which would not exclude women."[55]

Three women who attended the Wellesley conference—Nawal El
Saadawi from Egypt, Fatima Mernissi from Morocco, and Mallica
Vajrathon from Thailand—remembered it as "a painful clash." They
described the conflicts at Wellesley as a continuation of the "split"
seen at the International Women's Year conference. There, "women
from industrially developed countries" had engaged in discussions
about "the degrading economic conditions of women in developing
countries" but failed to address the underlying "economic/politi-
cal factors," including "the role of the multi-national corporation,"
that sustained the subordination of the global South. At Wellesley, they said, "mostly American 'scholars' were interpreting for us
our condition, our cultures, our religions and our experiences."[56]
In a follow-up to the conference, the feminist journal *Signs* published short "reflections" from a handful of participants. In one of
them, Bolanle Awe from the Nigerian Ministry of Education stated
bluntly that "participation of Third World scholars . . . was totally
inadequate."[57]

The problem was not only participation. It was also the failure
to recognize the hierarchies created in the colonial past and sustained in the postcolonial present. In another "reflection" published
in *Signs*, the Indian scholar and activist Vina Mazumdar wondered
whether "Third World Women" had been invited to the Wellesley
conference "only to provide data for U.S. scholars doing research
on the Third World? Was this yet another experiment in neocolonialism?" Right after the Wellesley conference ended, sixty-three of
the participants, a majority of them from the global South, met for
three additional days at the Wingspread conference center in Wisconsin. In their postconference report, they protested the limited
vision of experts who separated women's issues from "the broader
socio-economic features of underdevelopment." For them, WID was
part of the larger struggle for equity in the international order. They
insisted that analyses of women "must involve analysis of the causes
of underdevelopment rooted in colonialism and its sequelae." The
WID movement had to address "the neo-colonial situation as it

manifests itself in the power realities of the real world." Otherwise, conferences would "recreate . . . the power relationships between the developed and developing worlds."[58]

Some American participants offered their own critical assessments of the Wellesley conference, but from a different perspective. Within USAID, a report by a conference observer found the papers given by "foreign participants" as "generally of poor technical quality and ridden by 'Third World' tendentiousness." And at the Ford Foundation, which had joined USAID in contributing funds for the conference, Elinor Barber, head of its international women's program, described the conference as "troublesome," with "the dual character of academic conference and political event." Part of the problem, she wrote, was that "a good many Third World women at the conference" found "the actions of all Western developers suspect." They believed that "western scholars" could not have "any valid understanding of former colonial societies" and had "no real right to conduct their erroneous and condescending studies."[59]

The tensions festered in the field as well as at conferences. Another early WID grant, funded by USAID in 1976, included a study of rural women in Kenya, to be conducted by a White American researcher from the Washington-based International Center for Research on Women. But Kenya already had its own Women's Bureau, a government agency, which had unsuccessfully requested USAID funds. The head of the Kenyan Women's Bureau resisted the uninvited incursion of a foreign researcher. She wanted the money to come directly to her agency so that Kenyans could conduct research themselves. Eventually the situation grew testy enough that the USAID office in Nairobi asked the American woman sent to conduct the research not to return to Kenya, and when she insisted, USAID forbade her from having any contact with the "Kenyan women's leaders."[60] The episode exposed the friction generated by the unequal power relations. In postcolonial nations, policy makers requested foreign aid and pursued national economic development, but they also had a wary sensitivity to neocolonial condescension and its embedded racial hierarchies, and insisted on their nations' sovereignty, which included local participation and host-country control over how assistance funds were spent.

Resistance also came from within the US women's movement. Here, the women who worked in the WID office of USAID were suspect because they worked for the US government. In the years after the Vietnam War, leftists in the United States and elsewhere had an engrained suspicion of USAID and of the alleged benevolence of US foreign assistance, which had been deeply implicated in military interventions and counterinsurgency programs. The leftist critique of foreign aid extended to include the WID movement, at least in its incarnation in USAID. When she considered accepting her job in USAID's WID office, Elsa Chaney had her own doubts about working "in the heart of the beast." She argued, as she recalled, "with friends about being 'inside' (you'll be swallowed up, compromised, they said) or staying 'outside' to continue the radical critique of the whole development enterprise." But Arvonne Fraser convinced her that she could subvert from within. With "millions of dollars floating around . . . [Fraser] intended, she said, to get a lot of them for women."[61]

With similar reluctance, the anthropologist Ann Laura Stoler responded to an invitation to apply for a consultancy with USAID. As she wrote in a letter to Adrienne Germain, who worked at the Ford Foundation, "My first reaction was to refuse association immediately." She decided, though, to send her resumé. "It seems," she wrote, "if one is going to voice criticism one might as well do it where it will be heard." Germain agreed that it was "a tough decision whether to cooperate [with] them, but if all the 'good' people refuse, the situation will only get worse."[62] Irene Tinker, too, noted conflicts "between academics and policy analysts, between the scholarly research of one group and the applied research of the other." The tension, though, went beyond the divergent approaches of "scholarly" and "applied"; it also involved political differences, with vocal socialist- and Marxist-feminists working in academia and liberal feminists dominating in the US government. "Many academics," Jane Jaquette found, "seem convinced that working for governments is prima facie evidence of co-optation."[63]

In the United States and abroad, feminists on the left leveled critiques at the kind of development pursued in mainstream institutions. They agreed that development programs ought to include women, but they pushed for a more radical form of development that addressed labor, class, and global inequities. Incorporating women into existing development programs would not, they claimed, end poverty or women's subordination. After attending the Wellesley conference, for example, the Marxist-feminist anthropologist Eleanor Leacock, a professor at the City College of New York, called for a redefinition of what counted as development. "Women's oppression is inextricably bound up in an exploitative world system," she wrote, "in which development, as presently defined, is a part." For Leacock, "real development" involved "ending the system whereby rich nations continue to 'underdevelop' poor nations by consuming a huge proportion of the world's resources, while multinational corporations grossly underpay Third World workers." At the height of debates over the NIEO, left feminists, like other leftists, wanted structural change in economic relations. The kind of development that reinforced the existing international order could not suffice. Ester Boserup, who promoted the mainstream liberal version of development but with women included, also attended the Wellesley conference and, according to one account, "felt so under the gun."[64]

For their part, USAID staffers returned the critical gaze and rejected the leftist vision. At the Wellesley conference, one report noted, papers and discussions were "excessively theoretical," trafficked in "such generality as to deny the possibility of drawing useful conclusion[s] for down-to-earth situations," and "drew heavily on Marxist terminology and assumptions." Academic conferences, the report concluded, were "of doubtful usefulness for AID."[65] A Ford Foundation report noted similarly that "the academic character" of the Wellesley conference "grated on the non-academic participants who chafed at the lack of direct applicability" of the conference papers. Scholars soon complained that "serious research" on WID no longer had financial support from USAID. It was "being crowded out by . . . consulting firms and bureaucracies interested only in quick, dirty research." WID, one such scholar wrote, was now "fashionable and fundable, particularly in Washington," and "serious academics" were "being overlooked."[66]

In 1979, the conflicting visions came to a boil at the National Women's Studies Association conference, held that year at the University of Kansas. The WID office of USAID had sponsored panels, funded the travel for seven women from the global South, and displayed a photograph exhibit, all with the hope of inspiring more academic interest in WID research and programs. The women at USAID hoped to appeal to academic collaborators who could conduct social science research on development issues. An analyst in USAID's WID office, Kathleen Staudt, a former Peace Corps volunteer with a PhD in political science, recorded the uproar that ensued. After one of the panels, she wrote, USAID "was attacked as an 'oppressor,' 'enslaver,' 'CIA conduit,' and instrument to further capitalism." After another panel, critics condemned the USAID population control programs that aimed to "sterilize millions of women." Staudt heard that the USAID exhibit "would be trashed," but instead the critics staffed a table beside the exhibit with a sign reading "Feminists Against AID." And before the conference ended, the National Women's Studies Association passed a resolution banning USAID from future participation in any of its activities.[67] "We . . . were viewed," Staudt recalled later, "as tainted, as affiliates of the enemy because we worked in a government agency." But USAID was not just any government agency, and the protesters had a point: USAID supported repressive regimes, military interventions, counterinsurgency programs, and coercive population control. Staudt, though, saw herself as part of a progressive movement that aimed to reform the bureaucracy from within, and she took the attack personally. It was, she remembered, "a low point in my life."[68] In an article published shortly after the conference in the *Women's Studies Newsletter*, she suggested that her critics had an outdated understanding of USAID. "Are people completely unaware that the Women in Development office was set up to lessen the damage done to women in the development process . . . ?" she asked. "Do people not know about new directions in foreign aid emphasizing basic human needs . . . ?"[69]

Worldwide WID

The conflicts and confrontations were, to give them a positive spin, the signs of a vital and varied movement. In the second half of the 1970s, the WID movement took off in multiple directions. For many WID advocates the 1975 International Women's Year conference served as the galvanizing event. The conference's final document, the World Plan of Action, like the earlier UN resolution and the Percy amendment, called for including women in development programs. More important than the official deliberations, though, were the moments of connection among the hundreds of women who attended the conference, either in national delegations or as participants in the simultaneous NGO forum. Devaki Jain, an Indian WID activist, recalled the conference as "a defining moment" that "linked us to many friends and networks and gave us visibility within the international community." Gloria Scott, a UN official from Jamaica and an early advocate of WID, called the conference "an earth-moving event." And Adrienne Germain, from the Ford Foundation, described "an extraordinary sense of unity, shared experience and common cause" even as she acknowledged the "considerable political sparring and disagreement on particulars."[70]

Between 1975 and the end of the decade, more WID offices and programs opened in international institutions and government agencies. In 1976, the UN passed a resolution to use the money left in the International Women's Year fund to support women's programs in the poorest nations. In the years that followed, the commitment to WID in the UN expanded, and various UN agencies and affiliates inaugurated new WID endeavors. In 1975, the UN's Economic Commission for Africa established the African Training and Research Centre for Women, which served as a model for other regional WID programs, and in 1977, the United Nations Development Programme published its *Guidelines on the Integration of Women in Development* and followed it up three years later with a study of *Rural Women's Participation in Development*.[71]

In the last years of the decade, the International Labour Organization launched a major Programme on Rural Women, which eventually published forty-five studies on women's labor, income, and poverty in the global South. The ILO hired Ingrid Palmer, an

Australian economist, to inaugurate the project. Palmer tied the women's initiative directly to the ILO's commitment to the basic needs approach. Women, she said, "produce and deliver most of the goods and services required" to satisfy basic needs, but the ILO's variant of basic needs had ignored women as producers and seen them mostly as mothers. Palmer compared the unequal relations between women and men to the "unequal exchange . . . between rich and poor countries, between urban and rural areas, and between classes of households." A basic needs approach, she wrote, had to address the inequality "within households."[72]

Along with USAID, other national foreign aid agencies also took up WID endeavors. In the United States, the Peace Corps set up its own WID oversight committee in the late 1970s and eventually established a formal WID office.[73] Other donor nations—in Europe and also Canada and Australia—set up WID offices in their foreign assistance agencies. By the end of the decade WID representatives from the donor nations had met four times as an ad hoc group within the Development Assistance Committee of the Organisation for Economic Co-operation and Development.[74]

Meanwhile, women in the global South were generating their own international WID networks, in part through regional conferences. In 1977, the Bangladesh Institute of Law and International Affairs sponsored a five-day regional South and Southeast Asian seminar on women and development, funded by the Ford Foundation office in Dhaka. Participants came from India, Indonesia, Malaysia, Nepal, Pakistan, the Philippines, Sri Lanka, and Thailand, as well as Bangladesh.[75] Later in the year, the UN Economic Commission for Africa held a regional conference on WID. And the new UN Asian and Pacific Centre for Women and Development held its first meeting of experts and took up the question of the "basic needs of women." The meeting produced a report that called not only for "provision of basic goods and services," but also for "mobilization and structural change" that included "all oppressed groups," including women.[76]

WID activists from the global South held a range of political views. They were liberals and leftists; they were nationalists, internationalists, and third worldists. Some cooperated readily with the WID staffers in USAID, while others refrained. In general, they disagreed on whether they should seek foreign aid, with some "heavily relying" on it and others "outspokenly telling donors to keep out of women's projects." The quest for self-reliance and transnational South-South collaborations came conjoined with the need for resources that might help level the playing field between wealthier and poorer nations and between women and men. In any case, tensions intact, the WID movement snowballed with programs and conferences around the globe.[77]

By the end of the 1970s, WID advocates had created committees, divisions, and offices in virtually every development agency, organization, and foundation. In its overlapping constellations—academic and applied, left and liberal, South and North—the emerging WID movement intersected with and drew on the commitments of other development professionals. It rejected the trickle-down model of economic growth and focused on rural development, poverty, income, individual productivity, basic needs, and small-scale projects. But even though it grew out of prevailing trends, it had varying success in swaying the mainstream development institutions. As in USAID, supporters of WID found their way into the big bureaucracies and then wandered the halls in search of change.

The World Bank, for example, played a leading role in the global antipoverty campaigns but showed only minor interest in WID in the 1970s. In 1975, the Bank published a supportive pamphlet, *Integrating Women into Development*, and two years later persuaded Gloria Scott to leave the UN and take up a new position as the Bank's first advisor on WID. The Bank president Robert McNamara expressed support for WID case studies and seminars, in part because his wife Margaret took a concerted interest. But Scott had a tiny staff and little interaction with other World Bank employees. The Bank was a "white male establishment," she recalled later, with a "preponderance of ex-colonials." She "tried to spread the WID word" but "felt as if [she] were trying to push the world uphill."[78] The Bank staff, one study found, tended to see Scott's job "as a political or public relations position," created to showcase an interest in WID to the outside world without changing the Bank's priorities. Shortly before she left the post in 1985, Scott said that she "doubted the Bank's commitment." In an oral history interview, Montague

Yudelman, the director of the Bank's Agriculture and Rural Development department, confirmed her doubts. He remembered WID as a burden that confounded the Bank's staff. Environmentalism, he said (with some regret about the Bank's disinterest), was "just another thing that got in the way. And then women in development. Let's worry about women in development. . . . Nobody knew what to do about it." It was not until the late 1980s that the Bank made a greater commitment to WID.[79]

Within the United States, WID advocates had their greatest success in the 1970s at the Ford Foundation. From its founding in 1936 through the 1960s, the Ford Foundation had shown minimal interest in women. But in 1972, in response to the feminist movement, the foundation's president, McGeorge Bundy, appointed a Task Force on Women to study potential areas for grants. In the years that followed, the foundation devoted millions of dollars to national and international women's programs. It funded women's studies programs, litigation for women's rights, and projects for economic equity.[80] Elinor Barber chaired the International Division's committee on women's programs and turned the division's attention to WID in the mid-1970s. Along with USAID, Ford provided funds for the women's program of the Economic Commission for Africa, international travel for WID activists who attended the International Women's Year conference in Mexico City, and the 1976 Wellesley conference on WID. By the end of the decade, the International Division's women's program had placed improving "women's productive capacities and opportunities for employment" at the top of its list of priorities.[81]

At the Ford Foundation's New York headquarters, Barber worked closely with Adrienne Germain, who had come to Ford in 1972 from the Population Council, where she had already objected to the narrow focus of the population control movement. At Ford she moved from the population program to become the "circuit rider" who supported and monitored Ford's women's projects overseas. Along with Barber, Germain took up WID in the mid-1970s. In a *New York Times* op-ed, she wrote that women in "third world countries" were "producers, as well as mothers," and as such they were "key actors in the development process." "The important thing," she wrote in a letter, "is to recognize poor women have and deserve at least as much help as men get in increasing the productivity and efficiency of all their work." Like other mid-1970s WID advocates, Germain focused much of her effort "on the work of rural women, especially their agricultural and income-generating activities."[82]

Germain distinguished WID projects from what she (and others) described as relief or welfare programs. Development planners, she said, targeted women for welfare and not for new technology or training for jobs. These "welfare-oriented development programs," which included family planning, were "important but insufficient." They fostered "dependency" instead of self-reliance.[83] "Food supplements, health, and nutrition programs" were "not enough"; home economics training was "often worse than useless." Programs that promoted women's traditional craftwork were rarely economically sound. They involved "make-work projects that produce unmarketable items and skills which are sold at subsidized rates, if at all." Germain objected to the two-tier system that positioned men as producers and women as dependents. She called for "a self sustaining development effort" that gave women marketable skills.[84] Like other 1970s WID advocates, she had an abiding faith that equity for women relied on income-generating work. In 1980, though, her stance began to change. She suggested that the ultimate goal was "basic human rights" for women, including protection from "beatings by husbands" and "harassment by police." She began to question the "narrow economic projects concerned only about income." "Income," she wrote, "may be a first step but it is not sufficient."[85]

The Ford Foundation's early WID programs frequently overlapped, in public rhetoric and in the projects funded, with those in the US government. But in office correspondence the women at Ford cast a critical eye on USAID and the personnel involved. Germain was particularly blunt. Arvonne Fraser, she said, had good intentions but little experience. She hoped that Fraser would "mold AID's work on women in a more sensitive and appropriate way than she has in the past," but she also recognized "how hard it is to budge that bureaucracy in any direction."[86] John Gilligan, the head of USAID in the late 1970s, also came in for stinging critique. An article he wrote was, according to Germain, "simplistic," naive, and insensitive. He showed, she said, little concern for women's rights and missed the complexities, including "the multiple responsibilities and constraints poor women face."[87] Germain and others at Ford advised and cooperated with the WID section of USAID, but they saw themselves as more experienced, more sophisticated, and more attuned to the international scene and the hard realities of poverty.

From the mid-1970s on, the women at the Ford Foundation avoided some of the controversy that plagued USAID. The Ford Foundation frequently collaborated with the US government, and in parts of the global South it earned a reputation as an accomplice to hegemony. But because it was not a government agency, its employees were not quite so obviously connected to the US military, the CIA, and the explicit national self-interest that guided congressional appropriations. Its WID advocates thereby managed to sidestep at least some of the anti-American sentiment that attached to US government endeavors. Because the women at Ford funded women's studies programs in US universities, they had friends in academia and familiarity with the latest trends in feminist scholarship, and because they cultivated connections with WID activists around the globe, they had early ties to WID programs in the global South. After the International Women's Year conference, Barber and Germain saw that women in the global South were creating innovative programs of their own. In the second half of the 1970s, Germain built relationships with, among others, WID activists Vina Mazumdar and Ela Bhatt in India, Peggy Antrobus in Jamaica, and Rounaq Jahan in Bangladesh.

Germain looked for sites to promote the WID movement, and she found her best opportunity in Bangladesh. In the mid-1970s, the head of Ford's Dhaka office, George Zeidenstein, along with his wife Sondra, invited Germain to visit Bangladesh "and figure out what the Ford Foundation could do" for women. As Germain recalled, "that was the breakthrough really that I needed in order to move forward."[88] She spent eight weeks in Bangladesh in 1975, six weeks in 1976, and nine weeks in 1977. And then she made two or three trips per year through the last years of the decade. She looked for projects already in progress, reported on them in the New York headquarters, and supported women's programs within them.[89] Soon the Dhaka office had a reputation at Ford as a critical center for WID and a reputation in Bangladesh as a supporter of the nation's emerging WID movement. In the late 1970s, it provided funds for research on women and for skills training, cooperatives, and income-generating projects for rural women.[90]

The Mainstream Appeal

As the advocates of the WID movement secured a foothold in a range of national and international organizations, agencies, foundations, and institutions, they crafted a set of arguments that they used to win support in mainstream development circles. They distanced themselves from older notions of how women, as child rearers and child bearers, fit into development programs. But they did not simply discard the earlier policies; they built on them and relied on the commitments to them that other development planners already had. In that sense, the WID movement was less a rejection of past biopolitics than a new layer atop an accretion of older policies.

At its most basic, WID supporters made the case that their movement would contribute to economic development. They depicted women as "a vital human resource," displaced by programs that had focused on the productivity of men. WID, they argued, promoted more efficient use of the stock of human capital. As Adrienne Germain put it, "People are one of the few abundant development resources most third world countries have; they cannot afford to abuse and under-utilize fully half that resource." The sociologist Hanna Papanek suggested that WID advocates should consciously link their programs to the goal of "human resource development." She saw it as "politically useful in overcoming some kinds of opposition to women's participation." In a similar vein, Germain told Elinor Barber that "several of the [Ford Foundation] field offices are not interested in women's rights per se but they are concerned about the productive capacities of people, especially poor families." She suggested that Barber, in her memo to the field, avoid the phrase "women's programs" because it implied "a separation that may be counterproductive."[91]

WID supporters also situated their work within the global antipoverty discourse, which had growing traction in the 1970s. Economic growth, they acknowledged, had failed to reach the

poorest of the poor. And women, they said, were more impoverished than men and therefore in need of heightened attention. Here
they built on older modernization plans that focused on women
as child rearers and also on longstanding maternalist arguments
that positioned women as mothers and as more caring than men.
From early on, an argument in favor of WID programs hinged on a
"widespread complaint" that men spent their income on themselves
and did "not provide for their families."⁹² With this negative vision
of fathers, mothers needed their own income to lift their children
out of poverty.

To make the case more directly, WID advocates increasingly
turned to households in which women were the primary or sole
source of income. As Irene Tinker put it, "*One of every three families around the world is headed by a woman*. Women in all countries are the poorest of the poor." In 1978 two researchers, Mayra
Buvinic and Nadia H. Youssef, wrote an influential study, "Women-
Headed Households: The Ignored Factor in Development Planning," funded by the WID office of USAID. Male migration, death,
disability, and desertion had left increasing numbers of households
without male breadwinners. Buvinic and Youssef recognized that
"development planners" were now "trying to target their aid directly
to those most in need." Policies aimed at women household heads,
they wrote, "will prove to be a significant weapon in the struggle
against poverty."⁹³

The WID advocates had a more ambivalent approach to the
population control movement. They both relied on it and veered
away from it. In the 1970s they repudiated population control programs that coerced women and ignored their health. In the Ford
Foundation, USAID, and elsewhere, they found that "pushing con-
traceptives was not enough." They tried to shift the focus away from
women's fertility. Women, they said, "have many roles in addition
to motherhood that should be recognized and reinforced." Nonetheless, WID supporters remained heavily invested in the population control movement. At the same time that they rejected it in its
harsher forms, they drew on the lingering popularity of the movement and suggested repeatedly that WID programs would reduce
fertility. If motherhood remained women's primary occupation and
main source of social status, women would have multiple children,

leaving their families in poverty. And if women did not have efficient, productive, income-generating work, they would rely on large families for income from child labor. The WID supporters called for education, jobs, and training for women, and "other activities which offer alternate sources of personal security and life satisfaction." As one WID activist asserted, "educated, economically productive women" would "have fewer children," and they would also "enhance national output and welfare."[94]

The WID advocates made such arguments in published articles, unpublished reports, internal memos, congressional testimony, and private correspondence. And they won more allies in part because they convinced development planners that WID would advance their goals. In 1974, when USAID reviewed its population program, it reaffirmed that "lowering of fertility" was "an inherent aspect of development." And it called for "vigorous support" for "development programs that facilitate the creation of diversified roles" for women in the poorer nations. In 1977, World Bank president Robert McNamara made the connection more explicit: "The truth is that greater economic opportunity for women . . . would substantially reduce fertility. . . . Schools must make the point to young women that the ideal role of a girl is not to be the mother of a large and poor family but rather have a double role as mother of a small family and as a wage earner who contributes to the well-being of her family by economic employment."[95] In the mid-1970s, population control programs had substantial funding from governments and foundations. When WID advocates tied their programs to population control and fears of overpopulation, they demonstrated their own attachments to the reigning discourse, and they also gave men in power, like McNamara, more reason to support them.

By placing WID in the context of mainstream development concerns with productivity, poverty, and population, the WID supporters tried to deflect the critics who called them "cultural imperialists" and dismissed them as "women's libbers." Through the decade, they wrestled with the labels, which came from multiple points—left, center, and right—on the political spectrum. In the mid-1970s, the Peace Corps, in its internal deliberations on WID, included the question: "How do we know we're not just being culturally imperialistic, imposing our western (women's lib) trip on women in other countries?" The question came up again and again in various agencies and institutions. In response, WID advocates took up the mantra that WID was "*not* an issue of women's lib."[96]

The supporters of WID sometimes showed their irritation that they were held to a higher standard. Why, they asked, were they accused of interfering with the customs of other nations when population control programs and all the projects favoring men were not asked to explain their attempts to change local mores? When US programs supported agricultural training for men, provided child-rearing lessons for women, and encouraged smaller families, they attempted to export middle-class Euro-American ideals. Population control programs, in particular, intervened in customary practice at the most intimate level. In an internal memo, one USAID staffer said sarcastically that WID was "no more culturally imperialistic than a Lippes loop," an intrauterine birth control device. In a later memo, the same official again noted "the spurious argument that we can't mess around (suddenly!) with other folks' cultural values," and suggested that it "should be refuted . . . by pointing out that virtually every government has adopted the integration of women as official policy." With greater diplomacy, a USAID airgram sent to the field offices in Latin America acknowledged that WID was "in a sense social intervention," but, it said, "so are all economic development programs—ours, other donors, or fully indigenous ones—which attempt to produce social change."[97]

At a congressional hearing in 1978, the issue came up again. With Donald Fraser presiding, the staff from USAID's WID office testified, along with their allies, on "international women's issues," before the subcommittees on International Organizations and International Development of the House Committee on International Relations. The WID officials were directly instructed "to comment on whether the women in development idea is a product of American feminism and to what extent its export might be 'imperialistic.'" In response, and no doubt forewarned, Elsa Chaney insisted that WID was "not a product of U.S. feminism." Instead, it responded to "the situation of poor women and the needs of development." Another WID supporter responded more defensively. "When it comes to women, we should not 'fool around with' their culture," she said, "but everything else, we will interfere, and it is considered part of the development process. . . . [W]e are exporting a lot of our own cultural biases, but not necessarily women's lib. It is perhaps more of a male chauvinist bias that we are exporting." At the same hearings, Arvonne Fraser saw "a danger in saying it is safe to deal with the male sector of society and change that, but somehow it is not socially acceptable to change traditions for females."[98]

Some of the WID supporters expressed concerns about cultural imperialism, but others, including Fraser, believed that women's subordination made cultural change a positive good. Some "anthropologists and others," she later recalled, "were still arguing that cultures should not be disturbed. I thought that silly nonsense. Slavery had once been a part of every culture. Did we not want to abolish that?" But Fraser rarely distinguished between fighting for change in one's own nation and demanding change in someone else's. At the 1978 hearings, Dorothy Height, the long-time president of the National Council of Negro Women, had a more nuanced response. She drew an analogy to racial desegregation, suggesting that development, like democracy, required one to stand alongside those who pushed for social change. "It is not that we are imposing our views on others," she said. "Women's rights are human rights. . . . [T]he winds of change are blowing, and people are ready to move, and what we are doing is helping to support those forces which are ready to move."[99]

Like Dorothy Height, other US WID advocates increasingly tried to defuse the accusations of cultural imperialism by pointing to partners in the global South who also wanted change. While some WID activists from the South denounced US government policies and programs, many sought funds and alliances to support their own programs. These women tended to voice fewer concerns about intervening in local mores. At a conference in Sierra Leone, funded by the WID office of USAID, the Americans present expressed "reluctance to interfere with the prevailing values," but seven of the nine representatives from indigenous agencies in Sierra Leone and Liberia said that "their projects did attempt to influence values and attitudes of participating women." They also acknowledged that they hoped to raise women's status.[100]

In the United States and outside it, WID advocates did not necessarily see their work as feminist. In Bangladesh in the late

1970s, where her husband worked for the Ford Foundation, Martha (Marty) Alter Chen ran the women's program of the Bangladeshi organization BRAC (Bangladesh Rural Advancement Committee). As she recalled later, she saw herself as a feminist in her personal life and joined a feminist consciousness-raising group in Dhaka, but she understood BRAC's antipoverty work in a different light. In the villages, she found, it was class relations—seen in the power of local elites—that sustained the rural hierarchy that kept the poor impoverished. In BRAC's programs, women "were getting their consciousness raised à la Paulo Freire," Chen said, "not à la western feminism."[101] Freire, a Brazilian philosopher, was the author of *Pedagogy of the Oppressed*, an influential book that espoused active, democratic learning, in which the poor use what they know to come to a critical consciousness of the sources of their oppression. Freire's approach, called "conscientization," drew on Marxism, humanism, and anticolonialism. Like other WID programs, BRAC organized poor women into groups with goals that included technical training, enhanced productivity, income-earning work, and public services, and it recognized that women faced the particular constraints of unpaid household labor and "of limited social power and autonomy." But its ultimate aim was to bring poor women and men together "into a class federation to address the long-term systemic problems of economic domination by the rich."[102]

Other WID activists did envision their work as feminist but refrained from saying so publicly. In the US government, they often disguised their feminism behind more acceptable development claims. They worked to avoid the accusations of cultural imperialism by stressing the benefits of WID to existing development programs. It was about development, they said, not about imposing their own visions of gender equality. "Most of us were feminists," Elsa Chaney admitted later, "but we could not march under that banner. The choice was between equity and economic arguments. . . . We made a strategic decision to emphasize the latter."[103] At USAID, the WID staffers were semicloseted feminists, and in public at least, they insisted that WID programs were good development policy, not solely or even primarily aimed at women's rights, equality, or (a term used widely in the 1980s and after) "empowerment." The strategy seemed to work. By the end of the

1970s, the accusations of cultural imperialism had subsided, but they had not disappeared entirely. In 1979, Adrienne Germain still noted "the common reaction that an interest in 'women and development' is only 'women's lib' and culturally imperialistic."[104]

———————

By the end of the decade, the WID supporters had done what they could to legitimate their programs, and they had won at least lip service in virtually every corner of the development world. But they still wanted success stories. In development circles, everyone, it seems, had to promote their programs and projects. In order to win funding, one had to show a track record. Charities told success stories to attract donors, grant seekers wrote success stories into their proposals to demonstrate their competence, divisional staff in foundations and institutions used success stories to sell their higher-ups on the merits of their programs, and US government agencies reported success stories to persuade Congress, presidential administrations, and the public that they deserved taxpayers' money. Success stories served as a form of currency that bought respect, built reputations, and attracted future funders. And just as in the corporate world, the storytellers were tempted to inflate success in order to lure and keep investors.[105]

In their 1978 congressional testimony, the WID officials at USAID provided success stories to buy the good will of Congress. They acknowledged that progress thus far had been "modest," but they expressed optimism in the potential of their programs. As their key example, they referred repeatedly to the USAID grant for women in Upper Volta. WID officials had already touted the project a month before the congressional hearings in a special issue on "Women in Africa" in *Agenda*, a magazine published by the USAID Office of Public Affairs. USAID, the article noted, had committed more than a million dollars "to make credit and extension services available to women and to encourage their participation in small rural enterprises."[106] In their congressional testimony, the WID officials acknowledged that it was "not possible yet to point to concrete results," but they "anticipated at least 85 viable micro-projects . . . in the 60 villages." And they speculated, as development planners did, that they could reach "much wider areas" by replicating the program elsewhere.[107]

The Upper Volta project brought together the trinity of productivity, rural poverty, and women's income generation, and thus fulfilled the requirements of the New Directions mandate, the emerging concern with basic needs, and the Percy amendment. It would introduce "work-reducing/time-saving intermediate technologies" that would enhance women's "effectiveness within the non-monetary economy" and give "them more time to engage in production in the cash economy." And it would improve "family incomes" and "health and nutrition." The project thus coordinated well with the 1970s vocabulary of development.[108]

Two months after the congressional testimony, the Carter administration asked Arvonne Fraser to help plan a trip to Africa for President Carter's seventy-nine-year-old mother, known as "Miss Lillian," who had served as a nurse in the Peace Corps in her late sixties. Miss Lillian would receive a prize from the UN's Food and Agriculture Organization in Rome and then, in a publicity spectacle, head on to drought-stricken areas of Africa. US officials hoped that the trip might "express President Carter's interest in world hunger, the gap between rich and poor nations and the role of women in developing nations."[109] Fraser recommended that Miss Lillian visit Upper Volta. The nation "seemed a good place," she wrote, "for a number of reasons," including its "good women in development projects." It was also "easily accessible" and "visually attractive while [the] problems [were] obvious." And, as "an added attraction," it had "a notable and successful group of active women—both African and American." Miss Lillian visited in July, calling her trip a "mission of love," with Fraser as part of her entourage.[110]

But just a year later, the Upper Volta project no longer looked so promising. A 1979 report pointed to multiple problems. The grant had funded a "village survey" but the data collected were "unreliable." The project's staff had drafted and redrafted the forms for providing and monitoring loans, and had begun "discussions with village women with the aim of identifying potential loan activities." But no actual loans had yet been made. The project planners had misjudged both the number of local government agents and technicians available for the project and their skills and training.[111] The "project might sound good on paper," one behind-the-scenes evaluator acknowledged, but the project's managers—American and Voltaic—felt "powerless."[112] It was soon clear that, by any standards, including the project's own, it had failed. Without sufficient personnel, it could not provide training in income-generating activities. Of the $1.056 million budgeted for the project, USAID had allocated $288,000 for the loan fund. But in the end, with the bulk of the money spent, it had disbursed only 15 percent of the loan fund money. And women used the loans, when they got them at all, to fund their usual activities—such as making millet beer, producing bean paste, and reselling tobacco and kerosene—none of which required new training or technology and none of which had much potential for expanding income.[113] In 1984, when the WID division of USAID compiled an elaborate report on its first ten years of activity, the Upper Volta project, once its key success story, did not appear at all.[114]

In the late 1970s, the Ford Foundation stepped into the breach to find and publicize success stories. It planned a new initiative, an annual pamphlet series, titled *Seeds*. Sponsored by Ford, the Carnegie Corporation, and the Population Council, the pamphlets promised to "serve as a means of sharing information and sparking new project ideas based on the positive experiences of women," and they also intended to show "those in decision-making positions . . . that income-generating projects for and by women *are* viable and have important roles to play in development."[115] Earlier in the 1970s, most WID programs had focused on research, conferences, and outreach, but by the end of the decade there were projects on the ground, mostly small-scale projects that involved women working in agriculture, food preparation, handicrafts, and marketing. Each issue of the magazine would feature such "successful income generating projects for low income women." Adrienne Germain told her colleagues at Ford that she had identified a handful of projects—in Bangladesh, Guatemala, India, Jamaica, and Kenya—to showcase in the series. The first issue came out in 1980. It recounted how a group of women in rural Kenya had raised the funds to start a profit-making bus service and then opened a shop. This issue and others included photos of women at work, replacing an older visual trope, used by antipoverty campaigns, of distressed mothers depicted with needy children. The new photos aimed "not only to attract attention but to present an image of women as strong and capable."[116] Germain and her colleagues distributed the booklet to a mailing list of around 2,500.

By 1980, then, the WID movement had launched, and its advocates teetered between a hopeful vision of successful projects that alleviated the poverty of women and a realistic assessment of the divisions within their movement, the difficult dealings in bureaucracies, and the complexities involved in projects aimed at indigent women in the poorest nations. In the United States and elsewhere, they worked their way into the mainstream and made the kinds of strategic arguments that would appeal to more-established development experts.

Two major international commission reports help us measure the distance that the WID movement had traveled over the course of the 1970s. The 399-page Pearson report, *Partners in Development*, published in 1969, neglected women entirely. Even in its pages on population and birth control, the words "women" and "female" appear only once each, and women as producers made no appearance at all. In contrast, the Brandt report, *North-South: A Program for Survival*, published in 1980, had short subsections titled "Women in Society," "Development Depends on Women," "Women: Statistically Invisible," and "Special Hardships of Women." The report not only recognized women as economic actors, it also pointed to issues of equity in the distribution of labor and income. "Development with justice," the report stated, "calls urgently for measures that will give women access to better jobs; that will diminish the arduous tasks that hundreds of millions of women face in their domestic and agricultural occupations; and that will distribute more fairly between the sexes opportunities for creative work and economic advancement."[117]

In the same year, 1980, the World Bank positioned women as critical to the basic needs approach. Educating women and bringing them into the labor force, it claimed, could reduce population growth. Plus, women played a central role "in the production and use of goods . . . important in meeting [basic] needs." And in their spending patterns, women were "systematically oriented more toward basic needs than men."[118] The WID movement had made its mark. By 1980, foreign aid was in decline, and the NIEO's call for structural changes in the global economy had gone from a shout to a whisper. The language of basic needs still had some rhetorical punch, even if few expected the existing programs to actually end poverty. But the interest in women was rising, and it coincided with a growing privatization of development. In the late 1970s and early 1980s, more NGOs were turning to economic development and at the same time to women.

CHAPTER FOUR

Private Developments

IN OCTOBER 1984, BBC News broadcast a report on famine in Ethiopia. The report avoided the complex causes of famine, which included the repressive policies of the Ethiopian dictatorship as well as an unavoidable drought. Instead, it went straight for the heart with devastating footage of starvation and death. Critics today might cast the BBC coverage as "poverty porn," with its sensationalized exposure of helpless bodies in distress: "piles of dead children in shrouds, huge crowds of emaciated Ethiopians huddled in the desert, and an elderly man dying of starvation before the camera." But in 1984 it elicited, as it intended, the kinds of emotions—horror, pity, empathy—that provoke response. Hundreds of broadcasters replayed the televised suffering, and funds poured into Oxfam, Save the Children, Catholic Relief Services, and other organizations. In the United States, private charities collected $40 million in the last two months of the year. The public's "phenomenal response," the *New York Times* announced, had exceeded by far "the donations made in 1979 to relieve starvation in Cambodia or in 1973 during the last major drought in Africa." Donors included sixth-grade students in Brooklyn, the African Methodist Episcopal Church, and Chase Manhattan Bank.[1]

Earlier famines had also attracted funds with a magnetic pull. But this time there was something new beyond the BBC's wrenching report and the magnitude of donations. In Britain, the musicians Bob Geldof and James "Midge" Ure organized Band Aid, with forty big-name artists, and recorded the song "Do They Know It's

Christmas?" as a fundraiser for famine relief. The song sold a million copies in its first week on the market in late 1984. Soon after, Geldof and Ure formed a companion organization, Live Aid, which produced benefit concerts in London and Philadelphia in the summer following. Within a few months, the song and the concerts had raised $110 million.[2] Meanwhile, in the United States, the musician and activist Harry Belafonte and the musicians' manager Ken Kragen created another nonprofit, USA (United Support of Artists) for Africa. They enlisted producer Quincy Jones to pull together a star-studded roster of performers to raise money for the famine, which stretched beyond Ethiopia through the Sahel region, just south of the Sahara desert. The song they recorded, "We Are the World," written by Lionel Ritchie and Michael Jackson and released in March 1985, raised more than $50 million over the next year and a half. With their songs and concerts for disaster relief, Band Aid, Live Aid, and USA for Africa entered the megabusiness of celebrity fundraising for international crises.[3]

In the mid-1980s, "We Are the World" did not win universal acclaim; some listeners panned the song, which seemed more anodyne than artful. But for our purposes, the song and star power are mostly irrelevant. If we move beyond the music and follow the money instead, we can see the machinery of private foreign assistance in the late twentieth-century United States. USA for Africa raised funds for classic disaster relief, but where did the money go? Belafonte, Kragen, and Jones could organize the production of a song and sell the T-shirts and posters that went along with it, but they did not have the distribution networks for sending funds to Africa. On a two-week visit to Ethiopia, Tanzania, and Sudan, Kragen realized "that it's not just a question of sending more money or more food," and Belafonte confirmed that "the reality is certainly more complex than we anticipated."[4]

The problems were daunting. Without adequate transportation, bags of grain sat in storage. NGOs competed with one another for donors and government contracts, and they resented the pop star upstarts who had invaded their turf. And national governments siphoned off aid funds for their own purposes. In Ethiopia, in particular, food sent for famine relief went to support the military in a brutal civil war. Separatist rebels, too, turned the relief efforts to their own advantage. They ambushed relief convoys and made off with the food. With no experience in the field, USA for Africa decided to funnel its money through existing networks. It invited NGOs and UN agencies to submit proposals for grants, and it commissioned the United Nations Office for Emergency Operations in Africa along with InterAction, a new consortium of more than one hundred US NGOs, to vet the proposals that poured in.[5]

In the end, both USA for Africa and Band Aid/Live Aid joined the global antipoverty movement with its emphasis on small-scale, local, income-generating projects. That is, they chose to spend less money on immediate disaster relief, such as shipments of food and medicine, and more on "longer term recovery and development projects."[6] And some of the projects focused on women. Band Aid/Live Aid announced early on that it had "a special interest" in "women's projects," and USA for Africa fielded a number of proposals that directly targeted women, including a "women's training center" and "income-generating and labour-saving projects" in Ethiopia, "women's gardens" in Mali, and "women's extension and development" in Sudan.[7]

Funds were allocated, to give a more specific example, for a women's fish-processing project on the coast of Senegal. The Overseas Education Fund (OEF), a group that grew out of the League of Women Voters, had applied for the grant. It proposed to give women "entrepreneurs" in the town of MBao training, technology, and credit "to increase the profitability of their fish-drying and other enterprises and to improve their families' diets." This was not emergency relief; it was a WID (women in development) project designed to provide impoverished women with additional income. In an advertisement to raise funds so that "African women can take the next step to end hunger," the OEF stated, "Food relief from outside countries will save lives in the short run. But what about the long run?" The OEF president, Elise Fiber Smith, told the *Washington Post*, "We all really care about this long-term development."[8]

The fundraising for the famine highlights three significant trends in the global antipoverty campaigns of the late 1970s and 1980s. First, the privatization of foreign assistance with development channeled through NGOs. By the 1980s, many international NGOs had expanded well beyond disaster relief to undertake longer-term antipoverty development projects. In 1980, the executive director of CARE, a huge NGO that spent more than $200 million annually, noted the "trend away from the pure relief efforts" and toward "involvement in community improvement projects" in the global South. The US government encouraged the trend. In the 1970s and 1980s, USAID worked to outsource its local antipoverty projects via government grants and contracts with "private voluntary" groups. Older NGOs were moving, as one book title stated it, "beyond charity," and newer ones came on board to address the antipoverty turn and access the funding that came with it. With private donations and grants from governments and foundations, NGOs entered the vacuum created as bilateral foreign assistance came under fire. By the mid-1980s, even NGOs that raised funds explicitly intended for the relief of famine had jumped on the antipoverty development bandwagon.[9]

Second, antipoverty NGOs focused on supporting small-scale businesses, such as the fish-drying project in Senegal. They supplemented the language of "productivity" and "income generation" with increasing emphasis on "enterprise" and "business development." In the 1970s, development experts took a new interest in the informal economy and the small enterprises that composed it. In the 1980s, the Reagan administration encouraged the shift toward the private sector, small business, and training for the poor in marketing, management, and fiscal discipline. The poor were now seen less as workers and more as the owners and builders of their own businesses. Antipoverty development did not disappear in the 1980s; it took on new forms in a neoliberal era.

Third, the NGOs, new and old, turned to women. The WID movement had positioned women as critical to the global antipoverty movement. Private organizations took note. Some established women's organizations adapted to the changing times and adopted the antipoverty language that might win them government and foundation grants, and some new NGOs grew out of feminist activism. But the WID movement alone was not enough to turn a wide-ranging assortment of NGOs toward a focus on women. In the informal economy, the presence, and often predominance, of women was, it turned out, impossible to ignore. By the early 1980s, numerous NGOs—based in the United States and elsewhere—combined the promotion of the informal sector with growing attention to women as key to development programs. The NGOs involved varied in their experience, activities, reputations, and politics. But taken together, they and their funders saw women in the global South as diligent entrepreneurs who deserved income for themselves and their families. And they increasingly claimed that women were more responsible economic actors than men.

Beyond Charity

The Foreign Assistance Act of 1973, the same act that reoriented USAID toward local antipoverty projects and the same act that included the Percy amendment, which required the inclusion of women in development programs, also called on USAID to work more closely with private agencies. The relevant clause mandated that US government development programs "should be carried out to the maximum extent possible through the private sector, including . . . voluntary agencies."[10] The alliance between foreign assistance and the private sector had long-standing bipartisan backing. Throughout the postwar era, US policy makers had positioned private enterprise as a counter to communism and also as a way to offload the labor of economic development. Foreign aid programs routinely relied on private contractors and encouraged US businesses to invest in and build the private sector in the global South. In the 1960s, one historian writes, private investment was "a primary instrument of development policy."[11]

Like his predecessors, President Nixon hoped to promote US public-private collaboration. In 1969, he recommended the creation of a new government agency, the Overseas Private Investment Corporation, to provide incentives for US businesses to make investments, seen as risky, in the poorer nations. "We must," he said, "enlist the energies of private enterprise, here and abroad, in the cause of economic development." The Overseas Private Investment Corporation was established in 1971. It offered (and still offers today, as the US International Development Finance Corporation) insurance and loan guarantees for US investors in the global South. It protected businesses from nationalization and other political risks, and promised US government pay-outs in the case of loan defaults. It won the support of Democrats as well as Republicans, and so did the clause in the 1973 Foreign Assistance Act that endorsed foreign assistance via the private sector. NGOs did not describe their work as akin to that of profit-making contractors, corporations, and investors. Nonetheless, they could use their private status to tap into an agenda that had the seal of approval of both president and Congress.[12]

By 1973, the US government already had relationships with various American "private voluntary organizations," or PVOs, the term used then for what we now call NGOs. The Advisory Committee on Voluntary Foreign Aid (ACVFA), founded in 1946, registered nonprofit agencies that worked with the US government in projects overseas. At the start, most of the registered agencies engaged in postwar relief and refugee resettlement in Europe. Later, in the 1950s and after, they redirected their relief work from Europe to the global South. Eventually a few of the voluntary groups also joined in the Cold War–era technical assistance and community development programs. The charity CARE, for example, trained the first Peace Corps volunteers for a mission in Colombia, and then supported the Peace Corps elsewhere in Latin America, Asia, and Africa.[13]

The Vietnam War both cemented and sullied the relationship between the government and voluntary organizations. During the war, a number of NGOs worked hand in hand with the US military. CARE and Catholic Relief Services relied on the government for most of their revenue, and they actively promoted US Cold War foreign policy goals. As antiwar sentiment grew, they came under attack for using the guise of humanitarianism to cloak their involvement with military operations. Some NGO staff and volunteers opposed the war while they worked in Vietnam, but even they conceded that their charitable efforts abetted US military interventions. A former volunteer with Mennonite Central Committee remembered that "some of us . . . felt as though we were being used by U.S. policy makers to legitimize and make palatable a ruthless policy of destroying the fabric of Vietnamese society." In some ways, then, the Foreign Assistance Act of 1973 simply codified a dense (and troubling) entanglement that had run for decades.[14]

But the 1973 act also aimed to promote a different kind of collaboration. Through the 1960s, the largest American NGOs that worked overseas continued to devote their efforts primarily to humanitarian relief. They positioned themselves as charities that helped the hungry, ill, and displaced. Those that contracted with the US government focused heavily on food aid. Under Public Law (PL) 480, passed in 1954, they received government funds to send surplus agricultural products to poorer nations. The 1973 act changed the emphasis. It turned attention away from relief, rehabilitation, and food and toward longer-term development. It encouraged USAID to work with NGOs that would plan and implement small-scale antipoverty projects.[15]

USAID was already on board. In the year and a half before the act passed, it conducted studies on how it might involve NGOs more in its grassroots development programs. It created a new Office for Private and Voluntary Cooperation and sponsored East- and West-Coast conferences with US NGOs. With a declining budget and fewer personnel, it hoped to find "opportunities for possible use of private resources." Cooperation with NGOs could, it hoped, "maximize the use of diminishing AID dollars," augmenting government contributions with NGO resources supplied in part by private donors.[16] Projects managed by NGOs might also redistribute some of the labor involved and sidestep the complicated diplomatic protocols that government-run projects entailed. And they might help cleanse foreign assistance of the taint of national self-interest, military intervention, and bureaucratic bungling.

USAID officials sought, as they said, "to enlarge the role of voluntary agencies in development work," but they drew a distinction between the NGOs that focused on "traditional humanitarian goals and short-run objectives" and "those increasingly concerned with long-run developmental [goals]." To the director of the Office for Private and Voluntary Cooperation, the traditional NGOs addressed "the effects of underdevelopment rather than attempting to tackle the basic causes of underdevelopment." He clearly preferred the latter. NGOs, one USAID report stated, had "hovered about on the edge of the development scene." Now the agency planned "to encourage and to assist them to play more productive roles in the development picture."[17] With the Foreign Assistance Act of 1973, it had the green light to do so.

As usual, the Overseas Development Council (ODC) came out in support of USAID's initiatives and, more generally, of anything that might embellish US foreign aid. It had played a key role in pushing the Foreign Assistance Act of 1973 through Congress, and now it attempted to broadcast the call for more participation by NGOs. It requested and received a grant from USAID to hold workshops for NGOs that would help them "enhance their capacity to plan meaningful development activities." Eventually, it published a boosterish book, *Beyond Charity: U.S. Voluntary Aid for a Changing Third World*, that described the trend from relief to development and promoted NGOs, without an inkling of irony, as "missionaries for modernity." It positioned the global South as "the new frontier, as if manifest destiny had been extended from the American West to the world at large." The book dutifully pointed out some criticisms of NGOs, including "hidden motivations," "insensitive and poorly trained individual foreigners," and assistance that "strengthens the entrenched power elites at the expense of the downtrodden poor," but it skipped over the history of conversion, conquest, and imperialism that "missionaries" and "manifest destiny" evoked. Mostly it applauded NGOs and urged them to move "beyond charity" to participate in the new government-sponsored development programs. "The private and voluntary sector, whatever its shortcomings," it stated, "is a unique source of hope and promise as the people of the United States strive to reassert a constructive role in tomorrow's world."[18]

The registered NGOs were, for the most part, eager to comply. The ACVFA, comprising representatives from registered agencies, touted the NGOs' growing interest in development as well as their history of working with "the poorest parts of the populations."[19] It also claimed that leaders in the global South saw NGOs as "more acceptable" than US government agencies. NGOs, it suggested, were "considered less self-serving" and less likely to "generate suspicions as to motives and intent."[20] With the new emphasis on development, though, the largest NGOs worried that USAID might exclude them as relics from an earlier era. They objected to the distinctions that made them seem outdated. The executive director of CARE stated outright that his agency "very much resents any implication that it lacks a dedication to and an expertise in overseas development programming." And the executive director of Catholic Relief Services also balked. "If . . . the suggestion is made that our role in the humanitarian field makes our Agency unqualified to discuss, work and plan development," he wrote, "I must utterly and completely reject the inference." With new opportunities for government funding, the NGOs already working with the US government tended to want in.[21]

But the NGOs were a diverse group. They ranged, as the ODC noted, from "long-standing multi-million dollar enterprises," such as CARE and Catholic Relief Services, to "small agencies operating on a shoe-string budget." Some depended on government money; others refused it entirely. Even those that agreed to attend a government-funded ODC workshop on voluntary organizations and rural development, held in late 1974, remained leery of the morally suspect blend of humanitarian goals, geopolitics, and national self-interest. In the opening session of the workshop, participants wondered about "the degree of intimacy to be tolerated between the public and private sector" and expressed some distrust of the government. As the workshop report put it, "Viet Nam and Watergate have left their scars." In a series of "issues papers," drafted for discussion, ACVFA members also worried about their independence under government oversight. "Would government support" of development projects "subject them," one such paper asked, "to the vagaries of bureaucratic whim and development fads?"[22]

The NGOs had concerns about other governments as well. "Third World countries," another issue paper noted, were "less receptive" than they had been "to the policies and practices of the voluntary agencies from developed countries."[23] Host governments might trust NGOs more than they trusted the US government, but that hardly meant wholesale endorsement. Postcolonial leaders protected their national sovereignty, and they remained wary of interventions by US organizations as well as those by the US government. To the US NGOs, they seemed more "conscious of their emergent power" and "overly sensitive to charitable overtures from abroad," as well as "skeptical of the professed motives of voluntary agencies." And their "centralized social and economic planning" might conflict with "the micro-level projects of voluntary agencies."

In sum, the nations of the global South were "no longer so tolerant of well-intentioned outsiders as they once were."[24]

And NGOs expressed uneasiness, too, about their own finances. Many of them relied on disasters—with photos of starving children and stranded refugees—to pique the consciences of individual donors. "Would fund-raising prospects be diminished," they wondered openly, "if voluntary agencies were to emphasize development rather than relief activities in their public appeals?" Donors often contributed funds "out of a spontaneous charitable impulse in response to natural disasters" or through "poignant appeals in the media." NGO officials questioned whether long-term development could inspire the tug on the heartstrings that opened donors' wallets. They suspected that development projects would not generate the kinds of public support that "less controversial" relief efforts would.[25]

Despite their reservations, many NGOs found the lure of government support too appealing to reject. To reel them in, USAID offered two new kinds of grants. "Operational program grants" went to registered NGOs to plan and implement new on-the-ground antipoverty projects in the global South. "Development program grants" provided NGOs with funds to enter the international development field. NGOs could use those grants to build their institutional capacity to design and manage development projects. In the mid-1970s, USAID gave forty such grants that brought existing NGOs into the "New Directions" development programs that addressed the global poor. Some of them went to smaller NGOs, including the Overseas Education Fund, the group that planned the women's fish-processing project in Senegal just a few years later.[26]

Private WID

Because the 1973 Foreign Assistance Act also included the Percy amendment, USAID now had a mandate to integrate women into its development projects as well as to work with NGOs. The chair of ACVFA, Margaret Hickey, was happy to help. Hickey had spent her career as an advocate for women. In the 1940s, she had chaired the Women's Advisory Committee of the War Manpower Commission and served as president of the National Federation of Business and

Professional Women, and in the 1960s, she had served on President
Kennedy's Commission on the Status of Women and then chaired
President Johnson's Advisory Council on the Status of Women. She
was also the long-time editor of the "public affairs" section of the
popular magazine *Ladies' Home Journal*. In 1973, she had served
for more than twenty years on ACVFA and had just taken over as
chair. She took an active interest in the Percy amendment, and she
ushered a resolution endorsing it through the committee. The resolution promised "close cooperation" between NGOs and USAID "in
promoting equity and equal opportunity for men and women as a
basic principle of development." And it advertised NGOs as especially well suited to achieve the Percy amendment's goals. NGOs,
it stated, could "reach and organize women at the grassroots and
train women for productive employment." A separate organization
of NGOs, the American Council of Voluntary Agencies for Foreign
Service (ACVAFS, not to be confused with ACVFA), which was
not formally affiliated with the government, also worked to bring
NGOs into public-private collaborations in response to the Percy
amendment. With the encouragement of USAID, it formed a WID
subcommittee in 1975 to "focus on developing prototypes of projects and approaches which directly influence the status of women
in the L[ess] D[eveloped] C[ountrie]s." Individual NGOs, too,
approached USAID in search of the grants and contracts now available for WID.[27]

The phrase "beyond charity" captures the change for some
NGOs—a change that USAID, the ODC, CARE, and others noted
and promoted—but it also erases the multiple routes that NGOs
traveled in their move toward development projects that addressed
global poverty. In the case of WID, some of the US NGOs that
entered the field in the mid-1970s had never been charities. The
National Council of Negro Women, for example, was (and is) an
advocacy group, founded in 1935, by and for African American
women. In the late 1960s, it created antipoverty projects for rural
women in the US South, and it had earlier connections with elite
women overseas. In the 1970s, it came to WID from a sense of solidarity with Black women in Africa, a belief that its projects in the
rural United States could be replicated in rural Africa, and a search
for funding to sustain the organization. After it won a grant for

WID seminars during and after the International Women's Year conference in 1975, it hoped to expand its international reach. Over the course of a decade, USAID supplied around $1.7 million in support. The funds paid for a development program grant and a cluster of international endeavors, including a skills training center in Togo and a project for women in Swaziland to earn income by raising pigs.[28] Like the NCNW, various other NGOs converged on WID, drawn by some combination of their own politics, interests, and expertise, their connections with the US government and foundations, and their quest for financial support.

The Overseas Education Fund (OEF) was among the first NGOs to jump at the new opportunities for government funding and also the foremost NGO that USAID favored for its initial WID projects. Founded in 1947, it served as the international wing of the League of Women Voters, and as such, it focused most of its early efforts on citizen education, first in Europe and later in Latin America. In the 1960s and early 1970s, it worked with women's voluntary organizations overseas and brought middle- and upper-class women to the United States for seminars on leadership training. In 1973, its stated goal was "to encourage and assist . . . active and responsible citizen participation."[29] Based in Washington, DC, it fit well with the people-to-people international exchanges of Cold War foreign policy, and it received most of its funding from the US government.

The Cold War connection, it seems, was closer than most knew. In 1975, *CounterSpy* magazine published an exposé, revealing that at least three of the leaders of the OEF had given the CIA information on the foreign women who participated in its programs. According to *CounterSpy*, the director of the OEF's Latin American program worked hand in hand with a CIA officer, who was also the USAID director for Panama, and OEF's representative in Asia met with other CIA officers in South Korea. The magazine acknowledged, though, that most of the OEF board and staff had no knowledge of the intelligence gathering.[30] Still, the Cold War context, and the covert intelligence gathering, may have helped the OEF sustain its government support.

Like many NGOs, the OEF scrambled for the funds it needed to survive. In the early 1970s, it expanded its work in Asia as well as in Latin America, and it hoped to do more work "in the field," outside the United States, and "to reach younger and lower socio-economic groups." The Percy amendment provided the chance for the OEF to extend its reach and ease its chronic financial distress. The OEF was not the most obvious choice for antipoverty development programs, but it had friends in government who could help it position itself in the changing landscape. Clara Beyer, who had initiated the Percy amendment and worked at USAID, also served on the OEF's board of directors. In January 1974, a month after the foreign assistance bill was signed, she alerted the board that the amendment "requires AID to include programs for women, with emphasis on the rural and poor. She felt there was money there for new projects."[31] Over the next year, the OEF shifted its work with impressive speed, expressing increasing interest in global poverty and in work with indigent women. And it secured the funds it sought. In the second half of the 1970s, it landed USAID development and institutional program grants totaling over a million dollars, which allowed it to hire staff and "identify possible projects for implementation" in Latin America, Asia, and Africa. It used the grants to generate multiple proposals for specific projects, "so that if one is not funded we will have others in the mill."[32]

By the end of the 1970s, the OEF had won more than $4 million in additional USAID support for several of its projects. The grants included funds for, among other things, vocational training for women in Costa Rica, a community market and women's vocational training in Ecuador, training for women extension workers to promote health and income generation among poorer women in Sri Lanka, and the promotion of WID organizations in Zambia. The OEF now listed "promoting economic self-reliance for low-income women" as its key goal. A USAID report acknowledged the OEF's "past emphasis on middle-class women," but stated that "low-income women" now comprised "more than 90% of the 15,000 beneficiaries of the 11 new projects."[33]

The quick transformation combined sincere interest with a dose of opportunism, and it brought its own problems. For one, the OEF relied too heavily on government grants. From 1978 on, USAID pushed NGOs to supplement the public contributions with private gifts. In February 1978, it held a full-day meeting with NGOs that worked overseas, alerting them that they needed to raise at least 20 percent of their international projects' costs from private sources within the United States. The OEF attempted, with limited success, to win support from individual, corporate, and foundation donors. And the quality of the work came under question, too. At the Ford Foundation, Adrienne Germain was scathing. At the end of 1979, she told a colleague that she had "had contact with [OEF's] Washington-based staff for a number of years . . . and had reports on OEF overseas activities from Third World and other colleagues." Some of the problems she saw resulted from USAID's funding. When it gave money to develop proposals but not to implement them, it created "misunderstandings between OEF and the people they attempt to develop projects with overseas." But OEF shared the blame. "I am not impressed," Germain wrote, "by their staff, their philosophy (politics really), or their accomplishments to the extent I have seen them." It was a "classic" case, she said "of a well-intentioned institution with AID money stumbling through Third World countries with virtually nothing to offer making a mess of things." The criticism was harsh, but it captured the complicated public-private push and pull in which NGOs refashioned themselves, sometimes rapidly, to accommodate funders—in this case, USAID.[34]

And what pleased USAID changed over time. In the late 1970s, USAID, and the development field more generally, encouraged NGOs to pursue local, antipoverty "basic needs" programs, but the specific types of projects it favored shifted, at first subtly and then in more obvious ways. By the end of the 1970s, the buzzword "income generation," which had dominated in the first years of the WID movement, increasingly came conjoined with "small enterprise" and "entrepreneurship."

Poor Women as Entrepreneurs

In the 1970s, development economists and policy makers discovered the "informal sector" of precarious, labor-intensive, small-enterprise work, the kind of work that failed to register in official economic statistics. The ILO's *Employment, Incomes and Equality*, a report on Kenya published in 1972, labeled the sector "informal" and helped inspire a growing interest in it. The ILO saw promise in the informal sector, which it described as "economically efficient and profitable, though small in scale and limited by simple technologies, little capital, and lack of links with the other ('formal') sector." The ILO's informal economy included, among others, "petty traders, street hawkers, shoeshine boys . . . carpenters, masons, tailors . . . cooks and taxi-drivers" who had "the full range of basic skills needed to provide goods and services for a large though often poor section of the population." And it was immense. According to the ILO, the informal sector accounted for almost two-fifths of African employment outside of agriculture.[35] In the mid- and late 1970s, the ILO continued to publicize the informal sector in its World Employment Programme. It conducted studies in Kolkata, Jakarta, Bogotá, São Paolo, Lagos, and Abidjan, and encouraged "a new development strategy" to lift the "level of employment and labour productivity" in the informal sector.[36]

The new emphasis on the informal economy resonated widely in development circles of the late 1970s. It reflected the rejection of trickle-down theories and the endorsement of development programs that focused attention on the poorest of the global poor. It also registered a new attention to household economics, with surveys that attempted to measure local and home-based (and not simply national) production. And it responded to a rising alarm about population growth, the displacement of agricultural laborers, and the swell of migration from country to city. The ILO studies showed that many, maybe most, adult migrants to cities worked in the informal sector. Development projects in the informal economy meshed neatly, too, with the "small is beautiful" environmentalist vision that encouraged inexpensive, nonindustrial, "appropriate technology" to employ the poor in rural areas, small towns, and cities.[37]

Interest in informality reached across the political spectrum. For liberals, as one critic wrote, projects in the informal economy "appeared to offer the possibility of 'helping the poor without any major threat to the rich.'" For those on the left, they organized the subordinated petty producers who sold the minimally profitable goods and services that the mainstream capitalist sector relied on, and for those on the right, they rewarded the self-reliant individualists who lifted themselves by their bootstraps without government support. Accounts of the informal economy ranged in tone from outrage and pity to promotion and praise, but the debates over its merits only enhanced the growing consensus that it was central to the global economy. By the mid-1970s, the World Bank and the UN had added small-scale urban enterprise projects to their rural antipoverty programs. And by 1978, when the journal *World Development* published a special issue on the informal sector, the literature on it was extensive. It had, one of the journal's authors noted, "assumed enormous significance in urban development planning."[38]

That same year the US government joined in the trend with USAID's Small Enterprise Approaches to Employment project and, under its auspices, a subproject known as PISCES, or Program for Investment in the Small Capital Enterprise Sector. With PISCES, USAID hoped to uncover ways to channel more resources to the smallest enterprises. It found that "tens of millions of dollars" of foreign aid went to larger producers but "only a miniscule proportion of this assistance" went to "the hard core of the urban poor." Its "ultimate goal" was "to create jobs, increase incomes and productivity and generally redress the poverty" in the "urban informal sector."[39]

USAID contracted with three US NGOs to carry out the PISCES project. Under its rubric, ACCION International focused on Latin America, Partnership for Productivity on Asia, and the Development Group for Alternative Policies (DGAP) on Africa. The three NGOs convened workshops, conducted research, and compiled case studies on "approaches and methodologies . . . for working with the smallest enterprise needs of the urban poor."[40] They located and studied twenty-three projects—government programs, commercial bank ventures, and local NGO efforts—that already addressed the informal sector.

The PISCES project adopted the new language used in the informal-sector development field, which included a shift away from "wages" and toward "self-employment," and away from "workers" and toward "entrepreneurs" and "owners." It also underscored the rising importance of women. The three NGOs that conducted the study were relatively young. ACCION was founded in 1961 and Partners for Productivity in 1969. Both had developed community-level small-enterprise projects in the global South in the early 1970s.

DGAP was a new organization, incorporated in 1977, and more of a think tank concerned with policy than on-the-ground programs. In their origins, none of the three had special interest in women; they did not grow out of the WID movement or out of the women's movement more generally. They came to women through small enterprise. Through their own programs and through research for PISCES, they learned that the existing community projects "most commonly assisted women entrepreneurs," and they also discovered that "the smaller the business reached by a project, the larger the proportion of women business owners."[41]

In their PISCES investigations, the three US NGOs encountered women who made tortillas, candy, and costume jewelry, women who prepared food, raised chickens, and sold fruit, and women who spun, wove, sewed, crocheted, and patched in order to earn income. And they located new international, national, and local projects concerned with training these women in techniques of production, bookkeeping, sales, and credit. The National Christian Council of Kenya, for example, worked mostly with "extremely poor women" in its Small Business Scheme, started in Nairobi in 1975. It gave loans and taught accounting, "marketing, joint purchasing of materials . . . , licensing, cooperative registration, and how to get access to public services."[42] The UN Office of Technical Cooperation financed a similar project in Swaziland, beginning in 1976, that opened childcare centers and trained women "in manual production techniques and enterprise management" with the goal of "producing marketable products." It also provided loans for "simple tools and machines." Most of the women involved made sisal place mats or spun mohair into yarn.[43] In India, the Working Women's Forum, an NGO that registered in Madras (now Chennai) in 1978, aimed "to mobilize self-employed lower and lower-middle class working women." It protested police harassment, taught literacy, provided credit, and helped women "increase incomes . . . and get better conditions in the markets."[44]

Why the emphasis on women? The rise of the WID movement, and the feminist movement more generally, provides part of the answer, but other factors were just as important. When development experts trained their sight on the informal economy, women came into view. In some places, the adult, able-bodied men had left. They had gone to larger cities for wage work or migrated for agricultural or extractive labor. In Swaziland, for example, many of the men worked in South African mines, and the impoverished women who stayed behind, often with children, needed and wanted income. In other cases, the traditional primary breadwinners— husbands and fathers—were dead, disabled, or unemployed, or did not earn enough or share enough income to support their families. Women supported themselves and their households with small business endeavors, often those that allowed them to work in or near their homes. In the larger cities, men had easier access to wage work than did women. In its report on Manila, the PISCES team explained why it had interviewed three women for every man. "Men," they found, "seem not to be drawn to these small businesses."[45] In their hiring practices, employers tended to favor men for waged jobs, which had higher prestige and more regular income. Men could avoid the informal economy; women had fewer options. In the search for the smallest enterprises and the most indigent workers, women were hard to avoid.

Other unspoken factors may also have been at play. In the 1950s and 1960s, at the height of the Cold War, development theorists had worried that impoverished men would turn to revolution and communism. Impoverished women seemed less dangerous, which meant that modernizers felt less compelled to create the kinds of programs that they imagined would win their hearts and minds. But in the early 1970s, Nixon visited Beijing, opening relations with the People's Republic of China, and he eased Cold War hostilities with the Soviet Union through talks, summit meetings, arms limitation treaties, and trade. In the age of détente (and before the "war on terror"), US policy makers had fewer grounds to see destitute men in the global South as a threat to the international balance of power.

Through much of the 1970s, as Cold War anxieties ebbed in the United States, the fulfillment of basic needs played a larger role in discussions of foreign aid. With a focus on poverty, development experts not only had less reason to prioritize men; they also had more reason to notice women. Plus, with the new interest in the informal economy, a focus on hard-working women, without any mention of sex work, could cleanse the sector of its associations with illegality, crime, vice, and disorder.[46] For NGOs (and for donor governments as well), women—young women alone in the city, mothers left behind with children, widows—could have sentimental appeal in ways that men did not. They could inspire racialized fantasies of rescue and protection, what the literary theorist Gayatri Spivak has described as "white men saving brown women from brown men."[47]

Whatever the reason, the combined interest in small enterprise and women was widespread by the end of the 1970s, and additional NGOs entered the field. A wealthy married couple, Glen and Mildred Leet, for example, founded the Trickle Up Program in 1979 and quickly won support for it. Glen Leet had worked for the UN after World War II and then served as president of the charity Save the Children. In the 1970s, he was on the board of the OEF. Mildred Leet was a former president of the US National Council of Women and a former vice-president of the International Council of Women. She had served on the Women's Advisory Committee on Poverty of the US Office of Economic Opportunity. The Leets started Trickle Up with their own money on the assumption that poor people needed a tiny capital infusion to boost small businesses into something larger. They gave out $50 grants to small groups of applicants who filed a bare-bones business plan for self-employment, with a second grant of $50 if a follow-up report suggested some kind of business progress. The Leets worked through in-country coordinators, including churches, local NGOs, and Peace Corps volunteers, to locate grant recipients. They began on the Caribbean island of Dominica, where they funded ten projects, and then they expanded rapidly. Within ten years, they claimed to have assisted more than ten thousand enterprises in eighty-three nations.[48] From the start, the Leets billed Trickle Up as a program for men and women both, but they discovered that women applied for the grants more often than men did. Five years after they founded the program, 80 percent of their grants went to women.[49]

Trickle Up won backing from other donors, including the Dutch government and the UN Development Program. In the early 1980s, it also established a formal collaboration with the Peace Corps and soon much of its funding came from the US government. By the end of the decade, foundations and corporate sponsors—American Express, IBM, and J. P. Morgan—also chipped in. The support and acclaim came in part because the program captured the spirit of the

moment with its growing focus on indigent women, small enterprise, and the informal economy, and also because it promised to
alleviate poverty with only a piddling investment. The Leets envisioned poor people as potential "entrepreneurs who develop their
own enterprises, accumulate capital, stay in business, and create
wealth." Trickle Up, Mildred Leet stated, "learned from Third World
people that capital formation is more important than income generation as a means of climbing out of poverty."[50] Maybe, maybe not.
But most small businesses fail, and the Leets placed unusually high
expectations on a minuscule shot of seed capital and a bit of business training. Like other NGOs, Trickle Up advertised its success,
in this case with stories about and pictures of grant recipients and
with numbers of businesses started. The limited grants funded a
wide variety of local enterprises, including making bricks, packet-
ing tea, and selling eggs, charcoal, chili powder, ginger wine, and
mango jam. But without long-term follow-up, it was hard to dis-
cern whether they actually helped build income, productivity, or
sustainable business enterprise.

By the end of the 1970s, the Ford Foundation, too, took an interest in women and small enterprise. In its International Division,
Adrienne Germain added the urban informal economy to her
portfolio of WID programs in rural areas. She cultivated connections with NGOs in the global South and funded those she found
impressive. In India, the Ford Foundation worked with the Self-
Employed Women's Association (SEWA) from early on. SEWA was
founded in 1972 as part of the Gandhian Textile Labor Association
in Ahmedabad; later, in 1981, it split off as an independent organization. Its founder, Ela Bhatt, a lawyer, was inspired by Gandhi to
work with the poor. She had worked in the Labour Ministry of the
government of Gujarat and then moved to the women's branch of
the Textile Labor Association. There she created SEWA as a trade
union for self-employed women, including "seamstresses, used gar-
ment dealers, cart pullers, vegetable sellers," and others. Bhatt was a
charismatic activist who built her organization and promoted it bril-
liantly. In early 1975, she met with Kamla Chowdhry and Davidson
Gwatkin from Ford's New Delhi office, and later that year she met
Adrienne Germain at the International Women's Year conference in
Mexico City. At that point SEWA had around 6,500 members and
protested against exploitative middlemen and police harassment. It

had established cooperatives and a bank, and it had plans for child-care centers and legal aid services. It had a growing international reputation as a model program.[51]

On trips to India, Germain visited SEWA in 1976 and 1977, and she and Chowdhry encouraged Bhatt to apply for grants from Ford. Initially Bhatt demurred. She worried that the Indian government, which viewed the United States with suspicion, might not approve, and "she felt her work and SEWA's image" could "get tarnished with such assistance."[52] But in 1979 she accepted a small ($24,000) grant from Ford. It funded SEWA's expansion into rural areas to organize women who opened cotton pods, gathered firewood, and wove and dyed cloth. It also allowed SEWA to train organizers for its own work and for other NGOs. The first grant led to others. Over the next twenty-five years, the Ford Foundation gave SEWA more than $3 million in additional support, and SEWA's membership swelled to more than seven hundred thousand.[53]

The Trickle Up Program and SEWA differed substantially. The Leets were unabashed celebrants of capitalism. They talked up the benefits of hard work, investment, and capital accumulation. They gave out grants with the faith that minimal money and skill would allow an endeavor to flourish. Bhatt worked instead to organize the impoverished self-employed into unions and cooperatives. She ran a membership organization that addressed the structural constraints that women faced, social and legal as well as economic. But the two NGOs shared some features. Both hoped to increase the income of those engaged in the smallest enterprises, both encouraged self-employment and training in business skills in the informal economy, both focused on women, and both won support from funders in the mainstream of antipoverty development planning.

The Reaganomics of Global Poverty

In the fall of 1980, the election of Ronald Reagan sent shudders of trepidation through the NGOs and agencies that relied on the US government for international development funds. On the campaign trail, Reagan railed against big government. He promised to lower taxes, shrink the bureaucracy, and slash the US budget. He evinced, as one news report put it, "little interest in the third world," and he expressed skepticism about expenditure on foreign aid. Shortly after his election, he chose die-hard conservatives for his foreign aid transition team. The head of the team was Edwin J. Feulner Jr., the president of the Heritage Foundation, a right-wing think tank founded in 1973 that opposed government-funded foreign aid for antipoverty development.[54]

In January 1981, just days after Reagan's inauguration, David A. Stockman, the newly appointed director of the Office of Management and Budget, proposed deep cuts in the funds for foreign aid. The leaked document, the *Washington Post* reported, provoked "an explosive reaction from foreign aid supporters in Congress and from principal aid-giving nations around the world."[55] The proposed reduction was too much even for Secretary of State Alexander Haig, who fought it in what the press described as "the first major internal dispute of the new Administration." The battle ended quickly, though, in a compromise between the "zealous approach" to budget reduction, shaped by a Heritage Foundation study, and the State Department's expressed concern for the role of aid in national security. The administration aimed to cut economic aid but not to kill it, even if "the Caveman Right," as the historian Walter LaFeber labeled it, wanted to finish it off. Haig and his allies hoped to use aid for military more than economic development.[56] The compromise did not offer much to the advocates of the antipoverty programs of the 1970s.

The new administrator of USAID, M. Peter McPherson, a lawyer and a former Peace Corps volunteer, had served as a senior consultant on the Reagan campaign and had prepared a memo for the campaign on "a cheaper and more effective foreign aid program." He objected to "resource transfers" that were "arguably just doles" and called instead for more emphasis on technical training. After his appointment to USAID, McPherson tried to protect his agency from those who hoped to strangle it and also from those who hoped to preserve it in its 1970s form. He insisted that he had not given up on antipoverty development, but he hoped to realign development programs to fit with Reagan's world view. As one journalist summed it up, "the way to improve the conditions of the world's poor is to offer them private enterprise."[57]

The NGOs that relied on government funds had at least some minimal hope. Conservatives admired the private status of voluntary associations. Feulner, the mouthpiece of the Heritage Foundation, disliked aid in general because it supported "government as opposed to private structures." But he did not oppose disaster relief or even aid to the poorest nations if it was administered through "private voluntary organizations," which, he claimed, had "a much better track record in the third world." In April, 1981, McPherson, a more moderate Republican, met for two hours with ACVFA and around 170 NGO representatives and tried to reassure them. He urged "cost-effectiveness" and noted "limited resources," but said he had "no plans for revolutionary changes" in his agency. He wanted to bolster "cooperation with the private sector generally."[58] The new approach accelerated the privatization of foreign aid.

Under McPherson, USAID set up a new Bureau for Private Enterprise with $26 million in government money. The policy memorandum stated that the bureau aimed "to foster the growth of productive, self-sustaining income and job-producing private sectors." In short, USAID not only hoped to work more closely with private voluntary organizations, it also planned to give aid to "private business projects in the Third World." Money would go to banks and businesses rather than to governments, and nations of the global South would be encouraged "to increase the climate for private-sector investment."[59] Some conservative commentators found the Bureau of Private Enterprise inconsequential and considered McPherson too moderate; nonetheless, at USAID the center of activity shifted to initiatives that focused even more on privatized market-based programs.[60]

USAID's new enterprise approach supported agribusiness and commercial banks, but it also favored small businesses, which Reagan himself extolled. It emphasized technical assistance to build businesses in the private sector, and it preferred loans to foreign assistance grants, which were considered negatively as welfare programs and increasingly under attack. Career bureaucrats and various government-funded organizations soon accommodated to the new political climate. In some cases, they latched onto privatized aid strategically because the Reagan administration espoused it. They sometimes worked for real change that moved funds away from antipoverty development to, say, business management training, but they also "repackaged" existing programs, as one account noted, in which "'farmers' suddenly became 'rural entrepreneurs.'" In other cases, new Reagan appointees came into office and brought with them what one commentator called "a private-sector orientation to development, a preference for small business."[61]

Still, even though NGOs could leverage their private status, they noted "tensions" with USAID from early in the new administration. In March 1982, at an ACVFA conference with more than two hundred in attendance, twenty NGOs and NGO consortia submitted written statements outlining their concerns. They worried about their independence from US foreign policy, and they assumed (correctly) that the Reagan administration would subsume "basic human needs," now a priority of many NGOs, beneath "strategic and political interests." They wanted more USAID funds and less stringent requirements for supplementing government money with other donations, and they protested policy changes made without their input.[62]

With the changing administration, the supporters of WID had additional qualms. They had just begun to see the fruits of their efforts to win support in the US government, and they worried that Reagan's appointees would cut off the funding for projects that focused on women. As one WID advocate noted dryly, "the future of the women and development work in U.S. AID seems problematic under the Reagan Administration." Arvonne Fraser, the head of the WID section in USAID, knew that she had only a few months before a Republican appointee replaced her. In her remaining time, she remembered later, she did "everything in my power to firmly institutionalize women in development at AID."[63]

Since 1976, the OEF had sponsored the Coalition for Women in International Development (CWID), an advocacy group that included representatives from dozens of NGOs. With Reagan elected, CWID formed a "transition task force" to address the perceived threat. They engaged in discussions about how they might protect their projects. To court Republican women, the task force sent notes with "sincerest congratulations" to Elizabeth Dole, newly appointed as a White House assistant, and "heartiest congratulations" to Jeane Kirkpatrick, the incoming US ambassador to the

UN, and it asked to meet with them in hopes of winning their support for WID. Eventually, in the fall of 1981, it held a reception honoring Dole, Kirkpatrick, and other "women in leadership." Charles Percy, the liberal Republican who had sponsored the Percy amendment, was also an honoree.[64]

As it turned out, though, the Reagan administration offered its endorsement to WID goals. At USAID, McPherson promised to sustain the WID office. Paula Goddard, formerly with the Peace Corps and a supporter of WID, took on the role of the office's coordinator. In August 1981, to mark Women's Equality Day, the anniversary of women's suffrage, Secretary of State Haig sent a cable to all diplomatic posts giving "priority in our assistance programs . . . to encouraging the full participation of women in the development process."[65] At the Peace Corps, the WID coordinator Lael Stegall considered the cable "the strongest and best statement of any Secretary in recent years on the importance of women in development." Her boss, the new Peace Corps director Loret Miller Ruppe, recognized her own agency's "increased interest in WID both overseas and in Washington," and turned the agency's informal WID committee into a formal "core group."[66] The Reagan appointees, then, had no objections to programs that promoted the economic activities of indigent women, but they did favor some approaches more than others.

Here, too, small business had priority. Soon NGOs noted that it was "harder to get money for income generation programs."[67] The distinction between "income generation" and "business development" was fuzzy, and the two terms often appeared in tandem. But the advocates of the business approach increasingly described income-generation projects as skills training programs that failed to stand on their own. As one report put it, income-generation projects had left a "legacy of under-utilized communal workshops, craft outlets laden with unsold goods, and non-viable enterprises capitalized through seemingly endless subsidies." In contrast, "business development" paid more attention to management, efficiency, and profit and loss. It involved small-scale, self-sustaining, market-oriented activity with indigent clients recast as "business owners." The "crucial distinction," one supporter stated, was between "a business which can support itself through profits" and "an enterprise which generates cash but which will not become self-sufficient."[68]

With its eyes on the purse, the OEF tried to convince USAID that its own goals aligned with the agency's emphasis on the private sector and business development. In 1981, it launched its WIDTech Project, funded by USAID and the William and Flora Hewlett Foundation, to provide training for and consultation with agencies and organizations that aimed "to better the economic situations of women." WIDTech's staff worked with a range of projects, including several that addressed "financial management for small businesses." It advised the YWCA in Zimbabwe, for example, "on the development of small-scale enterprises."[69] In 1984, in a request for additional funds, the OEF stated directly that "the WIDTech project clearly addresses the priorities defined by the current U.S. administration." It was "helping local institutions create and manage small business projects," and it followed USAID's lead in promoting "private enterprise" and "institutional development." In accordance with the agency's policies, it offered training in "basic business and entrepreneurial skills."[70]

Within the OEF, some staff members resented and resisted the shift to business development. In the late 1970s, the OEF's projects had aimed "to create additional income for very poor beneficiaries," but, according to a USAID evaluation, the organization did not yet treat "women's productive activity . . . as business." In the early 1980s, as the OEF "positioned itself to compete . . . in the small enterprise development field," staff members argued over the new approach. The dissenters, who resisted the new business-development model, wanted the OEF to "focus . . . exclusively on the poorest," to work with groups or cooperatives instead of individual entrepreneurs, and to help poor women start new businesses instead of working with established entrepreneurs. They placed more emphasis on developing skills and organizations than on profitability. To avoid the business model, the dissenters eventually turned to projects on legal advocacy, education, and organizing.[71]

By the mid-1980s, though, the dissenters had lost, and the OEF had fully adopted the language of Reagan-era foreign assistance.

Renamed OEF International and no longer affiliated with the League of Women Voters, it touted itself as "the leading, U.S. based, private non-profit organization dedicated to providing Third World women with the training and technical assistance needed to improve their entrepreneurial abilities and economic conditions." It had established a US National Businesswomen's Committee, with "some 80 senior level corporate executive[s] and entrepreneurs" who agreed to support "the efforts of businesswomen in the Third World," and it held a $2 million contract, among others, with USAID "to foster the growth of women-owned businesses in Costa Rica and Honduras."[72] The OEF's board of trustees included prominent Democrats, such as Madeline Albright, Arvonne Fraser, and Maxine Waters, as well as prominent Republicans, such as Virginia Allan and Patricia Hutar. It was concertedly bipartisan, but it modified its projects to ride the political winds, and it increasingly won support from business boosters outside government as well as within it. In the 1980s it received some funding from J. P. Morgan & Co., which saw it as "a highly respected international development agency," and praise from conservative columnist Georgie Anne Geyer, who characterized it as "the most important single group helping Third World women help themselves."[73]

In its mid-1980s publicity materials, the OEF repeatedly highlighted its small-business orientation. It focused especially on a "success story" from its work in El Salvador. In 1979, the OEF had worked with "a group of 30 Salvadoran housewives" to "devise a means of generating income." With money from USAID, it provided technical assistance to increase the women's tomato crop and then helped start a small cooperatively-run factory to process tomato catsup and paste. At the 1985 UN World Conference on Women in Nairobi, women who represented Latin American NGOs addressed the "high level of imprisonment, torture, disappearance, and exile" in their homelands, but the OEF continued to promote its project in El Salvador with only minimal mention of the brutal civil war that lasted through the decade (and no mention of the US government's role in training the Salvadoran army's death squads). The OEF could have cast its tomato success story as an antipoverty, income-generating cooperative, none of which it denied or hid. But by the mid-1980s it was using the story to publicize its expertise in business development and to ask for private donations. The boldfaced headline from an especially blatant ad, published in *Newsweek*, stated: "We didn't teach her how to raise tomatoes. We taught her how to raise capital." US technical assistance was no longer about engineering—how to build an airport or run an electrical plant—it was about how to invest in and build a small business. The ad claimed that "women represent a . . . potential source of stability in their nations' economies—if they are given the opportunity to learn management, marketing, and agricultural skills." The OEF, an "organization of enlightened American women," provided the lessons and thereby contributed "to the advancement of humankind."[74]

The OEF was only one among many NGOs, but USAID assigned it "a larger policy significance" because it served as something of a test case. "Over the last several years," a USAID evaluation stated, "many relief and development agencies whose specialty is not economic or business programs have applied for and received AID grants for small enterprise development." Those agencies were "under pressure to define an approach to small enterprise." The OEF could serve as an example of the problems faced by NGOs "in transition toward small enterprise development."[75] As the OEF adapted, the evaluators at USAID did not object to its focus on women; in fact, they encouraged it to design "improved approaches to small enterprise development aimed at low-income women." The problems they identified were deficiencies in the OEF's planning and management, its costs, and its lack of technical expertise. For the El Salvador tomato processing plant, a USAID evaluator complained that the OEF "acts mainly as a broker to technical services and not the direct provider," and for the "women in business" project in Central America, another evaluator wanted the OEF to cut expenses and overheads, hold staff accountable for results, and raise more of its own funds. Despite the criticisms, USAID continued to supply most of the OEF's budget and support its WID projects through the 1980s. When the well ran dry, at the end of 1991, the OEF closed shop.[76]

As the OEF's history suggests, the privatization of development aid in the late 1970s and early 1980s was not exactly private. "NGOization," as it is now sometimes called, benefited in part from

We didn't teach her how to raise tomatoes.

We taught her how to raise capital.

OEF helps Third World women turn simple skills into income-producing businesses.

In El Salvador, for example, we helped a group of 30 housewives launch a cooperative that today produces catsup and sauces for supermarkets, restaurants, and hotels. Besides employing a substantial local labor force, they've brought their area electricity, water, and literacy.

In Africa, while food relief is saving lives this year, we're helping women to prevent hunger in the future by cultivating drought-resistant crops, preserving foods for dry spells, and actually selling surplus crops to buy equipment and seeds!

In the U.S., we're training refugee women to start up small businesses in their communities.

Women represent a powerful, and too often ignored, potential source of stability in their nations' economies —if they are given the opportunity to learn management, marketing, and agricultural skills.

There's no other organization like OEF. Formerly known as the Overseas Education Fund of the League of Women Voters, today OEF is an independent organization of enlightened American women contributing to the advancement of humankind.

You can share in this exciting and productive venture. With your contribution of $25 or more, you become an International Friend of OEF, and will be kept informed about our activities.

Please join us.

☐ I want to support your work. Enclosed is my tax-deductible contribution (please make payable to "OEF International"):
☐ $25 ☐ $50 ☐ $100 ☐ $250 ☐ More $_____
☐ Please send me more information.

Name_____

Address_____

City_____State_____Zip_____
Mail to: OEF International, 2101 L Street N.W., Suite 916N, Washington, D.C. 20037.

Women worldwide sharing their skills.

FIGURE 4.1. In 1985, the Overseas Education Fund placed a fundraising advertisement in *Newsweek*, touting its business-oriented development programs for women. (*Newsweek*, December 16, 1985)

a growing anti-statist suspicion of government programs, but it still relied heavily on funds from the United States and other donor governments. In 1983, for example, the US government provided $270 million of official development assistance to NGOs, excluding food aid and relief.[77] At roughly the same time that USAID turned to NGOs, so too did the European Community. In 1976, it set up a Liaison Committee with European NGOs and began a formal policy of funding them for development projects.[78]

International agencies and major foundations also turned to NGOs. The World Bank established its NGO committee in 1982. In the mid-1980s, it collaborated with NGOs on projects in sub-Saharan Africa, and at the end of the decade, when the Bank began to retreat from its market-oriented austerity policies, it funded NGO antipoverty programs to compensate for the damage done to public services by its own conditional loans. In the 1970s and 1980s, the UN and its subagencies also promoted more cooperation with NGOs. They preferred "to work through organizations in the nongovernmental rather than the public sector." And the Ford Foundation, too, "channeled most of its assistance to NGOs." It moved its grants away from governments and toward local NGOs, away from technocratic research and toward community-based, grassroots organizations.[79]

Like the US government, other donor governments, international agencies, and foundations hoped to tap into the labor and resources of private organizations and consultants, and remove the taint of "official aid" by channeling it through NGOs. In 1988, an OECD report, *Voluntary Aid for Development: The Role of Non-Governmental Organisations*, found that NGOs held "a comparative advantage . . . in their ability to work at the grass-roots level, to address basic human needs and to operate in remote areas often unserved by national governments or official donors."[80] Donors could allot funds to NGOs they trusted and bypass governments they considered corrupt, annoying, or incompetent. The OECD report summarized the trend toward privatized development. It noted the "interest nowadays in NGOs as 'development agencies'" and reflected on a series of mid-1980s meetings, seminars, conferences, evaluations, and studies that had pondered and promoted the antipoverty work of NGOs. Private voluntary organizations, it stated, "were often drawn to development by first providing relief in emergency situations" and then realized that "relief was not enough." Funds from donor governments "sustained the developmental element in the NGO sector." The "shock of the African famine" had furthered the public-private collaboration, and it had also fostered a growing recognition that "more of the initiative and implementation in the field can be taken over by . . . partners in the South."[81] Across the globe, a variety of NGOs, like the OEF, advertised their expertise and submitted proposals to fit the interests of the granting agencies.

WID, WAD, GAD

The history of the OEF shows that development NGOs that focused on women could accommodate to, survive, and even flourish in the neoliberal, business-oriented culture of the Reagan years. In the US government, the conservative policies of the decade narrowed some routes to addressing women's poverty and widened others. Elsewhere, though, the WID movement took on different forms. As social scientists and development experts relate the history, the WID movement actually stepped to the left, not the right, in the 1980s. It moved, some argue, from "women in development" to "women and development" to "gender and development": from WID to WAD to GAD. The different strands—which the WID–WAD–GAD chronology poses as change over time—were all there from the start and all there at the end of the 1980s. The changing terms mark a gradual shift in emphasis, from the early 1970s to the late 1980s, toward a more critical engagement with both development and gender. At its simplest, WID, seen in Ester Boserup's foundational work and the Percy amendment, proposed to integrate women into existing development programs. WAD, which reflected the impact of the NIEO, called for women's equality along with new forms of development that challenged the economic structures that subordinated the global South. GAD asked also for deeper changes in the gendered labor within the household, including childcare shared with men, and for greater attention to class differences among women. The advocates of GAD often posed it as a socialist-feminist critique of liberal feminist WID, an extension of the more radical redistributionist proposals of the 1970s, and an out-and-out rejection of the free-market policies that came to dominate in the US government, the World Bank, and the International Monetary Fund (IMF).[82]

The criticism of the early WID model emerged early on in academic circles through debates at conferences and articles in scholarly journals.[83] It reflected theoretical disputes as much as a disillusionment with on-the-ground WID projects. In 1982, Lourdes Benería and Gita Sen, both economists, published a widely cited article that captured the growing critique. They offered a Marxist-feminist vision of political economy. Women, they said, had been "superficially added to ongoing economic development programs" without addressing the hierarchies of class and gender. It was not enough, they said, to add women to modernization programs. Women's responsibility for unpaid reproductive labor—child rearing, household production, and other domestic work—doubled the workload of poor women who also worked for income, patriarchal families kept them dependent on men, and the capitalist division of labor subordinated them in exploitative jobs. Benería and Sen presented their analysis at a conference at Barnard College in 1980 and then published it in the US journal *Feminist Studies* in 1982.[84] At the time, Benería, who earned her PhD at Columbia, worked at the ILO, and Sen, with a PhD from Stanford, was an associate fellow at the Centre for Development Studies in Trivandrum (now Thiruvananthapuram), India. Their critical vision elaborated on earlier left-feminist arguments, and over the course of the 1980s, it reached into more development agencies and organizations.

It had some influence in the Ford Foundation, which upped its commitment to women's programs in the 1980s. The quantitative record is telling: from 1972 to 1979, Ford made 52 grants, totaling $5.1 million, that focused on women in "developing countries"; from 1980 to early 1988, it made 326 such grants and spent $22.4 million on them. The foundation spent more money in the 1980s but, on average, less on individual grants. Its funding shifted in emphasis from research in the 1970s to small-scale income-generation projects in the 1980s.[85] At the international level, Ford positioned itself, as a staff member said, "as a conduit, as a catalyst to build links between the governments, NGOs, and other donor agencies."[86] In Mali, it supported a "rural development organization" that worked on "small-scale projects, including soap making, market gardening, and goat raising." In India, it gave grants for women's work in "silk production and dairying." Like other development donors, it also turned its attention to the urban informal economy, with funds, for example, in Sudan for a small businesses project that promoted enterprise among women refugees.[87] Along with the kinds of WID projects supported by USAID, the Ford Foundation provided early grants to more progressive organizations that used the language of economic justice. In India it supported the Working Women's Forum of Madras as well as the Self-Employed Women's Association (SEWA) in Ahmedabad.

At the ILO, the GAD variant of WID found a stronger footing. Its Programme on Rural Women enlisted scholars from around the globe, including Lourdes Benería and other Marxist-feminists, to conduct a series of studies and seminars on women's labor in the global South. Like other WID advocates, the ILO program focused on impoverished women who needed and wanted income, but it challenged the WID model of integrating women into development projects, stressing instead that poor women were already "overworked" in reproductive and productive labor, and in need of "remunerative employment," not "entry into working life."[88] Its studies acknowledged the exploitation of women in the labor force, including poorly paid industrial workers in Singapore, sex workers in Thailand, plantation laborers in Malaysia, home-based craft workers in India, and agricultural workers in Mexico. Women were "over-integrated in development" and "over-burdened with work." Income-generating work was not inherently liberating.[89] The program encouraged women to organize into self-help associations and cooperatives. In practice, though, the ILO's technical assistance and advisory missions seemed similar to the programs supported by the Ford Foundation and other donor agencies. It worked, for example, on developing small enterprises for women in Kenya and for marketing farm produce in Ghana.[90] As one GAD advocate admitted, "it may be easier to develop GAD projects in the realm of research rather than in the realm of development practice or implementation."[91]

In the 1980s, much of the energy for the GAD approach came from the global South. In 1982, the Association of African Women for Research and Development and the Dag Hammarskjöld Foundation sponsored a seminar in Dakar, Senegal, that produced an early statement of GAD concerns. In the "Dakar Declaration on Another Development with Women," the seminar participants placed feminism within the NIEO and leftist visions of an alternative development. They called for a "new international economic and social order" with women's participation, elimination of "patriarchal relations and practices," an end to "discrimination and injustice based on race or ethnicity," and the mobilization of women.[92]

By mid-decade, new "poverty- and equity-oriented women's NGOs," as one commentator described them, had emerged "throughout the Third World."[93] One such organization, Development Alternatives with Women for a New Era (DAWN), quickly established itself as a key player in the international WID-WAD-GAD constellation. DAWN was founded in 1984 during a three-day meeting in Bangalore, funded by the Ford Foundation, to plan for the next UN Conference on Women, to be held in Nairobi the following year. By its own account, it brought together a global network of prominent "activists, researchers, and policymakers," mostly from the South, "to advocate alternative development processes." It addressed "problems of poverty and inequality" with a third worldist critique of colonialism, a leftist critique of capitalism, and a feminist critique of gender subordination. It advocated for structural changes in global and national economies, for basic needs antipoverty programs with local participation by the poor themselves, for better opportunities for women's employment and income earning in agriculture, wage work, and the informal sector, and for political mobilization by women's organizations, global networks, and coalitions.[94] It won early support from the development agencies of the social democratic governments of Norway, Sweden, and Finland and the Population Council, as well as the Ford Foundation. At the 1985 UN conference in Nairobi, it took a leading role in the NGO Forum, with a keynote presentation, panels, and workshops featuring its more critical version of GAD. As one US observer noted, "women of the South truly took over the women in development enterprise at the Nairobi world conference."[95]

In the 1980s, then, WID moved to the left as well as the right, and new organizations, like DAWN, joined the NGOs from the previous decade. By the end of the 1980s, staff in government agencies, international organizations, and NGOs—from the Reagan appointees who celebrated capitalism to the Marxist-feminists who denounced it—acknowledged that women deserved special attention in development programs. As in the 1970s, some made the instrumental case that programs for women would increase productivity, alleviate poverty, help children, and lower birth rates. In the late 1980s the World Bank, for example, under the leadership of a new president, Barber Conable, added women's issues to its list of priorities and gave more clout to the head of its women's division. It issued internal guidelines that supported "investing in women," in part as "a cost-effective route to broader development objectives such as improved economic performance, reduction of poverty, greater family welfare, and slower population growth."[96] Others, such as DAWN, placed more emphasis on social and economic equity.

But virtually everyone who advocated 1980s WID, WAD, or GAD programs made three interrelated arguments. First, they claimed, women were "disproportionately represented among the poor" and in need of income.[97] They repeatedly cited a UN statistic that one-third of the households in the world had no adult male income earners and acknowledged that development organizations could no longer promote an unworkable male-breadwinner ideal. In a letter to the executive director of CARE, the president of the Overseas Development Council, John W. Sewell, wrote, "Third World poverty is becoming increasingly feminized. . . . [T]he number of female-headed households has greatly increased both in absolute terms and as a percentage of all poor households." In a similar vein, in the foreword to a special issue on women of the journal *World Development*, John D. Gerhart, on the staff at the Ford Foundation, noted "an increase in temporarily divided families, abandoned families, never married women with children, and other departures

FIGURE 4.2. Development Alternatives with Women for a New Era (DAWN) had a third-worldist, leftist, feminist vision of the "women in development" movement. The back cover of this 1987 book states that it was "the result of a collective effort" by DAWN activists and researchers. (Courtesy of Monthly Review Press)

from 'traditional' family structures." Women as household heads were "in all countries . . . on the increase."[98]

Second, in the wake of the African famine, the supporters of WID, WAD, and GAD came to see women as the key suppliers of basic needs. In many African nations, women played a leading role in farming. They were, DAWN noted, the "main producers of food crops," the "main food processors and cooks," and "responsible for water and fuel collection." A USAID report spelled out the "implications for the food crisis in Africa." Women, it said, "could be the single most cost-effective available resource to alleviate this crisis, since they raise as much as 80 percent of the locally grown food crops." A 1990 pamphlet made the same point in its title: "Women: The Key to Ending Hunger." The author, Margaret Snyder, the former director of UNIFEM (the UN Development Fund for Women) and a former advisor to the UN Economic Commission for Africa, wrote that "women in the developing countries are the backbone of the rural food system. . . . [T]he responsibility for getting food for the family is shifting to women."[99]

Third, WID, WAD, and GAD supporters increasingly made the case that impoverished women were better investments than impoverished men. In antipoverty programs, women could be trusted to look after their children. The argument had appeared occasionally in the mid-1970s, but it came to the fore in the late 1970s and 1980s. At the Ford Foundation, Adrienne Germain noticed that "several argue that women are often more responsible than men in allocating their income to their family's health, nutritional and educational status." At the World Bank, Paul Streeten made a similar claim. "It appears," he wrote, "that women spend a larger share of their incomes on basic needs (foods, health care) than men." And at USAID, a report stated that "income under women's control . . . is most often spent for children's and the family's 'basic human needs,' especially among women with provider responsibilities."[100]

The positive focus on women suggested a skeptical assessment of men, usually implied with tactful reticence but sometimes stated outright. One article, which made the invidious distinction explicit, cited research in "India, Egypt, Morocco, Mexico, Guatemala, and Cameroon," all of which confirmed "men's tendency to withhold portions of their income" for personal consumption "even when families live in or near poverty." It quoted a study in which young men in Morocco spent their money on "clothes, cigarettes, cinema, prostitutes." Another study, on India, found that women with dependents spent money on themselves "only when absolutely necessary," but even when there was "not enough money to feed" their families, men found it "easy to ignore the problem" and met their "friends as usual at the tea or toddy shop." In "Women: The Key to Ending Hunger," Margaret Snyder also made overt comparisons that reflected poorly on men. "There is a good deal of evidence," she wrote, "that men tend to commit their incomes to consumer goods, prestige items or entertainment." In contrast, studies found "that women spend their incomes on nutrition and everyday subsistence." Male migrants, she noted, sometimes abandoned their families entirely, and in general men were less responsible when it came to supporting their children.[101]

During his first campaign for president, in 1976, Ronald Reagan repeatedly told the story of the welfare cheat, with the not-so-subtle implication that African American women stole from the government. Over the course of the late 1970s and 1980s, the notorious, racialized trope of the "welfare queen" spread widely, circulated in the press and by those who hoped to dismantle the social provisions of earlier decades.[102] In the same years, though, some liberals and leftists promoted a different picture of poverty, seen clearly among the advocates of international development. They situated impoverished women—in this case, overseas—as hardworking, resourceful mothers who sacrificed for their children. Unlike Reagan and his supporters and also unlike the Moynihan report of 1965, which described African American women as dominant matriarchs who reared delinquent sons, they removed the stigma from impoverished women and woman-headed households and did not attempt to revive a male-breadwinner ideal.

Over the course of two decades, the changing landscape of development and the WID, WAD, and GAD movements had promoted a striking reversal in the politics of gender. In the 1960s, modernization programs had mostly ignored women as backward or irrelevant. Development experts saw training, advice, and jobs for men as the route to economic progress. By the end of the 1980s, the anti-poverty basic needs approach, the recognition of women's work in the household and in the informal sector, the feminist quest for equity, and the decline of the male-breadwinner norm had shifted the gender valence. Women were now the responsible actors, and men were pushed to the side as spendthrifts, loafers, and deserters who could not be entrusted with money or the care of their children. As the scales shifted, government agencies, international organizations, and NGOs positioned women in the global South as the deserving poor.

———

In 1987, Judith Tendler, a professor of political economy at MIT, wrote the report "What Ever Happened to Poverty Alleviation?" for the Ford Foundation and published it two years later in the journal *World Development*. The report called for more antipoverty programs funded by the public sector, but it highlighted the hallmarks of 1980s development. Tendler featured six organizations, funded by the Ford Foundation, which she chose as especially "good performers." Five of the six organizations were NGOs; only one—a dairying project in India—was run by a government agency. The good performers shared certain characteristics. All reached significant numbers of impoverished people, all had competent organizational leadership, and all involved small enterprise, including "dairying, garbage-collecting, food hawking, food preparation, cigarette rolling," with viable markets for the goods and services sold. And four of the six focused solely on women. These included SEWA and the Working Women's Forum of Madras, as well as the dairying project and an NGO in Mumbai that organized women who prepared meals for factory workers.[103]

Tendler's report pointed to NGOization or the privatization of antipoverty programs, to feminization or the growing importance of WID, and to the focus on self-employment in the informal economy. The report also showcased something else. All six of the featured projects extended credit to impoverished borrowers. The largest of the six, the Grameen Bank in Bangladesh, had already won an international reputation. In 1986, it made loans to around

230,000 clients. Tendler did not include it as one of the women's programs, but in fact three-quarters of the bank's borrowers were women at the time she did her research.[104] By the late 1980s, antipoverty programs had increasingly turned to credit. In the years when many nations in the global South spiraled into debt and destitution, antipoverty advocates and WID supporters encouraged the poor, and especially women, to take out tiny loans. The promotion of credit for the smallest enterprises was emerging as the next big development trend.

PART III

The Microcredit Moment

Microfinance is simply everywhere. It is both the celebrity cause and the ordinary citizen's development tool.

—ANANYA ROY, *POVERTY CAPITAL: MICROFINANCE AND THE MAKING OF DEVELOPMENT*

CHAPTER FIVE

Macro Debt and Microcredit

IN JUNE 1988, 232 participants from forty-eight nations attended the International Conference on Microenterprise Development, held in Washington, DC. The World Bank, the Inter-American Development Bank, and USAID hosted the conference, and fourteen additional agencies contributed to the cost. In keeping with the times, most of the paper presenters wanted less government intervention and fewer regulations on small enterprises. And they returned repeatedly "to the lack of access to credit for microenterprises." Several speakers used the Grameen Bank as the prime example of success. It provided credit, one speaker noted, to people who were "arguably the poorest of the poor in one of the poorest nations in the world." In his own presentation, Muhammad Yunus, the bank's founder, acknowledged that "Grameen has attracted attention from all directions." He told the story of his bank's expansion and reported on its replication outside of Bangladesh. "Wherever there is the problem of poverty," he said, "Grameen appears like a possible solution." For those who hoped to replicate it, Yunus advised, "start the experimentation with the poorest women."[1]

In the 1970s and 1980s, as Yunus suggested, the global antipoverty movement turned to credit as a solution. Government agencies, international institutions, and NGOs provided funds to extend credit to impoverished individuals and especially to women. In many development projects, credit was already the norm. In rural areas, farmers regularly borrowed to buy seeds and fertilizer, and then repaid the loans after the harvest, and in urban areas business owners sought credit to purchase machinery and other capital goods, and home buyers took out loans for low-cost housing. Development programs had supported such credit for decades.[2] Now, with growing attention to the tiniest enterprises and the poorest women, antipoverty advocates called for credit for the most indigent people as well, those who lacked the collateral and cosigners to borrow from commercial banks. Microcredit provided financial services to people who were usually denied them, and it also fit comfortably with the 1980s anti-statist, private-sector, market-oriented approach. It offered an updated vision of a war on poverty that coincided with minimal government expenditure and with financialization in a neoliberal age.

The turn to microcredit came in the same years as a global crisis in debt. In much of the global South, public debt had mounted ominously through the 1970s. In the 1980s, with poorer nations on the brink of bankruptcy, the US government, the World Bank, and the IMF insisted on "structural adjustment loans," in which bailouts came conjoined with austerity policies that imposed fiscal discipline and market-oriented policies. Microcredit programs envisioned small-scale borrowing as the route to prosperity for poor women just as large-scale borrowing sank the economies of multiple nations. Microcredit advocates helped cleanse debt, something often seen as negative, by calling it credit, something often seen as positive, and they redefined debtors as entrepreneurs. Debt spelled danger, but credit held promise.

Dangerous Debt

For years, economists had been sounding the alarm. Nations in the global South were drowning in debt. Over the course of the 1960s, a rising proportion of foreign aid had come as loans, instead of grants. The proportion of loans grew from 13 to 50 percent of bilateral aid from the donor nations, and in the same years, interest rates had risen. The level of debt so threatened to bankrupt the poorer nations that even the moderate Pearson Commission report of 1969 noted its "explosive increase" and called for debt relief as "a legitimate form of aid."[3] In the 1970s, the threat loomed larger. The OPEC nations, flush with "petrodollars" from the spike in oil prices, deposited billions in US and European banks, and the banks recycled the money into commercial loans to the governments of the global South. When payments came due, the borrowing nations needed new loans to service the old. They negotiated with the IMF for conditional loans that mandated changes in their economic policies, and with the IMF's seal of approval they borrowed again from private banks. From the end of 1970 to the end of 1979, the debt of the nations labeled "developing" leapt from $70 billion to $300 billion. In the second half of the 1970s, as the Brandt Commission report noted, "many more countries were in arrears on their current payments, or were renegotiating—or trying to renegotiate—their debts with private banks."[4]

The "Volcker shock" of 1979 added the coup de grace. In an attempt to reduce double-digit inflation in the United States, the chair of the board of governors of the Federal Reserve, Paul Volcker, restricted the money supply, which raised interest rates, as he intended. In the United States, the policy controlled inflation but also pushed the nation into recession, with soaring levels of unemployment. The recession rippled across the globe, and in poorer nations it hit even harder. As international trade contracted and commodity prices dropped, the poorer nations had lower earnings from exports. They had diminishing funds for the kinds of social programs that benefited the poor, and they had less money with which to repay their debts. They tried to reschedule payments and negotiate additional loans. The rising interest rates made new loans costlier and also increased the burden of existing loans that had variable interest rates, which fluctuated with the market. By the end of 1981, the debt of developing countries had reached $630 billion, more than doubling in two years. As the debt mounted, the house of cards wobbled. Private bankers started to pull back. They expressed a new wariness, reluctant to loan to the global South.[5]

Despite repeated reports of impending collapse, it came as something of a surprise when Mexico announced, in August 1982, that it could not service its debt. Mexico had $81 billion in foreign debt, more than any other nation in the world, with around half of it due in the year ahead. Much of the money in question came from US banks. To head off default, the IMF, central banks, and private banks arranged new loans and new schedules for repayment. The US government contributed a loan of $1 billion for food imports and another billion in advance payment for Mexican oil.[6] The bailout came at a price. In return for its loans, the IMF imposed conditions that required Mexico to cut spending, reduce imports, and raise taxes. From the get-go, observers knew that the program would impose austerity and bring, as the *New York Times* noted, "higher unemployment, and a sharp drop in living standards."[7]

Such was the pattern that repeated as the debt crisis spread through Latin America and beyond. By the fall of 1982, Brazil and Argentina had entered into negotiations with the IMF to stave off default. Mexico, Brazil, and Argentina were not among the poorest nations, which explains why private banks had offered them substantial loans in the first place. But the financial devastation also reached into the poorest pockets of the globe. The non-oil-producing nations of sub-Saharan Africa were squeezed by a second surge in oil prices at the end of the 1970s and by the inflated price of imports from the global North. They had less private debt, but they still needed to borrow, especially with the dive in commodity prices, drop in exports, and drought in the Sahel. In the mid-1980s, the Organization of African Unity declared that most of the continent stood on the verge of "economic collapse."[8] By 1988, around thirty African nations had signed on to structural adjustment loans, some with the World Bank, which gave long-term loans for economic development, and some with the IMF, which offered short-term loans to address financial crises. The conditional loans forced governments to cut spending, devalue currency, eliminate food subsidies, reduce imports, privatize industry, and open their borders to foreign investment and trade. The shock therapy gutted social programs, including schooling and health care, and thereby increased the unpaid care labor performed by women at home. With rising unemployment, it also pushed more women and men into precarious enterprise in the informal sector.[9]

In an oral history interview, Robert McNamara remembered that he had initiated the World Bank's structural adjustment program in the late 1970s. He seemed to want credit for it. "The greatest contribution the Bank can make to a developing country," he said, "is in helping it formulate its macroeconomic policies and assisting it in implementing those policies." But conditional loans were not new in the 1970s. The IMF and the World Bank had been making loans conditioned on policy change—without the name "structural adjustment"—at least since the 1950s. And when the Bank introduced its new structural adjustment program in 1979, it had not yet solidified the forms of financial discipline and policy changes it would demand in return for loans. In general, McNamara wanted to speed up the Bank's lending, promote productivity, and encourage labor-intensive exports. At that point, US conservatives objected to the Bank's structural adjustment loans as central planning and "too much like foreign aid."[10]

After McNamara resigned from his post in 1981, his successor A.W. Clausen, former head of the Bank of America, aligned structural adjustment more closely with the free-enterprise, anti-statist policies of the IMF and the Reagan administration. He appointed Anne Krueger, an economics professor at the University of Minnesota, to replace Hollis Chenery as the Bank's chief economist. Krueger was, as the Bank's authorized history states, "a polemical conservative" who supported "heavy pro-markets, anti-interventionist" approaches. A news report on her appointment found that she wanted more Bank intervention into the economic policies of the poorer nations. For Krueger, the existing "structural adjustment initiative [did] not go far enough." Her approach reflected "the harder-nosed views on development . . . fashionable in Washington." McNamara may have launched the Bank's 1980s structural adjustment initiative, but Clausen and Krueger implemented it, made it routine, and steered it into the "Washington Consensus," a phrase coined later in the decade to refer to the ideological alignment of the World Bank, the IMF, and the US Department of the Treasury.[11]

The consensus had its limits. From early on, leftists, in Washington and outside it, protested the policies imposed by conditional loans. In fact, economists in the UN's Economic Commission for Latin America had been protesting the IMF's conditional loans since the 1950s. In the 1970s, with the alarming escalation in debt, the protests ramped up. In the United States, Cheryl Payer's 1974 book *The Debt Trap: The IMF and the Third World* provided an extended account that positioned IMF policies as "imperialist financial discipline" that impeded "autonomous national development" in the poorer nations. The Institute for Policy Studies (IPS) and its affiliate, the Transnational Institute, also issued warnings about the spiraling debt and blasted the IMF's response to it. In 1977, the economist Howard M. Wachtel, who taught at American University, wrote an eye-opening pamphlet published by the Transnational Institute that exposed how private banks had sought profits through massive loans to the global South and how the IMF had imposed austerity policies on the teetering debtor nations.[12] In 1980, the IPS joined with other progressive think tanks, including the Dag Hammarskjöld Foundation and the Third World Forum, to sponsor a major "South-North" conference in Tanzania, where economists and policy makers, mostly from the global South, addressed the impending crisis. The conference declaration denounced the IMF's conditional loans as "an unabashed form of external political intervention" and asked for a UN conference to "provide a universal, democratic, and legitimate forum for the negotiation of a new monetary system."[13]

More generally, as the debt crisis deepened, leaders of the global South objected repeatedly to the imposition of austerity conditions, with their echoes of colonial coercion. When the IMF and the World Bank mandated changes in the internal economic policies of nations, they encroached on national sovereignty and imposed ideologically freighted free-market solutions. The conditional loans seemed designed to favor the capitalists of the North and punish the South for global inflation, declining commodity prices, and rising interest rates. Some of the officials in poorer nations spent profligately, even corruptly, but structural adjustment programs held all of them responsible for economic conditions over which they had no control. Instead, it protected the foreign investors who had systematically drained wealth from the poorer to the richer nations. In a 1980 speech, Julius Nyerere declared that the IMF was not "an instrument of all its members" but rather "a device by which powerful economic forces in some rich countries increase their power over the poor nations of the world."[14] Structural adjustment policies undermined the leaders of the global South by curbing their control over their nations' economic policies, and the IMF's insistence on economic contraction further impoverished the poor. In a later (and often-cited) speech, in 1985, Nyerere asked, "Must we starve our children to pay our debts?"[15] The debtor nations had limited leverage, but they did win some concessions, in large part because collective default, a hovering threat, could have ruined some of the larger banks.

In response to the "deteriorating economic conditions," the members of the Brandt Commission regrouped and wrote a second report, *Common Crisis North-South: Cooperation for World Recovery*. The "failure to act," they said, could lead to "the disintegration of societies and create conditions of anarchy in many parts of the world." Like other liberals and leftists, they found that conditional loans had forced the poorest nations into too much "retrenchment" and saddled them with "an excessive share of adjustment." The commission placed its "highest priority" on "increased aid to the poorest countries," including "more official support" for antipoverty NGOs, and it wanted more loans on better terms with less stringent conditionality.[16]

In the mid-1980s, antipoverty NGOs, which had grown in number and clout, also organized in response to the mounting debt. Representatives from NGOs with "a commitment to social justice" joined to form the Debt Crisis Network in 1985. Members came from the IPS, Bread for the World, Development Group for Alternative Policies (DGAP), "religious organizations, unions, environmental groups," and more. They produced a booklet, *From Debt to Development: Alternatives to the International Debt Crisis*, published by the IPS, that called for debt relief, democratic participation and decision-making in international institutions, fair wages and fair prices for raw materials, regulation of private banks, and development programs that promoted jobs, housing, health care, and education. Some NGOs also pushed for change from inside the Bank. The World Bank's NGO Committee, established in 1982, met with Bank staff in 1985 and 1986 to address the impact of structural adjustment loans. A Bank report noted that "certain NGOs have expressed doubts about the commitment and effectiveness of multilateral development banks in reducing poverty."[17]

Meanwhile, in the US government, liberals in Congress drafted various bills to alleviate the debt burden. In 1986, Senator Bill

Bradley, a Democrat from New Jersey, proposed the plan for debt relief in Latin America that won the most attention. He called for lowering the interest rates on the existing loans of debtor nations by three percentage points over three years, forgiving three percent per year of the outstanding debt principal for three years, and providing $3 billion of new loans from the World Bank and other multilateral institutions in each of three years. His repeated use of the number three was, he granted, something of a gimmick, "a deliberate attempt to get attention." Bradley hoped to stem the tide of capital, the reverse transfer of funds, that flowed from the poorer nations to the wealthier and "address the fundamental problem of poverty and malnutrition." He was not a radical: he wanted conditional loans, private investment, and liberalization of trade, and he hoped the World Bank would take the lead in implementing his plan. He introduced it just after a new Bank president, Barber Conable, stepped into Clausen's shoes. Conable, though, rejected the Bradley Plan, and "and any generalized debt relief," within days of its announcement, and so did US Treasury officials. By this point, "third world debt" had risen to $1 trillion.[18]

Along with public pressure, it took private maneuvering to push the Bank and the IMF to address the impoverishment that accompanied their conditional loans. In the mid-1980s, researchers from UNICEF (United Nations Children's Emergency Fund), who studied "the impact of world recession on children," began consulting behind the scenes with the IMF and the Bank.[19] The UNICEF project reflected the ongoing presence of the 1970s "basic needs" approach. In the 1980s, the advocates of basic needs worked to preserve antipoverty projects in government agencies, NGOs, and international institutions, but they faded into the background as public debt came to the fore. As one UNICEF report stated it, "Not in a generation have expectations of world development, and hopes for an end to life-denying mass poverty, been at such a low ebb."[20] Even with diminished expectations, though, the antipoverty efforts continued. In 1980, James Grant left his position as head of the Overseas Development Council to serve as UNICEF's executive director, and he hired Richard Jolly, the former director of the Institute of Development Studies at the University of Sussex, as his deputy director. They worked in an agency that was not dominated by neoclassical economists, and they collaborated with

FIGURE 5.1. In the United States and elsewhere, liberals and leftists objected to the damaging austerity imposed by IMF and World Bank structural adjustment loans. This cartoon, in the *Los Angeles Times* in 1984, was reprinted in the booklet *From Debt to Development*, published by the leftist Institute for Policy Studies. (Dan Wasserman/*Los Angeles Times*/Tribune Content Agency)

antipoverty NGOs, heterodox researchers in the Society for International Development, and members of the World Bank staff who expressed concern that the Bank had abandoned its antipoverty campaign.[21]

At UNICEF, Jolly joined Giovanni Andrea Cornia, an Italian economist previously at UNCTAD, and Frances Stewart, a British economist who had helped write the World Bank's basic needs studies, to compile data on children—their malnutrition, ill health, and declining education—and push for a different kind of adjustment. Jolly, Cornia, and Stewart were left-leaning liberal insiders in economic development circles. They used their clout and connections to confer with the Bank and the IMF. In their attempt to budge the financial institutions, they refrained from repudiating structural adjustment; instead, they blamed economic recession for the toll on child welfare and called, with diplomacy, for different adjustment policies, in which "the human needs of the vulnerable will be protected." They saw "the moral outrage and action" that famine inspired, and they asked for a similar response "when the cause is economic, and the effects, although less dramatic, include rising infant deaths, mounting suffering, and permanent damage among millions."[22]

Eventually, in September 1987, the Bank announced a new "poverty task force" to attend to the "the social costs of economic adjustment."[23] The same year the UNICEF team published its influential collection of essays, *Adjustment with a Human Face: Protecting the Vulnerable and Promoting Growth.* Their vision, they wrote, added "a poverty alleviation dimension to adjustment, . . . the 'basic needs' approach to adjustment." They wanted "less conditionality," "less confrontational" restructuring, and "more expansionary" policies that maintained the incomes of the poor, protected their standards of living, and provided social services, including health care and education, to the most vulnerable. They also called for more aid, debt restructuring, and relief.[24]

The attempt to sustain the basic needs approach had other advocates as well. After McNamara resigned from the World Bank, Mahbub ul Haq left to serve as minister of commerce, planning, and finance in Pakistan, and then at the end of the 1980s he accepted a new job as special adviser to the United Nations Development Programme (UNDP). In the North-South Roundtable of the Society for International Development, which he chaired in the early 1980s, and at the UNDP, he helped reframe the basic needs approach as "human development," using indicators of well-being, such as literacy and life expectancy, to measure success in development programs. Haq worked with, among others, the Indian economist Amartya Sen and two of his former World Bank colleagues, Paul Streeten and Frances Stewart, to develop the UNDP's influential annual *Human Development Report.* In the first report, published in 1990, the researchers wrote, "Free market mechanisms may be vital for allocative efficiency, but they do not ensure distributive justice." They called for "food and health subsidies" to provide "an essential safety net in poor societies," and for debt relief and transfer of resources to the global South, especially to African nations. In its early years, the human development approach served, as one account described it, as "a credible international alternative to structural adjustment policies."[25]

The renewed attention to poverty had some impact. By the end of the 1980s, economists at the World Bank and the IMF had publicly acknowledged the detrimental impact of their loans. In 1988, the Bank's chief economist for Africa said, "We did not think that the human costs of these programmes could be so great and economic gains so slow in coming. . . . You can't just throw people out in the street, in the name of structural adjustment."[26] At the IMF, Davison L. Budhoo, a senior economist from Grenada, resigned from his job with a scathing open letter. In the attempt "to have the south 'privatised' or die," he wrote, "we ignominiously created bedlam in Latin America and Africa." The IMF, he told a reporter, "was never designed to help the Third World or end poverty."[27]

Conable, the Bank president, still promoted the private sector and adjustment policies, but he endorsed a revived concern with poverty. He also emphasized the environment and, as a Bank press release stated, "established women-in-development as a key priority for the Bank's operations world-wide." Pushed especially by the UNICEF report, the Bank made a commitment to "protecting the poor during adjustment," including maintaining funds "for primary education, primary health care and other programs benefiting the poor." For its 1990 World Bank report, it chose the theme of poverty, highlighting its reoriented initiatives.[28] But by then the damage had been done. In 1990, the nations of the global South owed $1.3 trillion in foreign debt. From 1982 to 1990, they had paid $418 billion more on their foreign debt interest and principal than they had taken in from official development assistance, export credits, and private investment and loans.[29] The critics of structural adjustment continued to detail the toll in human livelihood and economic decline during the "lost decade"—*la década perdida*, as it was known in Latin America—of the 1980s.

Promising Credit

Given the global preoccupation with escalating debt, it might seem odd that antipoverty advocates put so much stock in increasing credit, which is debt by another name. But so they did. At USAID, the PISCES project (Program for Investment in the Small Capital Enterprise Sector), launched in 1978, found credit as a key component in all but two of the twenty-three small-enterprise programs it studied in Africa, Asia, and Latin America. In the informal economy, credit seemed to be the missing ingredient that NGOs, banks, and governments could provide. For the PISCES researchers and for other microenterprise advocates, lack of capital was "the major impediment to increasing the efficiency of the informal sector," "the most pressing problem," and the "most critical need" identified by the self-employed themselves.[30] Credit was the solution, "the entry point for breaking the poverty cycle." It was also "the easiest and most inexpensive service to deliver to the [informal] sector."[31]

Credit programs had obvious appeal. They might provide the resources to start new enterprises and enlarge existing ones, repay exploitative money lenders who charged exorbitant rates of interest, purchase raw materials in bulk, and buy time- and labor-saving equipment. Because the borrowers repaid with interest, credit programs could possibly pay for their own costs, even with the heavy overhead for administering tiny loans. And they might flourish without expensive additional services. Some of the projects in the PISCES study combined credit with technical assistance, training, health care, and other components frequently found in antipoverty programs, but other "minimalist" programs offered credit alone and demonstrated, according to the study, that projects could "increase significantly the incomes of owners of existing micro-enterprises solely through extending credit." They could reach "larger numbers with very small amounts . . . at very low cost and high efficiency."[32] Plus, credit programs had an air of democratic participation when they allowed borrowers to determine how they used the borrowed funds; though, it turned out, many of the projects that the PISCES report described exercised "close supervision . . . over the expenditure of the loan monies." Nonetheless, microcredit promised to democratize finance by extending it to the poor people whom commercial banks routinely excluded.[33]

On its website, Accion International, the US NGO that supervised the PISCES project, claims, to the best of its knowledge, to have issued "the first loans that launched the field of microcredit." In 1973, in Recife, Brazil, it worked with a local affiliate to offer relatively small loans to businesses with fifteen or fewer employ-ees.[34] But Accion was not the first, and its initial loans did not go to the poorest. In various locales and in various guises, credit pro-grams for indigent borrowers had existed for decades in mutual aid associations, rotating credit groups, cooperatives, and credit unions as well as through loans from family, friends, shopkeepers, and others. In the early twentieth-century United States, philan-thropic loan societies undercut exploitative moneylenders with credit at lower interest rates for the urban poor. In El Salvador, in the 1950s, FEDECRÉDITO, a coordinating office for credit cooper-atives, moved beyond the routine lending for agriculture and began extending credit in markets to borrowers who could not qualify for commercial loans. And in 1960, a Maryknoll nun organized a credit cooperative for women as part of her missionary work in South Korea. It started with a single cooperative with 28 members, and three years later it had expanded to 6,900 members in fifty-two credit unions.[35] Many other such programs also offered loans to the poor before "microcredit" became a recognized term and a develop-ment movement.

Accion did not initiate microcredit, but it did play an early role in extending credit for small enterprises across Latin Amer-ica and in publicizing microcredit as a preferred form of antipov-erty development. It conducted studies, sponsored international workshops, assisted local affiliated organizations, guaranteed their loans, and wrote how-to guides for other NGOs that hoped to enter the field. By the mid-1980s, it had fourteen projects that provided loans to around twelve thousand "microentrepreneurs." In 1986, in a statement to the "microenterprise credit" hearings of the Select Committee on Hunger, Jeffrey Ashe, Accion's senior associate director and the lead author of USAID's PISCES proj-ect, promoted credit in "almost inconceivably small amounts" as a route to "income, production and employment." He and his organ-ization helped brand "micro"—"microentrepreneurs," "micro-enterprise," "micro-lending"—as the latest development trend, with credit as "perhaps the most cost effective way of alleviating poverty."[36]

In the late 1970s and early 1980s, women's NGOs were at least as central as Accion in elevating microcredit from its local sites to a global antipoverty movement. In the mid-1970s, the Self-Employed Women's Association in Ahmedabad, India, moved into the international spotlight and served as a model for other microcredit projects. SEWA started its credit program in 1972, the same year it was founded (and a year before Accion initiated its first small credit project in Brazil). The Indian government, as part of its poverty eradication campaign, had mandated that the national banks extend some of their loans to the indigent. But the banks hesitated. As Ela Bhatt, SEWA's founder, remembered, "The bankers were horrified at the lack of collateral, at the illiterate, uncouth manners of our members."[37] SEWA entered the credit field as an intermediary, helping illiterate women apply for loans, processing their applications, and overseeing repayment for the banks that supplied the money. In 1974, it opened its own bank, the Mahila SEWA Sahakari Bank (SEWA Women's Cooperative Bank). The bank gave tiny loans, sometimes only 50 rupees, or around $5 in 1975. The bank also started a savings program, in part to prevent husbands and sons from taking women's loan money.[38]

In the mid-1970s, the global women's movement elevated SEWA to the international platform. In 1975, Bhatt attended the UN's International Women's Year conference in Mexico City and presented her work at the "women in development" seminar, which took place in the week before the conference. She left Mexico with an international network of allies who saw credit as a critical problem for women and who knew her as a leader in the field. As her reputation grew, WID supporters and development experts traveled to Ahmedabad to learn about SEWA and its credit program.[39] Foundations, government agencies, and NGOs began to offer her funds to support her work. As a sign of her growing fame, Bhatt won the Magsaysay Award, the "Nobel Prize of Asia," in 1977 for her community service.

By the start of the 1980s, SEWA had enough of an international profile that USAID's Office of Urban Development commissioned a book-length study of its work. The 340-page report, completed in 1982, noted that "SEWA's reputation has made international funds more available to them than they perhaps would be to lesser known organizations." SEWA, it noted, expressed "a reluctance to accept funds and donations from local capitalists . . . to avoid conflicts of interest and pressure." It accepted foreign money selectively, including early support from the Ford Foundation, but it needed approval from the Indian government for grants from other governments' agencies, which could "expose an organization to political attacks and charges of being used as a vehicle of foreign 'infiltration.'" In the 1970s and early 1980s, SEWA's international support included funds from the Norwegian and Swedish governments, the Ford Foundation, and NGOs such as Oxfam.[40]

Among the people SEWA inspired was Michaela Walsh, an American who had worked in finance for fifteen years, including stints with Merrill Lynch in New York, Beirut, and London. Walsh worked her way up the ladder at Merrill Lynch, eventually left it, and became a partner in the first firm to trade mutual funds on the New York Stock Exchange. Through volunteer work with youth, she also entered the nonprofit realm. She decided, she wrote later, to close the "gap between my personal values and my work on Wall Street." By the time of the 1975 International Women's Year conference, she had taken a job as a program associate for the Rockefeller Brothers Fund, which sent her to Mexico City. As she remembered it, the conference "was a game-changer for my life, a complete paradigm shift."[41]

During the WID seminar and later in the conference sessions for NGOs, the issue of credit—and women's lack of access to it—came up repeatedly. In addition to Ela Bhatt, the Ghanaian businesswoman Esther Ocloo played a central role. Ocloo owned a successful food processing company, but she had started from scratch, in poverty, hawking homemade marmalade on the streets of Accra. She knew from experience that women had limited access to credit. At the Mexico City seminar, she made a plea for credit for women and then suggested an international "women's bank," and others present—UN delegates and NGO representatives—drafted a resolution for "a world bank for women." Nira Hardon Long, the head of USAID's WID office, described the call for a women's world bank as "the most surprising recommendation" of the seminar.[42] After the conference, Michaela Walsh used her experience in finance to run with the idea. She pulled together an international "Committee to Organize Women's World Banking" and worked with Ocloo, Bhatt, and others to create a new NGO.

Women's World Banking (WWB) was formally established in 1979 to provide guarantees to banks that made microloans to women. An avid promoter, Walsh convinced a range of donors, including the UNDP, the Rockefeller Brothers Fund, the Ford Foundation, the United Methodist Church, and Norwegian, Dutch, Swedish, and Canadian development agencies, to provide early support. In 1982, she also won a $500,000 loan plus more than $360,000 in grants from USAID.[43] WWB organized affiliates in Asia, Africa, and Latin America, and persuaded local banks to offer loans to women. It guaranteed half of the loan funds, and the affiliates guaranteed a quarter. The local bank that extended the credit assumed responsibility for the remaining 25 percent. At the end of the 1980s, WWB had forty-four affiliates in thirty-five nations. By that time, its programs were "no longer unique." It was, one assessment noted, "imitated or copied . . . to make it a sort of prototype of the new approach to development assistance."[44]

Walsh served as president of WWB, and Ocloo as first chair of its board of directors. Bhatt, a founding member, served on the board from the beginning and then chaired it in the late 1980s and early 1990s. She described WWB as "perhaps the most concrete result of the [UN] Women's Decade." It was, she wrote later, "bold enough to reclaim women's economic rights in the realm of formal banking."[45] In addition to loan guarantees and business training, WWB (and some of its affiliates) made occasional direct loans. The first such loan went to SEWA's bank for onlending to its members. In the WWB archives, the handwritten records indicate that the initial outlay funded around a hundred tiny loans that went to women whose work included knitting, sewing, embroidering, digging wells, making "chindi" rag rugs, and molding plaster of paris figurines.[46]

In the United States, other WID supporters also took up the cause of credit for impoverished women in the late 1970s and early 1980s. In the domestic feminist movement, the issue of credit already had resonance. Within the United States, activists had protested the denial of credit to women, who often had to get male cosigners in order to qualify for loans and credit cards. In a successful campaign, they had managed to change the law. The Equal Credit Opportunity Act, passed in 1974, stated that lenders could no longer discriminate against applicants on the basis of sex or marital status of anyone "who had the capacity to contract." It was soon amended to include race, religion, national origin, and age.[47] The US law offered nothing to American women (or men) who were too poor to qualify for conventional loans, but the push to enact it made credit a recognizable concern for those who supported gender equality. As microcredit moved to the center of international development circles, American WID supporters responded quickly to the call for credit equity for women in the global South. They conducted studies and wrote reports—funded by USAID, the Ford Foundation, and others—on "credit for rural women," "women's access to technology and credit," "giving women credit," and "organizing for credit," to draw from a handful of relevant titles, and they publicized existing local credit projects that served women in the global South. By the mid-1980s, in a review of its WID program, USAID noted its funding of credit programs for women in ten different nations.[48]

SEWA, WWB, and the slew of reports on women and credit show how microcredit won recognition at the intersections of the global WID and small-enterprise movements. The movements converged on the issue of extending credit to indigent women in the informal economy, and they won endorsements from a broad swath of the political spectrum. Ela Bhatt, a Gandhian trade unionist, could work with Michaela Walsh, a Wall Street veteran. The minutes of WWB board meetings suggest, predictably, that Bhatt kept her focus on poverty, while Walsh worried about attracting investors and finding self-sustaining income for WWB. At one board meeting on a "new strategy," for example, Walsh asked for a "focus on 'women in business'" and on "regional operations and the global institution." Bhatt countered that WWB needed to keep to its "original emphasis on low-income women" and their access to credit, ownership, and employment.[49] Even though they came to microcredit from different routes, they collaborated closely until Walsh retired in 1990. Elsewhere, too, WID supporters of various political stripes promoted microcredit as a women's issue. The Overseas Education Fund, wrangling for funds from the Reagan-era USAID, emphasized the private sector and advocated for "credit and business skills as tools for development" for women, and DAWN, the leftist WID organization rooted in the global South, called on governments to increase "the availability of credit for the self-employed women."[50] At least for a while, microcredit had wide appeal.

The Grameen Model

Microcredit was already on the international stage when Muhammad Yunus stepped in as its impresario. In the United States (and elsewhere), Yunus promoted and sold microcredit with more energy, skill, and appeal than anyone else. He came to the task already schooled in economics and US foreign policy. His American education began in 1965 when he made his first trip to the United States on a Fulbright scholarship for graduate study. He earned his PhD in economics at Vanderbilt University in 1971, the same year Bangladesh fought its brutal War of Liberation. In planned assaults, Pakistani soldiers massacred hundreds of thousands, probably millions, of Bengalis, and millions more fled to camps for refugees. In support of his homeland, Yunus headed to Washington, DC, to organize with other US-based Bengalis who hoped to halt the US military aid that supplied arms to Pakistan. That summer he lobbied Congress, studying its members and strategizing on how to persuade them of the justice of the nationalist cause. When Bangladesh won its independence from Pakistan, Yunus returned home and accepted a job as chair of the Department of Economics at Chittagong University.[51]

Born in genocide, Bangladesh was a nation in distress. A destructive cyclone in 1970 and the traumatic war in 1971 had devastated the country. The new government and local NGOs actively sought foreign aid, including funds for returning refugees, many of whom were widows. The government of India, the UN, and others moved into action to repair roads, railways, and bridges, supply food, and resettle refugees. Soon a multitude of multilateral institutions, government aid agencies, and transnational NGOs had programs on the ground, infusing funds into projects for relief and rehabilitation and for longer-term development. By the end of 1973, when the UN terminated its emergency relief operations, Bangladesh had received around $1.4 billion in funds.[52] And then the floods of 1974 ruined the crops and led to famine.

This was the context in which Yunus started a rural development project at Chittagong University. Disillusioned with conventional economics, which he now considered "useless," he turned his attention to local poverty. "I saw a horrible famine," he wrote later, "that provoked me to leave textbook economics behind and learn economics from the real lives of the poor."[53] He made his first experiment with microcredit in 1976. In his oft-told story, he met a woman who made bamboo stools in the village of Jobra near the university. She borrowed from middlemen to pay for the bamboo and then sold the stools back to them to repay her debt. She earned a net profit of two cents per day for her time and labor. Yunus had one of his students survey the village to see who else was caught in a spiral of debt and repayment. He then loaned around $27 of his own money to forty-two borrowers. His experiment seemed to suggest that tiny loans could free the poor from the traders, renters, and moneylenders who overcharged them for loans, equipment, and raw materials, and underpaid them for the goods they produced. Yunus imagined that successive small loans at commercial rates of interest, high enough to cover costs, would allow poor villagers to invest in their businesses and lift themselves out of poverty. Soon after, in 1977, he set up the Grameen Bank Project, which created branches to serve the poor within existing banks.[54]

Yunus was (and is) hard to pin down politically. He celebrated capitalism, especially its small-scale entrepreneurs, but he disliked the free-market ideologues who operated on universal theory instead of local trial and error. He favored market-oriented development but with a social conscience, which he saw as a curb on capitalist exploitation. He criticized the World Bank, its structural adjustment loans, and its fetishization of economic growth. He rejected its offer of a $200 million loan in 1986, but he softened on it somewhat in the 1990s when it supported microcredit and in 1993 accepted its offer of a $2 million grant for his bank. Still, even then, he rebuked the World Bank for the "conservatism at its core."[55] He aligned most, it seems, with the basic needs advocates, who rejected trickle-down economics and focused attention on the rural poor, and with those who paid increasing attention to the informal sector. But he put his efforts into providing loans, not grants, and into private enterprise rather than public services and redistribution.

He disliked traditional foreign aid programs, which he likened to welfare dependency and saw as boondoggles that benefited foreign donors and local elites, but he sought foreign and local funds for programs that directly reached the poor.

Yunus knew how to connect with, convince, and cultivate both the local officials and the foreign donors who poured into Bangladesh and looked for projects to fund. From early on, he worked with the Ford Foundation in its Dhaka office. It was, he remembered, an "international organization [that] had always come up with support when I asked for it." In 1977 Ford awarded Yunus $100,000 for his rural economics program, including a pilot project to test microcredit near Chittagong. In the early 1980s, it gave him $895,000 more for the Grameen Bank Project, including $770,000 to guarantee its loans, and it sent consultants from Chicago's South Shore Bank, a neighborhood development bank, to advise Yunus on management and auditing practices.[56] With the project on firmer footing, the International Fund for Agricultural Development (IFAD), a new UN agency established in 1977 to respond to the decade's famines, agreed to provide a $3.4 million loan, which the Bangladesh Central Bank matched. With the influx of money Yunus scaled his project up, with more borrowers and more branches in more districts of Bangladesh. By the fall of 1983, the Grameen project had eighty-six branches serving fifty-eight thousand borrowers. At that point, Yunus established the Grameen Bank as an independent financial institution, with its own branches, "designed to work exclusively for the rural poor."[57]

The bank expanded with impressive speed. By 1989, it had more than half a million borrowers in more than five hundred branches with a total staff of eight thousand. It loaned around $5 million per month, and it claimed a 98 percent recovery rate on the money loaned. It required its borrowers to join together in peer groups of five with access to further credit dependent on repayment. The groups exerted pressure on their members to pay off their loans on schedule, as did the groups' mandatory weekly meetings with Grameen staff. As the bank publicized its success, donors upped their contributions. By 1989, IFAD had contributed more than $50 million in loans and grants, the Norwegian government $8 million, the Swedish government almost $6.5 million, and the Ford

Foundation $4 million. Yunus made plans to double the number of branches and borrowers in the early 1990s.[58]

As the bank grew, so did the number of women borrowers. In 1976, when Yunus first experimented with credit for the poor, he made loans to men for the purchase of "rickshaws, cows, and equipment for muri [puffed rice] making." Only one woman—half of a husband-wife team who made and sold puffed rice—was directly involved in the early experiment. From the start, Yunus had hoped to give half of the loans to women, but he found it hard to involve indigent women, especially in the mixed-sex meetings, which men tended to dominate.[59] By that time, Yunus had already befriended Adrienne Germain, who made several trips to Bangladesh from Ford's New York office to promote WID programs. Yunus, Germain reported, "would be interested in developing projects with the women." Soon Yunus, like others involved in the small enterprise and microcredit movements, learned to organize women separately from men. The loans to women increased steadily. In 1980, a Ford Foundation consultant found that more than a third of Grameen's loans now went to women. Yunus was "obviously enthusiastic," she wrote, "about the women's component." Women, he told her, were "excited by their new independence," they repaid their loans "religiously," and they spent their "extra cash . . . on the next generation—food, schooling, clothing for their children—whereas the men like to spend it on themselves."[60] By the end of 1985, 65 percent of the Grameen Bank borrowers were women, and by 1989, 86 percent.[61]

In the mid-1980s, Yunus's version of microcredit was only one among many. Locally, the rural development program of the Bangladesh Rural Advancement Committee (BRAC), a major NGO with support from the Ford Foundation and others, and the credit project of Swanirvar, an organization funded mostly by the government of Bangladesh, also sponsored large-scale microcredit programs. USAID joined in with its own similar, smaller project in Bangladesh, the Women's Entrepreneurship Development Program, started in 1982 to offer credit to impoverished rural women.[62] In the rest of the world, Accion, SEWA, and WWB, among others, had won recognition for their microcredit work.

But the Grameen Bank had already eclipsed them all. It had an outsized reputation in the United States and internationally, in part because of its size. It had outpaced most of the similar programs in the number of borrowers and the amount of international funding. It also won attention for its less costly "minimalist" approach, which offered credit through the private sector without social services added on, and probably, too, for its seemingly apolitical stance, which called more for self-improvement than for structural change, unionization, or the critical consciousness of oppression known as "conscientization." In the 1980s, mainstream agencies, NGOs, and government officials saw it as a simple, inexpensive, and politically palatable model ready-made for replication.

Yunus himself played the starring role in publicizing the Grameen Bank. He knew how to promote his work with homespun anecdote and wit. He had what one admirer called "sales charm." Yunus, a USAID official noted, "is not an ordinary person. He's a very creative and almost charismatic leader." In the late 1970s and 1980s, he made several trips to the United States, where he met with Ford Foundation staff, spoke at conferences, visited and encouraged Grameen-like US microenterprise projects, and met with members of Congress. The US media took note from the mid-1980s. Early newspaper articles, headlined "Village Capitalism Betters Women's Lot," "Bangladeshi Landless Prove Credit-Worthy," and "Helping the Third-World's Poor Women," provided accounts of "an innovative program started by a visionary man."[63] What started as a trickle of news accounts mounted to a steady stream after Yunus testified in Washington.

In February 1986, Yunus traveled again to the United States with support from the Ford Foundation. He spoke at a World Bank conference on microenterprise, visited with Ford staff and others, and testified at hearings on "microenterprise credit" before the House Select Committee on Hunger and the Subcommittee on International Development. The hearings aimed to explore "the role of multilateral development banks," not the US government, "in providing finance for microenterprises." To kick them off, a Democrat, Stan Lundine from New York, and a Republican, Doug Bereuter from Nebraska, offered opening remarks. For Lundine, microcredit programs represented the new wave in development practice: "smaller scale" efforts, "the importance of the private sector," and "economic growth from the bottom up" with benefits for "the poorest of the poor." For Bereuter, they offered an easy corrective to the damaging impact of structural adjustment policies. "Austerity," he granted, had "taken a large toll." He supported the conditional loans to indebted nations "as a difficult but necessary medicine," but he looked for "innovative ways . . . to assist the poor." Microcredit was, he said, "an inexpensive way of providing funds for the poor in the economic sectors they know best" and "an optimal way to generate new income and jobs." And it aligned neatly "with the popular theme of assisting private sector growth."[64]

For his part, Yunus told his origin story: how he returned to Bangladesh after graduate study in the United States, how he rejected "economics from the textbooks," how he encountered the woman who earned "only 2 pennies" a day making bamboo stools, and how he established his bank. He recounted a success story about a "beggar woman" who borrowed one dollar and launched a business as "a trader in ribbons, hair clips, and bangles." "Every person," he claimed, "has the potentiality to translate into real income provided she can have an access to financial resources in the amount she needs." He urged "international funding agencies" to institute policies "conducive to making this credit available to the very poor." Yunus was the spellbinding storyteller, the raconteur who explained, as Lundine put it, "practical understanding of how things work to make a difference in the lives of people."[65]

Yunus won over the politicians. As a visitor from the global South, he already had a certain cachet. He could tell local stories from an insider's standpoint, and he could also help the supporters of foreign assistance dispel the image of foreign imposition or cultural imperialism. By courting Yunus and endorsing the Grameen Bank, they could change the negative optics in which they funded US NGOs to direct projects overseas and ignored indigenous organizations in the poorer nations. After his initial testimony, they invited Yunus to come back to Washington eight months later, in October 1986, to address "a forum on credit for the poor" sponsored once again by the House Select Committee on Hunger.[66] And they brought him back again in July 1987, this time to speak to a "members-only luncheon" on Capitol Hill with senators and representatives. In inviting his colleagues to the lunch, Representative Edward Feighan, a Democrat from Ohio, described Yunus as "a remarkable man" who was "demonstrating that providing credit to the very poorest people is the wave of the future in development."[67] By that time, Feighan and others had introduced three bills that required US foreign aid to support "credit for the poorest people." Feighan modeled his bill, he said, on the Grameen Bank.[68]

In the House the Self-Sufficiency for the Poor Act and the Comprehensive Microenterprise Credit Promotion Act, and in the Senate the Micro-Enterprise Loans for the Poor Act all required US government funding for microcredit overseas. In both the House and Senate, the sponsors were mostly Democrats, but they ranged widely from staunch progressives, such as Ron Dellums, Barbara Boxer, and Edward Kennedy, to at least a handful of dyed-in-the-wool conservatives, including John McCain, Mike DeWine, and Orrin Hatch. In the initial iterations, the bills differed in details— on, for example, how to determine the amount of funding and where the funds for the new loans would come from—but all agreed that microcredit benefited the poor and alleviated poverty. None of them asked for additional monies for USAID; they called instead for a reallocation of available funds, what one sponsor labeled "a bargain for U.S. taxpayers."[69]

Much of the impetus for the legislation came from a "citizens' lobby on hunger," an organization called RESULTS, founded in 1980 by Sam Daley-Harris, a former high-school music teacher who was moved by the news reports on famines. In the mid-1980s, Daley-Harris worked to raise money for IFAD. After he saw the Grameen Bank featured in an IFAD publicity film, he invited Yunus to testify before the House Select Committee on Hunger.[70] A few months later he helped draft the first bill that called for US foreign assistance funds for microcredit. To win support for the bill, RESULTS members—by one account, "more than 300 volunteers"—lobbied Congress and pressed newspapers to publish editorials. From November 1986 to December 1987, more than one hundred such editorials appeared in newspapers ranging from the *New York Times* and *Chicago Tribune* to the *Tulsa World* and *Orange County Register*.[71] In the course of the RESULTS campaign, Daley-Harris worked with Yunus to highlight the Grameen Bank as the most visible model of microcredit success. After one of his meetings with Congress, Yunus recalled, Daley-Harris put him on a telephone press conference with fourteen editorial writers. Yunus talked to them for an hour, and then fielded a second conference call with fourteen more. The editorials in support of the legislation frequently mentioned the Grameen Bank by name and recounted the success stories that Yunus had relayed.[72]

The lobbying seemed necessary in part because the bill, as Feighan said, "did not have high visibility on its own."[73] But it also worked to counter the objections of USAID. The first bill introduced had requested that USAID spend 10 percent of US foreign aid or $400 million, whichever was greater, on loans that would go to microcredit. Peter McPherson, the USAID administrator, argued that the microcredit programs would increase the debt burden of the poorer nations in the global South, decrease the flexibility of USAID in allotting resources, and create an administrative mess with too small a staff to oversee the actions of the local and US NGOs that would give out the microloans. USAID officials also argued that "marginally larger" loans to "slightly larger" businesses would do more to create employment for the poor than tiny loans to the smallest enterprises in the informal sector.[74] Eventually the House and Senate dropped the funding significantly to $50 million in 1988 and $75 million in 1989 but kept the mandate for microloans, of less than $300 each, to the poorest people in the poorer nations. When the bill passed as appropriations legislation in December 1987, Feighan credited the victory "almost exclusively" to RESULTS.[75]

Yunus's work with RESULTS on the 1987 bill, he recalled, caught the attention of CBS's *60 Minutes*. In 1989, interviewer Morley Safer and two television crews traveled to Bangladesh, interviewed Yunus, and visited villages where the loans were given. The twelve-minute segment aired in March 1990 and generated a tidal wave of new publicity for the Grameen Bank. Yunus continued to work with Sam Daley-Harris over the next decades.[76] Meanwhile, new projects attempted to replicate the Grameen Bank in, among other countries, Malaysia, the Philippines, Malawi, Mali, and Tanzania.[77] In the United States, "micro banks" sprang up in Chicago, in Pine Bluff, Arkansas, and on the Pine Ridge Indian Reservation in South Dakota. The US variant of microcredit built on a long-standing self-help ethos that had appeal in African American,

Native American, and immigrant communities, in the countercul-
ture, and also among politicians who promoted small business and
looked for alternatives to welfare. In the 1980s and after, it often
drew directly on the Grameen Bank experience.

The Arkansas project, the Southern Development Bancorporation, came with the active blessing of Governor Bill and Hillary
Clinton, who first met Yunus in Washington in 1986. At their invitation, Yunus traveled to Arkansas to help initiate the project. By
1988, it had $8 million in funding from the Winthrop Rockefeller
Foundation, the Ford Foundation, and private investors, including
Walmart. It was, one business magazine enthused, "the most radical experiment in rural economic development since the Tennessee
Valley Authority." Microcredit in Arkansas was, of course, no TVA. It
paled and shriveled in scale and ambition when compared with the
TVA's immense state-led investment in regional infrastructure and
agrarian reform.[78] But the hyperbolic description shows how microcredit was already trending as the next big thing in development, "a
dramatic new direction in foreign aid," the successor to modernization, the green revolution, population control, and basic needs.[79]

Empowering Women?

From the early 1980s, the supporters of microcredit featured
women as the central, and often sole, characters in the success stories they recounted. Some NGOs that took on microcredit, such
as SEWA and WWB, had intended women as their primary program beneficiaries from the start. Others, such as Accion and the
Grameen Bank, turned to women as they grew. In the US government, the congressional conference report that accompanied the
1987 microcredit legislation specifically called on USAID to give
special attention to "businesses owned by women." In 1988, in its
program guidelines in response to the legislation, USAID followed
suit. It stated that "programs should be designed ideally to . . .
seek out the smallest enterprises" and "make at least 50 percent
of their resources . . . available to women-owned and -operated
enterprises."[80]

In large part, the attention to women in microcredit programs
echoed the arguments made earlier by WID supporters and by

development experts concerned with the informal economy. Women who produced goods and sold them wanted, needed, and deserved loans without the inflated interest rates of local loan sharks, but commercial banks, which extended credit on less usurious terms, had ignored them. Women tended to be poorer than men, especially in single-parent households. They were the "poorest of the poor," the people who antipoverty advocates hoped to reach. They constituted the majority of microenterprise owners; that is, they ran most of the smallest businesses in the informal sector. "Poverty lending," one USAID study found, favors "producers with little or no assets—often women—more than those whose gender, status, and economic roles allow for . . . a higher level of asset accumulation."[81]

Microcredit advocates also returned repeatedly to the argument that women spent money to support their children instead of spending their income on themselves, "that men more than women squander disposable cash on items like alcohol, cigarettes, other stimulants, and gambling." Or as Yunus put it, "A man thinks of himself first. A woman thinks of her children." John Hatch, the president of FINCA, a US-based microcredit organization founded in 1984 with programs in Latin America, gave a similar argument more intensity by focusing on child mortality. "We have a situation," he said, "of 35,000 children dying every day, 14 million worldwide dying every year. . . . And I believe that the fastest way to prevent massive child die-off in the third world is by supporting their mothers." Microenterprise loans would, he believed, lead to a bit more income—"$5 or $10 extra per week"—for women that would "buy more food to narrow the nutritional gap." The reasoning assigned selfless virtue to mothers and built on, but refrained from questioning, a sexual division of labor in which women held responsibility for the well-being of children.[82]

In the era of global debt and structural adjustment, microcredit advocates also added a new layer of argument atop the old. In the stories and studies of microcredit, women were not only seen as more likely to spend their income on their children, they were also seen as more likely to repay their debts. Women, it seems, were better credit risks, more reliable than men. Yunus made the claim that "women had a much better pay-back record than men," and so did others. Michael Farbman, a staffer at USAID, told the Select Committee on Hunger that women were "excellent credit performers . . . better credit performers often than men in the same project."[83] Microcredit for the poor aimed to "create self-employment and income," but repayment rates, which were more easily recorded, routinely served as a proxy for success, "a clear and concise measure," as one account stated, "of good performance."[84] Repayment also replenished the cash supply that sustained the loan programs. Whether the loans benefited women economically or not, their higher repayment rates signaled sustainability, adding a further incentive to placing women at the heart of the microcredit movement.

By many accounts, microcredit fit the neoliberal moment.[85] In David Harvey's influential rendering, neoliberalism "holds that the social good will be maximized by maximizing the reach and frequency of market transactions, and it seeks to bring all human action into the domain of the market." By integrating women into financial markets and by training them as fiscal subjects, microcredit fulfilled the neoliberal promise. But it was a liberal variant of neoliberalism that expressed concern for poverty and extended financial services down the economic ladder, not simply through the free market, but through public-private collaborations of the mixed economy. In the 1980s, it used bilateral, multilateral, and private aid, funneled through NGOs, banks, and governments, to bring poor women into a private financial sector that had long excluded them.[86] It operated on the bet that the poor would benefit from entry into formal finance. At the macro level, the stakes were relatively low through the 1980s. The loans were small enough and few enough that debtors who failed to repay could be cut off without jeopardizing financial institutions. The tiny debts, it seemed, would not create a national or international crisis.

The advocates of microcredit took care to distinguish it from welfare and sometimes positioned it as welfare's replacement. "We must resist giveaways and handouts of all kinds," Yunus told reporters. For him, microcredit was "business." It was, one senator said, "not a hand-out but a hand-up," echoing a phrase repeatedly used during the domestic war on poverty.[87] In this line of thinking, loans, which had to be repaid, made poor women responsible, made them better economic actors and better citizens than did welfare, which allegedly made them dependent. The concern with "dependency" was widespread. In the context of foreign aid, it aligned with third worldist calls for national self-reliance. In the domestic US context, it fit neatly with the backlash against the welfare state and with a more general ethos that valorized self-help and the autonomous individual.[88] Government "handouts" damaged women; "business" trained them for participation in the market and society at large.

Microcredit shifted attention away from social services and other transfers of resources. It aimed to replace the basic needs approach with tiny loans, offered with the faith that they would lead to income, profit, and economic growth. Some sociologists who study the United States have suggested that "credit-based consumption" has served, insufficiently, as a market-based substitute for redistributive antipoverty programs. Policy makers who shaped foreign aid also saw credit—in this case, credit-based investment—as a market-oriented substitute for state expenditure on poverty alleviation. As a supportive report from the House Select Committee on Hunger stated directly, "The promotion of micro-enterprise development is nothing more than an expansion of capitalism."[89] And an inexpensive one at that.

In the Grameen Bank's version of microcredit, poor women were natural entrepreneurs. But if they were neoliberal subjects, they were also still women, still seen as mothers who supported their families. And they needed what Yunus and others called the "discipline" of repaying debts to help them gain "self-reliance, pride, and confidence." This vision of the woman entrepreneur was made explicit in the "16 decisions" that all Grameen Bank borrowers memorized and recited from 1984 on. The decisions included pledges to "discipline, unity, courage, and hard work," and also to pursue prosperity, upgrade housing, eat and sell vegetables, keep families small, minimize expenditure, educate children, use sanitary latrines, drink clean water, reject dowry, invest money for higher incomes, and engage in physical exercise. Just a few years earlier, in 1980, a World Bank brochure on "women in development" had declared that the informal sector kept women "barred from cultivating the attitudes toward work that modernization required."[90] But as the support for microcredit spread, the informal sector now became the crucial training ground for making women modern. The sixteen decisions offered a biopolitical primer for an updated version of motherhood that combined fiscal responsibility with older issues of hygiene, health, child rearing, population control, and income earning.

In the 1950s and 1960s, impoverished mothers were supposed to modernize their families via new child-rearing methods that shaped their sons into entrepreneurs. Now women themselves were the entrepreneurs whose road to prosperity came from borrowing and investing. Their financial inclusion brought new forms of surveillance. "Discipline," a Ford Foundation document stated, "is developed by mandatory attendance at weekly meetings, tightly scheduled loan repayments, group pressure, follow-up," and more.[91] The external economic surveillance came in tandem with demands for self-discipline in buying, selling, borrowing, repaying, and investing, and also lessons in the management of everyday life. The insistence on discipline suggested that microcredit's advocates did not envision women as the innovative risk takers of entrepreneurial lore. They tended to see women instead as dutiful mothers who added business activities onto their customary unpaid care labor. Microcredit's discipline was part of a long process of making poor women modern, in this case by bringing them into a regulatory regime of finance that no longer presumed that women could or should rely on a male breadwinner.

As in the WID movement, the microcredit supporters brought an upgraded picture of the poor. While conservatives vilified welfare recipients in the United States, the advocates of microcredit described poor women overseas as diligent and resilient, even if they needed instruction in self-discipline. The boosters of microcredit avoided the stigmatizing term "culture of poverty," which pathologized poor people of color as lazy and criminal; they preferred the less fraught "cycle of poverty," which they (and others) saw as the self-perpetuating economic constraints that held women and children back through no fault of their own. Congressman Mickey Leland, a liberal Black Democrat and civil rights activist from Texas, chaired the House Select Committee on Hunger, which adopted the "cycle of poverty" lingo. "The urban and rural poor in the developing world," he said, "are trapped in a vicious cycle of poverty, struggling on a daily basis to provide food and shelter for themselves and their families." Microcredit would allow them "to increase their incomes and join the economic mainstream." It offered "creative and cost-effective ways of helping the poor help themselves." Microcredit could "generate a significant surplus for poor people . . . beyond meeting their basic needs," another advocate testified, enough to break "the cycle of poverty."[92]

The supporters of microcredit focused on its perceived economic benefits—breaking free of the "cycle of poverty"—but even without economic success, they saw virtue in the extension of credit, especially for women. In 1985, a USAID study noted "the psychological gains that can come from the successful use and repayment of loans by those with little previous experience with the formal credit sector."[93] The "non-economic impacts" of microcredit included "increased self-confidence and motivation," "a feeling of self-worth and social acceptance," and, as Yunus put it, a fulfillment of "the potential locked inside of each and every human being."[94] The growing attention to women as entrepreneurs elevated a psychological discourse of self-improvement and self-actualization through the market. Earlier variants of development economics had also addressed psychology, but the attempts to change the mind-sets of the poor—their alleged fatalism, for example—had not usually addressed "self-confidence" and "self-worth," the lack of which had gendered, feminine overtones.

By the mid-1980s, the term "empowerment" had started to stand in for the range of benefits—economic and not—that supporters of microcredit perceived. For some, empowerment referred to the collective strength, the power in numbers that came from unions, social movements, and mass mobilization.[95] But for many it referred primarily to individual transformation, to a rising sense of power in interpersonal relationships. In the microcredit literature, it was a distinctly gendered term, used primarily in discussions of women. Articles praising microcredit suggested that husbands had more respect for entrepreneurial wives who brought in income, that local landowners greeted them instead of ignoring them, and that women now could "hold up their heads and . . . look strangers in the eye."[96] "Credit frees both men and women," Yunus stated, "but changes the situation of a woman more significantly

than it does for a man." The executive director of the US antihunger
NGO Bread for the World made a similar point: "Women, in many
cases, derive particular benefits from credit schemes, and are able
to improve their status generally in society in addition to earning
more income."[97] At the same time, then, that structural adjustment
loans vitiated national economies across the global South, loans to
impoverished women, if repaid, aimed to free them from the constraints of poverty, patriarchy, and personal self-doubt.

The claims for microcredit sounded too good to be true, and
from the start, skeptics, and even some avid supporters, voiced
their doubts. They pointed to the economic precarity of the smallest
businesses. Microenterprises often sold products in which demand
just could not be maintained. Handicraft producers confronted
a "highly variable market"; they could not depend on "a reliable
source of income." (One WID activist asked early on, "How many
baskets does the world need?")[98] In other areas, small producers
faced "competition by large-scale firms" and "static final demand if
the local economy is not expanding," and in the export sector, they
encountered "forces well beyond their control or understanding."[99]
With unpredictable shifts in the market, debt could oppress women
who had no reserves to fall back on.

Plus, not every woman had the entrepreneurial talent, luck,
drive, or desire to scale up a microbusiness. "Many of the poor," one
microcredit supporter cautioned, "prefer to have stable employment rather than bearing the risks and responsibilities of running
their own businesses." The risks were real, the pay-off iffy. FINCA's
John Hatch admitted that "eight of the ten women that we lend
to . . . will never be per se an entrepreneur creating a business
that grows and creates employment."[100] And in its policy guidelines, USAID concluded that microcredit alone "only rarely produced self-sustaining gains; increases in income were short-lived."
Instead, as an agency study concluded, microcredit might "easily
end up bolstering the power of local elites" who could raise prices
for raw materials and other supplies to capture the loaned funds.[101]

USAID, the Ford Foundation, and others wondered whether
microcredit would have any real impact on poverty. A number of
critics suspected that only larger enterprises, even slightly larger

enterprises, could create employment.[102] In 1989, Marty Chen, working as a Ford Foundation consultant, evaluated its programs for women in Bangladesh. The foundation had funded three large microcredit NGOs—the Grameen Bank, BRAC, and Proshika—all of which had "international reputations for their creativity, effectiveness, and scale" and all of which worked with "poor and landless women." The NGOs had "legitimized and popularized the concept of credit for traditional subsistence activities," but none of them, the report concluded, had "achieved significant breakthroughs in helping women move to higher productivity or higher return activities."[103]

Moreover, the very thing that made women appealing as microcredit borrowers—that they seemed to spend on their children and not on themselves—also made them troublesome for microcredit programs. When women used their loans for family consumption, they withdrew funds that lenders wanted them to invest in their businesses. In 1982, a Ford Foundation study found that one of BRAC's microcredit projects in Bangladesh failed because "female members used the credit obtained to subsidise their family consumption rather than for income-generating purposes." And in 1985, a USAID study of a project in Kenya noted that the impoverished microenterprise "owners had to consume most of the profits to meet family needs." A few years later, another Ford study concluded that once women had achieved their "basic consumption goals," they avoided business "expansion and upgrading," which would bring "substantially greater risk and headaches."[104] Despite the discipline imposed on borrowers, their family obligations and personal preferences could interfere with the capital accumulation that the lenders banked on.

And the discipline posed its own problems. A Ford Foundation staffer who supported the Grameen Bank wondered nonetheless whether "the highly acclaimed Grameen 'discipline' could lead to regimentation," whether its "easy-to-use slogans . . . could become indoctrination," and whether "the innovative use of social pressure" to repay loans "could create a new elite based on the power to control." Would women become "'targets' rather than participants"? Would "identification with the Bank" divide "members and non-members" and create "disparities among the poor"?[105] The questions mounted over the course of the 1980s, but they hardly dampened the enthusiasm for microcredit or for women as its principal clients.

In the US government, the commitment to microcredit ramped up steadily through the 1990s. In 1994, USAID, in cooperation with members of Congress, launched a Microenterprise Initiative. It promised to build microenterprise programs, work with US NGOs, and emphasize "reaching women and the very poorest." At the same time, USAID's Micro and Small Enterprise Development Program provided US guarantees "to encourage developing country banks to open lending windows to both small and micro businesses."[106] The Clinton administration, with the vocal support of Bill and Hillary Clinton, kept the focus on microcredit, the private sector, and the liberal variant of neoliberalism. In his move to slash the federal budget, President Clinton reduced the funds for foreign aid generally, but the budget for microcredit shot up.[107] In "much poorer countries," he said, microcredit had brought "new dignity and better lives for women and children, especially."[108]

In addition to the US-based microcredit NGOs—such as Accion, WWB, and FINCA—the larger international US NGOs also joined what USAID now called "the microcredit revolution." In the 1990s, the evangelical Christian NGO World Relief carried out a $4 million microcredit project, mostly in Africa, with $1.7 million in funds from USAID. It reached fifty-six thousand people, 94 percent of them women. In 1991, CARE, one of the largest international NGOs, claimed that microcredit was "its fastest growing portfolio." In the mid-1990s, it received more than $7 million in USAID grants for its microcredit activities. It developed a program in Niger that it planned to convert "into a profit making bank."[109] The list could go on. In 1997 alone, USAID spent $114 million on microcredit programs. It reported that 1.4 million "poor clients had active loans." Two-thirds of them were women. Dozens of NGOs, in the United States and abroad, received USAID grants to implement the projects, among them Save the Children, Catholic Relief Services, and World Vision. Save the Children's economic development specialist told a reporter, "It's credit as a social movement. It's economic empowerment."[110]

The World Bank, apparently, had come to agree. In 1995, in concert with USAID, IFAD, the UNDP, the Asian and African Development Banks, and several others, it launched a consortium of donors, the Consultative Group to Assist the Poorest. CGAP aimed to promote microcredit, coordinate donors, research "best practices," and "mainstream microfinance within World Bank operations." Within a year, it had a budget of $250 million. Yunus remembered that the World Bank had "considered us a bit of a joke before," but with CGAP it had "legitimised the idea of micro-credit."[111] He served as the first chair of CGAP's advisory board but soon balked at the Bank's top-down technocratic approach. "We had no idea," he said, "that money earmarked for micro-credit would end up in the hands of consultants—not in the hands of the poor women." A "guy who has never seen a micro-credit program in his life becomes a consultant and tells you this is the way you should do it."[112]

By that time, Yunus was an international celebrity. In 1995, he spoke at the UN's Fourth World Conference on Women in Beijing. In 1996, he appeared at the Gorbachev Foundation's "State of the World" forum, along with Mahbub ul Haq, environmental activist Vandana Shiva, and others. Haq spoke on human development and basic needs. "Rescuing people from poverty," he said, "would mean a trade-off between investment in arms and investment in people." Shiva warned of foreign monopolies and the rising "jobless rate" in "free market economies." But it was Yunus, with his well-rehearsed story of his bank's origins, who left his listeners "teary-eyed."[113] A few months later, the right-wing Heritage Foundation sponsored a lunch for journalists with Yunus as the featured speaker. "One of the beauties of microcredit's arrival," a reporter wrote, "is its staying power across the political spectrum."[114]

In February 1997, the first International Microcredit Summit convened in Washington, DC, organized by RESULTS, the lobbying group that promoted microcredit in Congress. First Lady Hillary Clinton served as cochair, along with the prime minister of Bangladesh Sheikh Hasina and Queen Sofia of Spain. More than 2,900

FIGURE 5.2. Muhammad Yunus, the Bangladeshi economist who founded the
Grameen Bank, played the leading role in promoting microcredit globally.
(Richard Ellis/Alamy Stock Photo)

delegates from 137 nations attended. "We have assembled to launch
a global movement," the summit's "Plan of Action" stated, "to reach
100 million of the world's poorest families, especially the women of
those families, with credit for self-employment and other financial
and business services, by the year 2005."[115] James Gustave Speth,
the head of the UNDP, saw "the microcredit revolution" as "paving
the way for a radically new approach to poverty reduction." He
announced a $41 million program, MicroStart, to support "micro-
finance institutions operating in developing countries." James
Wolfensohn, president of the World Bank, told the delegates that
"microcredit programs brought the vibrancy of the market economy to the poorest villages and people of the world."[116]

Hillary Clinton, Muhammad Yunus, Ela Bhatt, and a slew of
other world leaders, UN officials, NGO directors, and corporate
executives also gave speeches and statements. Clinton claimed that
microcredit was "a macro idea . . . an invaluable tool in alleviating poverty, promoting self-sufficiency and stimulating economic

activity." She praised the work of both Yunus and Bhatt. Yunus, now dubbed the "godfather" of microcredit, celebrated the movement's success. The summit, he said, "wants to end poverty in the world." Bhatt, never a minimalist, was not convinced that credit and business enterprise could actually end poverty. "Without the active participation of the poor, and especially poor women," she stated, "poverty will not be reduced." She acknowledged that "the poor want access to credit," but even more, she said, "they want ownership of productive assets." She called for "savings instruments," "business development services," and "insurance for health care, child care, and shelter" for the poor, and she asked for "support to poor peoples' organizations."[117] Her speech hinted, but only hinted, at behind-the-scenes divisions. A Ford Foundation memo described the tensions at an Asian regional preparatory meeting for the summit, held in Malaysia in the fall. Many "were concerned about what they perceived to be the simplistic message of the Summit—micro credit as *the* strategy for poverty alleviation—and the overall focus on the Grameen Bank as *the* model."[118]

At the conference itself, the president of Uganda, Yoweri Museveni, expressed the most skepticism in a speech that one reporter described as "almost a reality check to the lofty ideals." He reminded his listeners that microcredit did not address the causes of poverty, including the protectionist trade policies of the United States and Europe. "Let's eliminate [the causes]," he said, "and then we can talk about credit."[119] Just as pointed and much more acid was the coverage of the summit in the *Times of India*. "Hail to the saviour, the saviour has arrived," journalist Shahnaz Anklesaria Aiyar wrote. "Mandarins from a dozen international donor agencies have 'discovered' yet another 'strategy' for poverty alleviation—delivering microcredit services to poor women for their 'economic empowerment.' Targets have been set, goals announced. . . . [H]allelujah! It's empowerment time!" Despite the sarcasm, Aiyar, a feminist, did not oppose "empowerment," but she saw it as more complicated. It took time, commitment, and participation, not "the micromanaging or fast forwarding of development." It was "a long process of working towards radical shifts in power equations between women and men." And now, she said, it was "also a tag-on to the officialese of the gender development jet set."[120]

At the end of the 1990s, microcredit, along with its language of empowerment, was, as Aiyar wrote, "getting fashionable." But as microcredit supporters got louder, so did the chorus of critics, who now had more pronounced concerns than their counterparts in the 1980s. Microcredit, the doubters argued, did not address basic needs. It could "divert scarce aid funds from more mundane development goals like health and education improvement."[121] The critics worried that "micro-finance evangelism" promoted a one-size-fits-all model for poverty alleviation that treated poor women simply as entrepreneurs and supported them in low-income enterprises that would not end poverty. They wondered whether the reigning metrics of repayment rates, number of borrowers, and financial sustainability deflected attention from the actual impact of microcredit on the well-being of borrowers, and they suspected that credit programs made poor women dependent on NGOs and did not help the poorest people at all. "Some of the poorest borrowers," studies found, "became worse off as a result of micro-enterprise credit."[122] As for empowerment, they noted that many women "had partial, limited or no control over their loans, passing the money over to husbands—sometimes by choice, sometimes by force." They recounted instances in which husbands beat their wives after the women returned home late from a loan meeting, failed to get a loan, or refused to hand over loan money. Microcredit, they found, could reside within existing gender hierarchies instead of undermining them. And they expressed concern that the larger NGOs might stress quantity instead of quality, displace smaller, local social and financial networks, respond to the whims of foreign donors, and lose touch with their clients as they focused on scale. The organizers of the Microcredit Summit, with their "almost spiritual mission," the critics said, had overstated their case.[123] They now encountered pushback. Whether credit would lift women out of poverty, leave them in debt, or do something else entirely was still an open question. The debate had just begun.

The Development
of Poverty

*The distribution of wealth is one of today's most widely discussed and
controversial issues.*

—THOMAS PIKETTY, *CAPITAL IN THE TWENTY-FIRST CENTURY*

IN THE FALL OF 2006, Muhammad Yunus and the Grameen Bank
won the Nobel Peace Prize. "Micro-credit," the Nobel Committee
stated, was "an important liberating force" for women and would
have to "play a major part" in ongoing efforts to end world poverty.
By that point, the Grameen Bank had nearly seven million borrowers, 97 percent of them women. The bank no longer needed donors.
With a high repayment rate, it now sustained itself. The bank had
moved from microcredit to "microfinance," the preferred term for a
range of services that included but went beyond the minimal loans
for small enterprises in the informal sector. It extended housing
and student loans, held savings accounts, created pension funds,
and sold insurance. With outside funds, Yunus had also started a
cell phone company and a nutritional yogurt factory, intended to
employ and help the poor, and he had plans to open ophthalmology
hospitals.[1]

In his Nobel lecture, Yunus once again told the story of the
bank's origins and its subsequent growth. But with his own entrepreneurial bent, he now had something else to sell. In addition to

microfinance, he called for "social business." Yunus asked investors to "change the character of capitalism radically" by replacing "maximization of profit" with "doing good to people and the world." Social businesses would provide services such as health care, education, or microfinance. Private investors would recoup their capital but reinvest their profits to sustain, expand, and improve the enterprise. Yunus, attuned to his day, pitched a plan to merge business and philanthropy with minimal drag on the state. He expressed his support for capitalism, free markets, and globalization but asked for rules to tame the "free-for-all" in which the rich "elbowed out" the poor. He opposed "financial imperialism" but wanted foreign investment. Social businesses could help build "strong economies in the poor countries by protecting their national interest from plundering companies."[2] Just as selfless women who spent their income on their children were the virtuous poor, so selfless investors who spent their profits on the poor were the virtuous rich.[3]

When the UN proclaimed 2005 the "International Year of Microcredit," and the next year when Yunus and the Grameen Bank won the Nobel Prize, the surge of publicity brought new rounds of acclaim. In 2006, after winning the Nobel Prize, Yunus returned to the United States and celebrated his achievement on *The Daily Show* with Jon Stewart, *The Oprah Winfrey Show*, and *PBS News-Hour*, among others.[4] The press joined in with laudatory stories. Microcredit, the *New York Times* reported, "raises an entire village's standard of living. . . . [I]t produces higher incomes and better-fed children." And the conservative *National Review* claimed that Yunus's work had "lifted an untold number from what must have seemed irredeemable poverty."[5]

But by then the microcredit bubble had grown so big that it simply had to burst. Yunus's call for social business, along with the expansive range of programs now offered by the Grameen Bank, suggested that he himself knew that microcredit alone would not accomplish all that it had promised.[6] The skeptics came on stronger. From the right, John Tierney, a libertarian columnist for the *New York Times*, wrote of the "limit to how much money villagers can make selling eggs to one another." He placed his faith in the global market, called for factory jobs, and claimed that Walmart, with its imports from impoverished nations, did more to end poverty than the Grameen Bank. From the left, Alexander Cockburn, a Marxist columnist for the *Nation*, agreed that "microloans don't make any sort of macro-difference." They were "micro-Band-Aids," he said. But he looked to the state, not to Walmart and its sweatshop suppliers, for poverty alleviation. Microfinance had let governments off the hook, he said, allowing them to retreat from "their most basic responsibilities to poor citizens"; it had made "the market a god."[7]

Earlier critics, too, had wondered whether microcredit could make a serious dent in global poverty. Now more of them also asked, "does it do harm?" In 2006, in the month before the Nobel Committee announced its prize, the *Times of India* carried an article headlined "Death by Microcredit." In the Indian state of Andhra Pradesh, microfinance institutions had charged "usurious interest rates" and intimidated their clients "with forced loan recovery practices." A number of rural debtors, possibly more than two hundred, had committed suicide. Their rising debt suggested "that a large proportion of microcredit clients" were "worse off after accessing loans." Other reports reached similar conclusions. A Bangladeshi economist studied the Grameen Bank and concluded "that nearly 80 per cent of the women beneficiaries of the bank had got themselves into debt traps." Women borrowed from one microcredit program in order to pay off another. Women were not empowered, he found. "There is no surge of women in local leadership positions, no jobs are being created because of this, nor are women getting any social security benefit like health [or] education."[8]

In the United States, the damaging press mounted in the wake of microcredit's reinvention as for-profit business. Following the logic of private sector aid, some microfinance institutions had turned from the NGO model, which relied on donors, and adopted a profit-making model that appealed to investors. These were not Yunus's social businesses, which asked investors to rein in their profit motives, although for-profit founders often framed themselves as socially conscious benefactors. Instead, the new businesses attracted investors who looked for a windfall. In Mexico, Banco Compartamos started as an NGO in 1990 and incorporated as a business in 2000. With its initial public offering in 2007, it raked in $458 million. "Private Mexican investors, including the bank's top executives," the *New York Times* reported, "pocketed $150 million from the sale." Microcredit promoters had to admit that it did not look good when the wealthy reaped their fortunes from the world's poor. One "microfinance consultant" noted, "Not only are they making obscene profits off poor people, they are in danger of tarnishing the rest of the industry."[9]

In 2010, the tide turned decisively. Private microcredit companies, the press reported, had spread through Africa, Asia, and Latin America. The "rush of private capital" had created "overheated microfinance markets" that "led to repayment crises in Bosnia, Nicaragua, Morocco, and Pakistan."[10] Private companies had extended "loans to poor villagers at exorbitant interest rates and without enough regard for their ability to repay."[11] An Indian government agency reported more than seventy suicides by indebted women and men, once again in Andhra Pradesh, from March through November of 2010. "Microfinance was supposed to empower women," one Indian economist noted. "These women ended up becoming slaves." The photos that accompanied a *New York Times* report on the story omitted the usual visual trope of microcredit—smiling women producing goods by hand—and turned to photos of devastated women, staring grimly, empty-handed, in the wake of family and financial disaster.[12]

Much of the public alarm centered on SKS Microfinance (now known as Bharat Financial Inclusion), a huge for-profit lender that had raised more than $350 million in stock sales in its initial public offering in 2010. SKS's founder, Vikram Akula, with an MA from Yale and a PhD from the University of Chicago, had sold some of his own shares in the company for around $13 million. Yunus was appalled. On a panel with Akula at the Clinton Global Initiative, held in New York City, he said, "Microcredit is not about exciting people to make money off the poor. That's what you're doing. That's the wrong message completely." For his part, Akula defended himself with a rescue fantasy. He argued that only commercial capital could raise enough money to help "all the people who need it. . . . We need more than one approach with 3 billion people to save."[13]

But did microcredit "save" the poor? A creeping disillusionment with the entire enterprise—profit making and nonprofit—inched its way into scholarship. Ethnographers, economists, and others found that some microcredit clients built their businesses, others used their loans to tide themselves through a crisis, still others spiraled into debt, and most remained poor. Borrowers took out multiple loans from different lenders and competed with one another in markets saturated with tiny businesses. Microcredit institutions pressured strapped clients to repay their loans and sometimes confiscated their meager assets, including their homes, when they could not. Furthermore, microcredit's promotion of carefully curated success stories attracted resources that might have gone to other antipoverty programs, and its inflated claims allowed the state to abdicate its role in providing services for the poor.[14]

For good reason, proponents of microcredit saw it as a tool for giving poor people the same assistance in expanding an enterprise that wealthier people routinely enjoy, and, also for good reason, detractors saw it as a trap that sent poor people into debt with unsustainable businesses and predatory collectors who shamed borrowers into repaying loans at the expense of their well-being. Economists who conduct randomized controlled experiments staked out the middle ground. At MIT, the Abdul Latif Jameel Poverty Action Lab, a highly regarded team with clout in mainstream development circles, concluded that "microcredit and other ways to help tiny businesses" could provide some benefits to those who had no options for income outside the informal economy, but "we are kidding ourselves if we think that they can pave the way for a mass exit from poverty." Another set of such studies also found a "lack of transformative effects on the average borrower" and only minimal evidence (in only one out of four studies) that microcredit increased "female decision making and/or independence within the household."[15] In the 2010s, an emerging scholarly consensus came to conclude that microcredit might sometimes help impoverished women, but it had not and would not end their poverty or empower them. And, indeed, it does seem strange that going into debt, through the equivalent of a credit card with a minuscule credit limit, would lead to general prosperity and gender equality.

Development fads come and go, but they rarely disappear. Microcredit is no longer the latest thing, but it remains big business today. In 2015, the World Bank estimated the microfinance industry "at $60–100 billion, with 200 million clients," and it noted, too, that "critics cite modest benefits associated with microcredit, overindebtedness, and a trend toward commercialization that is less focused on serving the poor." In the same fiscal year, USAID "invested $280 million in microenterprise activities in 35 countries." A majority—58 percent—of the borrowers were women. It also held "114 active microfinance guarantees" that could "leverage $755 million in private sector capital" to support microenterprise.[16] US philanthropists—Bill and Melinda Gates of Microsoft, Michael and Susan Dell of Dell Computers—contribute to microfinance programs, now dubbed "financial services for the poor" or "financial inclusion," and middle-class American donors help sustain US-based NGOs, such as FINCA and the online crowdfunder Kiva, with around 4.5 million borrowers between them. A recent FINCA brochure features smiling women of color, dressed in colorful clothes, holding the products they sell, along with endorsements from actress Natalie Portman and rock singer Bono. "You can help fight global poverty," it tells us, "one tiny loan at a time."[17]

———

In the 1970s, when development experts rejected the trickle-down economics of modernization, they could hardly have guessed that the war on global poverty would be fought "one tiny loan at a time." The boldest among them had asked for structural changes to remove the inequities in the global economy and proposed significant transfers of resources, perhaps through an international tax, from the world's wealthy to the world's poor. From South and North, they had called for state action and international collaboration to narrow the "widening gap" between the rich and poor nations, provide for basic needs, and eliminate global poverty. They had pushed for gender equality, sometimes simply as inclusion within existing development programs but sometimes as a serious rethinking of the gendered division of labor and the systemic features that subordinated women. In the United States and elsewhere, some of them had worked their way into government agencies and international institutions, and with at least some limited success, they had promoted policies that internationalized a war on poverty and a movement for gender equity. In the US government, they had codified their antipoverty aims in the "New Directions" mandate of the 1973 Foreign Assistance Act and their "women in development" goals in the same act's Percy amendment.

By the end of the 1970s the sense of possibility had shrunk, as conservative opposition grew and a global economic crisis left wealthier nations stagnant and poorer nations plummeting into debt. In the United States, the Carter administration, despite some initial promise, disappointed the antipoverty advocates, and the election of Ronald Reagan blocked the roads that had already narrowed. At the Cancún conference in 1981, the Reagan administration rejected any significant transfer of resources from North to South. The NIEO had lost whatever momentum it had in the mid-1970s, and the World Bank had turned to conditional loans that demanded fiscal austerity in the global South and thereby cut the life support to social provisions for the poor.

But if some routes closed, neither the war on global poverty nor the movement for gender equality came to a stop. Some leftist and liberal development advocates redirected their efforts through UN agencies and progressive think tanks, research institutes, NGOs, and commissions. Within the United States, some others adjusted to the times and retrofitted their programs to follow the turn to the private sector, small business, and "the magic of the marketplace."[18] In this rendering of development, microcredit could serve as an inspiration, with women in a central role as the deserving and entrepreneurial poor. The neoliberal ethos repudiated redistribution, but it could accommodate paler variants of the antipoverty and feminist movements. It reoriented them away from the state and toward the market. It rejected structural changes to the global economy and focused instead on expanding the market's inclusion, shrinking the role of the state, and changing the conduct of the poor.

The genealogy that runs from modernization to microcredit tracks an accretion of biopolicies that accompanied the war on global poverty. The preferred routes to improving a population and an economy expanded over time from producing more food and fewer children to incorporating women as income earners to recasting them as entrepreneurs whose prosperity and empowerment derived from borrowing and investing "one tiny loan at a time." Successive development programs reflected a broader ideological shift that moved from a male-breadwinner family model to the normalization of the household in which the mother served as the primary responsible earner. In the international arena, as in the United States, antipoverty advocates suspected that fathers—at least among the poor—would not take economic responsibility for their children. In the same years that mass incarceration of men devastated African American communities, microcredit programs sidelined poor men in the global South not as criminal but as selfish and unreliable. Poor women were now expected to combine unpaid care labor with income-earning businesses that might support their children, and impoverished men were increasingly written off.[19]

Today, two decades into the twenty-first century, the UN, the World Bank, USAID, and many others continue to call, as they should, for the end of global poverty and the empowerment of women. A new cohort of corporate philanthropists has joined them. The charity of corporations and their wealthy executives, channeled through foundations and NGOs, has partially supplanted the foreign aid of the second half of the twentieth century. To give just one well-known example, the shoe manufacturer Nike, under scrutiny for the exploitative labor practices of its contractors in Asia, attempted to cleanse its reputation with a new campaign of corporate social responsibility. In 2004, it established the Girl Effect, on "a single premise: that the most effective way to break the cycle of global poverty is to improve the situation of adolescent girls." In 2010, the Girl Effect spelled out its simplistic biopolitical wager with an advertiser's hype: "an educated girl will stay healthy, save money, build a business, empower her community, lift her country, and save the world." As the sociologist Sarah Babb has written, "we live in a world that has mostly come to accept market capitalism as the only viable option."[20] Lost along the way were serious proposals to redistribute wealth or change the rules that govern the global economy.

Over the past thirty years, and for a range of reasons, poverty has indeed declined. Most importantly perhaps, state-led economic growth, especially in China, has reduced by millions the number of people living below the World Bank's International Poverty

Line, currently set at living on less than $1.90 per day. Nonetheless, in the World Bank's latest estimate, 736 million people were still living in extreme poverty in 2015, including 41 percent of the population of sub-Saharan Africa.[21] The current UN development campaign, its Sustainable Development Goals, aims "to eradicate extreme poverty for all people everywhere" by the year 2030. The World Bank set a similar goal "of reducing extreme poverty to less than 3 percent of the world's population by 2030."[22] It all sounds strangely familiar. In the 1970s the World Bank and others had proposed to end "absolute poverty" by meeting basic needs by the year 2000.

At its worst, the history of development is a tale of technocratic hubris, coercion, repression, corruption, bungled projects, and self-interest, and even at its best, it seems, it is a story of inflated expectations, unintended consequences, and disappointing outcomes. We could easily dismiss it all in a round of condemnation. But the historian Frederick Cooper reminds us that critique is not enough. "Critiques," he writes, "do not bring piped water to people who lack it; they do not ease the burdens of women caught between rural patriarchies and urban exploitation; they do not distribute readily available antidotes to childhood diarrhoea and malaria in areas of high infant mortality."[23] And, on a more general level, they do not bring equity, justice, or an end to poverty. However tempting it is to toss the baby out with the bathwater, we would do well to hold on to the worthier aspirations.

Why limit the choice to a free market skewed toward the wealthy or the palliative measures of charity, corporate philanthropy, and self-interested foreign aid? In this day of deepening inequality and rampant xenophobia, it might seem naïve to imagine other options. But not so long ago, activists, experts, policy makers, and others, collaborating across the globe, set their sights higher. A number of "influencers," from Europe and the global South, charmed and cajoled Americans, including those who held political power, pushing and pulling them to consider new options. Today, a variety of activists across the globe carry on their legacy by proposing "alter-globalization" policies—to cancel the debt of poorer nations, provide universal basic income, close tax havens, promote fair trade, protect workers, regulate transnational corporations—that could redistribute wealth and power between nations and within them. For almost twenty years now, the World Social Forum, headquartered in Brazil, has provided an annual gathering for those who look for alternative policies. Among the many proposals, some have revived the call for an international tax. The organization Attac, for example, founded in 1999, promotes "global taxes to finance access to common goods." It asks for taxes on the profits of transnational corporations, carbon taxes on polluters, and taxes on "financial transactions" and "large private estates." And in his recent blockbuster book *Capital in the Twenty-First Century*, French economist Thomas Piketty calls for "a progressive annual tax on global wealth."[24]

In the study of history, there is always the question of what we choose to remember. We should, of course, remember the cautionary tales that remind us that a half-century of antipoverty projects have failed to end global poverty and that plans to empower women have failed to end their subordination. We should also remember that current calls for women's empowerment and an end to poverty are steeped in the legacies of neoliberal retrenchment. But we might also recall the push to transfer resources, the claims for gender equity, and the proposals to change those global economic structures that have kept some nations and millions of people poor. If we remember those audacious plans, we might imagine anew a just redistribution.

ACKNOWLEDGMENTS

I BEGAN THIS PROJECT a dozen years ago when I visited my sister, who was conducting research in Rwanda. We traveled together to Ethiopia, where the signs of foreign aid dotted the landscape. In Addis Ababa, we passed the offices of large NGOs, such as Save the Children and Doctors Without Borders, and smaller NGOs, including one for people with HIV/AIDS. In the countryside, we saw a water tank donated by a Scandinavian Lutheran church and the rusting remnants of a decades-old USAID water reclamation project, and we spotted USAID jeeps speeding across the rural stretch. Some of the signs—literal signs that advertised projects and often their donors—announced programs for women.

On a main road in Addis Ababa, the Former Women Fuelwood Carriers Association, an NGO, provides jobs weaving cloth and grinding grain to women who once carried firewood on their backs from the hills outside the capital. (Photo by author)

When I returned to Connecticut, I went to the USAID website and plugged the word "women" into its search engine. I landed at a "women in development" page, now replaced with other similar pages on "women's economic empowerment." Another page (also defunct) held links to dozens of "gender stories," sorted from A to Z, from Afghanistan to Zambia. Each link led to a short "success story" about US-funded projects targeted at women. A brief one-sentence history claimed, "USAID's commitment to the full inclusion of women dates back to 1973, when the United States Congress passed the 'Percy Amendment.'" That sentence served as the springboard for this book.

While I researched and wrote, I incurred a slew of debts. First thanks go to my sister Beth for joining me on the journey that piqued my historical interest, for accompanying me on a final research trip to Dhaka, and for all things sisterly before, after, and in between. Beth is an accomplished traveler and excellent company even when stranded in gridlocked traffic. Friends, acquaintances, and strangers shared sources, leads, citations, reading recommendations, and their own works in progress. Thanks to Paul Adler, Eileen Boris, Brenda Chalfin, Dorothy Sue Cobble, Wai Chee Dimock, David Engerman, Michael Franczak, Lily Geismer, Lucia Hulsether, Sergio Infante, Sam Klug, Lisa Levenstein, Kris Manjapra, Alan Mikhail, Durba Mitra, Samuel Moyn, Orlando Patterson, and Corinna Unger. Thanks, too, to those who invited me to give talks and participate on panels, and to those who asked questions afterwards that pushed me to think harder. And wholesale gratitude to those who read and commented on conference papers, draft chapters, or the manuscript in toto. They showed me how to make the book better, and I apologize now for not following all of their sound advice. Thank you, Dorothy Sue Cobble, Nick Cullather, David Engerman, Susan Ferber, Regina Kunzel, Priya Lal, Stephen Macekura, Katherine Marino, Samuel Moyn, Amy Offner, Jocelyn Olcott, Pat Swope, and Corinna Unger. You'll see your mark in these pages.

Friends, family, and colleagues kept me company, offered advice, and inspired me with their own impressive scholarship. At Yale, I benefited especially from conversations with Rohit De, Kate Dudley, David Engerman, Crystal Feimster, Joanne Freeman, Inderpal Grewal, Greta LaFleur, Naomi Lamoreaux, Katie Lofton, Mary Lui,

Alan Mikhail, Ali Miller, Sam Moyn, and Graeme Reid, and also from my brilliant graduate student advisees and the undergraduate students in my seminar, "The Problem of Global Poverty." Outside of Yale, Anne Boylan, Margot Canaday, George Chauncey, Dorothy Sue Cobble, Nancy Hewitt, Kathi Kern, Regina Kunzel, Joan Kobori and Elliot Meyerowitz, and the Swope-Kukla clan, among others, heard about a book in progress and politely refrained from asking, "haven't you finished it yet?"

Like other historians, I put in solitary hours researching in archives, in libraries, at home, and increasingly online. But nothing is more instructive than talking to people with long-time practical experience in the fields I study. Thank you to all who took the time to educate me, especially Martha (Marty) Chen and Orlando Patterson, who related their own histories of working with antipoverty programs. In Dhaka, I appreciated the welcoming staff at the Grameen Bank and the Yunus Centre. Nurjahan Begum graciously shared her memories of her early involvement with the Grameen project, and the charismatic Muhammad Yunus generously carved out a chunk of a day to respond gamely to every question I asked.

Many others eased the way from first glimmer to finished book. Librarians and archivists guided me to sources. Lucas Buresch, then at the Rockefeller Archives Center, and Sherrine M. Thompson at the World Bank Archives deserve special mention for their expert help. Yale University provided critical institutional support, and at the start of the project, so did the American Council for Learned Societies and the John Simon Guggenheim Memorial Foundation. The Radcliffe Institute for Advanced Study provided the perfect venue for a year of writing, with the added benefit of the camaraderie of my fellow fellows. And at the end of the process, Eric Crahan, Priya Nelson, Thalia Leaf, Maia Vaswani, Jenny Wolkowicki, and their team at Princeton University Press gave the good advice that shaped the manuscript into a book.

As I sit to write these acknowledgments, housebound at the peak of a global pandemic, the United Nations estimates that half a billion people might sink into poverty by the year's end. Another reminder, if we need one, of inequality in our current precarious day. For making my own precarious life better in all the important ways, thank you, Pat Swope.

Abbreviations Used in the Notes

ARCHIVAL REPOSITORIES

FFR	Ford Foundation Records, Rockefeller Archive Center, Sleepy Hollow, New York
GU	Special Collections, Georgetown University, Washington, DC
ILO	International Labour Organization Archives, Geneva, Switzerland
JCPL	Presidential Papers of Jimmy Carter, Jimmy Carter Presidential Library, Atlanta, GA
MHS	Minnesota Historical Society, Saint Paul
NARA	National Archives and Record Administration, College Park, MD
NYPL	New York Public Library, Manuscripts and Archives Division
PU	Seeley G. Mudd Manuscript Library, Princeton University
SL	Schlesinger Library, Radcliffe Institute for Advanced Study, Harvard University
UM	Hornbake Library, Special Collections, University of Maryland
UMSL	Thomas Jefferson Library, University of Missouri, St. Louis
WBGA	World Bank Group Archives, Washington, DC

ARCHIVAL COLLECTIONS

AFP	Arvonne S. Fraser Papers, MHS
AGC	Adrienne Germain Correspondence Files, USAIP/Rural Poverty and Resources, FFR
AGO	Adrienne Germain Office Files, International Division, FFR
BWP	Barbara Ward Papers, GU
CARE	CARE Records, NYPL
CBCA	Clara M. Beyer Collection, Additional Papers, 1959–79, SL
DFP	Donald M. Fraser Papers, MHS
DPF	Asia/BA Dhaka Program Staff Files, FFR
EBC	Elinor Barber Correspondence Files, FFR
EBO	Elinor Barber Office Files, International Division, FFR
ESF	Ernest Stern Files, WB IBRD/IDA 43–09, WBGA
FG	Ford Foundation Grants, FFR
FR	Ford Foundation Reports, FFR
MHP	Margaret Hickey Papers, Western Historical Manuscript Collection—St. Louis, UMSL
MLC	Mildred R. Leet Collection, SL

OCL   Office of Congressional Liaison, JCPL
OEF   Overseas Education Fund Papers, UM
PBF   Special Assistant to the President—Peter Bourne's Files, JCPL
PCWH   Presidential Commission on World Hunger, JCPL
PC/WID   Records of the Peace Corps, 1961–2000, RG 490, Women in Development Program Files, NARA
POML   Press Office—Media Liaison Office, JCPL
SEF   Domestic Policy Staff—Stu Eizenstadt's Files, JCPL
USAID/WID   Records of the United States Agency for International Development, RG 286, USAID headquarters, Bureau for Policy and Program Coordination, Office of Women in Development, NARA
WCP   William D. Clark Papers, WB IBRD/IDA 80, WBGA
WEP   World Employment Program Files, ILO
WFGP   Women in the Federal Government Project, SL
WHP   Wilma Scott Heide Papers, SL
WIDC   Women in Development Collection, UM
WWB   Women's World Banking Records, MC 198, Public Policy Papers, PU

ONLINE COLLECTIONS

APP   American Presidency Project, www.presidency.ucsb.edu
DEC   United States Agency for International Development, Development Experience Clearinghouse, https://dec.usaid.gov/dec/home/Default.aspx
FRUS   *Foreign Relations of the United States*, https://history.state.gov/historicaldocuments/ebooks
WBOHP   World Bank Group Archives Oral History Program, https://oralhistory.worldbank.org/

Introduction

1. J. R. Goddard, "Michael Harrington: Peripatetic Ideologist Views the Unaffluent American," *Village Voice*, March 22, 1962, quoted in Maurice Isserman, *The Other American: The Life of Michael Harrington* (New York: PublicAffairs, 2000), 175. On the number of copies sold, see also Isserman, "Michael Harrington: Warrior on Poverty," *New York Times*, June 19, 2009.

2. Michael Harrington, *The Vast Majority: A Journey to the World's Poor* (New York: Simon and Schuster, 1977), 13, 27.

3. Gunnar Myrdal, *The Challenge of World Poverty: A World Anti-Poverty Program in Outline* (New York: Random House, 1970); Barbara Ward, J. D. Runnalls, and Lenore D'Anjou, *The Widening Gap: Development in the 1970's* (New York: Columbia University Press, 1971). Pope Paul VI used the phrase the "widening gap" in his 1967 encyclical on development: "Populorum Progressio: Encyclical of Pope Paul VI on the Development of Peoples," Libreria Editrice Vaticana, March 26,

1967, http://w2.vatican.va/content/paul-vi/en/encyclicals/documents/hf_p-vi_enc
_26031967_populorum.html. See also Julius K. Nyerere, speech at Howard University, August 1977, reprinted in "Destroying World Poverty: President Nyerere Speaks," *Southern Africa* 10, no. 7 (September 1977): 7.

4. On conservative aspersions on women on welfare in the 1970s, see, for example, Josh Levin, *The Queen: The Forgotten Life behind an American Myth* (New York: Little, Brown, 2019).

5. As many have noted, programs for international development began well before economists created the subfield of development economics. Colonial officials and missionaries, for example, engaged in various attempts to change economic conditions in Asia, Africa, the Caribbean, and Latin America. The literature on development is extensive. For now-classic critical accounts of the history of international development, see Arturo Escobar, *Encountering Development: The Making and Unmaking of the Third World* (Princeton, NJ: Princeton University Press, 1995); Gilbert Rist, *The History of Development: From Western Origins to Global Faith* (London: Zed Books, 1997); Timothy Mitchell, *Rule of Experts: Egypt, Techno-Politics, Modernity* (Berkeley: University of California Press, 2002). For recent overviews, see Stephen J. Macekura and Erez Manela, eds., *The Development Century: A Global History* (Cambridge: Cambridge University Press, 2018); Corinna R. Unger, *International Development: A Postwar History* (London: Bloomsbury Academic, 2018); Sara Lorenzini, *Global Development: A Cold War History* (Princeton, NJ: Princeton University Press, 2019). For recent historiographic assessment, see Joseph Morgan Hodge, "Writing the History of Development (Part 1: The First Wave)," *Humanity: An International Journal of Human Rights, Humanitarianism, and Development* 6, no. 3 (Winter 2015): 429–63, and "Writing the History of Development (Part 2: Longer, Deeper, Wider)," *Humanity: An International Journal of Human Rights, Humanitarianism, and Development* 7, no. 1 (Spring 2016): 125–74. On early development, see, for example, Amanda Kay McVety, "Wealth and Nations: The Origins of International Development Assistance," in Macekura and Manela, *Development Century*, 21–39.

6. On US modernization programs, see, for example, Stephen G. Rabe, *The Most Dangerous Area in the World: John F. Kennedy Confronts Communist Revolution in Latin America* (Chapel Hill: University of North Carolina Press, 1999); Michael E. Latham, *Modernization as Ideology: American Social Science and "Nation Building" in the Kennedy Era* (Chapel Hill: University of North Carolina Press, 2000); David C. Engerman, Nils Gilman, Mark H. Haefele, and Michael E. Latham, *Staging Growth: Modernization, Development, and the Global Cold War* (Amherst: University of Massachusetts Press, 2003); Nils Gilman, *Mandarins of the Future: Modernization Theory in Cold War America* (Baltimore, MD: Johns Hopkins Press, 2003); Bradley R. Simpson, *Economists with Guns: Authoritarian Development and U.S.-Indonesian Relations, 1960–1968* (Stanford, CA: Stanford University Press, 2008); Nick Cullather, *The Hungry World: America's Cold War Battle against Poverty in Asia* (Cambridge, MA: Harvard University Press, 2010); David Ekbladh, *The Great American Mission: Modernization and the Construction of an American World Order* (Princeton, NJ: Princeton University Press, 2010); Michael E. Latham, *The Right Kind of Revolution: Modernization, Development, and U.S. Foreign Policy from the Cold War to the Present*

(Ithaca, NY: Cornell University Press, 2011); Amanda Kay McVety, *Enlightened Aid: U.S. Development as Foreign Policy in Ethiopia* (New York: Oxford University Press, 2012); Thomas C. Field Jr., *From Development to Dictatorship: Bolivia and the Alliance for Progress in the Kennedy Era* (Ithaca, NY: Cornell University Press, 2014); Daniel Immerwahr, *Thinking Small: The United States and the Lure of Community Development* (Cambridge, MA: Harvard University Press, 2015); David C. Engerman, *The Price of Aid: The Economic Cold War in India* (Cambridge, MA: Harvard University Press, 2018); Amy C. Offner, *Sorting Out the Mixed Economy: The Rise and Fall of Welfare and Developmental States in the Americas* (Princeton, NJ: Princeton University Press, 2019).

7. Tom Wolfe, "The 'Me' Decade and the Third Great Awakening," *New York Magazine*, August 23, 1976.

8. See, for example, Bruce J. Shulman and Julian E. Zelizer, eds., *Rightward Bound: Making America Conservative in the 1970s* (Cambridge, MA: Harvard University Press, 2008); Laura Kalman, *Right Star Rising: A New Politics, 1974–1980* (New York: W. W. Norton, 2010). For a useful recent historiographic essay on the 1970s, see Suleiman Osman, "Glocal America: The Politics of Scale in the 1970s," in *Shaped by the State: Toward a New Political History of the Twentieth Century*, ed. Brent Cebul, Lily Geismer, and Mason B. Williams (Chicago: University of Chicago Press, 2019), 241–60. Osman sees new global and local political identities rising in the 1970s, with "antistatist and anticorporate impulses on both the left and right" (244).

9. See, for example, Beth Bailey and David Farber, eds., *America in the Seventies* (Lawrence: University Press of Kansas, 2004); Stephen Tuck, "Introduction: Reconsidering the 1970s—the 1960s to a Disco Beat," *Journal of Contemporary History* 43, no. 4 (October 2008): 617–20, as well as the other articles on the 1970s in this issue of the journal; Dan Berger, ed., *The Hidden 1970s: Histories of Radicalism* (New Brunswick, NJ: Rutgers University Press, 2010); Thomas Borstelmann, *The 1970s: A New Global History from Civil Rights to Economic Inequality* (Princeton, NJ: Princeton University Press, 2012), chap. 2; Kirsten Swinth, *Feminism's Forgotten Fight: The Unfinished Struggle for Work and Family* (Cambridge, MA: Harvard University Press, 2018).

10. An Act to Amend the Foreign Assistance Act of 1961, Pub. L. No. 93-189, 22 U.S.C. § 2151 (1973).

11. A few US historians have begun to study economic development in the 1970s. See, for example, Stephen J. Macekura, *Of Limits and Growth: The Rise of Global Sustainable Development in the Twentieth Century* (Cambridge: Cambridge University Press, 2015); Patrick Allan Sharma, *Robert McNamara's Other War: The World Bank and International Development* (Philadelphia: University of Pennsylvania Press, 2017); the articles in Nils Gilman, ed., "Toward a History of the New International Economic Order," special issue, *Humanity: An International Journal of Human Rights, Humanitarianism, and Development* 6, no. 1 (Spring 2015); Michael Franczak, "Human Rights and Basic Needs: Jimmy Carter's North-South Dialogue, 1977–81," *Cold War History* 19, no. 4 (2018): 447–64; Paul Adler, "Creating 'The NGO International': The Rise of Advocacy for Alternative Development, 1974-1994,"

in Macekura and Manela, *Development Century*, 305–25. For brief overviews, see Latham, *Right Kind of Revolution*, chap. 6; Ekbladh, *Great American Mission*, chap. 7.

12. For a brief overview that takes this approach, see Frederick Cooper, "Writing the History of Development," *Journal of Modern European History* 8, no. 1 (2010): 5–23. See also Christy Thornton, "'Mexico Has the Theories': Latin America and the Interwar Origins of Development," in Macekura and Manela, *Development Century*, 263–82.

13. Several historians have pointed to the mutual influence of domestic policy and foreign aid. David Ekbladh, for example, outlines the influence of the Tennessee Valley Authority on later modernization programs. Gabriel Rosenberg tracks the career of the US-government-sponsored 4-H Club in overseas rural development. Sheyda Jahanbani and Daniel Immerwahr show how the War on Poverty borrowed from the Peace Corps and community development programs. Amy Offner examines how US New Dealers shaped development in Colombia and how US officials and businessmen brought foreign development programs back to the United States during and after the War on Poverty. Ekbladh, *Great American Mission*; Gabriel N. Rosenberg, *The 4-H Harvest: Sexuality and the State in Rural America* (Philadelphia: University of Pennsylvania Press, 2015), chap. 6; Sheyda Jahanbani, "One Global War on Poverty: The Johnson Administration Fights Poverty at Home and Abroad," in *Beyond the Cold War: Lyndon Johnson and the New Global Challenges of the 1960s*, ed. Francis J. Gavin and Mark Atwood Lawrence (New York: Oxford University Press, 2014), 97–117; Immerwahr, *Thinking Small*, chap. 5; Offner, *Sorting Out the Mixed Economy*. For the mutual imbrication of foreign and domestic community development policy, see also Alyosha Goldstein, *Poverty in Common: The Politics of Community Action during the American Century* (Durham, NC: Duke University Press, 2012).

14. As the historian Jeremy Adelman has written recently, "there is growing evidence that Washington was importing development ideas, taking cues from the rest of the world." Jeremy Adelman, "Epilogue: Development Dreams," in Macekura and Manela, *Development Century*, 332. On importing ideas and programs more generally, see, for example, Daniel T. Rodgers, *Atlantic Crossings: Social Politics in a Progressive Age* (Cambridge, MA: Harvard University Press, 2000); Mark Philip Bradley, *The World Reimagined: Americans and Human Rights in the Twentieth Century* (New York: Cambridge University Press, 2016); Andrew Preston and Doug Rossinow, eds., *Outside In: The Transnational Circuitry of U.S. History* (New York: Oxford University Press, 2017).

15. Thanks to Corinna Unger for suggesting in an email that "the underlying pluralism of development thought" became "more visible" in the 1970s and 1980s.

16. Dag Hammarskjöld Foundation, *What Now? Another Development: The 1975 Dag Hammarskjöld Report* (Uppsala: Dag Hammarskjöld Foundation, 1975).

17. I refer here to twentieth-century US conceptions of race. Many Latin Americans, for example, had different versions of racial classification and did not see much of their region's populace as people of color. On development as "determinedly colourblind," see Sarah White, "Thinking Race, Thinking Development," *Third World Quarterly* 23, no. 3 (2002): 407–19, quote 407.

18. On rural productivity, see, for example, Cullather, *Hungry World*; Tore C. Olsson, *Agrarian Crossings: Reformers and the Remaking of the US and Mexican Countryside* (Princeton, NJ: Princeton University Press, 2017); Offner, *Sorting Out the Mixed Economy*. On women's labor, see, for example, Eileen Boris, *Making the Woman Worker: Precarious Labor and the Fight for Global Standards, 1919–2019* (New York: Oxford University Press, 2019), chap. 3; Dorothy Sue Cobble, *For the Many: A Global History of American Feminism* (Princeton, NJ: Princeton University Press, forthcoming), chap. 11. On credit, see, for example, Rosenberg, *4-H Harvest*, 199–203.

Chapter 1

1. John F. Kennedy, "Inaugural Address," January 20, 1961, APP.

2. UN General Assembly, Resolution 1710 (XVI), United Nations Development Decade: A Programme for International Economic Co-operation (I), A/RES/1710(XVI) (Dec. 19, 1961), https://digitallibrary.un.org/record/204609?ln=en; George D. Woods, "The Development Decade in the Balance," *Foreign Affairs* 44, no. 2 (January 1966): 206. See also "Decade of Disappointment," *New York Times*, November 15, 1967.

3. See Michael E. Latham, *Modernization as Ideology: American Social Science and "Nation Building" in the Kennedy Era* (Chapel Hill: University of North Carolina Press, 2000), and *The Right Kind of Revolution: Modernization, Development, and U.S. Foreign Policy from the Cold War to the Present* (Ithaca, NY: Cornell University Press, 2011); Bradley R. Simpson, *Economists with Guns: Authoritarian Development and U.S.-Indonesian Relations, 1960–1968* (Stanford, CA: Stanford University Press, 2008); Nick Cullather, *The Hungry World: America's Cold War Battle against Poverty in Asia* (Cambridge, MA: Harvard University Press, 2010); David Ekbladh, *The Great American Mission: Modernization and the Construction of an American World Order* (Princeton, NJ: Princeton University Press, 2010); Thomas C. Field Jr., *From Development to Dictatorship: Bolivia and the Alliance for Progress in the Kennedy Era* (Ithaca, NY: Cornell University Press, 2014); Daniel Immerwahr, *Thinking Small: The United States and the Lure of Community Development* (Cambridge, MA: Harvard University Press, 2015); David C. Engerman, *The Price of Aid: The Economic Cold War in India* (Cambridge, MA: Harvard University Press, 2018); Amy C. Offner, *Sorting Out the Mixed Economy: The Rise and Fall of Welfare and Developmental States in the Americas* (Princeton, NJ: Princeton University Press, 2019).

4. On the intellectual arguments undermining modernization, see especially Nils Gilman, *Mandarins of the Future: Modernization Theory in Cold War America* (Baltimore, MD: Johns Hopkins Press, 2003), chap. 6; Latham, *Right Kind of Revolution*, chap. 6.

5. Walter Trohan, "Report from Washington: Johnson's Goal to End World Poverty," *Chicago Tribune*, September 3, 1966; "Grand Assize for Aid?" *Economist*, November 4, 1967, 491; Robert D'A. Shaw, "A New Look in Foreign Aid," *New York Times*, January 30, 1972; "U.S. Official Development Assistance Flows," ca. 1975, box 149.C.12.4F, folder: Notebook 1, DFP. For the constant dollar figures on foreign

aid over time, see also Foreign Aid Explorer, USAID, https://explorer.usaid.gov/aid
-trends.html.

6. Charles S. Maier, "The Politics of Productivity: Foundations of American International Economic Policy after World War II," *International Organization* 31, no. 4 (Autumn 1977): 607–33.

7. Patricia Blair, interview with William Clark, October 4, 1983, p. 3, WBOHP; Commission on International Development, *Partners in Development: Report of the Commission on International Development* (New York: Praeger, 1969), vii.

8. Commission on International Development, *Partners in Development*, 3, 4, 5.

9. See, for example, Barbara Ward, "To Widen the Base of World Wealth," *New York Times*, March 14, 1954.

10. John F. Kennedy, "Address and Question and Answer Period at the Economic Club of New York," December 14, 1962, APP; Commission on International Development, *Partners in Development*, 9.

11. Commission on International Development, *Partners in Development*, 9, 19.

12. Didier Fassin, *Humanitarian Reason: A Moral History of the Present* (Berkeley: University of California Press, 2012), 4. Fassin uses the phrase "humanitarian government" to refer to "the deployment of moral sentiments in contemporary politics" (1).

13. Commission on International Development, *Partners in Development*, 7, 8, 9, 10.

14. David R. Francis, "Foreign Aid Because It's Right," *Christian Science Monitor*, October 2, 1969; Edward Cowan, "Pearson Views Foreign-Aid Report as a 'Sermon,'" *New York Times*, October 2, 1969; Pearson quoted in Kevin Brushett, "Partners in Development? Robert McNamara, Lester Pearson, and the Commission on International Development, 1967–1973," *Diplomacy and Statecraft* 26, no. 1 (2015): 90.

15. "The Pearson Report: The End of Aid," *Washington Post*, October 5, 1969; Carl K. Eicher, review of *Partners in Development: Report of the Commission on International Development* by Lester B. Pearson, *American Journal of Agricultural Economics* 52, no. 4 (November 1970): 622; Thomas Balogh, "The Challenge of World Poverty," *New York Times*, July 19, 1970; [Charles Elliott], *Partnership or Privilege? An Ecumenical Reaction to the Second Development Decade* (Geneva: Committee on Society, Development and Peace, n.d., ca. 1970), 31, 33.

16. Despite her titles—Lady Jackson, Baroness Jackson—Ward was not an aristocrat by birth: in 1956, her husband (from whom she separated in the early 1970s) was knighted, and she was made a life peer in 1976 with the title Baroness Jackson of Lodsworth. On Ward's life, see especially Jean Gartlan, *Barbara Ward: Her Life and Letters* (London: Continuum, 2010); Michael J. Walsh, "Ward [Married Name Jackson], Barbara Mary, Baroness Jackson of Lodsworth (1914–1981), Journalist and Economist," *Oxford Dictionary of National Biography*, September 23, 2004, www.oxforddnb.com/view/10.1093/ref:odnb/9780198614128.001.0001/odnb -9780198614128-e-31801.

17. Barbara Ward, *The Rich Nations and the Poor Nations* (New York: W. W. Norton, 1962), 144.

18. "Lyndon's Other Bible," *Time*, September 3, 1965, 21; Lady Bird Johnson quoted in Gartlan, *Barbara Ward*, 120.

19. See Robert W. Oliver, *George Woods and the World Bank* (Boulder, CO: Lynne Rienner, 1995), 241–42; Blair, interview with William Clark, 13.

20. M. A. Farber, "One Department at Columbia Rejected Miss Ward for Post," *New York Times*, December 17, 1967.

21. Gartlan, *Barbara Ward*, 151, 158, 159.

22. The conference participants are listed in the back of the conference report: See Barbara Ward, J. D. Runnalls, and Lenore D'Anjou, *The Widening Gap: Development in the 1970's* (New York: Columbia University Press, 1971), 347–54. The list includes 121 participants in Williamsburg and an additional 76 in New York City. The *Washington Post* report gives higher figures (137 attendees from 39 nations in Williamsburg and another 100 in New York): Bernard D. Nossiter, "McNamara Hits Foreign Aid Cuts," *Washington Post*, February 21, 1970.

23. Judith Hart, "We Are Unlikely to Be Moved," *Guardian*, December 30, 1971.

24. Barbara Ward, J. D. Runnalls, and Lenore D'Anjou, "The Columbia Declaration," in Ward, Runnalls, and D'Anjou, *Widening Gap*, 11, 12, 13. The appendix of *The Widening Gap*, pp. 347–54, indicates which of the conference participants signed the declaration. Of the 197 listed participants, 101 signed. Based on their listed affiliations and on Internet searches, at least 46 of the conference participants came from the global South; 31 of the 46 signed the declaration.

25. Joan Nelson (conference participant) quoted in Devesh Kapur, John P. Lewis, and Richard Webb, eds., *The World Bank: Its First Half Century*, vol. 1, *History* (Washington, DC: Brookings Institution, 1997), 221n18; Blair, interview with William Clark, 13; W. W. Rostow, *Eisenhower, Kennedy, and Foreign Aid* (Austin: University of Texas Press, 1985), 180.

26. Bernard D. Nossiter, "Experts View Rich-Poor Gap Dismally," *Washington Post*, February 23, 1970.

27. Samir Amin, "Development and Structural Change: African Experience," in Ward, Runnalls, and D'Anjou, *Widening Gap*, 331.

28. Commission on International Development, *Partners in Development*, 3.

29. Teresa Hayter, *Aid as Imperialism* (Harmondsworth, UK: Penguin Books, 1971), 9. On the origins of dependency theory, see Joseph L. Love, "The Origins of Dependency Analysis," *Journal of Latin American Studies* 22, no. 1 (February 1990): 143–68. For classic and influential statements of dependency theory, see Andre Gunder Frank, "The Development of Underdevelopment," *Monthly Review* 18, no. 4 (September 1966): 17–31; Fernando Henrique Cardoso and Enzo Faletto, *Dependency and Development in Latin America* (Berkeley: University of California Press, 1976 [expanded version of 1971 Spanish-language text]).

30. Harry Magdoff, *The Age of Imperialism: The Economics of U.S. Foreign Policy* (New York: Monthly Review Press, 1969), 139, 167. On copies sold, see Douglas Martin, "Harry Magdoff, Economist, Dies at 92," *New York Times*, January 9, 2006.

31. "'Imperialist' Jibe from Youth Rejected at Development Parley," *Christian Science Monitor*, March 3, 1970; A. D. Horne, "Aid at Crossroads: A Lively Encounter," *Washington Post*, March 10, 1970.

32. Africa Research Group, *International Dependency in the 1970's: How America Underdevelops the World* (Cambridge, MA: Africa Research Group, 1970).

33. Samuel P. Huntington, "Foreign Aid for What and for Whom," *Foreign Policy* 1 (Winter 1970–71): 188, 189. For more on Huntington's views, see Gilman, *Mandarins of the Future*, 228–34.

34. See, for example, 118 Cong. Rec. 31,123–24, and 32,327–29 (1972). In an article in the conservative *National Review*, James Burnham called Bauer "perhaps the foremost authority" in the field of foreign aid: James Burnham, "The Domestic Aid Program," *National Review*, December 3, 1971, 1344.

35. Peter T. Bauer, "The Case against Foreign Aid," *Wall Street Journal*, October 3, 1972.

36. Peter T. Bauer, *Dissent on Development: Studies and Debates on Development Economics* (London: Weidenfeld and Nicolson, 1971), 326.

37. Shaw, "New Look in Foreign Aid."

38. Fred L. Zimmerman, "Opposition on Cambodia May Delay Bills to Lift U.S. Funds to International Units," *Wall Street Journal*, May 7, 1970; James M. Naughton, "Proposal for Reform Likely to Gain," *New York Times*, October 31, 1971.

39. Bergsten paraphrased in document 129, *FRUS, 1969–1976*, vol. 4, *Foreign Assistance, International Development, Trade Policies, 1969–1972*.

40. "U.S. Officials Charged with Lax Supervision of Peruvian Highway Project," *Wall Street Journal*, December 27, 1971; Jack Anderson, "Millions Wasted in Viet Pacification," *Washington Post*, January 22, 1972.

41. Arthur Ellis, "Steichen Focuses Lens on Poverty," *Washington Post*, April 11, 1964; "Graham Asks Fight on World Poverty," *New York Times*, May 25, 1964; "Aiding Poor Urged," *Hartford Courant*, November 12, 1964; Robert C. Doty, "Pope Paul Donates His Jeweled Tiara to Poor of the World," *New York Times*, November 14, 1964; Martin Luther King Jr., Nobel Lecture, December 11, 1964, NobelPrize.org, Nobel Media AB, https://www.nobelprize.org/prizes/peace/1964 /king/lecture.

42. Foundational document quoted in Gartlan, *Barbara Ward*, 132; Norris quoted in "Pope Will Preside over Council," *Washington Post*, November 6, 1964. On the establishment of the secretariat, see Gartlan, *Barbara Ward*, chap. 7; "Vatican Joining War on Poverty," *Sun* (Baltimore, MD), May 10, 1966.

43. Paul VI, "Populorum Progressio, Encyclical of Pope Paul VI on the Development of Peoples," Libreria Editrice Vaticana, March 26, 1967, www.vatican.va /content/paul-vi/en/encyclicals/documents/hf_p-vi_enc_26031967_populorum.html; William R. MacKaye, "Pope Bids Rich Nations Attack World Poverty," *Washington Post*, March 29, 1967; "A Blessing for Secular Error," *Wall Street Journal*, March 30, 1967. Pope Paul VI is perhaps better known for his conservative stance on birth control, which disappointed liberal Catholics.

44. Commission on International Development, *Partners in Development*, 144. Barbara Ward had suggested the 1 percent figure in 1954: Barbara Ward, *Faith and Freedom* (New York: W. W. Norton, 1954), 250.

45. World Council of Churches, *World Conference on Church and Society: Christians in the Technical and Social Revolutions of Our Time* (Geneva: World Council of

Churches, 1967), 92; World Council of Churches, *The Uppsala Report 1968: Official Report of the Fourth Assembly of the World Council of Churches, Uppsala July 4–20, 1968* (Geneva: World Council of Churches, 1968), 46, 47, 48, 51, 129.

46. On SODEPAX, see especially George H. Dunne, *King's Pawn: The Memoirs of George H. Dunne, S. J.* (Chicago: Loyola University Press, 1990), 309–80; Hella Pick, "Call for New Look at World Poverty," *Guardian*, October 20, 1970. For the SODEPAX critique of foreign aid (including the Pearson report), see [Elliott], *Partnership or Privilege?*

47. [Elliott], *Partnership or Privilege?* 33.

48. Gustavo Gutiérrez Merino, "The Meaning of Development: Notes on a Theology of Liberation," in *In Search of a Theology of Development: Papers from a Consultation on Theology and Development*, by Consultation on Theology and Development (Cartigny, Switzerland) (Geneva: Ecumenical Centre, Publications Department, 1970), 120, 151. Gutiérrez had presented a version of the paper a year earlier at a conference in Peru; he presented a revised (and subsequently published) version at the SODEPAX conference. The English-language version most commonly read today is a different translation, circulated under the title "Notes for a Theology of Liberation."

49. Committee on Society, Development and Peace, *The Challenge of Development: A Sequel to the Beirut Conference of April 21–27, 1968, Montreal, Canada, May 9–12, 1969* (Geneva: Committee on Society, Development and Peace, 1969), 23; Hugh O'Shaughnessy, "Vatican Conservatives Abort Plan to Tackle World Poverty," *Washington Post*, April 22, 1972. On SODEPAX's troubles with the Vatican, see also Dunne, *King's Pawn*.

50. David E. Bell to McGeorge Bundy, "Grantee: World Council of Churches," June 1, 1971, in FG 69–157, reel 1945. On the budget cut, see O'Shaughnessy, "Vatican Conservatives Abort Plan."

51. Gerard Van Bilzen, *The Development of Aid* (Newcastle upon Tyne, UK: Cambridge Scholars, 2015), 335; Ward quoted in Raymond Fletcher, "Poverty War," *Guardian*, October 21, 1968; "Students Give Aid," *Atlanta Constitution*, March 30, 1969; John Budd, "The Internationalists," *Guardian*, October 29, 1974. On British NGOs, see also Matthew Hilton, "International Aid and Development NGOs in Britain and Human Rights since 1945," *Humanity: An International Journal of Human Rights, Humanitarianism, and Development* 3, no. 3 (2012): 449–72; on the Haslemere Group, see also Kevin O'Sullivan, "Feed the World or Fight for Justice (or Both)?" *Humanity Journal* blog, April 30, 2015, http://humanityjournal.org/blog/feed-the -world-or-fight-for-justice-or-both.

52. On Myrdal's early interest in international welfare, see Samuel Moyn, "Welfare World," *Humanity: An International Journal of Human Rights, Humanitarianism, and Development* 8, no. 1 (Spring 2017): 175–83; Samuel Moyn, *Not Enough: Human Rights in an Unequal World* (Cambridge, MA: Harvard University Press, 2018), 104–9; Isaac Nakhimovsky, "An International Dilemma: The Postwar Utopianism of Gunnar Myrdal's *Beyond the Welfare State*," *Humanity: An International Journal of Human Rights, Humanitarianism, and Development* 8, no. 1 (Spring 2017): 185–94; Simon Reid-Henry, "From Welfare World to Global Poverty," *Humanity: An*

International Journal of Human Rights, Humanitarianism, and Development n8, no. 1 (Spring 2017): 207–26.

53. Gunnar Myrdal, *The Challenge of World Poverty: A World Anti-Poverty Program in Outline* (New York: Random House, 1970), xi, xii, xiii.

54. Myrdal, 362, 363, 368; Balogh, "Challenge of World Poverty."

55. "60,000 May Join Hunger Walks," *Los Angeles Times*, February 25, 1973; Robert D. McFadden, "Thousands Walk in Poverty Fight, *New York Times*, May 9, 1971. Full disclosure: if my memory serves me correctly, I participated in one such walk when I was in high school. On the Food and Agriculture Organization's Freedom from Hunger campaign in Europe, see Kevin O'Sullivan, "A 'Global Nervous System': The Rise and Rise of European Humanitarian NGOs, 1945–1985," in *International Organizations and Development, 1945–1990*, ed. Marc Frey, Sönke Kunkel, and Corinna R. Unger (New York: Palgrave Macmillan, 2014), 202–4.

56. David R. Francis, "Youths Call for Antipoverty Fight," *Christian Science Monitor*, November 16, 1970. On the walks in Canada, see Tamara Myers, "Local Action and Global Imagining: Youth, International Development, and the Walkathon Phenomenon in Sixties' and Seventies' Canada," *Diplomatic History* 38, no. 2 (April 2014): 282–93.

57. Richard Jolly, "The Aid Relationship: Reflections on the Pearson Report," in Ward, Runnalls, and D'Anjou, *Widening Gap*, 292; Dudley Seers, "What Are We Trying to Measure?" *Journal of Development Studies* 8, no. 3 (April 1972): 24. Seers wrote an earlier version of this essay under the title "The Meaning of Development." He presented it first as a talk at the Society for International Development meeting in November 1969.

58. On modernization as global and transnational, see David C. Engerman and Corinna R. Unger, "Introduction: Towards a Global History of Modernization," *Diplomatic History* 33, no. 3 (June 2009): 375–85, and the other articles in the same issue of *Diplomatic History*. See also Corinna R. Unger, *International Development: A Postwar History* (London: Bloomsbury Academic, 2018); Sara Lorenzini, *Global Development: A Cold War History* (Princeton, NJ: Princeton University Press, 2019).

59. Seers referred generically, for example, to "various poverty lines in India, where there has been much work on this question": Seers, "What Are We Trying to Measure?" 36.

60. Dharam Ghai, "The World Employment Programme at ILO" (excerpts from Dharam Ghai, "Building Knowledge Organizations: Achieving Excellence," unpublished MS, 1999) International Labor Organization, https://www.ilo.org/wcmsp5/groups/public/---dgreports/---inst/documents/genericdocument/wcms_193047.pdf. On the Institute of Development Studies at the University of Sussex and its involvement with the WEP, see, for example, Richard Jolly, "A Short History of IDS: A Personal Reflection," IDS Discussion Paper 388, Institute of Development Studies, January 28, 2008, 22–25, https://www.ids.ac.uk/publications/a-short-history-of-ids-a-personal-reflection/.

61. International Labour Office, *Towards Full Employment: A Programme for Colombia, Prepared by an Inter-Agency Team Organised by the International Labour*

Office (Geneva: International Labour Office, 1970), 14; Director General to ILO Governing Body, November 1974, document GB 194/2/12, WEP file 1001-0:1.

62. UN Department of Economic and Social Affairs, *Attack on Mass Poverty and Unemployment: Views and Recommendations of the Committee for Development Planning* (New York: UN, 1972), 8; "The Foundation and the Less Developed Countries: The Decade of the Seventies," March 1972, pp. 2, 4, FR 003307, record group FA739, series: Catalogued Reports, box 147, folder 003307.

63. Quoted in Vernon W. Ruttan, *United States Development Assistance Policy: The Domestic Politics of Foreign Economic Aid* (Baltimore, MD: Johns Hopkins University Press, 1996), 107.

64. Albert Fishlow, "Brazilian Size Distribution of Income," *American Economic Review* 62, no. 2 (March 1972): 402; Irma Adelson and Cynthia Taft Morris, *Economic Growth and Social Equity in Developing Countries* (Stanford, CA: Stanford University Press, 1973), 189.

65. 15 members of House Foreign Relations Committee to President Nixon, April 11, 1973, box 149.G.13.8F, folder: Foreign Aid 1973 (1), DFP. On Barbara Ward's participation, see Committee on Foreign Affairs, "Foreign Aid Reform Plan: An Overview," July 1973, box 149.G.13.8F, folder: Foreign Aid 1973 (1), DFP. On the 1973 "New Directions" legislation, see especially Rolf H. Sartorius and Vernon W. Ruttan, "The Sources of the Basic Human Needs Mandate," *Journal of Developing Areas* 23, no. 3 (April 1989): 331–62; Congressional Research Service, "The New Directions Mandate and the Agency for International Development," in *AID's Administrative and Management Problems in Providing Foreign Economic Assistance: Hearing before a Subcommittee of the Committee on Government Operations, House of Representatives*, 97th Cong. 112–59 (1981). On Fraser's liberal approach to foreign affairs (and especially human rights), see Barbara J. Keys, *Reclaiming American Virtue: The Human Rights Revolution of the 1970s* (Cambridge, MA: Harvard University Press, 2014), esp. chaps. 4, 6, and 7.

66. "Overhauling Aid," *New York Times*, June 5, 1973; "House Panel Stressed Aid to Poorest Nations," *Washington Post*, May 31, 1973. The number of cosponsors is listed as 26 in House Comm. on Foreign Affairs, Mutual Development and Cooperation Act of 1973, H.R. Rep. No. 93-388, at vii (1973).

67. James P. Grant to Donald M. Fraser, May 26, 1973, box 149.G.13.8F, folder: Foreign Aid 1973 (2), DFP.

68. *Mutual Development and Cooperation Act of 1973, Hearings before the Committee on Foreign Affairs, House of Representatives*, 93rd Cong. 473, 475, 483, 488 (1973), hearing ID: HRG-1973-FOA-0050 (statement and testimony of James Grant).

69. *Mutual Development and Cooperation Act of 1973, Hearings*, 498 (1973) (statement of Edgar Owens); *Foreign Economic Assistance, 1973, Hearings before the Committee on Foreign Relations*, 93rd Cong. 268 (1973), hearing ID: HRG-1973-FOR-0021 (statement of Theodore M. Hesburgh).

70. Congressional Research Service, Foreign Affairs Division, *The Reorganization of U.S. Development Aid: Comparison and Summary Analysis of Some Official and Unofficial Proposals, Prepared for the Committee on Foreign Affairs* (Washington, DC: Government Printing Office, 1973), 38.

71. *Foreign Economic Assistance, 1973, Hearings before the Committee on Foreign Relations*, 93rd Cong. 264, 265 (1973) (statement of Hesburgh); *Mutual Development and Cooperation Act of 1973, Hearings* (statement of Owens).

72. House Comm. on Foreign Affairs, Mutual Development and Cooperation Act of 1973, H.R. Rep. No. 93-388, at 12, 105 (1973).

73. An Act to Amend the Foreign Assistance Act of 1961, Pub. L. No. 93-189, 22 U.S.C. § 2151 (1973). On Nixon's views on USAID, see, for example, "Memorandum of Conversation," February 11, 1970, document 125, *FRUS, 1969–1976*, vol. 4.

74. "FY 1976 Program Budget Submission Guidance," Airgram from AID/W, June 22, 1974, pp. 2, 4, 6, box 5, folder: Percy Amendment—A.I.D. Directives to Overseas Missions on the Percy Amendment, CBCA.

75. Congressional Research Service, "New Directions Mandate," 66, 74, 75. From fiscal year 1973–74 to fiscal year 1979–80, the percentages changed as follows: from 38% to 65% of USAID development assistance in the agricultural, rural development, and nutrition category; from 26% to 72% of proposed USAID projects naming the poor as intended beneficiaries; from 16% to 27% of total aid going to Africa.

76. "Foundation and the Less Developed Countries," 9.

77. Commission on International Development, *Partners in Development*, 214.

78. Group of 77, "First Ministerial Meeting of the Group of 77: Charter of Algiers," Algiers, October 10–25, 1967, The Group of 77 at the United Nations, www.g77.org /doc/algier-1.htm.

79. John Lewis, Richard Webb, and Devesh Kapur, interview with Robert S. McNamara, April 1, May 10, and October 3, 1991, p. 61, WBOHP. See also Sarah Babb, *Behind the Development Banks: Washington Politics, World Poverty, and the Wealth of Nations* (Chicago: University of Chicago Press, 2009).

80. On the Bank's changing understanding of poverty and development, see especially Robert L. Ayres, *Banking on the Poor: The World Bank and World Poverty* (Cambridge, MA: MIT Press, 1983); Martha Finnemore, "Redefining Development at the World Bank," in *International Development and the Social Sciences: Essays on the History and Politics of Knowledge*, ed. Frederick Cooper and Randall Packard (Berkeley: University of California Press, 1997), 203–27; Rob Konkel, "The Monetization of Global Poverty: The Concept of Poverty in World Bank History, 1944–90," *Journal of Global History* 9, no. 2 (July 2014): 276–300; Patrick Allan Sharma, *Robert McNamara's Other War: The World Bank and International Development* (Philadelphia: University of Pennsylvania Press, 2017).

81. Spiral Notebook 3, April 1, 1968, p. 6, box 1, WB IBRD/IDA 80, WCP. On McNamara's passionate commitment to poverty alleviation, see, for example, Kapur, Lewis, and Webb, *World Bank*, 1:219.

82. "McNamara Warns Affluent Nations," *Atlanta Constitution*, February 21, 1970.

83. Robert S. McNamara, "Address to the Board of Governors," September 24, 1973, pp. 6, 7, 9, 11, 27, The World Bank, https://documents.worldbank.org/en/publication/documents-reports/documentdetail/930801468315304694 /address-to-the-board-of-governors-by-robert-s-mcnamara.

84. Julius Duscha, "World Bank's Profit-Turning Do-Gooder," *New York Times*, July 8, 1973; McNamara quoted in Joseph Lelyveld, "McNamara's Style at the World Bank," *New York Times*, November 30, 1975.

85. Deborah Shapley, *Promise and Power: The Life and Times of Robert McNamara* (Boston: Little, Brown, 1993), 507.

86. Shapley, *Promise and Power*, 507; Lewis, Webb, and Kapur, interview with Robert S. McNamara, 24.

87. Mahbub ul Haq, *The Poverty Curtain: Choices for the Third World* (New York: Columbia University Press, 1976), 6.

88. Robert Asher, interview with Mahbub ul Haq, December 3, 1982, pp. 2, 3, WBOHP.

89. Kapur, Lewis, and Webb, *World Bank*, 1:241; Lewis, Webb, and Kapur, interview with Robert S. McNamara, 81. On Haq as author of McNamara's 1973 speech in Nairobi, see William H. Becker and Marie T. Zenni, interview with Shahid Javed Burki, June 27 and 28 and July 2, 2002, p. 3, WBOHP.

90. Robert Asher, interview with Hollis B. Chenery, January 27, 1983, pp. 7, 8, WBOHP.

91. Hollis Chenery, Montek S. Ahluwalia, C.L.G. Bell, John H. Duloy, and Richard Jolly, *Redistribution with Growth: Policies to Improve Income Distribution in Developing Countries in the Context of Economic Growth, A Joint Study by the World Bank's Development Research Center and the Institute of Development Studies at the University of Sussex* (Oxford: Oxford University Press, 1974), v, xiii.

92. Chenery et al., *Redistribution with Growth*, xvii, xviii. On the ILO's "redistribution from growth," see International Labour Office, *Employment, Incomes and Equality: A Strategy for Increasing Productive Employment in Kenya, Report of an Inter-Agency Team Financed by the United Nations Development Programme and Organised by the International Labour Office* (Geneva: International Labour Office, 1972), 109–14; Kapur, Lewis, and Webb, *World Bank*, 1:263.

93. Chenery et al., *Redistribution with Growth*, xviii.

94. Lewis, Webb, and Kapur, interview with Robert S. McNamara, 73; Chenery et al., *Redistribution with Growth*, xix, 161, 174.

95. Kapur, Lewis, and Webb, *World Bank*, 1:310, 315.

96. Lelyveld, "McNamara's Style at the World Bank."

97. Kapur, Lewis, and Webb, *World Bank*, 1:326.

98. Ernest Stern, Senior Adviser, Development Policy, to Michael Lipton, November 2, 1973, ESF.

99. Ayres, *Banking on the Poor*, 99.

100. International Bank for Reconstruction and Development, *The Assault on World Poverty: Problems of Rural Development, Education and Health* (Baltimore, MD: Johns Hopkins University Press, 1975), 3.

101. Edgar Owens, "'Community Development' and AID's New Legislation," n.d., ca. 1974, p. 2, box 5, folder: Percy Amendment Working Committee Background Reports for Subcommittee on Agriculture, Nutrition, and Rural Development, CBCA; John M. Cohen and Norman T. Uphoff, "Rural Development Participation,"

International Agriculture: A Newsletter from the New York State College of Agriculture and Life Sciences, Cornell University, 5, no. 1 (January 1978): 1, in box 2, folder: U, AGO; Vernon W. Ruttan, "Integrated Rural Development Programmes: A Historical Perspective," *World Development* 12, no. 4 (1984): 398. In fact, CD programs were concerned with productivity; see, for example, Engerman, *Price of Aid*, 137–40.

102. For figures on US nonmilitary aid over time, see, for example, Catherine Gwin, "U.S. Relations with the World Bank," in *The World Bank: Its First Half Century*, vol. 2, *Perspectives*, ed. Devesh Kapur, John P. Lewis, and Richard Webb (Washington, DC: Brookings Institution, 1997), 214.

103. See, for example, Ernest Feder, "Capitalism's Last-Ditch Effort to Save Underdeveloped Agricultures: International Agribusiness, the World Bank, and the Rural Poor," *Journal of Contemporary Asia* 7, no. 1 (January 1977): 56–78; Cheryl Payer, "The World Bank and the Small Farmers," *Journal of Peace Research* 16, no. 4 (1979): 293–312.

104. See, for example, Peter T. Bauer and Basil S. Yamey, "World Wealth Distribution: Anatomy of the New Order," in *The First World and the Third World: Essays on the New International Economic Order*, ed. Karl Brunner (Rochester: Center for Research in Government Policy and Business, University of Rochester, 1978), 205.

105. For a summary of mid-1970s critical commentary, see Haq, *Poverty Curtain*, 206. On pushback from the global South, see chapter 2.

106. Congressional Research Service, "New Directions Mandate," 242, 244; Ayres, *Banking on the Poor*, 102–5, 134–35.

107. Congressional Research Service, "New Directions Mandate," 360, 402–6; Ayres, *Banking on the Poor*, 126–28.

108. Sharma, *Robert McNamara's Other War*, 118, 120, 123.

109. Finnemore, "Redefining Development at the World Bank," 220.

110. David R. Francis, "World Poverty Called Key Issue," *Christian Science Monitor*, April 26, 1972.

111. Barbara Ward, *Human Settlements: Crisis and Opportunity* (Ottawa: Information Canada, 1974), 10–11.

Chapter 2

1. Michael Harrington, *The Vast Majority: A Journey to the World's Poor* (New York: Simon and Schuster, 1977), 33.

2. Harrington, 29, 71.

3. Harrington, 142, 150, 180.

4. Andrew Silk, "The Perils of Compassion," *Nation*, February 4, 1978, 123; Harrington, *Vast Majority*, 182, 213.

5. Silk, "Perils of Compassion," 124; Robert Lekachman, "The Other World," *New York Times*, November 27, 1977.

6. UN General Assembly, Resolution 3201, Declaration on the Establishment of a New International Economic Order, A/RES/S-6/3201 (May 1, 1974), http://www.un-documents.net/s6r3201.htm.

7. David Winder, "A Reordered World Economy? UN Adopts Plan of Nonaligned States," *Christian Science Monitor*, May 3, 1974.

8. UN General Assembly, Resolution 3202, Programme of Action on the Establishment of a New International Economic Order, A/RES/S-6/3202 (May 1, 1974), http://www.un-documents.net/s6r3202.htm.

9. On Prebisch, see, for example, Joseph L. Love, "Raúl Prebisch and the Origins of the Doctrine of Unequal Exchange," *Latin American Research Review* 15, no. 3 (1980): 45–72; Cristóbal Kay, "Raúl Prebisch," in *Fifty Key Thinkers on Development*, ed. David Simon (London: Routledge, 2006), 199–205. Prebisch headed ECLA from 1949 to 1962.

10. On Bandung and the NIEO, see, for example, Bret Benjamin, "Bookend to Bandung: The New International Economic Order and the Antinomies of the Bandung Era," *Humanity: An International Journal of Human Rights, Humanitarianism, and Development* 6, no. 1 (Spring 2015): 33–46.

11. On the prehistory of the NIEO, see Daniel J. Whelan, "'Under the Aegis of Man': The Right to Development and the Origins of the New International Economic Order," *Humanity: An International Journal of Human Rights, Humanitarianism, and Development* 6, no. 1 (Spring 2015): 93–108; Johanna Bockman, "Socialist Globalization against Capitalist Neocolonialism: The Economic Ideas behind the New International Economic Order," *Humanity: An International Journal of Human Rights, Humanitarianism, and Development* 6, no. 1 (Spring 2015): 109–28.

12. The phrase "trade union of the poor," often attributed to Nyerere, was used by more than one commentator. See, for example, Mahbub ul Haq, Turkeyen Third World Lectures, Georgetown, Guyana, November 1975, reprinted in *The Third World and the International Economic Order* (Washington, DC: Overseas Development Council, 1976), 1; Julius K. Nyerere, speech at Howard University, August 1977, reprinted in "Destroying World Poverty: President Nyerere Speaks," *Southern Africa* 10, no. 7 (September 1977): 7. On the NIEO, see also Adom Getachew, *Worldmaking after Empire: The Rise and Fall of Self-Determination* (Princeton, NJ: Princeton University Press, 2019), chap. 5.

13. C. Fred Bergsten, "The Threat from the Third World," *Foreign Policy* 11 (Summer 1973): 121.

14. Winder, "Reordered World Economy?"

15. Martin G. Berck, "UN Approves Controversial Aid Program," *Newsday*, May 2, 1974.

16. Daniel P. Moynihan, "The United States in Opposition," *Commentary*, March 1, 1975, https://www.commentarymagazine.com/articles/the-united-states -in-opposition/; "Memorandum from the Economic Policy Board to President Ford," May 1975, document 291, *FRUS, 1969–1976*, vol. 31, *Foreign Economic Policy, 1973–1976*; "A Word to the Third World," *Wall Street Journal*, July 17, 1975. For more on conservative opposition to the NIEO, see, for example, Quinn Slobodian, *Globalists: The End of Empire and the Birth of Neoliberalism* (Cambridge, MA: Harvard University Press, 2018), chap. 7; Michael Franczak, "Losing the Battle, Winning the War: Neoconservatives versus the New International Economic Order, 1974–82," *Diplomatic History* 43, no. 5 (2019): 867–89.

17. "Memorandum of Conversation," May 24, 1975, document 292, *FRUS, 1973–1976*, vol. 31.

18. Quoted in Victor McFarland, "The New International Economic Order, Interdependence, and Globalization," *Humanity: An International Journal of Human Rights, Humanitarianism, and Development* 6, no. 1 (Spring 2015): 226. On Kissinger's approach to the NIEO, see also Daniel J. Sargent, *A Superpower Transformed: The Remaking of American Foreign Relations in the 1970s* (New York: Oxford University Press, 2015), 175–82; Daniel J. Sargent, "North/South: The United States Responds to the New International Economic Order," *Humanity: An International Journal of Human Rights, Humanitarianism, and Development* 6, no. 1 (Spring 2015): 201–16.

19. Patrick Sharma, "Between North and South: The World Bank and the New International Economic Order," *Humanity: An International Journal of Human Rights, Humanitarianism, and Development* 6, no. 1 (Spring 2015): esp. 193.

20. James P. Grant, introduction to *Beyond Dependency: The Developing World Speaks Out*, ed. Guy F. Erb and Valeriana Kallab (New York: Praeger, 1975), x, xii.

21. Adrienne Germain, "Conversation with Mildred Marcy and Virginia Allan 3/28/75—International Women's Year," p. 2, box 2, folder 32, EBO.

22. See, for example, Roger D. Hansen, *A "New International Economic Order"? An Outline for a Constructive U.S. Response* (Washington, DC: Overseas Development Council, 1975).

23. Crawford D. Goodwin, "The Overseas Development Council: A Ten-Year Review for the Ford Foundation," January 17, 1978, pp. 18, 19, FG 74–288, reel 236.

24. "A Discussion on North-South Economic Relations: Summary Report on the Princeton Meeting," September 1978, pp. 2, 4, FG 74–288, reel 236.

25. Jan Pronk and Altaf Gauhar, "North-South Dialogue," *Third World Quarterly* 3, no. 2 (April 1981): 197, 198.

26. Dag Hammarskjöld Foundation, *What Now? Another Development: The 1975 Dag Hammarskjöld Report* (Uppsala: Dag Hammarskjöld Foundation, 1975), 12, 63, 64.

27. Peter Adamson, "Consensus on Crisis," *New Internationalist* 32 (October 1975): 3. Historian Kevin O'Sullivan has aptly characterized the *New Internationalist* as "more than liberal but less than Marxist"; see Kevin O'Sullivan, "The Search for Justice: NGOs in Britain and Ireland and the New International Economic Order, 1968–1982," *Humanity: An International Journal of Human Rights, Humanitarianism, and Development* 6, no. 1 (Spring 2015): 178.

28. Orlando Letelier and Michael Moffitt, *The International Economic Order* (Washington, DC: Transnational Institute, 1977), 53. On the IPS and the NIEO, see Paul Adler, "'The Basis of a New Internationalism?': The Institute for Policy Studies and North-South Politics from the NIEO to Neoliberalism," *Diplomatic History* 41, no. 4 (September 2017): 665–93. In addition to leftists, a few American religious commentators also endorsed the NIEO as an issue of Christian justice. See, for example, Ronald J. Sider, *Rich Christians in an Age of Hunger: A Biblical Study* (New York: Paulist Press, 1977), 144–46.

29. Harrington, *Vast Majority*, 215, 232, 253, 254.

30. Robert C. Christopher, "The World's New Cold War," *Newsweek*, June 16, 1975, 37; Reginald Herbold Green and Hans W. Singer, "Toward a Rational and Equitable New International Economic Order: A Case for Negotiated Structural Changes," *World Development* 3, no. 6 (June 1975): 427, 428.

31. James P. Grant to Theodore M. Hesburgh, October 15, 1975, p. 4, FG 76–177, reel 1358.

32. Flora Lewis, "Rich and Poor: Shifting Ties," *New York Times*, June 3, 1977; Roger D. Hansen, "North-South Policy: What's the Problem?," *Foreign Affairs* 58, no. 5 (Summer 1980): 1110, 1115.

33. C. Clyde Ferguson Jr., "The Politics of the New International Economic Order," *Proceedings of the Academy of Political Science* 34, no. 4 (1977): 154.

34. Barbara Ward, letter to the editor, *Times* (London), January 14, 1977, 2:61, BWP.

35. Jimmy Carter, "Address before the United Nations General Assembly," March 17, 1977, APP.

36. Quoted in "Editorial Note," document 265, *FRUS, 1977–1980*, vol. 3, *Foreign Economic Policy*. On the ODC and Carter, see Michael Franczak, "Human Rights and Basic Needs: Jimmy Carter's North-South Dialogue, 1977–81," *Cold War History* 19, no. 4 (2018): 447–64. On Carter's foreign policy more generally, see, for example, Odd Arne Westad, *The Global Cold War: Third World Interventions and the Making of Our Times* (Cambridge: Cambridge University Press, 2005); Nancy Mitchell, *Jimmy Carter in Africa: Race and the Cold War* (Stanford, CA: Stanford University Press; Washington, DC: Woodrow Wilson Center, 2016).

37. Barbara Ward to Robert McNamara, September 6, 1977, 2:61, BWP; Harrington, *Vast Majority*, 20.

38. "Nyerere Seeks Clarification," *Times of India*, August 16, 1977; Stephen S. Rosenfeld, "Carter's Engagement with the Third World," *Washington Post*, March 24, 1978. For Nyerere's speech, see "Destroying World Poverty."

39. "Talking Points for Your Meeting on Foreign Assistance," March 8, 1977, box 102, folder: Foreign Assistance, 3/7–22/77, Bourdeaux Subject Files, OCL; "President Orders Thorough Review of Foreign Aid," press release, July 7, 1977, box 209, folder: Foreign Assistance, SEF.

40. Memorandum from Guy Erb of the National Security Council staff to the President's assistant for national security affairs (Brzezinski), February 11, 1978, document 295, *FRUS, 1977–1980*, vol. 3. See also Memorandum from the undersecretary of state for economic affairs (Cooper) to President Carter, July 3, 1978, document 310, *FRUS, 1977–1980*, vol. 3.

41. According to Roger Hansen, the Carter administration had rejected "almost all Southern proposals for the consideration of significant structural reforms." Hansen, "North-South Policy," 1120.

42. For succinct statements of the basic needs approach, see Richard Jolly, "The World Employment Conference: The Enthronement of Basic Needs," *Development Policy Review* A9, no. 2 (October 1976): 31–44; Paul P. Streeten, "Basic Needs: Premises and Promises," *Journal of Policy Modeling* 1 (1979): 136–46.

43. Streeten, "Basic Needs," 144–45.

44. On measurements and indices, see Norman Hicks and Paul Streeten, "Indicators of Development: The Search for a Basic Needs Yardstick," *World Development* 7 (1979): 567–80.

45. Donella H. Meadows, Dennis L. Meadows, Jørgen Randers, and William W. Behrens III, *The Limits to Growth: A Report for the Club of Rome's Project on the Predicament of Mankind* (New York: Universe Books, 1972), 183.

46. Marc Nerfin, "Report of the [1975 Dag Hammarskjöld] Project Director," December 16, 1975, 1001-04-0:2, WEP. The UN's concern with environmental issues was relatively new. The UNEP was established in 1972.

47. "The Cocoyoc Declaration," *Development Dialogue* 2 (1974): 94, 91. On Ward and the Cocoyoc Declaration and, more generally, on the merging of environmentalism and basic needs development, see Stephen J. Macekura, *Of Limits and Growth: The Rise of Global Sustainable Development in the Twentieth Century* (New York: Cambridge University Press, 2015), chap. 6, esp. 223–26.

48. Marc Nerfin, "Outline of an Enquiry into the Imperatives for International Co-operation to Meet Fundamental Human Needs without Transgressing the 'Outer Limits,'" November, 1974, 1001-04-0:1, WEP.

49. Dag Hammarskjöld Foundation, *What Now?* 1, 13, 26.

50. International Labour Organization, *Meeting Basic Needs: Strategies for Eradicating Mass Poverty and Unemployment* (Geneva: International Labour Office, 1977), 10.

51. A. Pathmarajah to Louis Emmerij et al., January 30, 1975, 1001-04-0:1, WEP; A. Pathmarajah to Louis Emmerij, July 20, 1975, 1001-02:3, WEP.

52. International Labour Organization, *Employment, Growth and Basic Needs: A One-World Problem* (Geneva: International Labour Office, 1976), 40.

53. International Labour Organization, *Meeting Basic Needs*, 12, 13; "Discussions on First Draft WEC Policy Document: Visit to New York, Washington and Ottawa (11–21 December 1975)," 1001-02:4, WEP; Louis Emmerij with Peter Adamson, "The Writing on the Wall," *New Internationalist* 43 (September 1976): 24; Harrington, *Vast Majority*, 242. USAID, though, was more "broadly supportive" of the ILO position, but had "reservations on the ILO's Basic Needs Strategy because it appears to overweight redistribution . . . relative to . . . an employment oriented development strategy." See John E. Murphy to Donald M. Fraser, June 4, 1976, in 149.G.9.8F, folder: Foreign Aid—1976, DFP.

54. International Labour Organization, *Meeting Basic Needs*, 12, 13, 24.

55. Graciela Chichilnisky, "Development Patterns and the International Order," *Journal of International Affairs* 31, no. 2 (Fall/Winter 1977): 290. See also Amílcar O. Herrera, Hugo D. Scolnik, Graciela Chichilnisky, Gilberto C. Gallopin, Jorge E. Hardoy, Diana Mosovich, Enrique Oteiza, et al., *Catastrophe or New Society? A Latin American World Model* (Ottawa: International Development Research Centre, 1976).

56. Jan Tinbergen, Antony J. Dolman, and Jan van Ettinger, *Reshaping the International Order* (New York: E. P. Dutton, 1976), 162.

57. Robert S. McNamara, "The World's Poor: Life on $100 a Year," *Los Angeles Times*, October 22, 1976; Devesh Kapur, John P. Lewis, and Richard Webb, *The World*

Bank: Its First Half Century, vol. 1, *History* (Washington, DC: Brookings Institution, 1997), 266.

58. Clyde H. Farnsworth, "World Bank Alters Strategy to Focus on Aid to Very Poor," *New York Times*, June 6, 1977; Barry Newman, "Missing the Mark: In Indonesia, Attempts by World Bank to Aid Poor Often Go Astray," *New York Times*, November 10, 1977.

59. On Streeten, see especially Francis Wilson, "Paul Patrick Streeten," in Simon, *Fifty Key Thinkers on Development*, 252–58.

60. Reprinted in Mahbub ul Haq, *The Poverty Curtain: Choices for the Third World* (New York: Columbia University Press, 1976), 35.

61. Robert Asher, interview with Hollis B. Chenery, January 27, 1983, p. 15, WBOHP; Robert Asher, interview with Mahbub ul Haq, December 3, 1982, p. 7, WBOHP; Stephen S. Rosenfeld, "On Inequality among Nations," *Washington Post*, October 22, 1976.

62. Asher, interview with Mahbub ul Haq, 22; John Lewis, Richard Webb, and Devesh Kapur, interview with Robert S. McNamara, April 1, May 10, and October 3, 1991, p. 81, WBOHP.

63. On Haq's career, see Khadija Haq and Richard Ponzio, eds., *Pioneering the Human Development Revolution: An Intellectual Biography of Mahbub ul Haq* (New Delhi: Oxford University Press, 2008).

64. Louis Emmerij, Richard Jolly, and Thomas G. Weiss, *Ahead of the Curve: UN Ideas and Global Challenges* (Bloomington: Indiana University Press, 2001), 75.

65. Streeten, "Basic Needs," 142; Guy Standing, "Basic Needs and the Division of Labour," *Pakistan Development Review* 19, no. 3 (August 1980): 214. On the ways that development agencies recast political problems as technical and apolitical, see James Ferguson, *The Anti-Politics Machine: "Development," Depoliticization, and Bureaucratic Power in Lesotho* (Cambridge: Cambridge University Press, 1990); Tania Murray Li, *The Will to Improve: Governmentality, Development, and the Practice of Politics* (Durham, NC: Duke University Press, 2007).

66. Standing, "Basic Needs and the Division of Labour," 214, 222.

67. Gamani Corea, "UNCTAD and the New International Economic Order," *International Affairs*, April 1977, 187.

68. Nyerere, "Destroying World Poverty," 7; Vijay Prashad, *The Poorer Nations: A Possible History of the Global South* (London: Verso, 2012), 93; Harrington, *Vast Majority*, 181; USAID, Office of Rural Development and Development Administration, *The "New Directions" Mandate: Studies in Project Design, Approval and Implementation*, vol. 2, January 23, 1978, p. 134, document PN-AAN-448, DEC. As the historian Priya Lal has noted, "A key theme of African socialism was its immediate emphasis on meeting what later came to be termed the 'basic needs' of average people rather than achieving aggregate economic growth." Priya Lal, "Decolonization and the Gendered Politics of Developmental Labor in Southeastern Africa," in *The Development Century: A Global History*, ed. Stephen J. Macekura and Erez Manela (Cambridge: Cambridge University Press, 2018), 176. On the World Bank's support for Tanzania's antipoverty goals in the 1970s, see Sean Delehanty, "From Modernization

to Villagization: The World Bank and Ujamaa," *Diplomatic History* 44, no. 2 (2020): 289–314.

69. Orlando Patterson, "The Realities of Intervention in Alienated Cultures: A Jamaican Case Study," in *Private-Public Partnership: New Opportunities for Meeting Social Needs*, ed. Harvey Brooks, Lance Liebman, and Corinne S. Schelling (Cambridge, MA: Ballinger for the American Academy of Arts and Sciences, 1984), 131. Patterson recounts the difficulties of implementing the project in urban Jamaica. In a personal conversation, May 12, 2016, he told me that the name of the USAID accountant assigned to the project later appeared on a list of CIA agents.

70. Hans Singer, "The New International Economic Order: An Overview," *Journal of Modern African Studies* 16, no. 4 (1978): 546; Ajit Singh, "The 'Basic Needs' Approach to Development vs the New International Economic Order: The Significance of Third World Industrialization," *World Development* 7, no. 6 (June 1979): 586, 587.

71. The other participants from the global South mentioned in the report were Juan Somavía, a Chilean scholar and diplomat, Bagicha S. Minhas, an Indian economist, and Donald O. Mills, the Jamaican ambassador to the UN and chair of the Group of 77. "Meeting Basic Human Needs: The U.S. Stake in a New Development Strategy: A Report of the 26ᵗʰ Anniversary International Development Conference, February 7–9, 1978, Washington, D.C.," 14, 16, box 2, folder 49, SL 564, MHP. For similar critical comments from the global South, see Samuel Moyn, *Not Enough: Human Rights in an Unequal World* (Cambridge, MA: Harvard University Press, 2018), 138–39. Moyn sees the basic needs approach as "a turn away from distributive equality" (145). In its stronger variants, I see basic needs as redistributive, working in tandem with broader calls for structural change. See Joanne Meyerowitz, "Born-Again Equality," *Law and Political Economy*, May 14, 2018, https://lpeproject.org/blog/born-again-equality/.

72. On the economic assistance provided by the USSR, China, and other socialist nations, see, for example, Sara Lorenzini, *Global Development: A Cold War History* (Princeton, NJ: Princeton University Press, 2019), chap. 7.

73. "U.S. Official Development Assistance Flows," box 149.C.12.4F, folder: Notebook 1, DFP; John W. Sewell and the Staff of the Overseas Development Council, *The United States and World Development: Agenda 1980* (New York: Praeger, 1980), 224. In 1960, the UN had asked for a contribution of 1% of national income but that figure (also a pipe dream) included private investments as well as government contributions. In 1970, the UN recalibrated the figure to 0.7% of donor nation GNP as the target for official development assistance, or ODA. ODA does not include private capital. On the target history, see "The 0.7% ODA/GNI Target—a History," OECD, n.d., accessed September 11, 2020, http://www.oecd.org/dac/stats/the07odagnitarget-ahistory.htm.

74. Roger D. Hansen and the Staff of the Overseas Development Council, *The U.S. and World Development: Agenda for Action 1976* (New York: Praeger, 1976), ix; John W. Sewell and the Staff of the Overseas Development Council, *The United States and World Development: Agenda 1977* (New York: Praeger, 1977), 120.

75. "The Overseas Development Council, 1973 through 1977; 1978 through 1982: Report of a Task Force to ODC's Board of Directors," February 1978, p. III-9, FG 74–288, reel 236. On Hesburgh and the ODC's influence, see Franczak, "Human Rights and Basic Needs."

76. Claire Sterling, "The Making of the Sub-Saharan Wasteland: How to Spend Hundreds of Millions of Dollars to Help People Starve," *Atlantic*, May 1974, at https:// www.theatlantic.com/magazine/archive/1974/05/the-making-of-the-sub-saharan -wasteland/482175/. For a recent account of 1970s relief efforts in the Sahel, see, for example, Gregory Mann, *From Empires to NGOs in the West African Sahel: The Road to Nongovernmentality* (Cambridge: Cambridge University Press, 2015), chap. 5.

77. Dan Morgan, "Key Aspects Unclear: Food Meeting Outlines Plan to End Hunger," *Washington Post*, November 17, 1974.

78. "Report to the NCC Governing Board from the Coordinating Council for Hunger Concerns," May 4–6, 1977, box 15, folder: National Council of Churches, General Records-Subject File, PCWH; Arthur Simon, *The Rising of Bread for the World: An Outcry of Citizens against Hunger* (New York: Paulist Press, 2009), 87. On Food First, see, for example, Francis Moore Lappé and Joseph Collins, *World Hunger: Ten Myths* (San Francisco: Institute for Food and Development Policy, 1979).

79. Richard Gold to Daniel Shaughnessy, September 22, 1978, box 15, folder: NGOs-PVOs/Commission General Records—Subject File, PCWH; William Aiken and Hugh La Follette, eds., *World Hunger and Moral Obligation* (Englewood Cliffs, NJ: Prentice-Hall, 1977). On philosophers, see also Moyn, *Not Enough*, 148–52.

80. "The Second Carter-Ford Presidential Debate," October 6, 1976, Commission on Presidential Debates, http://www.debates.org/index.php?page=october-6-1976 -debate-transcript. Jimmy Carter, "Foreign Assistance Programs Message to the Congress," March 17, 1977, APP; "The President's News Conference," June 13, 1977, APP; "Visit of President Julius K. Nyerere of Tanzania: Remarks of the President and President Nyerere at the Welcoming Ceremony," August 4, 1977, APP; "World Conference on Religion and Peace: Remarks at a White House Reception for Conference Participants," September 6, 1979, APP.

81. Carter, "Address before the United Nations General Assembly."

82. "U.S. Studies Linking Basic Needs to Rights," *Hartford Courant*, July 12, 1977. On US support for basic needs at the Conference on International Economic Cooperation and OECD, see "President Orders Thorough Review of Foreign Aid"; Development Coordination Committee, "Foreign Assistance Study," October 4, 1977, p. 16, box 209, folder: Foreign Assistance Study (1), SEF. On Carter and human rights, see, for example, Samuel Moyn, *The Last Utopia: Human Rights in History* (Cambridge, MA: Harvard University Press, 2010), 154–61; Barbara J. Keys, *Reclaiming American Virtue: The Human Rights Revolution of the 1970s* (Cambridge, MA: Harvard University Press, 2014), chaps. 9 and 10.

83. John E. Rielly, ed., *American Public Opinion and U.S. Foreign Policy 1975* (Chicago: Chicago Council on Foreign Relations, 1975), 26, 27.

84. Jimmy Carter, "Memorandum for the Heads of Executive Departments and Agencies on World Hunger Working Group," September 30, 1977, APP.

85. Development Coordination Committee, "Foreign Assistance Study," 34; "PRM 8-Track III, US Relations with the Developing Countries: The Next Twelve Months," September 13, 1977, p. 14, box 253, folder: Policy Review Committee on Foreign Aid, SEF; Brookings Institution, "Interim Report: An Assessment of Development Assistance Strategies, Summary of Recommendations," ca. October 1977, box 253, folder: Policy Review Committee on Foreign Aid, SEF.

86. "PRM 8-Track III, US Relations with the Developing Countries," 15. Emphasis in original.

87. "Gilligan Stresses Need for Shift in Aid Policy," press release, September 27, 1977, box 33, folder: Gilligan, John J.—International Development Strategies, PBF.

88. Dan Oberdorfer, "Carter Tells Agencies to Plan Larger Foreign Aid Program," *Washington Post*, June 29, 1977; Don Shannon, "Foreign Aid Reorganization Inches Along," *Los Angeles Times*, April 26, 1978.

89. On the "appropriate technology" movement, see Macekura, *Of Limits and Growth*, chap. 4.

90. Patrick Buchanan, "Tough Talk for Third World Beggars," *Chicago Tribune*, May 10, 1979.

91. Rosenfeld, "Carter's Engagement with the Third World." See also Robert Kleiman, "Carter Again Defers Large Foreign Aid Increases, *New York Times*, January 22, 1978; Ann Crittenden, "The Realpolitik of Foreign Aid," *New York Times*, February 26, 1978; Dan Morgan, "Foreign Aid Funds Stay Mainly in U.S.," *Washington Post*, March 5, 1978.

92. "For the President's Meeting with the Leadership," n.d., ca. Spring 1978, box 221, folder: Foreign Aid, 3/24/78–5/31/78, Bob Beckel's Subject Files, OCL; "Excerpts of Remarks by the President: Meeting with Religious Leaders," July 31, 1978, box 15, folder: Foreign Aid, 1977–1980 (1), Jim Purks' Subject Files, POML.

93. Ann Crittenden, "Foreign Aid Has Friends Back Home: Businessmen," *New York Times*, July 30, 1978. The development economist Ester Boserup noted that "private export industries in donor countries come to form a powerful pressure group in favour of additional aid tied to procurement in the donor country." See Ester Boserup, "Absorptive Capacity for Foreign Aid," in *Foreign Aid to Newly Independent Countries*, ed. Boserup and Ignacy Sachs (The Hague: Mouton, 1971), 7–8.

94. Crittenden, "Foreign Aid Has Friends Back Home"; Morgan, "Foreign Aid Funds Stay Mainly in U.S."; "Foreign Aid: Background Report by Office of Media Liaison, The White House Press Office," July 11, 1979, box 15, folder: Foreign Aid, 1977–1980 (1), Jim Purks' Subject Files, POML.

95. Jimmy Carter, "Presidential Commission on World Hunger Statement," October 5, 1978, APP; "Memorandum from Secretary of Agriculture Bergland, the President's Special Assistant for Health Issues (Bourne), the President's Assistant for National Security Affairs (Brzezinski), the President's Assistant for Domestic Affairs and Policy (Eizenstat), the Director of the Office of Management and Budget (McIntyre), and the Chairman of the Council of Economic Advisers (Schultze) to President Carter," February 17, 1978, document 244, *FRUS, 1977–1980*, vol. 2, *Human Rights and Humanitarian Affairs*; "Using the Launching of the Presidential

Commission on Hunger and the Commission Itself to Build Up the Foreign Assistance Constituency," September 1, 1978, box 40, folder: Briefing Material (Linowitz), Records of Commissioners and Staff—Linowitz's Subject File, PCWH.

96. Presidential Commission on World Hunger, *Overcoming World Hunger: The Challenge Ahead, Report of the Presidential Commission on World Hunger, An Abridged Version* (Washington, DC: Government Printing Office, 1980), 17, 18, 19.

97. Presidential Commission on World Hunger, 19. On the interagency review of the commission report, see "Memorandum from the Acting Director of the International Development Cooperation Agency (Erb) to President Carter," August 15, 1980, document 277, *FRUS, 1977–1980*, vol. 2.

98. Sewell and Staff of the Overseas Development Council, *United States and World Development: Agenda 1980*, 14, 17; "Paper Prepared by Thomas Thornton of the National Security Council Staff, n.d., ca. December 1980, document 354, *FRUS, 1977–1980*, vol. 3; Hansen, "North-South Policy," 1124, 1126.

99. Gunnar Myrdal, *The Challenge of World Poverty: A World Anti-Poverty Program in Outline* (New York: Random House, 1970), 365. On the history of the idea of international taxation, see Myron I. Frankman, "International Taxation: The Trajectory of an Idea from Lorimer to Brandt," *World Development* 24, no. 5 (1996): 807–20. The better-known Tobin tax, a tax on foreign-exchange transactions proposed in 1972 by economist James Tobin to reduce the fluctuations in exchange rates, was not originally intended for economic development assistance or the transfer of resources from North to South.

100. "Cocoyoc Declaration," 94. A similar approach to international taxation appears in the Dag Hammarskjöld Foundation's *What Now?* 18, 19, 120.

101. UN General Assembly, Resolution 3362, Development and International Economic Co-operation, A/RES/S-7/3362 (Sep. 16, 1975), http://www.un-documents.net/s7r3362.htm; Tinbergen, Dolman, and Van Ettinger, *Reshaping the International Order*, 210, 216, 217. Haq and Grant repeated the call for international taxation in their own publications. See Haq, *Poverty Curtain*, 194–97; James P. Grant, "Perspectives on Development Aid: World War II to Today and Beyond," *Annals of the American Academy of Political and Social Science* 442 (March 1979): 9.

102. Eleanor B. Steinberg and Joseph A. Yager with Gerard M. Brannon, *New Means of Financing International Needs* (Washington, DC: Brookings Institution, 1978), 195. The book also recommended other international taxes intended for environmental protection, not necessarily for generating funds for global redistribution.

Earlier, in August 1976, Maurice Strong had joined with other environmentalists and UN officials in a public demonstration—a fifty-mile journey from UN headquarters in New York to the New Jersey shore on the square-rigged sailing ship *Barba Negra*—that ended with the adoption of the Barba Negra Appeal, a statement that asked that a portion of revenues from ocean-floor minerals be used especially "to aid development" and "fight pollution." On the Barba Negra Appeal, see 123 Cong. Rec. 2071 (1977) (Robert W. Edgar, "A Proposal to President-Elect Carter").

103. Mahbub ul Haq to Barbara Ward, November 8, 1976, and Barbara Ward to Mahbub ul Haq, November 22, 1976, 3:1, BWP; "Delhi Announcement of Brandt

Commission," press release, December 22, 1977, p. 2, box 11, folder: Brandt Commission, General Records—Subject File, PCWH.

104. Leonard Silk, "McNamara's Commitment to War on World Poverty," *New York Times*, September 29, 1977.

105. Independent Commission on International Development Issues, *North-South, A Programme for Survival: Report of the Independent Commission on International Development Issues* (Cambridge, MA: MIT Press, 1980), 8; William Clark, Spiral Notebook 3, p. 52, box 1, WCP; "Some Minimum Conditions for Ensuring Brandt Commission Attracts Widespread Third World Support and Effectively Contributes to N-S Dialogue," ca. 1978, 11:1, BWP.

106. On funding for the commission, see Independent Commission on International Development Issues, *North-South*, 304. The Carter administration "verbally approved" the effort, but the US government did not contribute funds. On verbal approval, see David R. Francis, "'Marshall Plan' for Third World?," *Christian Science Monitor*, March 15, 1977.

107. Clark, Spiral Notebook 3, p. 52; "Delhi Announcement of Brandt Commission," 5.

108. Quotes relating to the South in William Clark, "Notes of Conversation between R.S. McNamara and Willy Brandt in Bonn," March 7, 1979, p. 3; 1:7, WCP; quotes relating to the North in William Clark, "Brandt Commission Report—World Bank Implications," February 5, 1980, p. 6, 1:7, WCP.

109. Independent Commission on International Development Issues, *North-South*, 271.

110. Independent Commission on International Development Issues, 273, 274, 291.

111. Independent Commission on International Development Issues, 278, 281.

112. Melvyn B. Krauss, "Brandt Report Is Irrelevant to Third World," *Wall Street Journal*, August 28, 1980. A few years later, Krauss expounded further in his Manhattan Institute book *Development without Aid: Growth, Poverty and Government* (New York: McGraw-Hill, 1983).

113. Ronald Reagan, "Remarks at the Annual Meeting of the Board of Governors of the World Bank Group and International Monetary Fund," September 29, 1981, APP; Ronald Reagan, "Remarks at a Luncheon of the World Affairs Council of Philadelphia in Philadelphia, Pennsylvania," October 15, 1981, APP.

114. "The President in Cancun," *Boston Globe*, October 22, 1981; Alan Riding, "22 Leaders Gather for Two-Day Cancún Meeting," *New York Times*, October 22, 1981; Gerald McCarthy, "Cancun Opens in Air of Discord," *Irish Times*, October 23, 1981.

115. Alan Riding, "Mexicans Go All Out for Talks in Cancún," *New York Times*, October 18, 1981. On the meeting in Cancún, see also Greg Grandin, *Empire's Workshop: Latin America, the United States, and the Rise of the New Imperialism* (New York: Metropolitan, 2006), 185–87; Prashad, *Poorer Nations*, 76–83; Vanessa Ogle, "State Rights against Private Capital: The 'New International Economic Order' and the Struggle over Aid, Trade, and Foreign Investment," *Humanity: An International Journal of Human Rights, Humanitarianism, and Development* 5, no. 2 (Summer 2014): 224–25.

116. Hobart Rowen and Lee Lescaze, "North-South Chiefs Plan More Talks: Cancun Dialogue to Be Continued in U.N. Forum," *Washington Post*, October 24, 1981.

117. Bernard D. Nossiter, "Parley in Cancún: Next Step by World's Leaders in Doubt," *New York Times*, October 25, 1981; Carl T. Rowan, "Cancun: The Wealthy Disdain the Poor," *New York Amsterdam News*, October 31, 1981.

118. Robert Amdur, "Global Distributive Justice: A Review Essay," *Journal of International Affairs* 31, no. 1 (1977): 81. See also Moyn, *Not Enough*, chap. 6.

119. Mahbub ul Haq, "Negotiating the Future," *Foreign Affairs* 59, no. 2 (Winter 1980): 415; Irving Howe and Michael Harrington, "Voices from the Left," *New York Times*, June 17, 1984.

Chapter 3

1. "Strengthening Women's Roles in Development," 2, 10, 12, USAID project 686–0211, May 25, 1976, document PD-AAC-166, DEC.

2. Adrienne Germain, "Poor Rural Women: A Policy Perspective," *Journal of International Affairs* 30, no. 2 (Fall/Winter, 1976–77): 161.

3. Michael Adas, *Dominance by Design: Technological Imperatives and America's Civilizing Mission* (Cambridge, MA: Harvard University Press, 2006), 260. On community development programs and women, see Daniel Immerwahr, *Thinking Small: The United States and the Lure of Community Development* (Cambridge, MA: Harvard University Press, 2015), 86, 92–93. On the masculinism of modernization theory, see also María Josefina Saldaña-Portillo, *The Revolutionary Imagination in the Americas and the Age of Development* (Durham, NC: Duke University Press, 2003), chap. 2. In the 1950s and 1960s, a small group of US women, active in international labor circles, paid more attention to women workers in the global South. See Dorothy Sue Cobble, *For the Many: A Global History of American Feminism* (Princeton, NJ: Princeton University Press, forthcoming), chap. 11.

4. Nancy Rose Hunt, *A Colonial Lexicon: Of Birth Ritual, Medicalization, and Mobility in the Congo* (Durham, NC: Duke University Press, 1999), 270, 271.

5. Kathryne Sheehan Hughes, *Wash Dishes Right: An Aid to Extension and Village Workers in Many Countries*, FES AID Sanitation Series 4 (Washington, DC: Federal Extension Service, US Department of Agriculture in cooperation with the Agency for International Development, US Department of State, 1963), 8. This pamphlet and eight others in the same series and by the same author, published from 1962 to 1964, are available online at DEC. On home economics in African socialist development projects in Tanzania and Zambia, see Priya Lal, "Decolonization and the Gendered Politics of Developmental Labor in Southeastern Africa," in *The Development Century: A Global History*, ed. Stephen J. Macekura and Erez Manela (Cambridge: Cambridge University Press, 2018), 173–93.

6. Germain, "Poor Rural Women," 163. On teaching homemaking in the global South, see also Gabriel N. Rosenberg, *The 4-H Harvest: Sexuality and the State in Rural America* (Philadelphia: University of Pennsylvania Press, 2015), chap. 6.

7. David C. McClelland, *The Achieving Society* (Princeton, NJ: D. Van Nostrand, 1961), 36, 356. On McClelland, see also Nils Gilman, *Mandarins of the Future: Modernization Theory in Cold War America* (Baltimore: Johns Hopkins University Press, 2003), 97–100; Sara Fieldston, *Raising the World: Child Welfare in the American Century* (Cambridge, MA: Harvard University Press, 2015), 141–42, 149–50, 153–54, 157–58.

8. Michel Foucault, *The History of Sexuality*, vol. 1, *An Introduction* (New York: Pantheon,1978), 140, 146.

9. See Fieldston, *Raising the World*, esp. chap. 6.

10. USAID, Civic Participation Division, Office of Policy Development and Analysis, Bureau for Program and Policy Coordination, "Participation of Women in Development: A Background Paper on the New Foreign Assistance Act Provision (Percy Amendment)," February 11, 1974, p. 10, box 5, folder: General Information, Women in Development, 1975–1987, Series 1, WIDC; Paul R. Ehrlich, *The Population Bomb* (New York: Ballantine Books, 1968); Matthew Connelly, *Fatal Misconception: The Struggle to Control World Population* (Cambridge, MA: Harvard University Press, 2008), 259. On the difference between eugenics and population control—on "the focus on rates rather than kinds of people"—see also Michelle Murphy, *The Economization of Life* (Durham, NC: Duke University Press, 2017), 42.

11. Connelly, *Fatal Misconception*, 231, 289, 290.

12. See Connelly, esp. chap. 8.

13. Ray Vicker, "The Problem that Won't Go Away," *Wall Street Journal*, August 23, 1974. See also Connelly, *Fatal Misconception*, esp. chaps. 7 and 8; Rebecca Sharpless, interview with Adrienne Germain, June 19–20, September 25, 2003, Population and Reproductive Health Oral History Project, Sophia Smith Collection, Smith College.

14. Ronald Kotulak, "Population Bomb Defused," *Chicago Tribune*, February 15, 1978.

15. Stephen S. Rosenfeld, "A New Slant on Population Crisis," *Washington Post*, April 28, 1978.

16. *International Women's Issues: Hearing and Briefing before the Subcommittees on International Organizations and International Development of the Committee on International Relations, House of Representatives*, 95th Cong. 38 (1978) (statement of Elsa Chaney).

17. *International Protection of Human Rights: The Work of International Organizations and the Role of U.S. Foreign Policy: Hearing before the Subcommittee on International Organizations and Movements, Committee on Foreign Affairs, House of Representatives*, 93rd Cong. 474 (1973) (testimony of Irene Tinker). For a slightly later influential statement of the WID challenge to conventional economics, see Marilyn Waring, *If Women Counted: A New Feminist Economics* (San Francisco: Harper and Row, 1988).

18. Adrienne Germain, minutes of meeting December 6, 1974, with Esther [*sic*] Boserup, January 14, 1975, FR 7803; Nadia H. Youssef, "Women in Development: Urban Life and Labor," in *Women and World Development*, ed. Irene Tinker, Michèle Bo Bramsen, and Mayra Buvinic (New York: Praeger, 1975), 71.

19. Irene Tinker, "A Tribute to Ester Boserup: Utilizing Interdisciplinarity to Analyze Global Socio-Economic Change," presented at Global Tensions Conference, Cornell University, March 9–10, 2001, https://irenetinker.com/publications -and-presentations/ester-boserup; Ester Boserup to Gunnar Myrdal, January 1960, p. 9, Ester and Mogens Boserup Papers, Acc. 1998/94, Department of Manuscripts, Royal Danish Library, Copenhagen. Many thanks to Sam Klug for sharing a copy of this letter. On Boserup's career and scholarship, see also Ester Boserup, *My Professional Life and Publications, 1929–1998* (Copenhagen: Museum Tusculanum, 2000).

20. Ester Boserup, *The Conditions of Agricultural Growth: The Economics of Agrarian Change under Population Pressure* (London: G. Allen and Unwin, 1965).

21. Ester Boserup, *Woman's Role in Economic Development* (New York: St. Martin's, 1970), 53, 54, 56. For an influential critique of Boserup's book, see Lourdes Benería and Gita Sen, "Accumulation, Reproduction, and Women's Role in Economic Development: Boserup Revisited," *Signs* 7, no. 2 (Winter 1981): 279–98.

22. Boserup, *Woman's Role in Economic Development*, 5.

23. On India, see Indian National Congress, National Planning Committee, *Woman's Role in Planned Economy (Report of the Sub-Committee)* (Bombay: Vora, 1947). On the ILO, see Eileen Boris, *Making the Woman Worker: Precarious Labor and the Fight for Global Standards, 1919–2019* (New York: Oxford University Press, 2019), chap. 3; Cobble, *For the Many*, chap. 11. On the Economic Commission for Africa, see Margaret C. Snyder and Mary Tadesse, *African Women and Development: A History* (London: Zed Books, 1991), 32. On Sweden, see Karin Himmelstrand, "Can an Aid Bureaucracy Empower Women?" in *Women, International Development, and Politics: The Bureaucratic Mire*, ed. Kathleen Staudt (Philadelphia, PA: Temple University Press, 1990), 104.

24. Ester Boserup, "Women's Role in Economic Development," *Development Digest* 9, no. 2 (April 1971): 97–122.

25. UN General Assembly, Resolution 2626, International Development Strategy for the Second United Nations Development Decade, A/RES/25/2626 (Oct. 24, 1970), http://www.un-documents.net/a25r2626.htm; *Report of the Interregional Meeting of Experts on the Integration of Women in Development, United Nations Headquarters, 19–28 June 1972* (New York: United Nations, 1973); Margaret Snyder, "The Politics of Women and Development," in *Women, Politics, and the United Nations*, ed. Anne Winslow (Westport, CT: Greenwood, 1995), 97.

26. Ester Boserup and Christina Liljencrantz, *Integration of Women in Development* (New York: United Nations Development Programme, 1975). On the WID caucus in the Society for International Development, see Irene Tinker, "Women in Development," in *Women in Washington: Advocates for Public Policy*, ed. Tinker (Beverly Hills: Sage, 1983), 228–29. On the OECD meeting, see Elizabeth Johnstone to Clara Beyer, March 22, 1973, box 3, folder: ILO Geneva, CBCA. On the International Women's Year conference in Mexico City, see Jocelyn Olcott, *International Women's Year: The Greatest Consciousness-Raising Event in History* (New York: Oxford University Press, 2017).

27. Program of National Foreign Policy Conference for Leaders of Nongovernmental Organizations, September 18–19, 1973, 13:21, WHP; Irene Tinker, "Challenging Wisdom, Changing Policies: The Women in Development Movement," in *Developing Power: How Women Transformed International Development*, ed. Arvonne S. Fraser and Irene Tinker (New York: Feminist Press, 2004), 70–71, esp. 70. In addition, see Kathleen Staudt, *Women, Foreign Assistance, and Advocacy Administration* (New York: Praeger, 1985), 33–34; Arvonne Fraser, *She's No Lady: Politics, Family, and International Feminism* (Minneapolis: Nodin, 2007), 161–62; Tinker, "Women in Development," 229–32. In a later recollection, Tinker remembered the woman who denounced the State Department officials at the conference as the president of the Washington, DC, chapter of the National Organization for Women; email from Irene Tinker to author, January 12, 2017.

28. Meg McGavran Murray and Blanche Coll, interview with Clara M. Beyer, September 1980, 37, WFGP; Clara Beyer to Elizabeth Johnstone, March 13, 1973, box 3, folder: ILO Geneva, CBCA; Tinker, "Women in Development," 230. On Beyer, see also "Clara Beyer, 98, Dies; Key New Deal Official," *New York Times*, September 28, 1990; Joanne Meyerowitz, "Clara Beyer's Gen(d)erations," *Radcliffe Magazine*, Summer 2016, 8–9.

29. Jean Joyce, interview with Mildred Marcy, 1983, 157, WFGP. See also Tinker, "Challenging Wisdom," 70–71; Staudt, *Women, Foreign Assistance, and Advocacy Administration*, 33–34; Fraser, *She's No Lady*, 161–62; Tinker, "Women in Development," 229–32; Dorothy Robins-Mowry, interview with Mildred Marcy, February 15, 1991, p. 31, in Foreign Affairs Oral History Collection of the Association for Diplomatic Studies and Training, http://www.loc.gov/item/mfdipbib000744.

30. Committee on Foreign Affairs, US House of Representatives, and Committee on Foreign Affairs, US Senate, *Legislation on Foreign Relations with Explanatory Notes* (Washington, DC: Government Printing Office, 1974), 13.

31. Clara Beyer to Elizabeth Johnstone, October 29, 1973, series: Women's Questions, file WN 1-1-61, Jacket 2, ILO. Thanks to Eileen Boris for a copy of this letter.

32. Tinker, "Challenging Wisdom," 71.

33. Tinker, 71; Fraser, *She's No Lady*, 162. The same year that Congress passed the Percy amendment, it also passed another provision of the same Foreign Assistance Act that prohibited the use of foreign aid funds to pay for abortions. The abortion provision attracted less attention from the old-line women's organizations and more attention from the newer feminist groups. See Committee on Foreign Affairs, US House of Representatives, and Committee on Foreign Affairs, US Senate, *Legislation on Foreign Relations*, 13; Tinker, "Challenging Wisdom," 71.

34. Clara Beyer to Arthur Z. Gardiner, February 22, 1974, and "Report of the Percy Amendment Working Committee," June 18, 1974, p. 1, both in box 5, folder: Percy Amendment—Report of the A.I.D. Percy Amendment Working Committee, 6-18-74, CBCA.

35. "U.S. Department of Labor's Involvement in Improving the Status of Women in Developing Countries," n.d., ca. 1974, box 3, folder: AID/W O/LAB, 1974, CBCA;

"Draft Project Submission Data, Pan-African Women's Centre and African Women's Development Task Force," 1974, box 3, folder: Economic Commission on Africa Project, CBCA.

36. Philip Sperling to Nan Frederick, April 2, 1974, p. 3, box 5, folder: Percy Amendment—Background Papers on Ongoing A.I.D. Programs that Impact on Women, March–April 1974, CBCA; Arthur D. Silver to Nira H. Long, April 5, 1974, p. 2, box 5, folder: Percy Amendment—Background Papers on Ongoing A.I.D. Programs that Impact on Women, March–April 1974, CBCA; Airgram from AID/W on "FY 1976 Program Budget Submission Guidance," June 22, 1974, p. 8, box 5, folder: Percy Amendment—A.I.D. Directives to Overseas Missions on the Percy Amendment, CBCA.

37. "Women's Role in Development Stressed," [USAID] *Front Lines*, April 18, 1974, box 5, folder: Percy Amendment—Establishing Authorities Early Background Papers Set-Up Percy Committee, 1972–6/74, CBCA; "Report of the Percy Amendment Working Committee," 4.

38. "Report of the Percy Amendment Working Committee," 4.

39. Margaret C. Snyder to Clara Beyer, April 11, 1974, box 5, folder: Percy Amendment—Working Committee Background Papers for Subcommittee on National Planning and Employment, CBCA; Lorraine J. Simard to Nira H. Long, June 11, 1974, copy of Kissinger's June 7 testimony before the Senate Foreign Relations Committee, box 5, folder: Percy Amendment—Establishing Authorities Early Background Papers Set-Up Percy Committee, 1972–6/74, CBCA.

40. "'Percy Amendment' Becomes Official Aid Policy," press release, September 16, 1974, 9:160, SL 236, MHP. On Long, see "Nira Hardon Long Gets Federal Post," *Los Angeles Sentinel*, October 24, 1974.

41. Long paraphrased in Minutes of Advisory Committee on Voluntary Foreign Aid, September 16, 1974, 9:178, SL236, MHP.

42. On the NCNW grant, see box 1, folder: 0658001 (G), NCNW Conf Mexico, USAID/WID. For more on NCNW's WID programs, see Rebecca Tuuri, *Strategic Sisterhood: The National Council of Negro Women in the Black Freedom Struggle* (Chapel Hill: University of North Carolina Press, 2018), chap. 8.

43. Nira Long, "SOG Presentation—Women in Development," March 12, 1975, p. 14, box 7, folder: AID Women in Developing Countries, CBCA.

44. Tinker, "Challenging Wisdom," 73.

45. "Coalition for Women in International Development," n.d., ca. 1978, box 58, folder: Coalition Meetings, 1978, OEF; Staudt, *Women, Foreign Assistance, and Advocacy Administration*, 75.

46. Arvonne S. Fraser, "Seizing Opportunities: USAID, WID, and CEDAW," in Fraser and Tinker, *Developing Power*, 167.

47. Adrienne Germain to Marty Chen, September 24, 1977, p. 2, box 1, folder: Sept. 1977—AG Chrons, AGO.

48. Fraser, *She's No Lady*, 186; Jane S. Jaquette, "Crossing the Line: From Academia to the WID Office at USAID," in Fraser and Tinker, *Developing Power*, 191.

49. Jaquette, "Crossing the Line," 194.

50. Elsa M. Chaney, "Full Circle: From Academia to Government and Back," in Fraser and Tinker, *Developing Power*, 205; Charles H. Percy to John J. Gilligan, February 2, 1978, box 145.E.12.2F, folder: Samples 1978, AFP.

51. Tinker, "Challenging Wisdom," 73; Sharpless, interview with Adrienne Germain, 62. In addition to USAID, the seminar was sponsored by the UN Development Programme, the UN Institute for Training and Research, and the Mexican National Council on Science and Technology.

52. Joan M. Goodin, "U.S. Delegation to United Nations World Conference on International Women's Year: A Report," July 14, 1975, p. 10, box 8, folder: International Conference on Women's Year, Mexico City, 6/19–7/2/75, CBCA.

53. On the International Women's Year conference and the NIEO, see Olcott, *International Women's Year*, 208–10, 218; Joyce, interview with Mildred Marcy, 163–64; Roland Burke, "Competing for the Last Utopia? The NIEO, Human Rights, and the World Conference for the International Women's Year, Mexico City, June 1975," *Humanity: An International Journal of Human Rights, Humanitarianism, and Development* 6, no. 1 (Spring 2015): 47–61. The *World Plan of Action for the Implementation of the Objectives of the International Women's Year* is available online at http://www.un.org/womenwatch/daw/beijing/otherconferences/Mexico /Mexico%20conference%20report%20optimized.pdf; on the NIEO, see, for example, paragraph 2.

54. "Sen. Percy Moderates Forum on Women and Development Assistance," *Women Today*, July 7, 1975, p. 86, box 8, folder: International Conference on Women's Year Mexico City, 6/19–72/75, U.S. Center, CBCA; see also Olcott, *International Women's Year*, 166.

55. Roxann A. Van Dusen to David I. Steinberg, June 9, 1976, box 2, folder: 0668006—Wellesley, USAID/WID; Judith W. Gilmore to Allan R. Furman, June 16, 1976, box 146.E.12.1B, folder: AID Legislation 1977, AFP.

56. Nawal El Saadawi, Fatima Mernissi, and Mallica Vajrathon, "A Critical Look at the Wellesley Conference," *Quest* 4, no. 2 (1978): 102, 103.

57. Bolanle Awe, "Reflections on the Conference on Women and Development: I," *Signs* 3, no. 1 (Autumn 1977): 315.

58. Vina Mazumdar, "Reflections on the Conference on Women and Development: IV," *Signs* 3, no. 1 (Autumn 1977): 324; Lourdes Casal, Suad Joseph, Achola Pala, and Ann Seidman, "Women and Development: A Wingspread Workshop Convened by Center for Research and Development, Wellesley College, in Cooperation with the Johnson Foundation," June 1976, unpublished report, p. 3, 5:154, SL 564, MHP. For an earlier era—the 1920s and 1930s—Katherine Marino has written about somewhat similar conflicts over priorities between women's rights activists in the United States and the global South. In Latin America, she finds, feminists condemned US imperialism, called for the equality of nations, and rejected the US feminists who tried to assume leadership of an international movement; see Katherine M. Marino, *Feminism for the Americas: The Making of an International Human Rights Movement* (Chapel Hill: University of North Carolina Press, 2019).

59. Richard Birnberg to Alfred D. White, June 14, 1976, box 2, folder: 0668006—Wellesley, USAID/WID; Elinor G. Barber, "Wellesley and Wingspread Conferences," June 14, 1976, pp. 1, 4, FR 7780.

60. Federation of Organizations for Professional Women, "History of the Development of the Grant Prior to Start of Grant Period, " typewritten report, June 18, 1976, box 1, folder 0668002—3 Country Study—General 1, USAID/WID.

61. Chaney, "Full Circle," 203.

62. Ann Stoler to Adrienne Germain, November 24, 1978, and Adrienne Germain to Ann Stoler, December 8, 1978, both in 2:S (2/2), AGO.

63. Tinker, "Women in Development," 237; Jaquette, "Crossing the Line," 199.

64. Eleanor Leacock, "Reflections on the Conference on Women and Development: III," *Signs* 3, no. 1 (Autumn 1977): 320; Suellen Huntington to Elinor Barber, March 13, 1976, 3:38, EBO. For a later and influential left- feminist critique of mainstream WID programs, see Lourdes Benería and Gita Sen, "Class and Gender Inequalities and Women's Role in Economic Development—Theoretical and Practical Implications," *Feminist Studies* 8, no. 1 (Spring 1982): 157–76. For a more recent assessment of left-feminist structuralist critiques of WID, see Naila Kabeer, *Reversed Realities: Gender Hierarchies in Development Thought* (London: Verso, 1994), chap. 3.

65. Richard Birnberg to Alfred D. White, June 14, 1976.

66. Barber, "Wellesley and Wingspread Conferences," 3; Hanna Papanek to Elinor Barber, April 10, 1978, 3:54, EBO.

67. Kathleen A. Staudt to Arvonne Fraser, June 16, 1979, box 146.E.12.2F, folder: Miscellaneous, 1976–1979, AFP.

68. Kathleen Staudt, "Straddling Borders: Global to Local," in Fraser and Tinker, *Developing Power*, 319.

69. Kathleen A. Staudt, "In Defense of AID," *Women's Studies Newsletter* 7, no. 3 (Summer 1979): 8.

70. Devaki Jain, "A View from the South: A Story of Intersections," in Fraser and Tinker, *Developing Power*, 134; Gloria Scott, "Breaking New Ground at the UN and the World Bank," in Fraser and Tinker, *Developing Power*, 21; Adrienne Germain, "Women at Mexico: Beyond Family Planning Acceptance," *Family Planning Perspectives* 7, no. 5 (September–October 1975): 235.

71. On the UN, see Snyder, "Politics of Women and Development," 95–116; on the African Training and Research Centre for Women, see Snyder and Tadesse, *African Women and Development*, chap. 7; on the United Nations Development Programme, see United Nations Development Programme, *Rural Women's Participation in Development* (New York: United Nations, 1980).

72. Ingrid Palmer, "Rural Women and the Basic-Needs Approach to Development," *International Labour Review* 115, no. 1 (January–February 1977): 97, 103, 104. On the ILO program, see also Zubeida M. Ahmad and Martha F. Loutfi, "International Labour Office Programme on Rural Women," December 1980, 10-4-04:9, WEP; Boris, *Making the Woman Worker*, chap. 4.

73. "Peace Corps," January 1, 1981, box 10, folder: PC WID Office, History and Chron, 1981, PC/WID. From 1976 on, the WID movement had made inroads into the

Peace Corps bureaucracy. But it was not until 1978 that the Percy amendment was officially incorporated into the Peace Corps Act, which led to the creation of a Peace Corps WID oversight committee and in 1982 a Peace Corps WID office.

74. Arvonne S. Fraser, memorandum on ad hoc Women in Development Donor Group, October 14, 1980, 1:5, EBO. On the OECD subcommittee on WID, see Fraser, "Seizing Opportunities," 170.

75. On the seminar in Bangladesh, see news clippings in FR 007630.

76. Quoted in Boris, *Making the Woman Worker*, 120.

77. Petra Reyes to Susan Goodwillie, memorandum on [Economic Commission for Africa] Regional Conference on the Implementation of National, Regional and World Plans of Action for the Integration of Women in Development, October 24, 1977, p. 4, FR 007911.

78. Scott, "Breaking New Ground," 22.

79. Nüket Kardam, *Bringing Women In: Women's Issues in International Development Programs* (Boulder, CO: Lynne Rienner, 1991), 77, 78; Robert Oliver, interview with Montague Yudelman, July 18, 1986, p. 20, WBOHP. Yudelman's comments about WID seem to reflect his acknowledgment of the blinders at the World Bank. His wife, Sally Watters Yudelman, was a feminist who tried to promote WID issues at the Inter-American Foundation. That foundation, she said, hired women but did little for WID; Sally W. Yudelman, "The Inter-American Foundation and Gender Issues: A Feminist View," in Staudt, *Women, International Development, and Politics*, 129–44.

80. On the Ford Foundation's financing of the US women's movement, see Susan M. Hartmann, *The Other Feminists: Activists in the Liberal Establishment* (New Haven, CT: Yale University Press, 1998), chap. 5.

81. Ford Foundation, *Women in the World: A Ford Foundation Position Paper* (New York: Ford Foundation, 1980), 35. On Ford's International Division's commitment to WID, see also Kardam, *Bringing Women In*, chap. 4; Cornelia Butler Flora, "Incorporating Women into International Development Programs: The Political Phenomenology of a Private Foundation," in *Women in Developing Countries: A Policy Focus*, ed. Kathleen A. Staudt and Jane S. Jaquette (New York: Haworth, 1983), 89–106; Ford Foundation, *Created Equal: A Report on Ford Foundation Women's Programs* (New York: Ford Foundation, 1986); Cornelia Butler Flora, "The Ford Foundation and the Power of International Sisterhood," in Fraser and Tinker, *Developing Power*, 277–87. On Ford's support for the women's program of the Economic Commission for Africa, see Snyder and Tadesse, *African Women and Development*, 76; Adrienne Germain to Mel Fox, January 6, 1976, 2:30, EBO.

82. Adrienne Germain, "A Major Resource Awaiting Development: Women in the Third World," *New York Times*, August 26, 1975; Adrienne Germain to Denis de Tray, September 8, 1976, 2:D, AGO; Adrienne Germain to D. E. Bell, January 4, 1978, p. 3, box 1, folder: AG Chrons—Jan. 1978, AGO.

83. Germain, "Major Resource"; Germain, "Poor Rural Women," 163.

84. Adrienne Germain to James Grant, April 17, 1979, box 1, folder: AG Chrons—April 1979, AGO; Germain, "Poor Rural Women," 163; Adrienne Germain to Jeff Puryear, November 29, 1979, box 1, folder: AG Chrons—November 1979, AGO.

85. Adrienne Germain to David Smock, April 29, 1980, 2:26, EBO.

86. Germain to Marty Chen, September 24, 1977.

87. Adrienne Germain to David Bell/Oscar Harkavy, July 31, 1978, 2:G, AGO.

88. George Zeidenstein to Eugene S. Staples, November 18, 1972, 4:76, EBC; Sharpless, interview with Adrienne Germain, 65.

89. See, for example, Adrienne Germain, "Women's Roles in Bangladesh Development: A Program Assessment," April 1976, FR 003708.

90. See, for example, Martha Chen, "Review of the Ford Foundation's Programming for Women in Bangladesh," November 1989, box 2, folder: Marty Chen, 1989, DPF. For more on WID in Bangladesh, see chapter 5.

91. "Women's Role in Development Defined," [USAID] *Front Lines*, September 26, 1974, 3; Germain, "Major Resource"; Hanna Papanek, "Development Planning for Women," *Signs* 3, no. 1 (Autumn 1977): 19, 20; Adrienne Germain to Elinor Barber, March 3, 1978, box 1, folder: 3/78, AGO.

92. Irene Tinker and Michèle Bo Bramsen, "Proceedings of the Seminar on Women in Development (Mexico City, June 15–18, 1975)" in Tinker, Bramsen, and Buvinic, *Women and World Development*, 148.

93. Irene Tinker, "Basic Human Needs: The Equity Revolution," March 15, 1977, box 146. E.12.1B, folder: AID Advice Memos," AFP; Mayra Buvinic and Nadia H. Youssef, "Women-Headed Households: The Ignored Factor in Development Planning," March 1978, iii, document PN-AAF-595, DEC.

94. Elinor Barber and Adrienne Germain, "The Percy Amendment," May 20, 1974, FR 7789, p. 3; Germain, "Women at Mexico," 237; "Report of the Sub-Committee on Health, Population, and Family Planning," p. 7, in "Report of the Percy Amendment Working Committee"; Rae Lesser Blumberg, "Fairy Tales and Facts: Economy, Family, Fertility, and the Female," in Tinker, Bramsen, and Buvinic, *Women and World Development*, 21.

95. Jarold A. Kieffer, "A.I.D. Population Assistance Program Strategies, Priorities, and Issues—FY 1975–1976," pp. 10, 17, October 7, 1974, 11:212, SL 236, MHP; McNamara quoted in Nüket Kardam, "The Adaptability of International Development Agencies: The Response of the World Bank to Women in Development," in Staudt, *Women, International Development, and Politics*, 116. See also *International Women's Issues: Hearing and Briefing* (statement of George A. Dalley, deputy assistant secretary for international organization affairs, Department of State), 5.

96. "Sample Questions," n.d., ca. 1976; Linda Muller to John Dellenback, "Peace Corps Directors' Conference Presentation—'Women in International Development,'" August 9, 1976, p. 2; both in box 9, folder: PC WID Office History and Chron, 1974–1977, PC/WID.

97. Arthur D. Silver, "Women, Development, and A.I.D.," July 6, 1973, p. 6, box 5, folder: Percy Amendment, Establishing Authorities, Early Background Papers, Set-Up Percy Committee, 1972–6/74, CBCA; Silver to Nira H. Long, April 5, 1974; LA Working Group on the Percy Amendment, AID/AA/LA, USAID airgram, July 25, 1974, p. 4, 11:214, SL 236, MHP.

98. *International Women's Issues: Hearing and Briefing* (statement of Elsa Chaney), 14, 20; (statement of Coralie Turbitt) 58–59; (statement of Arvonne Fraser) 85.

99. Fraser, *She's No Lady*, 172–73; *International Women's Issues: Hearing and Briefing* (statement of Dorothy Height), 59–60.

100. "Final Report of the Workshop on the Involvement of Women in the Development Project Implementation Process, Freetown, Sierra Leone, October 11–14, 1977," January 13, 1978, p. 6, box 2, folder: 0678009 Transcentury—Participants, USAID/WID.

101. Martha Alter Chen, interviewed by author, March 1, 2016.

102. Martha Alter Chen, *A Quiet Revolution: Women in Transition in Rural Bangladesh* (Cambridge, MA: Schenkman, 1983), 83.

103. Chaney, "Full Circle," 204. See also Kathleen Staudt, "Gender Politics in Bureaucracy: Theoretical Issues in Comparative Perspective," in *Women, International Development, and Politics*, 23; Jaquette, "Crossing the Line," 193.

104. Adrienne Germain to Alexander Shakow, January 22, 1979, box 1, folder: Jan. 1979, AGO.

105. For a critical account of "success stories" in the development field, see William Paddock and Elizabeth Paddock, *We Don't Know How: An Independent Audit of What They Call Success in Foreign Assistance* (Ames: University of Iowa Press, 1973).

106. *International Women's Issues: Hearing and Briefing*, 23 (statement of Elsa Chaney); "Women in Africa: What Is the Impact of Development?," [USAID] *Agenda* 1, no. 2 (February 1978): 2.

107. *International Women's Issues: Hearing and Briefing*, 42, 109.

108. *International Women's Issues: Hearing and Briefing*, 41, 42.

109. "Miss Lillian Feels for Sand in Her Shoes," *Afro-American*, July 29, 1978.

110. Arvonne S. Fraser to Alexander Shakow, May 15, 1978, box 146.E.12.2F, folder: Samples 1978, AFP; "Peanuts Greet Miss Lillian on African 'Mission of Love,'" *Atlanta Constitution*, July 30, 1978. Carter also visited Morocco, Senegal, the Gambia, and Mali.

111. Carolyn Barnes, "Report on 'Strengthening Women's Roles in Development,'" USAID project 686–0211, February 14, 1979, pp. 7, 9, document PD-AAH-995, DEC.

112. Sheila Reines to Arvonne Fraser, April 12, 1979, box 146.E.12.6F, folder: ASF's Trip to Upper Volta Sahel Info 1979, AFP.

113. Thomas Stickley, "Credit Consultancy Report on 'Strengthening Women's Roles in Development': Credit (Revolving Fund) Activity," USAID project 686–0211, October 1980, p. 2, document PD-AAW-668, DEC; Linda Postle, "Project Completion Report on 'Strengthening Women's Roles in Development,'" USAID project 686–0211, September 1982, p. 5, document PD-BAL-906, DEC.

114. See Office of Women in Development, Bureau for Program and Policy Coordination, Agency for International Development, *Women in Development: The First Decade, 1975–1984, A Report to the Committee on Foreign Relations United States Senate and the Committee on Foreign Affairs United States House of Representatives* (Washington, DC: USAID, ca. 1985).

115. Kristin Anderson, Judith Bruce, Adrienne Germain, and Ann Leonard, group letter announcing pamphlet series, box 1, folder: March 1978, AGO.

116. Elinor Barber and Adrienne Germain to Howard Dressner, May 16, 1977, 2:29, EBO; "Proposal to the Ford Foundation for Support of the Seeds Documentation Project on Women's Productive Roles and Economic Empowerment," January 1994, FG 860-0708-2. For the list of identified projects, see Adrienne Germain to ID Committee on Women, May 3, 1977, 2:29, EBO. On the older visual "Madonna-and-child" trope, see Laura Briggs, "Mother, Child, Race, Nation: The Visual Iconography of Rescue and the Politics of Transnational and Transracial Adoption," *Gender and History* 15, no. 2 (August 2003): 179–200.

117. Independent Commission on International Development Issues, *North-South, A Programme for Survival: Report of the Independent Commission on International Development Issues* (Cambridge, MA: MIT Press, 1980), 59.

118. [Mahbub ul Haq and Shahid Javed Burki], *Meeting Basic Needs: An Overview* (Washington, DC: World Bank, Policy Planning and Program Review Department, 1980), 15.

Chapter 4

1. Michael Buerk and Mohammed Amin, "BBC News, 10/23/84," YouTube, November 13, 2009, https://www.youtube.com/watch?v=XYOj_6OYuJc; Sally Bedell Smith, "Famine Reports Show Power of TV," *New York Times*, November 22, 1984; Kathleen Teltsch, "2-Month U.S. Total to Help Ethiopians Reaches $40 Million," *New York Times*, January 1, 1985. For an older critique of "poverty porn," see Jørgen Lissner, "Merchants of Misery," *New Internationalist*, June 1, 1981, https://newint .org/features/1981/06/01/merchants-of-misery. Other photography theorists have imagined photographs of catastrophe as testimony or witness that demands political action. See, for example, Ariella Azoulay, *The Civil Contract of Photography* (Cambridge, MA: MIT Press, 2008). For an account of the US government's involvement in the relief effort, see Alexander Poster, "The Gentle War: Famine Relief, Politics, and Privatization in Ethiopia, 1983–1986," *Diplomatic History* 36, no. 2 (April 2012): 399–425. For a classic and influential account on famines more generally, see Amartya Sen, *Poverty and Famines: An Essay on Entitlement and Deprivation* (Oxford: Clarendon, 1981).

2. Organisation for Economic Co-operation and Development, *Voluntary Aid for Development: The Role of Non-Governmental Organisations* (Paris: OECD, 1988), 33.

3. "USA for Africa Overcomes Resentment with Results," *Hartford Courant*, January 8, 1987; on Band Aid/Live Aid and critical commentary on celebrity fundraising, see, for example, Tanja R. Müller, "The Long Shadow of Band Aid Humanitarianism: Revisiting the Dynamics between Famine and Celebrity," *Third World Quarterly* 34, no. 3 (2013): 470–84.

4. Clifford D. May, "'We Are the World' Meets a Continent of Misery," *New York Times*, June 26, 1985.

5. On USA for Africa's work with InterAction and the United Nations Office for Emergency Operations in Africa, see 1190:23 and 24, and 1241:4, CARE.

6. Peter J. Davies, InterAction, to Members of the Africa Emergency Subcommittee, December 2, 1985, 1241:4, CARE. See also "Famine Relief Audit Issued," *New York Times*, March 12, 1986. InterAction was established in 1984 as a merger of two older consortia: the American Council of Voluntary Agencies in Foreign Service (ACVAFS) and Private Agencies in International Development (PAID). See, for example, Victoria Irwin, "New Unity for Humanitarian Groups," *Christian Science Monitor*, June 18, 1984.

7. On Band Aid/Live Aid, see Davies to Members of the Africa Emergency Subcommittee. On USA for Africa, see "Project Proposals for the Country of Ethiopia," March 18, 1986, 1190:23; Charles La Meunière, "UN Agency Projects for Submission to USA for Africa," March 21, 1986, 1190:24; "Project Proposals for the Country of Mali," March 18, 1986, 1190:23; "INTERACTION/UNOEOA Submission to USA for Africa for Sudan," February 21, 1986, 1190:23; InterAction/OEOA/USA for Africa, "Status Report on US/AF Grants for Recovery and Development," August 26, 1986, 1190:24; all in CARE.

8. OEF International, "OEF Receives USA for Africa Grant to Deliver Training, Technology and Credit to Senegalese Women Entrepreneurs," press release, May 1, 1987, box 6 (no folder), OEF; OEF International, "African Women Can Take the Next Step to End Hunger," advertisement, box 68 (no folder), OEF; Steve Coll, "Live Aid and the Swirl of Criticism," *Washington Post*, November 22, 1985.

9. Louis Samia, Executive Director of CARE, to Daniel Shaughnessy, February 19, 1980, box 11, folder: CARE, PCWH; John G. Sommer, *Beyond Charity: U.S. Voluntary Aid for a Changing Third World* (Washington, DC: Overseas Development Council, 1977). On the 1970s rise of international NGOs more generally, see, for example, Akira Iriye, *Global Community: The Role of International Organizations in the Making of the Contemporary World* (Berkeley: University of California Press, 2002), chap. 5; Thomas Davies, *NGOs: A New History of Transnational Civil Society* (London: Hurst, 2013), chap. 3; Gregory Mann, *From Empires to NGOs in the West African Sahel: The Road to Nongovernmentality* (Cambridge: Cambridge University Press, 2015). On "NGOization" of women's projects, see Victoria Bernal and Inderpal Grewal, eds., *Theorizing NGOs: States, Feminisms, and Neoliberalism* (Durham, NC: Duke University Press, 2014).

10. Foreign Assistance Act of 1973, Pub. L. No. 93-189, 81 Stat. 445 (1973).

11. Amy C. Offner, *Sorting Out the Mixed Economy: The Rise and Fall of Welfare and Developmental States in the Americas* (Princeton, NJ: Princeton University Press, 2019), 154. On the 1950s, see Burton I. Kaufman, *Trade and Aid: Eisenhower's Foreign Economic Policy, 1953-1961* (Baltimore, MD: Johns Hopkins University Press, 1982).

12. Richard Nixon, "Special Message to the Congress on Foreign Aid," May 28, 1969, APP. For a recent account of US private investment in the global South in the 1970s, see, for example, Vanessa Ogle, "Archipelago Capitalism: Tax Havens, Offshore

Money, and the State, 1950s–1970s," *American Historical Review*, December 2017, 1431–58.

13. On the longer history of US government and NGO collaboration, see Rachel M. McCleary, *Global Compassion: Private Voluntary Organizations and U.S. Foreign Policy since 1939* (New York: Oxford University Press, 2009), esp. chaps. 2–4. On CARE and the Peace Corps, especially in Colombia, see Heike Wieters, *The NGO CARE and Food Aid from America, 1945–80: "Showered with Kindness"?* (Manchester: Manchester University Press, 2017), chap. 7. See also Michael Barnett, *Empire of Humanity: A History of Humanitarianism* (Ithaca, NY: Cornell University Press, 2011), chap. 6. For consistency, I have used the abbreviation NGO in this chapter, even though PVO was commonly used in the United States in the 1970s and 1980s.

14. Earl Martin, "Refugees without Hope," *St. Louis Post-Dispatch*, August 8, 1973. On CARE in Vietnam, see Delia T. Pergande, "Private Voluntary Aid and Nation Building in South Vietnam: The Humanitarian Politics of CARE, 1954–61," *Peace and Change* 27, no. 2 (April 2002): 163–97; on Catholic Relief Services in Vietnam, see Scott Flipse, "The Latest Casualty of War: Catholic Relief Services, Humanitarianism, and the War in Vietnam, 1967–1968," *Peace and Change* 27, no. 2 (April 2002): 245–70; on Mennonite Central Committee in Vietnam, see the articles in *Intersections: MCC Theory and Practice Quarterly* 5, no. 2 (Spring 2017), https://mcc.org/sites/mcc.org/files/media/common/documents/intersectionsspring2017web_0.pdf.

15. McCleary, *Global Compassion*, chaps. 4 and 5. On the rising influence of environmental NGOs in 1970s development circles, see Stephen J. Macekura, *Of Limits and Growth: The Rise of Global Sustainable Development in the Twentieth Century* (Cambridge: Cambridge University Press, 2015). On earlier overlaps (and the permeable boundary) between humanitarian relief and development assistance, see Julia F. Irwin, "The 'Development' of Humanitarian Relief: US Disaster Assistance Operations in the Caribbean Basin, 1917–1931," in *The Development Century: A Global History*, ed. Stephen J. Macekura and Erez Manela (Cambridge: Cambridge University Press, 2018), 40–60.

16. USAID Bureau for Population and Humanitarian Assistance, "A.I.D. and the Independent Voluntary Sector: A Progress Report," January 3, 1973, pp. 1, 2, document PD-ACS-320, DEC.

17. John A. Ulinski Jr. to members of Advisory Committee on Voluntary Foreign Aid, n.d., ca. July 1973, 8:152, SL 236, MHP; USAID Bureau for Population and Humanitarian Assistance, "AID and the Private and Voluntary Organizations," September 24, 1973, pp. 6, 7, document PN-ADW-873, DEC.

18. James P. Grant to Jarold A. Kieffer, June 26, 1974, 8:157, SL 236, MHP; Sommer, *Beyond Charity*, 1, 2, 7.

19. Margaret Hickey to Daniel S. Parker, December 21, 1973, 8:153, SL 236, MHP.

20. Advisory Committee on Voluntary Foreign Aid, "A Look to the Future: The Role of Voluntary Agencies in International Assistance," April 1974, p. 102, 10:200, SL 236, MHP.

21. Frank L. Goffio to Jarold A. Kieffer, January 7, 1974, 8:154, SL 236, MHP; Edward E. Swanstrom to Jarold A. Kieffer, January 10, 1974, 8:155, SL 236, MHP.

22. Overseas Development Council, "Report on Rural Development Workshop, December 2–4, 1974," 9:162, SL 236, MHP; Issues Paper no. 5, ca. January–February 1975, p. 4, 11:218, SL 236, MHP.

23. Issues Paper no. 3, p. 2, ca. January–February 1975, 11:218, SL 236, MHP.

24. Issues Paper no. 4, pp. 6–7, ca. January–February 1975, 11:218, SL 236, MHP.

25. Issues Paper no. 5, p. 4.

26. USAID Bureau for Population and Humanitarian Assistance, "Policy Directions," April 17, 1974, 8:156, SL 236, MHP.

27. Advisory Committee on Voluntary Foreign Aid, "Transcript of Proceedings," September 11, 1974, p. 137, 2:64, SL 371, MHP; John A. Ulinksi Jr. to Nira Long, February 18, 1975, p. 2, 9:180, SL 236, MHP. On Margaret Hickey, see "Margaret A. Hickey, Women's Leader, 92," *New York Times*, December 10, 1994; "Preliminary Inventory: Margaret Hickey Papers," State Historical Society of Missouri, April 23, 2020, https://files.shsmo.org/manuscripts/saint-louis/S0236.pdf.

28. "Development Program Grant for the National Council for Negro Women," June 4, 1975, document PD-AAQ-622, DEC; "Aid Contract No. AID/PHA-G-1120 to the National Council of Negro Women to Develop a Systematic International Program by Establishing an International Division," July 14, 1975, document PD-FAB-191, DEC; Elinor G. Barber and Richard Horovitz to Katharine McKee and Laketch Dirasse, November 28, 1979, 3:50, International Division, EBO. For NCNW's WID programs, see also Rebecca Tuuri, *Strategic Sisterhood: The National Council of Negro Women in the Black Freedom Struggle* (Chapel Hill: University of North Carolina Press, 2018), chap. 8.

29. "OEF Goal," July 1973, box 13, folder: OEF Minutes, Board Meetings, 1972–1974, OEF. The OEF separated from the League of Women Voters in 1961, but remained affiliated with it until the mid-1980s.

30. "The Inside Story of the Overseas Education Fund," *CounterSpy*, Winter 1975, 10–18.

31. Minutes, board of directors meeting, January 27, 1972, box 13, folder: OEF Minutes, Board Meetings, 1972–1974, OEF; Minutes, board of directors meeting, January 31, 1974, box 13, folder: OEF Minutes, Board Meetings, 1972–1974, OEF.

32. "Development Program Grant for the Overseas Education Fund, 1975–1978," p. 23, document PD-FAB-705, DEC; Program Development Committee to OEF Board, "Long-Range Plan," January 1978, p. 2, box 13, folder: Board Minutes, 1976–1979, OEF. On the OEF, see also Elise Fiber Smith, "Women Empowering Women through NGOs," in *Developing Power: How Women Transformed International Development*, ed. Arvonne S. Fraser and Irene Tinker (New York: Feminist Press, 2004) 249–61.

33. USAID, "Project Evaluation, Overseas Education Fund of the League of Women Voters Institution Development Grant, Report on Year 1," January 1980, document PD-AAN-262, p. 11. DEC; USAID, additional document attached to "Project Evaluation, Overseas Education Fund of the League of Women Voters Institution Development Grant, Report on Year 1," January 1980, document XD-AAN-262A, DEC. For a list of OEF's USAID projects and their funding, see appendix A of document PD-AAN-262, cited above.

34. Adrienne Germain to Peter Weldon, December 4, 1979, box 1, folder: December 1979, AGO. On the February 1978 USAID meeting, see "Board Briefing," April 1978, box 13, folder: Board Minutes, 1976–1979, OEF.

35. International Labour Office, *Employment, Incomes and Equality: A Strategy for Increasing Productive Employment in Kenya* (Geneva: International Labour Office, 1972), 5, 225. Development economists often cite the work of anthropologist Keith Hart as an influence on the ILO. In the early 1970s, Hart addressed the contributions small-scale entrepreneurs made to the economy and called on development economists to consider the informal sector in their analyses. In its study of Kenya, the ILO drew on the paper Hart presented at the conference "Urban Unemployment in Africa," held at the Institute of Development Studies at the University of Sussex in 1971. See Keith Hart, "Small-Scale Entrepreneurs in Ghana and Development Planning," *Journal of Development Studies* 6, no. 4 (July 1970): 104–20; Keith Hart, "Informal Income Opportunities and Urban Employment in Ghana, *Journal of Modern African Studies* 11, no. 1 (March 1973): 61–89. On Hart's influence, see, for example, Ray Bromley, "Introduction—the Urban Informal Sector: Why Is It Worth Discussing?" *World Development* 6, nos. 9–10 (1978): 1036.

36. S. V. Sethuraman, "The Urban Informal Sector: Concept, Measurement and Policy," *International Labour Review* 114, no. 1 (July–August 1976): 80.

37. See especially E. F. Schumacher, *Small Is Beautiful: Economics as if People Mattered* (New York: Harper and Row, 1973), pt. 3.

38. Bromley, "Introduction—the Urban Informal Sector," 1036; Caroline O. N. Moser, "Informal Sector or Petty Commodity Production: Dualism or Dependence in Urban Development?" *World Development* 6, nos. 9–10 (1978): 1042. The liberal and Marxist views are debated in the articles in the *World Development* special issue (*World Development* 6, nos. 9–10 [1978]); for the conservative view, see, for example, the account of Hernando de Soto's work in Mario Vargas Llosa, "In Defense of the Black Market," *New York Times*, February 22, 1987; Hernando de Soto, "Structural Adjustment and the Informal Sector," in *Microenterprises in Developing Countries: Papers and Proceedings of an International Conference Held in Washington, D.C., USA, 6–9 June 1988*, ed. Jacob Levitsky (London: Intermediate Technology, 1989), 3–12.

39. USAID, "PISCES Phase I, Program Description," pt. 1, p. 5, and annex A, p. 3, August 1978, 1365:7, CARE.

40. Jeffrey Ashe, Jason Brown, Peter H. Fraser, Douglas A. Hellinger, Fred M. O'Regan, and William R. Tucker, *The Pisces Studies: Assisting the Smallest Economic Activities of the Urban Poor* (Washington, DC: Office of Urban Development, Bureau for Science and Technology, Agency for International Development, International Development Cooperation Agency, 1981), vii.

41. Ashe et al., ix.

42. Ashe et al., 32, 69.

43. Ashe et al., 129.

44. Ashe et al., 349, 376.

45. Ashe et al., 270.

46. The early studies of women's work in the informal economy rarely addressed sex work. For an exception, see Pasuk Phongpaichit, *From Peasant Girls to Bangkok Masseuses* (Geneva: International Labour Organization, 1982). This study treated women's sex work as "an entrepreneurial move designed to sustain the family units of a rural economy" (74–75).

47. Gayatri Chakravorty Sprivak, "Can the Subaltern Speak?" originally published in 1988, reprinted in Rosalind C. Morris, ed., *Can the Subaltern Speak? Reflections on the History of an Idea* (New York: Columbia University Press, 2010), 269. On the United States, see, for example, Emily S. Rosenberg, "Rescuing Women and Children," *Journal of American History* 89, no. 2 (September 2002): 456–65.

48. See Wolfgang Saxon, "Glen Frazier Leet Dies at 89; Helped Aspiring Entrepreneurs," *New York Times*, April 12, 1998; Daniel E. Slotnik, "Mildred Leet, 88, Who Helped Empower the Poor, Dies," *New York Times*, May 8, 2011; Kathleen Teltsch, "Couple Using $100 Grants to Foster Self-Help," *New York Times*, September 12, 1982; United Nations Development Program, "Trickle Up Program," ca. 1989, box 5, folder: Video/UNDP 1989—TUP, MLC.

49. Jane Anderson, "Private Volunteer Groups Aid Third-World Women," *Christian Science Monitor*, August 9, 1984.

50. Mildred Robbins Leet, "How Women Create Wealth through the Trickle Up Program," April 1985, pp. 2, 7, box 2, folder: T/MRL/Writings, MLC. On the formal agreement with the Peace Corps, see Susan Scull to Sarah Wright and Sue McCabe, August 31, 1983, box 10, folder: PC WID Office, History and Chron 1983, PC/WID. On US government funding, see Thomas H. Fox, "NGOs from the United States," *World Development* 15, Supplement (Autumn 1987): 17. On corporate and foundation sponsors, see Trickle Up Foundation, *Global Report for the Year Ending 1987* (New York: Trickle Up Program, 1988), 1, https://trickleup .org/1987-global-report/.

51. Davidson R. Gwatkin, "Self-Employed Women's Association (SEWA)," February 20, 1975, p. 3, 4:78, EBC.

52. Kamla Chowdhry, "Status of women, Ahmedabad Visit July 29, 1977," August 1, 1977, FG 795–0283, reel 4071.

53. On the 1979 grant, see FG 795–0283, reels 4071 and 5128. On the total grants to SEWA, see "Ford Grants Unrestricted," Excel spreadsheet, available at Rockefeller Archive Center. On SEWA membership in 2004, see Ela R. Bhatt, *We Are Poor But So Many: The Story of Self-Employed Women in India* (New York: Oxford University Press, 2006), 16.

54. Frank C. Balance, "Reagan and the Third World," *Christian Science Monitor*, December 30, 1980. See also Cass Peterson, "Reagan's Team on Foreign Aid Reflects the New Right's Influence," *Washington Post*, November 30, 1980.

55. John M. Goshko and Hobart Rowen, "Plan to Cut Foreign Aid Is Softened," *Washington Post*, February 1, 1981.

56. Juan de Onis, "Haig Fights Proposal for Drastic Reduction in Foreign Assistance," *New York Times*, January 31, 1981; Goshko and Rowen, "Plan to Cut Foreign

Aid Is Softened"; Walter LaFeber, "Wielding the Foreign-Aid Weapon," *Newsday*, April 12, 1981.

57. M. Peter McPherson to Ronald Reagan, "A Cheaper and More Effective Foreign Aid Program," May 19, 1980, 2:48, SL 564, MHP; Christopher Madison, "Exporting Reaganomics—the President Wants to Do Things Differently at AID," *National Journal*, May 29, 1982, 960.

58. "Foreign Aid: Debating the Uses and Abuses," *New York Times*, March 1, 1981; Advisory Committee on Voluntary Foreign Aid, "Summary Meeting Report," April 7, 1981, p. 1, 2:39, SL 564, MHP.

59. Madison, "Exporting Reaganomics," 961, 963.

60. See, for example, Nicholas Eberstadt, *Foreign Aid and American Purpose* (Washington, DC: American Enterprise Institute for Public Policy Research, 1988), 51–57.

61. Richard Newfarmer, "A Look at Reagan's Revolution in Development Policy," *Challenge* 26, no. 4 (September–October 1983): 39; Sally W. Yudelman, "The Inter-American Foundation and Gender Issues: A Feminist View," in *Women, International Development, and Politics: The Bureaucratic Mire*, ed. Kathleen Staudt (Philadelphia, PA: Temple University Press, 1990), 136. On the adoption of the small-business model in the Peace Corps, see Susan Scull to Carolyn Doppelt Gray, July 21, 1983, box 10, folder: PC WID Office, History and Chron, 1983, PC/WID.

62. Private Agencies in International Development (PAID), "Comments on Proposed AID Policy Statement on Programs of Private and Voluntary Organizations," March 16, 1982, pp. 1–2, in "Public Report of Meeting, March 25–26, 1982, Cooperation between American Corporations and Private Voluntary Organizations in the Developing World," by USAID, Advisory Committee on Voluntary Foreign Aid, pp. 136–137, document PN-AAL-172, DEC.

63. Joan Dunlop, "Whither Women and Development?" May 1981, p. 4, FR 007790; Arvonne Fraser, *She's No Lady: Politics, Family, and International Feminism* (Minneapolis: Nodin, 2007), 207.

64. Leah Janus to Elizabeth Dole, January 9, 1981, and Leah Janus and Willie Campbell to Jean[e] Kirkpatrick, January 29, 1981, both in box 58, unlabeled folder on transition task force 1981, OEF; Minutes of the task force, Coalition on Women in Development, November 12, 1981, box 58, folder: 1981 Task Force on International Development, OEF.

65. Alexander Haig to All Diplomatic Posts, August 26, 1981, box 9, folder: WID History, Percy Amendment, PC Act, etc., PC/WID.

66. Lael Stegall to Loret Ruppe et al., October 1, 1981, box 10, folder: PC WID Office, History and Chron—1981, Women in Development Program Files, PC/WID; "Peace Corps Women in Development Statement of Purpose," p. 1, box 13, folder: Women in Development, Women in Development Program Files, PC/WID.

67. Advisory Committee on Voluntary Foreign Aid, Women in Development Subcommittee, minutes of the June 15, 1983, meeting, p. 2, 1190:28, CARE.

68. Jeffrey Ashe, *The PISCES II Experience: Local Efforts in Micro-Enterprise Development*, vol. 1 (Washington, DC: USAID, 1985), i, ii; Advisory Committee on

Voluntary Foreign Aid, Women in Development Subcommittee, minutes of the June 15, 1983 meeting.

69. Overseas Education Fund, "Technical Advisory Service for International Women's Development Organizations and the Affiliated Indigenous Organizations: Final Evaluation," May 1983, pp. 2, 15, 20, box 12 (no folder), OEF.

70. Overseas Education Fund, "WIDTech: Training for Action," January 20, 1984, p. 5, box 12, Folder: WIDTech Chron File 1984, OEF.

71. Cheryl A. Lassen, "The Transition from Income Generation towards Small Enterprise Development: An Evaluation of the OEF Women-in-Business Program in Costa Rica and Honduras," April 1988, p. 38, document PD-ABA-936, DEC.

72. OEF International, "Impact and Effectiveness of the Caribbean Basin Initiative: Women and Small Business Participation," statement at Hearings of the Subcommittee on Oversight, House Committee on Ways and Means, February 25 and 27, 1986, pp. 1, 2, document PN-ABF-183, DEC.

73. "Low-Income Women Trained to Run Businesses," *Morgan News*, May 1987, box 68 (no folder), OEF; Georgie Anne Geyer, "Third World Businesswomen Learn to Help Themselves" (syndicated column; clipping), ca. September 1986, box 68 (no folder), OEF.

74. Overseas Education Fund, "El Castano's Success Story," May 1983, box 12 (no folder), OEF; Caroline Pezzulo, "For the Record . . . Forum '85: The Non-Governmental World Meeting for Women, Nairobi, Kenya," September 1986, p. 7, box 58, folder: Coalition, 2/5/87 meeting, OEF; OEF International advertisement, *Newsweek*, December 16, 1985.

75. Lassen, "Transition from Income Generation towards Small Enterprise Development," 6.

76. Thomas A. McKay, "Action Memorandum for the Assistant Administrator, FVA," March 20, 1984, p. 3, document PD-AAP-520, DEC; "USAID Project Evaluation Summary, Rural Women's Production Center," December 31, 1985, p. 3, document PD-AAS-567, DEC; Lassen, "Transition from Income Generation towards Small Enterprise Development," 45. On USAID's share of OEF's budget, see OEF International, "Seeds of Promise: 1986 Annual Report," 15, document PN-AAX-649, DEC. On the demise of OEF International, see Willie Campbell to Friend of OEF, November 1991, 86:5, WWB.

77. Organisation for Economic Co-operation and Development, *Voluntary Aid for Development*, 154. On state funding of European NGOs, see Kevin O'Sullivan, "A 'Global Nervous System': The Rise and Rise of European Humanitarian NGOs, 1945–1985," in *International Organizations and Development, 1945–1990*, ed. Marc Frey, Sönke Kunkel, and Corinna R. Unger (New York: Palgrave Macmillan, 2014), 196–219.

78. On the European Community, see Commission of the European Communities, "Introduction to, and the General Conditions of, the Scheme for the Cofinancing of Micro-Projects by the Commission of the European Communities (CEC) with European Non-Governmental Organizations (NGOs) in the Developing Countries," January 1978, 10:89, BWP; "Report on Relations with Non-Governmental Organizations

(NGOs) Active in the Field of Development, with Special Reference to the Cofinancing of Projects (1977)," March 3, 1978, 10:89, BWP; see also O'Sullivan, "Global Nervous System," 209.

79. Mayra Buvinic, "Investing in Poor Women: The Psychology of Donor Support," *World Development* 17, no. 7 (1989): 1049. On the World Bank, see Organisation for Economic Co-operation and Development, *Voluntary Aid for Development*, 98–100. On the UN, see also Sönke Kunkel, "Contesting Globalization: The United Nations Conference on Trade and Development and the Transnationalization of Sovereignty," in Frey, Kunkel, and Unger, *International Organizations and Development*, 252. On the Ford Foundation, see also Kathleen D. McCarthy, "From Government to Grass-Roots Reform: The Ford Foundation's Population Programmes in South Asia, 1959–1981," *Voluntas: International Journal of Voluntary and Nonprofit Organizations* 6, no. 30 (October 1995): 292–316.

80. Organisation for Economic Co-operation and Development, *Voluntary Aid for Development*, 102–3.

81. Organisation for Economic Co-operation and Development, 14, 28, 132. On concerns about the overly cozy relationship between donor governments and NGOs, see Michael Edwards and David Hulme, "Too Close for Comfort? The Impact of Official Aid on Nongovernmental Organizations," *World Development* 24, no. 6 (1996): 961–73.

82. On WID, WAD, and GAD, see, for example, Eva M. Rathgeber, "WID, WAD, GAD: Trends in Research and Practice," *Journal of Developing Areas* 24 (July 1990): 489–502; Jane L. Parpart, "Who is the 'Other'? A Postmodern Feminist Critique of Women and Development Theory and Practice," *Development and Change* 24 (1993): 439–64; Valentine M. Moghadam, "Feminisms and Development," *Gender and History* 10, no. 3 (November 1998): 590–97.

83. For an early example, see the discussion of the 1976 conference at Wellesley in chapter 3.

84. Lourdes Benería and Gita Sen, "Class and Gender Inequalities and Women's Role in Economic Development—Theoretical and Practical Implications," *Feminist Studies* 8, no. 1 (Spring 1982): 157.

85. Nüket Kardam, *Bringing Women In: Women's Issues in International Development Programs* (Boulder, CO: Lynne Rienner, 1991), 89, 91.

86. Quoted in Kardam, 94.

87. Ford Foundation, *Created Equal: A Report on Ford Foundation Women's Programs* (New York: Ford Foundation, 1986), 34–35.

88. Martha F. Loutfi, "Rural Women," August 28, 1981, 10-4-04:11, WEP.

89. Zubeida M. Ahmad and Martha F. Loutfi, "International Labour Office Programme on Rural Women," December 1980, p. 11, 10-4-04:9, WEP. On the Programme on Rural Women, see also Zubeida M. Ahmad and Martha F. Loutfi, *Women Workers in Rural Development: A Programme of the ILO* (Geneva: International Labour Office, 1985); Eileen Boris, "Mothers, Household Managers, and Productive Workers: The International Labor Organization and Women in Development," *Global Social Policy* 14, no. 2 (2014): 200–202.

90. "Annual Report on ILO/ECA/SIDA/75/RAF Handicrafts and Small-Scale Industries Unit at African Training and Research Centre for Women, UNECA, January to 31 December 1981," pp. 5, 11, 10-4-04:12, WEP.

91. Rathgeber, "WID, WAD, GAD," 499.

92. "The Dakar Declaration on Another Development with Women," *Development Dialogue* 1982, nos. 1–2 (1982): 12.

93. Sally W. Yudelman, "The Integration of Women into Development Projects: Observations on the NGO Experience in General and in Latin America in Particular," *World Development* 15, Supplement (Autumn 1987): 180.

94. Gita Sen and Caren Grown, *Development, Crises, and Alternative Visions: Third World Women's Perspectives* (New York: Monthly Review, 1987), 9, 18.

95. Elsa M. Chaney, "Full Circle: From Academia to Government and Back," in Fraser and Tinker, *Developing Power*, 208. See also Devaki Jain, "A View from the South: A Story of Intersections," in Fraser and Tinker, *Developing Power*, 135–36; Pezzullo, "For the Record . . . Forum '85," 11; Dorothy Sue Cobble, *For the Many: A Global History of American Feminism* (Princeton, NJ: Princeton University Press, forthcoming), chap. 12.

96. World Bank 1989 guidelines quoted in Kardam, *Bringing Women In*, 51. One study found that the World Bank promoted WID as a means to population reduction, USAID addressed WID as a means to economic growth, and the ILO saw WID as an issue of gender equality; Buvinic, "Investing in Poor Women," 1047.

97. World Bank 1989 guidelines quoted in Kardam, *Bringing Women In*, 51.

98. John W. Sewell to Philip Johnston, January 7, 1987, 1190:2, CARE; John D. Gerhart, foreword to "Beyond Survival: Expanding Income-Earning Opportunities for Women in Developing Countries," ed. Caren A. Grown, special issue, *World Development* 17, no. 7 (1989): 933.

99. Sen and Grown, *Development, Crises, and Alternative Visions*, 57; Rae Lesser Blumberg, "Executive Summary: Making the Case for the Gender Variable: Women and the Wealth and Well-Being of Nations," October 1989, p. 2, document PN-ABJ-556, DEC; Margaret Snyder, "Women: The Key to Ending Hunger," *Hunger Project Papers* 8 (August, 1990): 4.

100. Adrienne Germain to W. O. Sweeney, May 30, 1978, box 1, folder: AG Chrons, May 1978, AGO; Paul Streeten, "Basic Needs in the Year 2000," *Pakistan Institute of Development Economics* 19, no. 2 (Summer 1980): 140; Blumberg, "Executive Summary: Making the Case for the Gender Variable," 2.

101. Judith Bruce, "Homes Divided," *World Development* 17, no. 7 (1989): 986; Joan P. Mencher, "Women's Work and Poverty: Women's Contribution to Household Maintenance in South India," in *A Home Divided: Women and Income in the Third World*, ed. Daisy Dwyer and Judith Bruce (Stanford, CA: Stanford University Press, 1988), 100, 114; Snyder, "Women: The Key to Ending Hunger," 14.

102. Josh Levin, *The Queen: The Forgotten Life behind an American Myth* (New York: Little, Brown, 2019), chap. 6.

103. Judith Tendler, "What Ever Happened to Poverty Alleviation?," paper presented at conference on Support for Microenterprises, Washington, DC, June 6–9, 1988, pp. 6, 27, document PN-ABA-440, DEC. The report was written in 1987 for the

Ford Foundation in its review of its Livelihood, Employment, and Income Generation Programs. It was published in article form in the proceedings of a 1988 conference—Levitsky, *Microenterprises in Developing Countries*, 26–56—and as an article in *World Development* 17, no. 7 (1989): 1033–44.

104. On the number of borrowers and proportion of women in 1986, see Organisation for Economic Co-operation and Development, *Voluntary Aid for Development*, 63; Muhammad Yunus, "Grameen Bank: Organization and Operation," in Levitsky, *Microenterprises in Developing Countries*, 161.

Chapter 5

1. Jacob Levitsky, "Summary Report of Conference," xxiii; Henry R. Jackelen, "Banking on the Informal Sector," 134–35; Muhammad Yunus, "Grameen Bank: Organization and Operation," 155, 156; all in Jacob Levitsky, ed., *Microenterprises in Developing Countries: Papers and Proceedings of an International Conference Held in Washington, D.C., USA, 6–9 June 1988* (London: Intermediate Technology, 1989).

2. On earlier development projects that provided credit for farmers, see, for example, Nick Cullather, *The Hungry World: America's Cold War Battle against Poverty in Asia* (Cambridge, MA: Harvard University Press, 2010); on development projects that included credit for home buyers, see, for example, Nancy Kwak, *A World of Homeowners: American Power and the Politics of Housing Aid* (Chicago: University of Chicago Press, 2015).

3. Commission on International Development, *Partners in Development: Report of the Commission on International Development* (New York: Praeger, 1969), 153, 167.

4. Independent Commission on International Development Issues, *North-South, A Programme for Survival: Report of the Independent Commission on International Development Issues* (Cambridge, MA: MIT Press, 1980), 238, 223.

5. Independent Commission on International Development Issues, *Common Crisis North-South: Cooperation for World Recovery/The Brandt Commission 1983* (Cambridge, MA: MIT Press, 1983), 45; Laurie Cohen, "Banks Wax Cautious as Economies Slump," *Hartford Courant*, August 10, 1982.

6. Robert A. Bennett, "Mexico Seeking Postponement of Part of Debt," *New York Times*, August 20, 1982; David Simpson, "$8 Bn Bid to Save Mexico," *Guardian*, August 19, 1982.

7. Alan Riding, "Mexico Agrees to Austerity Terms for $3.84 Billion in I.M.F. Credit," *New York Times*, November 11, 1982.

8. Edward A. Gargan, "Rise in Africa Debt Worrying Banks," *New York Times*, August 26, 1985.

9. Salim Lone, "Africa's Unyielding Economic Crisis," *Guardian*, September 17, 1988.

10. John Lewis, Richard Webb, and Devesh Kapur, interview with Robert S. McNamara, April 1, May 10, and October 3, 1991, p. 85, WBOHP; Art Pine, "Clausen Holds World Bank's Course," *Wall Street Journal*, May 13, 1982. On McNamara and structural adjustment loans, see Patrick Allan Sharma, *Robert McNamara's Other*

War: The World Bank and International Development (Philadelphia: University of Pennsylvania Press, 2017), chap. 7. On the IMF's earlier conditional loans, see, for example, Cheryl Payer, *The Debt Trap: The IMF and the Third World* (New York: Monthly Review, 1974); Bradley R. Simpson, *Economists with Guns: Authoritarian Development and U.S.-Indonesian Relations, 1960–1968* (Stanford, CA: Stanford University Press, 2008), 88–92, 109–12.

11. Devesh Kapur, John P. Lewis, and Richard Webb, *The World Bank: Its First Half Century*, vol 1, *History* (Washington, DC: Brookings Institution, 1997), 339, 511; Alex Brummer, "World Bank Names Woman for Top Spot," *Guardian*, May 12, 1982. Nonetheless, conservatives in the Reagan administration criticized Clausen for not adhering strictly enough to free markets and the private sector; see Clyde H. Farnsworth, "A Troubled Rule at the World Bank," *New York Times*, September 2, 1984. On the Washington consensus and the World Bank, see also Sarah Babb, "The Washington Consensus as Transnational Policy Paradigm: Its Origins, Trajectory and Likely Successor," *Review of International Political Economy* 20, no. 2 (2013): 268–97.

12. Payer, *Debt Trap*, x; Howard M. Wachtel, *The New Gnomes: Multinational Banks in the Third World* (Washington, DC: Transnational Institute, 1977). On the IPS and debt in the 1970s, see Paul Adler, "'The Basis of a New Internationalism?': The Institute for Policy Studies and North-South Politics from the NIEO to Neoliberalism," *Diplomatic History* 41, no. 4 (September 2017): 665–93.

13. "The Arusha Initiative: A Call for a United Nations Conference on International Money and Finance," *Development Dialogue* 1980, no. 2 (July 1980): 14, 17.

14. Julius Nyerere, "No to IMF Meddling," *Development Dialogue* 1980, no. 2 (July 1980): 8.

15. Quoted in Jonathan Power, "Must We Starve Our Children?" *Los Angeles Times*, July 14, 1985. For late 1980s debates among global South leaders, see Vijay Prashad, *The Poorer Nations: A Possible History of the Global South* (London: Verso, 2012), 99–105.

16. Independent Commission on International Development Issues, *Common Crisis North-South*, 1, 20, 21, 75, 81.

17. Kapur, Lewis, and Webb, *World Bank*, 1:367.

18. Hobart Rowen, "Bradley Challenges Baker on Third World Debt," *Washington Post*, July 6, 1986; Hobart Rowen, "Conable Favors Baker Initiative over Bradley Plan," *Washington Post*, July 22, 1986. On the US Treasury, see Carl Hartman, "Bradley Plan Seen Hurting U.S. Banks," *Washington Post*, July 31, 1986.

19. Richard Jolly and Giovanni Andrea Cornia, eds., *The Impact of World Recession on Children* (Oxford: Pergamon, 1984).

20. The quote is from a 1981 UNICEF *State of the World's Children* report, quoted in Richard Jolly, "Adjustment with a Human Face: A UNICEF Record and Perspective on the 1980s," *World Development* 19, no. 12 (1991): 1809.

21. On concerns within the Bank, see Kapur, Lewis, and Webb, *World Bank*, 1:352.

22. Giovanni Andrea Cornia, Richard Jolly, and Frances Stewart, eds., *Adjustment with a Human Face*, vol. 1, *Protecting the Vulnerable and Promoting Growth* (Oxford: Clarendon, 1987), 6, 141.

23. Mark Tran, "World Bank Hits Commercial Banks," *Guardian*, September 18, 1987.

24. Cornia, Jolly, and Stewart, *Adjustment with a Human Face*, 1:7, 278, 285, 290.

25. United Nations Development Programme, *Human Development Report* (New York: Oxford University Press, 1990), 3; Khadija Haq and Richard Ponzio, eds., *Pioneering the Human Development Revolution: An Intellectual Biography of Mahbub ul Haq* (New Delhi: Oxford University Press, 1998), 8. On the North-South Roundtable and "human development," see Richard Jolly, "Society for International Development, the North-South Roundtable and the Power of Ideas," *Development* 50, S1 (2007): 47–58.

26. Lone, "Africa's Unyielding Economic Crisis."

27. Quoted in Naomi Klein, *The Shock Doctrine: The Rise of Disaster Capitalism* (New York: Picador, 2007), 205; Anthony Swift, "IMF Whistleblower: 'We Make or Break Human Life Every Day of Every Year,'" *New Internationalist*, November 5, 1988, https://newint.org/features/1988/11/05/moonlight.

28. "World Bank Acts to Enhance the Economic Status of Asia's Women," press release, October 31, 1988, box 6, folder: Organizations—World Bank—1980–89, Series 1, WIDC; Kapur, Lewis, and Webb, *World Bank*, 1:365. On the Bank's late-1980s growing interest in women, see also Barbara Herz, "The World Bank New Approach to Women in Development," March 1987, box 6, folder: Organizations—World Bank—1980–89, Series 1, WIDC. For an example of the Bank's post-1990 neoliberal antipoverty efforts, see Tania Murray Li, *The Will to Improve: Governmentality, Development, and the Practice of Politics* (Durham, NC: Duke University Press, 2007), chap. 7.

29. Susan George, *The Debt Boomerang: How Third World Debt Harms Us All* (London: Pluto Press with the Transnational Institute, 1992), xv.

30. Jeffrey Ashe, Jason Brown, Peter H. Fraser, Douglas A. Hellinger, Fred M. O'Regan, and William R. Tucker, *The Pisces Studies: Assisting the Smallest Economic Activities of the Urban Poor* (Washington, DC: Office of Urban Development, Bureau for Science and Technology, Agency for International Development, International Development Cooperation Agency, 1981), 189, 217, 374.

31. Ashe et al., 189, 374.

32. Ashe et al., 28, 183.

33. Ashe et al., 151. On democratizing finance, see Ananya Roy, *Poverty Capital: Microfinance and the Making of Development* (New York: Routledge, 2010).

34. "Our History," Accion, n.d., accessed September 17, 2020, https://www.accion.org/about/history/.

35. Lucia Hulsether, "Liberated Market: On the Cultural Politics of Capitalist Humanitarianism," PhD dissertation, Yale University, 2020, chap. 2; Ashe et al., *Pisces Studies*, 172; Amanda Izzo, *Liberal Christianity and Women's Global Activism: The YWCA of the USA and the Maryknoll Sisters* (New Brunswick, NJ: Rutgers University Press, 2018), 146.

36. *Microenterprise Credit: Joint Hearing before the Select Committee on Hunger and the Subcommittee on International Development Institutions and Finance of the Committee on Banking, Finance and Urban Affairs, House of Representatives,*

99th Cong. 9, 41 (1986) (statement of Jeffrey Ashe). See also "Inside Accion: News from the Americas," Fall 1990, 77:4, WWB.

37. Ela Bhatt, "Women and Small Scale Enterprise Development in a New Era," paper presented at the International Institute of Development, Ottawa, October 27, 1987, p. 4, FR 011400.

38. Kalima Rose, *Where Women Are Leaders: The SEWA Movement in India* (London: Zed Books, 1992), 174; Jyotsna Sreenivasan, *Ela Bhatt: Uniting Women in India* (New York: Feminist Press, 2000), chap. 6.

39. Jennefer Sebstad, *Struggle and Development among Self Employed Women: A Report on the Self Employed Women's Association, Ahmedabad, India* (Washington, DC: Office of Urban Development, Bureau for Development Support, Agency for International Development, 1982), 258, document PN-AAK-591, DEC.

40. Sebstad, 259–62.

41. Michaela Walsh with Shamima De Gonzaga and Lilia C. Clemente, *Founding a Movement: Women's World Banking, 1975–1990* (New York: Cosimo Books, 2012), 4, 10.

42. Margaret C. Snyder and Mary Tadesse, *African Women and Development: A History* (Johannesburg: Witwatersrand University Press, 1995), 91; Nira Hardon Long, "Report of the World Conference of the International Women's Year," July 28, 1975, box 8, folder: International Conference on Women's Year, Mexico City, 6/19–7/2/75, CBCA. On Ocloo, see also Douglas Martin, "Esther Ocloo, 83, Pioneer in Microloans to Help Women Become Entrepreneurs, Dies," *New York Times*, March 10, 1992. For the statement on credit in the UN report, see *Report of the World Conference of the International Women's Year, Mexico City, 19 June-2 July 1975* (New York: United Nations, 1976), 82. On credit at the UN's 1975 International Women's Year conference, see also Jocelyn Olcott, *International Women's Year: The Greatest Consciousness-Raising Event in History* (New York: Oxford University Press, 2017), 227, 228.

43. Cameron L. Smith and Bruce A. Tippett, "Evaluation of Women's World Banking," draft report prepared for USAID, International Science and Technology Institute, Inc., February 1985, p. i, 9:4, WWB. Accion provided help in the planning stages and contributed $3,000 toward the cost of incorporating WWB; see Walsh, *Founding a Movement*, 147.

44. Development Finance Consultants, Ltd., "Women's World Banking: Ten-Year Assessment," September 1989, pp. 4–6, 27:9, WWB.

45. Stichting Women's World Banking, "Three Year Business Plan," August 1, 1982, pp. 18–19, 6:3, WWB; Bhatt quoted in Rose, *Where Women Are Leaders*, 198; Bhatt quoted in Walsh, *Founding a Movement*, inside front cover.

46. Handwritten loan history reports, 48:6, WWB.

47. Equal Credit Opportunity Act of 1974, 15 U.S.C. §1691 (2011), https://www.govinfo.gov/content/pkg/USCODE-2011-title15/html/USCODE-2011-title15-chap41-subchapIV.htm. See Louis Hyman, "Ending Discrimination, Legitimating Debt: The Political Economy of Race, Gender, and Credit Access in the 1960s and 1970s," *Enterprise and Society* 12, no. 1 (March 2011): 200–232.

48. Mayra Buvinic, Jennefer Sebstad, and Sondra Zeidenstein, "Credit for Rural Women: Some Facts and Lessons," August 1979, document PN-AAH-427, DEC; Ilsa Schumaker, Jennefer Sebstad, and Mayra Buvinic, "Limits to Productivity: Improving Women's Access to Technology and Credit," May 1980, document PN-AAJ-919, DEC; Judith Bruce, "Market Women's Cooperatives: Giving Women Credit in Nicaragua," *Seeds* (1982), and Marty Chen, "The Working Women's Forum: Organizing for Credit and Change in Madras, India," *Seeds* (1984), both reprinted in Ann Leonard, ed., *Seeds: Supporting Women's Work in the Third World* (New York: Feminist Press, 1989); Office of Women in Development, Bureau for Program and Policy Coordination, Agency for International Development, *Women in Development: The First Decade, 1975–1984, A Report to the Committee on Foreign Relations United States Senate and the Committee on Foreign Affairs United States House of Representatives* (Washington, DC: USAID, ca. 1985), 20, 21. The first two studies were funded by USAID through the International Center for Research on Women. The *Seeds* case studies were funded by the Carnegie Corporation, the Ford Foundation, and others. In its ten-year review of its WID programs, the ten USAID-funded credit projects mentioned were in Bangladesh, Botswana, Burkina Faso, Dominica, Indonesia, Kenya, Lesotho, Peru, the Philippines, and Thailand.

49. Minutes of the board of trustees annual meeting, May 22–23, 1987, pp. 20–21, 6:7, WWB.

50. Barbara Morrison Reno, ed., *Credit and Women's Economic Development: A Dialogue among Entrepreneurs, Bankers and Development Specialists on Issues Related to Credit for Business Enterprise* (Washington, DC: World Council of Credit Unions, in collaboration with Overseas Education Fund, 1981), vi, document PN-AAJ-909, DEC; Gita Sen and Caren Grown, *Development, Crises, and Alternative Visions: Third World Women's Perspectives* (New York: Monthly Review, 1987), 86.

51. David Bornstein, *The Price of a Dream: The Story of the Grameen Bank and the Idea that Is Helping the Poor to Change Their Lives* (New York: Simon and Schuster, 1996), 121.

52. "Annex III: The Economy," p. 1, from report no. P-1461-BD, June 5, 1974, folder: Contacts with member countries: Bangladesh-Correspondence 02, folder ID: 1770953, reference code: WB IBRD/IDA 03 EXC-10-4549S, sub-fond: Records of President Robert S. McNamara, fond: Records of the Office of the President, WBGA.

53. Joan M. Dunlop, "Chittagong University, Bangladesh," February 28, 1976, p. 1, 34:1, WWB; Muhammad Yunus, "Credit and Ingenuity Can Save the Children," *Los Angeles Times*, July 9, 1990.

54. Muhammad Yunus, *Banker to the Poor: Micro-Lending and the Battle against World Poverty* (New York: PublicAffairs, 1999), chaps. 4, 5, 6.

55. Ela Dutt, "World Bank to Try New Remedies," *India Abroad*, December 10, 1993. See also Bornstein, *Price of a Dream*, 238–53. On the World Bank, see Alex Counts, *Give Us Credit* (New York: Times Books, 1996), 178–83.

56. Yunus, *Banker to the Poor*, 112; Adrienne Germain to Franklin Thomas, March 11, 1984, pp. 2, 3, FG 08100579; Ken Marshall to Peter Geithner, March 30, 1986, FG 08100578.

57. Yunus, *Banker to the Poor*, 112–13; quote from Grameen Bank, *Annual Report 1984* (Dhaka: Grameen Bank, 1985), 3, http://www.grameen.com/wp-content /uploads/bsk-pdf-manager/GB-1984.pdf. Some accounts state that the World Bank rejected an early request for support from Yunus. See, for example, "Giving Poor Credit for Better Living Standard," *Guardian*, October 23, 1985. Yunus denied it. See *Microenterprise Credit: Joint Hearing*, 8 (statement of Muhammad Yunus).

58. William D. Carmichael to Franklin A. Thomas, recommendation for grant to Grameen Bank, May 11, 1989, pp. 4, 7, FG 08500787. On the contributions from IFAD, Norway's NORAD, and Sweden's SIDA, see "Grameen Bank Project," IFAD, n.d., accessed September 17, 2020, https://www.ifad.org/en/web/operations/project /id/161/country/bangladesh.

59. Adrienne Germain, "Visit to Chittagong University, March 21 and 22, 1977," April 12, 1977, FR 007630. I learned of Yunus's early attempts to include women as half of the borrowers from Nurjahan Begum, who worked with Yunus from 1977 on; conversation with Nurjahan Begum, July 23, 2019, Yunus Centre, Dhaka.

60. Adrienne Germain, "Visit to Chittagong University"; Ruth B. Dixon, "Programming for Women in the Ford Foundation Bangladesh: Report of a Consultancy, 19 May–19 June 1980," annex VII, p. 19, box 1, folder: Dixon, Ruth, AGC. In the early 1980s, Germain moved to Dhaka as head of the Bangladesh field office and continued to work with Yunus.

61. Grameen Bank, *Annual Report 1985* (Dhaka: Grameen Bank, 1986), 3, http:// www.grameen.com/wp-content/uploads/bsk-pdf-manager/GB-1985.pdf; Carmichael to Thomas, recommendation for grant to Grameen Bank, 4.

62. Muzammel Hoque and Zia U. Ahmed, "A Review of Microenterprise Credit Programs in Bangladesh," May 1989, document PN-ABF-100, DEC; Marguerite Berger and Martin Greeley, "A Women in Development Implementation Plan for USAID/Bangladesh," April 1987, pp. 12–15, box 7, folder: Project Design and Evaluation—Design and Planning, 1977–1988 and Undated (2), Series 1, WIDC.

63. Mary Houghton quoted in Bornstein, *Price of a Dream*, 253; *Banking on the Poor: Hearing before the Select Committee on Hunger, House of Representatives*, 100th Cong. 32 (1987) (testimony of Michael Farbman); Carol Kleiman, "Village Capitalism Betters Women's Lot," *Chicago Tribune*, October 31, 1983; "Bangladeshi Landless Prove Credit Worthy," *Washington Post*; February 19, 1984; Mayra Buvinic, "Helping the Third-World's Poor Women," *Christian Science Monitor*, July 15, 1985.

64. *Microenterprise Credit: Joint Hearing* (statements of Stan Lundine and Doug Bereuter) 1–3.

65. *Microenterprise Credit: Joint Hearing* (statements of Muhammad Yunus and Stan Lundine), 4, 5, 7, 9.

66. Colman McCarthy, "Third World Bank Lends a Hand," *Washington Post*, November 2, 1986.

67. Dennis DeConcini, Edward F. Feighan, and Benjamin Gilman, "Luncheon with Founder of Grameen Bank," July 19, 1987, in FG 08200806; Edward F. Feighan, "Lunch with Dr. Mohammed [*sic*] Yunus, Founder and Managing Director of Grameen Bank in Bangladesh," 133 Cong. Rec. H6392 (daily ed., July 21, 1987).

68. "Self-Sufficiency for the Poor Act of 1987," 133 Cong. Rec. E284 (daily ed., January 28, 1987); "More Food, Less Cement," *Cleveland Plain Dealer*, February 3, 1987.

69. 133 Cong. Rec. S8803 (daily ed., April 9, 1987) (statement of Dennis DeConcini). For bills and sponsors, see Self-Sufficiency for the Poor Act of 1987, H.R. 910, 100th Cong. (1987–88), www.congress.gov/bill/100th-congress/house-bill/910; Comprehensive Micro-Enterprise Credit Promotion Act of 1987, H.R. 1032, 100th Cong. (1987–88), www.congress.gov/bill/100th-congress/house-bill/1032; A Bill Entitled the "Micro Enterprise Loans for the Poor Act," S. 998, 100th Cong. (1987–88), www .congress.gov/bill/100th-congress/senate-bill/998. On the process of reconciling the bills, see USAID, "Experiments in Small- and Microenterprise Development," n.d., ca. 1991, chap. 6, document PN-ABG-834, DEC.

70. Conversation with Muhammad Yunus, July 22, 2019, Yunus Centre, Dhaka.

71. Colman McCarthy, "Leading the Charge against Hunger," *Washington Post*, May 8, 1988. On RESULTS, see also "Let's Get Tiny Loans to the World's Poor," *New Options* 37 (March 30, 1987), in 90:12, WWB; Kristin Helmore, "Results: A Lobby Group that Lives Up to Its Name," *Christian Science Monitor*, October 24, 1988. Twenty-seven such editorials are copied in FG 08200806.

72. Yunus, *Banker to the Poor*, 146–47. For a few examples of editorials that mention the Grameen Bank, see, for example, "Foreign Aid: The U.S. Tries to Mix in a Dose of Self-Sufficiency for the Poor," *Detroit Free Press*, January 23, 1987; "A Modest Proposal," *Santa Barbara News-Press*, February 3, 1987; "Congress Should Support Measure to Designate Aid for Poor Nations," *Fort Lauderdale News*, February 5, 1987; "Small Loans Get Big Results," *San Jose Mercury News*, February 10, 1987; all copied in FG 08200806.

73. Feighan quoted in Helmore, "Results: A Lobby Group that Lives Up to Its Name."

74. M. Peter McPherson to Edward F. Feighan, February 5, 1987, in *Micro-Enterprise Development Legislation: Hearing before the Subcommittee on International Economic Policy and Trade of the Committee on Foreign Affairs, House of Representatives*, 100th Cong. 148–50 (1987); Dennis Brennan responses in *Banking on the Poor: Hearing*, 137.

75. Feighan quoted in Helmore, "Results: A Lobby Group that Lives Up to Its Name."

76. Yunus, *Banker to the Poor*, 149.

77. Yunus, chap. 9; Kristin Helmore, "Banking on a Better Life," *Christian Science Monitor*, March 15, 1989. Yunus still serves on the board of directors of RESULTS.

78. "'Micro Bankers' Help the Poor Make Money," *New York Times*, September 3, 1990; David Osborne, "Bootstrap Banking," *Inc.*, August 1, 1987, www.inc.com /magazine/19870801/8543.html. See also Yunus, *Banker to the Poor*, chap. 10; *Access and Availability of Credit to the Poor in Developing Countries and the United States: Staff Report of the Select Committee on Hunger, U.S. House of Representatives, December 1987* (Washington, DC: Government Printing Office, 1988), pt. 2. On the Clintons and microcredit, see Lily Geismer, "Agents of Change: Microenterprise, Welfare

Reform, the Clintons, and Liberal Forms of Neoliberalism," *Journal of American History* 107, no. 1 (June 2020): 107–31.

79. Edward Feighan quoted in Clyde H. Farnsworth, "Micro-Loans to the World's Poorest," *New York Times*, February 21, 1988.

80. USAID, "Policy Determination: Microenterprise Development Program Guidelines," October 10, 1988, p. 3, document PN-AAV-466, DEC.

81. Cheryl Lassen, "Poverty Lending: Something Distinct within Micro Enterprise Credit," September 1990, p. 31, document PN-ABG-154, DEC.

82. Lassen, 31; Yunus quoted in Brian Sullam, "Bangladesh Banker Helps the Poor Help Themselves," *Baltimore Sun,* June 1, 1988; *Microenterprise Development: Hearing before the Subcommittee on International Economic Policy and Trade of the Committee on Foreign Affairs, House of Representatives*, 101st Cong. 54 (1990) (statement of John Hatch).

83. Sullam, "Bangladesh Banker"; *Banking on the Poor: Hearing* (testimony of Michael Farbman), 30. See also Seth Mydans, "A Bank Battles Poverty," *New York Times*, July 12, 1987; Rounaq Jahan, "Women and Development in Bangladesh: Challenges and Opportunities," March 1989, p. 16, FR 013962.

84. Yunus, "Credit and Ingenuity Can Save the Children"; Judith Tendler, "What Ever Happened to Poverty Alleviation?" paper presented at conference on Support for Microenterprises, Washington, DC, June 6–9, 1988, p. 18, document PN-ABA-440, DEC.

85. See, for example, Milford Bateman, *Why Doesn't Microfinance Work? The Destructive Rise of Local Neoliberalism* (London: Zed Books, 2010); Lamia Karim, *Microfinance and Its Discontents: Women in Debt in Bangladesh* (Minneapolis: University of Minnesota Press, 2011).

86. David Harvey, *A Brief History of Neoliberalism* (New York: Oxford University Press, 2005), 3. For a useful recent overview of the term "neoliberalism," see Kim Phillips-Fein, "The History of Neoliberalism," in *Shaped by the State: Toward a New Political History of the Twentieth Century*, ed. Brent Cebul, Lily Geismer, and Mason B. Williams (Chicago: University of Chicago Press, 2019), 347–62. For a recent account of the rise of neoliberalism in US politics, see Gary Gerstle, "The Rise and Fall (?) of America's Neoliberal Order," *Transactions of the Royal Historical Society* 28 (December 2018): 241–64. On neoliberalism in US foreign assistance, see, for example, Michael E. Latham, *The Right Kind of Revolution: Modernization, Development, and U.S. Foreign Policy from the Cold War to the Present* (Ithaca, NY: Cornell University Press, 2011), 175–82. On liberal variants of neoliberalism, see Geismer, "Agents of Change." For a critical account of our understanding of the roots of neoliberalism, see Amy C. Offner, *Sorting Out the Mixed Economy: The Rise and Fall of Welfare and Developmental States in the Americas* (Princeton, NJ: Princeton University Press, 2019), 283–85.

87. Yunus, "Credit and Ingenuity Can Save the Children"; Mydans, "Bank Battles Poverty"; 133 Cong. Rec. S8803 (daily ed., April 9, 1987) (statement of Dennis DeConcini).

88. On the concern with "dependency" in the United States, see Alice O'Connor, *Poverty Knowledge: Social Science, Social Policy, and the Poor in Twentieth-Century U.S. History* (Princeton, NJ: Princeton University Press, 2009), chap. 10.

89. Monica Prasad, *The Land of Too Much: American Abundance and the Paradox of Poverty* (Cambridge, MA: Harvard University Press, 2012), xiv; *Access and Availability of Credit to the Poor*, 21. On the "trade-off" between credit and welfare in the United States, see also Greta R. Krippner, *Capitalizing on Crisis: The Political Origins of the Rise of Finance* (Cambridge, MA: Harvard University Press, 2011); Prasad, *Land of Too Much*, chap. 9.

90. Yunus, *Banker to the Poor*, 135–37; World Bank, *Women in Development* (Washington, DC: World Bank, 1980), 4.

91. Recommendation for grant to Bangladesh Bank, May 21, 1981, p. 6, FG 08100578.

92. 133 Cong. Rec. E376 (daily ed., February 5, 1987) (statement of Mickey Leland); *Banking on the Poor: Hearing* (statement of David C. Richards), 10. On "cycle of poverty," see also Ashe et al., *Pisces Studies*, 189; *Banking on the Poor: Hearing*, 2 (statement of Mickey Leland); 133 Cong. Rec. S8804 (daily ed., April 9, 1987) (statement of Patrick Leahy); *Access and Availability of Credit to the Poor*, v. The phrase "cycle of poverty" or "circle of poverty" was not new in the 1970s. It was sometimes used in place of "culture of poverty" in the 1960s.

93. Robert W. Hunt, "Private Voluntary Organizations and the Promotion of Small-Scale Enterprise," July 1985, p. 13, document PN-AAL-055, DEC.

94. Ashe et al., *Pisces Studies*, 45; Yunus quote in *Microenterprise Development: Hearing* (statement of Muhammad Yunus), 15. See also Khalid Shams, Noeleen Heyzer, and Ismael Getubig, "What We Can Learn from Grameen Bank" [1989], in *Collected Essays and Stories from Grameen Dialogue, Newsletter Issues #1–50*, ed. Khalid Shams (Dhaka: Grameen Trust, 2005), 13.

95. See, for example, Sen and Grown, *Development, Crises, and Alternative Visions*, 89.

96. Helmore, "Banking on a Better Life." See also Elora Shehabuddin, "Social Impact of Grameen Bank," in Shams, *Collected Essays*, 21–30.

97. *Microenterprise Development: Hearing* (statement of Muhammad Yunus), 15; *Microenterprise Credit: Joint Hearing* (statement of Arthur Simon), 56.

98. Ashe et al., *Pisces Studies*, 44; Maryanne Dulansey, quoted in Elsa M. Chaney, "Full Circle: From Academia to Government and Back," in *Developing Power: How Women Transformed International Development*, ed. Arvonne S. Fraser and Irene Tinker (New York: Feminist Press, 2004), 208.

99. Ashe et al., *Pisces Studies*, 44.

100. Alfred A. Whittaker to Microenterprise Advisory Committee, May 4, 1988, p. 3, 95:3, WWB; *Microenterprise Development: Hearing* (statement of John Hatch), 56.

101. USAID, "Policy Determination: Microenterprise Development Program Guidelines," 9; Hunt, "Private Voluntary Organizations and the Promotion of Small-Scale Enterprise," 14.

102. "Research on Microenterprise Development," ca. 1984, 80:8, WWB.

103. Martha Chen, "Review of the Ford Foundation's Programming for Women in Bangladesh," November 1989, p. 11, box 2, folder: Marty Chen, 1989, DPF.

104. T. Scarlett Epstein, "An Action-Oriented Study of the Role of Women in Rural Development," 1982, p. 5, FR 011521; Hunt, "Private Voluntary Organizations and the Promotion of Small-Scale Enterprise," 13; Katharine McKee, "Micro-level Strategies for Supporting Livelihoods, Employment, and Income Generation of Poor Women in the Third World—The Challenge of Significance," May 1988, p. 14, FR 011400.

105. Carmichael to Thomas, recommendation for grant to Grameen Bank, 6.

106. Curt Tarnoff, "Microenterprise and U.S. Foreign Assistance, CRS Report for Congress," August 19, 1996, pp. 5, 8, document PB-AAJ-354, DEC.

107. On the Clinton administration and foreign assistance, see Carol Lancaster, *Foreign Aid: Diplomacy, Development, Domestic Politics* (Chicago: University of Chicago Press, 2006), 85–91. On rising funds for microenterprise, see USAID, "Reaching Down and Scaling Up: Meeting the Microenterprise Development Challenge: U.S. Agency for International Development Microenterprise Results Reporting for 1997," September 1998, p. 14, document PD-ABR-637, DEC.

108. William J. Clinton, "Remarks on Presenting the Presidential Awards for Excellence in Microenterprise Development," January 30, 1997, APP.

109. USAID, "Reaching Down and Scaling Up," 11; USAID, "World Relief Corporation, 1993–1998 Matching Grant for Microenterprise Development, Final Evaluation," December 1998, p. ii, document PD-ABT-056, DEC; Brent Bowers, "Third-World Debt that Is Almost Always Paid in Full," *Wall Street Journal*, June 7, 1991; Michele Singletary, "Loans Foster Spirit of Self Help," *NABJ Journal* 12, no. 9 (November 1994): 7. On CARE, see also USAID, Grant 624-0272-G-00-1071-00, "Program Description of CARE/Maradi Micro Enterprise Development Project," 1991, document PDF-CZ-570, DEC.

110. USAID, "Reaching Down and Scaling Up," v, 11, 14; Singletary, "Loans Foster Spirit of Self Help."

111. "The Microcredit Summit, Declaration and Plan of Action, February 2–4, 1997," 1, fn2, box 147, WWB; Jennifer Scott, "Lending to the Poor Can Be Profitable: Grameen Banker," *Times of India*, February 6, 1996.

112. Nancy Yoshihara, "Muhammad Yunus: Championing the Right to Credit for Poor Women around the World," *Los Angeles Times*, January 25, 1998. On CGAP, see also Tarnoff, "Microenterprise and U.S. Foreign Assistance," 4.

113. Viji Sundaram, "State of the World Forum," *India West*, October 11, 1996.

114. Skip Kaltenheuser, "Fitting Microcredit into a Macro Picture," *Christian Science Monitor*, February 5, 1997.

115. "Microcredit Summit, Declaration and Plan of Action," front cover.

116. Aziz Haniffa, "High-Level Support Proclaimed for Microcredit," *India Abroad*, February 14, 1997. For the range of UN involvement in microfinance in the late 1990s, see UN General Assembly, "Role of Microcredit in the Eradication of Poverty: Report of the Secretary-General," A/53/223, August 10, 1998, https://digitallibrary.un.org /record/262753?ln=en.

117. "The Microcredit Summit Report, February 2-4, 1997," 29, 11, 14, 15, box 147, WWB. On Yunus as "the godfather of the movement," see Fred Hiatt, "Penny-Wise Loan Policy," *Washington Post*, January 20, 1997.

118. Jane Rosser to Susan Berresford and Barry Gaberman, May 15, 1997, p.1, Ford Grant 08200806.

119. Aziz Haniffa, "World Leaders Call for Expanding Loans to Poor," *India Abroad*, February 14, 1997.

120. Shahnaz Anklesaria Aiyar, "Women and Microcredit: Can a Mantra Deliver Empowerment?" *Times of India*, February 26, 1997.

121. Aiyar, "Women and Microcredit"; Paul Lewis, "Small Loans May Be Key to Helping Third World," *New York Times*, January 26, 1997.

122. Ben Rogaly, "Micro-Finance Evangelism, 'Destitute Women,' and the Hard Selling of a New Anti-Poverty Formula," *Development in Practice* 6, no. 2 (May 1996): 105.

123. Sue Wheat, "Banking on a Better Future," *Guardian*, January 29, 1997. On violence against women, see especially Aminur Rahman, *Women and Microcredit in Rural Bangladesh: Anthropological Study of the Rhetoric and Realities of Grameen Bank Lending* (Boulder, CO: Westview, 1999), 120-26. For a review of 1990s critical commentary on microcredit in Bangladesh, see Elora Shehabuddin, *Reshaping the Holy: Democracy, Development, and Muslim Women in Bangladesh* (New York: Columbia University Press, 2008), chap. 4.

Epilogue

1. "The Nobel Peace Prize for 2006," press release, Nobel Prize website, October 13, 2006, https://www.nobelprize.org/prizes/peace/2006/press-release/. On the Grameen Bank in 2006, see Muhammad Yunus, "Nobel Lecture," Nobel Prize website, December 10, 2006, https://www.nobelprize.org/prizes/peace/2006/yunus/26090-muhammad-yunus-nobel-lecture-2006-2/.

2. Yunus, "Nobel Lecture." In 1966, David Lilienthal spelled out an earlier variant of "social entrepreneurship," which also called on the private sector to create businesses to address social problems. See Amy C. Offner, *Sorting Out the Mixed Economy: The Rise and Fall of Welfare and Developmental States in the Americas* (Princeton, NJ: Princeton University Press, 2019), 182.

3. Yunus's emphasis on selfless maternalism and paternalism fits neatly with Wendy Brown's recent gloss on neoliberalism as activating "traditional morality in place of legislated social justice." Wendy Brown, *In the Ruins of Neoliberalism: The Rise of Antidemocratic Politics in the West* (New York: Columbia University Press, 2019), 21.

4. Ameet Sachdev, "Nobel Winner's Bank Has Chicago Interest," *Chicago Tribune*, November 22, 2006.

5. "How to Fight Poverty: 8 Programs that Work," *New York Times*, November 16, 2006; "The Week," *National Review*, November 6, 2006, p. 14.

6. Yunus has continued to expand his antipoverty programs beyond microcredit. The Yunus Centre in Bangladesh now trains nurses, supports younger entrepreneurs who build businesses that create jobs, and promotes larger social businesses. It also installs solar systems for homes without electricity. Muhammad Yunus with Karl Weber, *A World of Three Zeros: The New Economics of Zero Poverty, Zero Unemployment, and Zero Net Carbon Emissions* (Dhaka: University Press Limited, 2017); for recent updates, https://www.muhammadyunus.org/.

7. John Tierney, "Shopping for a Nobel," *New York Times*, October 17, 2006; Alexander Cockburn, "The Myth of Microloans," *Nation*, November 6, 2006. On Walmart's "benefiting from forced labor and other abusive practices," see Rachel Abrams, "Retailers like H&M and Walmart Fall Short of Pledges to Overseas Workers," *New York Times*, May 31, 2016.

8. Sudhirendar Sharma, "Death by Microcredit," *Times of India*, September 16, 2006; Aasha Khosa, "Grameen Bank Can't Reduce Poverty: Economist," *Business Standard*, April 2, 2007.

9. Elisabeth Malkin, "Microloans, Big Profits," *New York Times*, April 5, 2008.

10. Vaishnavi Chandrashekhar, "In India, Warnings of a Microfinance Bubble," *Christian Science Monitor*, June 30, 2010.

11. Lydia Polgreen and Vikas Bajaj, "Microcredit is Imperiled in India by Defaults," *New York Times*, November 18, 2010.

12. Yoolim Lee and Ruth David, "Spate of Suicides Point to Stresses from Microcredit," *News India-Times*, January 7, 2011; Polgreen and Bajaj, "Microcredit is Imperiled in India by Defaults" (photos in online version of the same article: Lydia Polgreen and Vikas Bajaj, "India Microcredit Faces Collapse from Defaults," *New York Times*, November 17, 2010, https://www.nytimes.com/2010/11/18/world/asia/18micro.html).

13. Megha Bahree, "A Big Split over Microfinance," *Forbes*, October 1, 2010, https://www.forbes.com/global/2010/1011/companies-akula-yunus-iskenderian -clinton-global-big-split.html#7270510c1898.

14. For a brief review of the early scholarly literature, see Lamia Karim, *Microfinance and Its Discontents: Women in Debt in Bangladesh* (Minneapolis: University of Minnesota Press, 2011), xxvi–xxx. Karim provides a damning ethnographic account of microcredit in Bangladesh. For an account of critical commentary on microcredit in the early twenty-first-century press, see Ananya Roy, *Poverty Capital: Microfinance and the Making of Development* (New York: Routledge, 2010), chap. 3. For more recent critical accounts of microcredit, see also Milford Bateman and Kate Maclean, eds., *Seduced and Betrayed: Exposing the Contemporary Microfinance Phenomenon* (Albuquerque: University of New Mexico Press, 2016); Sohini Kar, *Financializing Poverty: Labor and Risk in Indian Microfinance* (Stanford, CA: Stanford University Press, 2018).

15. Abhijit V. Banerjee and Esther Duflo, *Poor Economics: A Radical Rethinking of the Way to Fight Global Poverty* (New York: PublicAffairs, 2011), 234; Abhijit Banerjee, Dean Karlan, and Jonathan Zinman, "Six Randomized Evaluations of Microcredit: Introduction and Further Steps," *American Economic Journal: Applied Economics* 7, no. 1 (2015): 3, 13.

16. "Does Microfinance Still Hold Promise for Reaching the Poor?," World Bank, March 30, 2015, http://www.worldbank.org/en/news/feature/2015/03/30/does -microfinance-still-hold-promise-for-reaching-the-poor; "2015 Microenterprise Results Report," USAID, n.d., ca. 2015, pp. 2, 5, https://www.usaid.gov/sites/default /files/documents/1865/MicroenterpriseResultsReportingFY2015_0.pdf.

17. "Over 1 Billion People around the World Survive on $2.50 a Day, or Less," FINCA fundraising brochure, Spring 2020, in author's possession. On Kiva, see, for example, Inderpal Grewal, *Saving the Security State: Exceptional Citizens in Twenty-First-Century America* (Durham, NC: Duke University Press, 2017), 79–85.

18. Ronald Reagan, "Radio Address to the Nation on United States-Soviet Relations," September 29, 1984, APP. The full sentence reads: "The growing economic interdependence of our world is creating a ripple effect of good news for those countries committed to sensible policies—policies which allow the magic of the marketplace to create opportunities for growth and progress, free from the dead weight of government interference and misguided protectionism."

19. For a recent account that questions the widely circulated statistic claiming "that women spend ninety per cent of their income on their children," see Kathryn Moeller, "The Ghost Statistic that Haunts Women's Empowerment," *New Yorker*, January 4, 2019.

20. "Our Story," Girl Effect, n.d., accessed September 18, 2020, https://global .girleffect.org/who-we-are/our-story; 2010 statement quoted in Michelle Murphy, *The Economization of Life* (Durham, NC: Duke University Press, 2017), 117; Sarah Babb, "The Washington Consensus as Transnational Policy Paradigm: Its Origins, Trajectory and Likely Successor," *Review of International Political Economy* 20, no. 2 (2013): 286. In 2015, Girl Effect became an independent organization, no longer affiliated with the Nike Foundation. On the Girl Effect, see also Kathryn Moeller, *The Gender Effect: Capitalism, Feminism, and the Corporate Politics of Development* (Oakland: University of California Press, 2018). For a critical account of corporate philanthropy more generally, see Anand Giridharadas, *Winners Take All: The Elite Charade of Changing the World* (New York: Vintage, 2019).

21. World Bank Group, *Piecing Together the Poverty Puzzle: Poverty and Shared Prosperity 2018* (Washington, DC: International Bank for Reconstruction and Development/The World Bank, 2018), 1, 2, https://openknowledge.worldbank.org /bitstream/handle/10986/30418/9781464813306.pdf.

22. United Nations, "Goals: 1, End Poverty in All Its Forms Everywhere," UN Sustainable Development Goals website, n.d., accessed September 18, 2020, https://sdgs .un.org/goals/goal1; World Bank Group, *Piecing Together the Poverty Puzzle*, 1.

23. Frederick Cooper, "Writing the History of Development," *Journal of Modern European History* 8, no. 1 (2010): 6.

24. "What We Do," Attac, n.d., accessed September 18, 2020, https://www.attac .org/en/we-fight; Thomas Piketty, *Capital in the Twenty-First Century* (Cambridge, MA: Harvard University Press, 2014), 665.

Abdul Latif Jameel Poverty Action Lab, 225
ACCION International: microcredit work by, 203, 208, 216; PISCES project carried out by, 155–56, 194–95; WWB, support for, 283n43
ACVFA. *See* Advisory Committee on Voluntary Foreign Aid
Adelman, Irma, 38
Adelman, Jeremy, 239n14
Advisory Committee on Voluntary Foreign Aid (ACVFA), 145, 147–48, 162–63
African Americans: Ferguson, C. Clyde, Jr., 63; Leland, Mickey, 212; Long, Nira Hardon, 111; mass incarceration of male, 228; National Council of Negro Women (NCNW), 150 (*see also* National Council of Negro Women (NCNW)); self-help ethos in communities of, 207–8; "welfare cheats," women branded as, 2, 177; Young appointed as first Black US ambassador to the UN, 65
African Development Bank, 217
Agriculture, U.S. Department of, 100–101
Ahooja-Patel, Krishna, 95
Aiyar, Shahnaz Anklesaria, 219–20
Akula, Vikram, 224
Albright, Madeleine, 166
Allan, Virginia, 109–10, 166
Allende, Salvador, 74
Alliance for Progress, 15
"alter-globalization" policies, 229–30
American Council of Voluntary Agencies for Foreign Service (ACVAFS), 150
American Express, 158
American Freedom from Hunger Foundation, 34–35
Amin, Samir, 26
Anderson, Jack, 29

antipoverty discourse/efforts. *See* global poverty, campaigns against
Antrobus, Peggy, 128
Argentina, 186
Ashe, Jeffrey, 195
Asian Development Bank, 217
Association of African Women for Research and Development, 173
Attac, 230
Awe, Bolanle, 118

Babb, Sarah, 228
Band Aid, 140–42
Bangladesh: Germain and the WID movement in, 128–29; Grameen Bank in (*see* Grameen Bank); microcredit NGOs in, limited impact of, 215; war, natural disasters, and famine in, 50, 78, 200; War of Liberation, 200
Bangladesh Institute of Law and International Affairs, 124
Bangladesh Rural Advancement Committee (BRAC), 133–34, 203, 215
Barba Negra Appeal, 258n102
Barber, Elinor, 119, 126, 128–29
basic needs approach to global poverty: Carter administration support for, 66, 79–81; Ford administration opposition to, 70; fragmentation of, 91; the global debt crisis and, 190–93; microcredit and, 220; the NIEO and, 75–77, 80; as one option for redistribution, 55–56, 66–68; support for, 68–71; the Upper Volta project and, 97; women in development and, 124, 138–39 (*see also* women in development (WID) movement); the World Bank and, 55, 67, 71–75, 77, 138–39
Bauer, Peter T., 28
BBC News: report on famine in Ethiopia, 140

Belafonte, Harry, 141
Benería, Lourdes, 171–72
Bereuter, Doug, 204–5
Bergsten, C. Fred, 29, 58
Beyer, Clara, 109–12, 152
Bharat Financial Inclusion, 224
Bhatt, Ela: background and career of, 159; on the bankers' reaction to SEWA members, 196; Ford Foundation, acceptance of funding from, 160; Germain and, 128; as "influencer," 7; at the International Microcredit Summit (1997), 218–19; at the International Women's Year conference, 196–97; Women's World Banking, activities at, 198–99
biopolitics, 102, 129, 212, 227–28
Black Americans. See African Americans
Bono, 226
Boserup, Ester: The Conditions of Agricultural Growth, 105; as "influencer," 7; Integration of Women in Development: Why, When, How (with Christina Liljencrantz), 108; Mexico City WID seminar, attendance at, 116; Myrdal and, 105; private export industries in donor countries as pressure groups, 257n93; Wellesley conference, attendance at, 121; WID, foundational work for, 170; Woman's Role in Economic Development, 105–8
Bosnia, 224
Boxer, Barbara, 206
Bradley, Bill, 189–90
Brandt, Willy, 87–89
Brandt Commission: conservative reaction to, 90–91; establishment of, Pearson Commission and, 87–89; report of (see North-South: A Program for Survival (Brandt Commission)); second report of: Common Crisis North-South: Cooperation for World Recovery, 189; the summit, 91–92; universal taxation, call for, 90
Brazil: the debt crisis and negotiations with the IMF, 186; inequality in, study of, 38
Bread for the World, 78, 189, 214

Britain: antipoverty efforts in, 33; dominance of free-market advocates in Thatcher's, 91; support for the NIEO in the New Internationalist, 61–62
Brookings Institution: basic needs approach, report supporting, 80; international taxation, conference and book supporting, 86–87
Brown, Wendy, 290n3
Brown & Root Overseas Inc., 29
Budhoo, Davison L., 193
Bundy, McGeorge, 126
Burki, Shahid Javed, 72
Burnham, James, 243n34
Buvinic, Mayra, 130

Canada, 198
CARE: annual spending of, 143; "beyond charity" change in NGOs promoted by, 150; microcredit in the portfolio of, 216; the Peace Corps and, 145; USAID initiatives, concerns regarding, 147–48; US Cold War foreign policy goals promoted by, 145
Carnegie Corporation, 137
Carnegie Endowment for International Peace, 60
Carter, Jimmy: basic needs policies and, 79–84; hunger as touchstone for, 79–80; North-South relations, evolution of position on, 64–65; the ODC and, 78; Presidential Commission on World Hunger, 83–84
Carter, "Miss Lillian," 136
Carter administration: antipoverty advocates disappointed by, 227; basic needs approach to global poverty of the, 66, 79–81; foreign assistance, giving up on, 84–85; "Miss Lillian"'s trip to Africa, 136; NIEO, rejection of, 65–66; Policy Review Committee, 80; population control movement, backing away from, 104; WID division of USAID, support for, 114
Castro, Fidel, 92
Catholic Church: Commission for Justice and Peace, the Vatican's, 31; global poverty initiatives by, 30–33;

population control programs, opposition to, 104
Catholic Relief Services, 140, 145, 148, 216
Central Intelligence Agency (CIA), 151
Chamber of Commerce, U.S., 83
Chaney, Elsa, 104, 114–15, 120, 132, 134
Chen, Martha (Marty) Alter, 134, 215
Chenery, Hollis, 46–47, 187
Chile: dominance of free-market advocates in Pinochet's, 91; World Bank loans and, 74
China, People's Republic of: economic development programs, investment in, 77; poverty reduction in, 228–29
China, Republic of, 91
Chowdhry, Kamla, 159–60
Christian Aid, 33
Clark, William, 18, 25, 43
Clausen, A. W., 187, 281n11
Clinton, Bill, 208, 216
Clinton, Hillary, 208, 216–19
Clinton administration: microcredit and neoliberalism, focus on, 216
Club of Rome: *The Limits to Growth*, 68; *The Limits to Growth*, retreat from in favor of basic needs approach, 71; RIO report, 86
Coalition for Women in International Development (CWID), 114, 163–64
Cockburn, Alexander, 223
Cocoyoc Declaration, 69–70, 75, 85–86
Cocoyoc symposium, 68–69
Cold War: Carter and, 82; foreign assistance and, 19, 99, 145, 157; foreign assistance and the waning of, 2, 8–9, 17, 40, 49, 58, 157; modernization and, 3; North-South split as the new, 63; the OEF and, 151
Collins, Joseph, 78
Colombia, 37
Columbia Conference on International Economic Development (1970), 23–26, 44–45, 90
Columbia Declaration, 25–26, 38, 42, 46
Commission on International Development (Pearson Commission), 19, 87–89. *See also* Pearson report *(Partners in Development)*

community development (CD) programs, 15–16, 49
Conable, Barber, 174, 190, 193
Conference on International Economic Co-operation (1977), 63–65, 79
Consultative Group to Assist the Poorest (CGAP), 217
Cooper, Frederick, 229
Corea, Gamani, 75
Cornia, Giovanni Andrea, 191
Costa Rica: vocational training for women in, USAID funding for, 152; women-owned businesses, OEF funding to support, 166
credit: extension of as trend in anti-poverty programs, 178–79, 183–84; the promise of, 193–200. *See also* microcredit
cultural imperialism, 131–35
cycle of poverty, 212–13

Dag Hammarskjöld Foundation: basic needs approach supported by, 68–70, 75; GAD concerns, support for, 173; as incubator for development plans, 8; international equity and the new international economic order, support for, 61; "South-North" conference in Tanzania (1980), sponsorship of, 188
"Dakar Declaration on Another Development with Women," 173
Daley-Harris, Sam, 206–7
DAWN. *See* Development Alternatives with Women for a New Era
debt: the basic needs approach and the global debt crisis, 190–93; of the global South in 1990, 193; structural adjustment loans and the global debt crisis, 6, 184–93, 214. *See also* credit; microcredit
Debt Crisis Network, 189
Debt Trap, The: The IMF and the Third World (Payer), 187–88
Dell, Michael, 226
Dell, Susan, 226
Dellums, Ron, 206
Denmark, 77
dependency, 211

dependency theory, 26–27, 54
development: credit and, 178–79, 183–84
(*see also* credit; microcredit); history
of from modernization to microcredit,
226–30; the informal economy and,
153–56, 211–12; liberation theology
as critique of, 32; microcredit and
(*see* microcredit); as modernization
(*see* modernization policies/theory);
population and women as childbear-
ers, focus on, 102–4; public-private
collaboration on, 144–49 (*see also*
nongovernmental organizations
(NGOs)); reorientation towards global
poverty, 17–26 (*see also* global poverty,
campaigns against); trickle-down
economics and, rejection of, 17, 36–41,
51, 226; as twentieth-century term
for economic interventions against
poverty, 3; WID and, 129 (*see also*
women in development (WID) movement); women as childrearers, focus
on, 100–102
Development Alternatives with Women
for a New Era (DAWN), 173–76,
199–200
Development Group for Alternative Policies (DGAP), 155–56, 189
DeWine, Mike, 206
Dole, Elizabeth, 163–64
Dominica, 158
Dunne, George, 32

Echeverría, Luis, 117
economic development. *See* development
Ecuador, 152
Ekbladh, David, 239n13
Elliott, Charles, 32
El Salvador: FEDECRÉDITO, coordinating credit cooperatives and extending
credit by, 195; tomato raising and processing project, OEF promotion of,
166–68
Emmerij, Louis, 70
Equal Credit Opportunity Act of 1974,
198–99
Ethiopia: famine in, 140–41; famine relief
diverted to the military or separatist

rebels, 141–42; women in, NGO
projects targeting, 142
European Community, Liaison Committee
with European NGOs, 169

famine: African, perspective on women
in the wake of, 176; in Bangladesh, 50,
78 (*see also* Bangladesh); in Ethiopia,
140–42; fundraising for relief of, 140–44;
reported in American newspapers,
29–30; in the Sahel, 50, 78, 141
Fanon, Frantz, 13, 53
Farbman, Michael, 210
Fassin, Didier, 20, 241n12
Feighan, Edward, 205–7
feminism/feminists: credit for women as
an issue for, 198; as cultural imperialists, WID and, 131–35; development
pursued in mainstream institutions,
critiques of, 120–21; equal employment opportunities for women, attention brought to, 107; GAD and, 173;
Marxist-feminists, 104–5, 120–21,
171–72, 174; Percy amendment, appeal
of, 116; population control programs,
opposition to, 103–4. *See also* gender
Ferguson, C. Clyde, Jr., 63
Feulner, Edwin J., Jr., 161–62
FINCA, 209, 216, 226
Finnemore, Martha, 51
Fishlow, Albert, 38
Food First (Institute for Food and Development Policy), 78
Ford administration: opposition to the
NIEO, 117
Ford Foundation: Bangladesh Institute
of Law and International Affairs WID
seminar sponsored by, 124; Brookings
conference on international taxation,
funding of, 86; Columbia conference,
funding of, 23; credit equity for
women in the global South, funding
of reports on, 199; DAWN, funding
of meeting that founded, 173; "discipline" associated with microcredit,
212, 215; economic development programs, internal review of funding of,
37; Grameen Bank, funding support

for, 202–3; International Microcredit Summit, tensions preceding, 219; microcredit, limitations of and doubts about, 214–15; NGOs, collaboration with, 169; Overseas Development Council (ODC), funding of, 38, 61; population control programs, backing of, 103; *Seeds* pamphlet series, 137–38; Self-Employed Women's Association (SEWA), support for, 159–60, 197; SODEPAX, support for, 32–33; Southern Development Bancorporation, funding for, 208; third world mistrust of the United States, report on, 42; USAID and, 127–28; Wellesley conference, funding of, 126; Wellesley conference, reaction to, 119, 121; "What Ever Happened to Poverty Alleviation?" (Tendler), 178; the WID movement, increasing support for in the 1980s, 171–72; the WID movement, support for, 126–29, 137–38; Women's World Banking, support of, 198; Yunus, financial support of, 202, 204. *See also* Germain, Adrienne

foreign aid: antipoverty strategy, obstacles to and limitations of, 49–52; antipoverty strategy, reorientation towards, 18–26 (*see also* global poverty, campaigns against); basic needs and (*see* basic needs approach to global poverty); critique from the left, 26–27, 50; critique from the right, 27–28, 50; "dependency," concerns about, 211; for development (*see* development); microcredit as (*see* microcredit); for modernization (*see* modernization policies/theory); US (*see* US foreign aid)

Foreign Assistance Act of 1973: abortions, prohibition of using foreign aid funds to pay for, 263n33; goals of, 5; New Directions mandate of (*see* New Directions mandate); the Percy Amendment to (*see* Percy Amendment); privatization of development programs, mandating of, 144–45; from relief to development, change in public-private collaboration, 145–47; signing of, 111

Foucault, Michel, 102
Fraser, Arvonne: Chaney, recruitment of for WID division of USAID, 120; co-ordinator of the WID division of USAID, appointment as, 114; defense of WID, cultural imperialism issue and, 133; Germain's view of, 127; institutionalization of women in development at AID, efforts toward, 163; "Miss Lillian" Carter's visit to Upper Volta, planning of, 136; OEF board of trustees, position on, 166; Percy amendment, lobbying for, 111; photo of, 115
Fraser, Donald M., 38–39, 111, 114, 132
Freire, Paulo, 134
Fundación Bariloche, *Catastrophe or New Society? A Latin American World Model*, 71

Gandhi, Indira, 92
Gates, Bill, 226
Gates, Melinda, 226
Geldof, Bob, 140–41
gender: empowerment of women through microcredit, 213–14, 220; gender equity and alleviation of global poverty, interconnected histories of, 226–28; reversal in the politics of, 177–78; women *versus* men for antipoverty investments, 176–77; women *versus* men for microcredit programs, 208–10, 215, 220. *See also* feminism/feminists; women; women in development (WID) movement
gender and development (GAD), 170–77
General Agreement on Tariffs and Trade (GATT), 92
Gerhart, John D., 174, 176
Germain, Adrienne: Bangladesh, work in, 128–29; cooperation with USAID, question of, 120; dismissals of WID noted by, 135; human capital, WID as utilization of, 129; on the International Women's Year conference, 123; OEF, criticism of, 153; SEWA, work with and funds for, 159–60; USAID, criticism of, 127–28; as a WID advocate at the Ford Foundation, 126–27;

Germain, Adrienne (*continued*)
  WID success stories publicized in pamphlet series, 137–38; women as more responsible than men in allocating family income, arguments for, 176; women in the global South, building relationships with, 128; Yunus and, 203
Geyer, Georgie Anne, 166
Ghana, 172
Gilligan, John J., 80–81, 114–15, 127
Girl Effect, 228
global poverty, campaigns against: antipoverty strategy of the 1970s, obstacles to and limitations of, 49–52; in Britain, 33; Christian initiatives, 30–33; credit and, 178–79, 183–84, 211 (*see also* credit; microcredit); current goals, familiarity of, 229; history of US involvement in the 1970s and 1980s, 2–3; humanitarian argument supporting, 20; internationalization of poverty into a global problem, 51; Johnson's War on Poverty and, 29–30; longer history of, 3; microcredit and (*see* microcredit); in the Pearson report, 17–26; redistributive approaches of the second half of the 1970s, 55–56 (*see also* basic needs approach to global poverty; New International Economic Order (NIEO)); rejection of trickle-down economics and, 36–42; trends of the late 1970s and 1980s, 142–44; in the United States, 34–36; WID and, 129–30 (*see also* women in development (WID) movement); women as superior to men in, 176–77; at the World Bank, 43–49 (*see also* World Bank). *See also* development; modernization policies/theory; poverty
global South: antipoverty programs of the 1970s, tepid reception to, 50; austerity conditions, objections to imposition of, 188–89; bilateral aid from the US suspect in, 42, 148; credit equity for women, call for, 199; cultural change supported by women in, 133; the debt crisis and the consequences of austerity, 184–93; debt owed by in 1990, 193;

dependency theory applied to, 26–27; divisions within the WID movement, suspicions directed at USAID and, 116–19; economists from included in the Columbia conference, 23, 26; GAD approach to WID in, 173–74; New International Economic Order written and supported in, 55–58 (*see also* New International Economic Order (NIEO)); nongovernmental organizations (NGOs) suspect in, 148–49; political views of WID activists in, 124–25; the UN as multilateral institution of choice in, 42–43; usage of the term, 12
Goddard, Paula, 164
Goodin, Joan, 117
Gorbachev Foundation, 217
Graham, Billy, 30
Grameen Bank: in Bangladesh, limited impact of, 215; borrowers in 2006, number and gender of, 221; criticisms of, 222–23; establishment and rapid growth of, 202–4; international fame of, 178, 183, 206–8; *60 Minutes* segment on, 207; Nobel Peace Prize awarded to, 221; poor women as entrepreneurs, view of, 211; "16 decisions" borrowers memorized and recited, 211–12; women, increasing percentage of loans going to, 203, 208
Grameen Bank Project, 201–2
Grant, James P., 38–39, 60, 78, 85–86, 190
green revolution, 15–16
Gremillion, Joseph, 30–31
G-77 (Group of 77), 42, 57, 117
Gutiérrez, Gustavo, 32
Gwatkin, Davidson, 159

Haig, Alexander M., Jr., 92, 161, 164
Hammarskjöld Foundation. *See* Dag Hammarskjöld Foundation
Hansen, Roger D., 78, 84–85, 252n41
Haq, Mahbub ul: basic needs approach, reframing of, 192; basic needs approach, support for, 72–76; Brandt Commission and, 87, 93; as "influencer," 7; international tax, support

for, 85–86; McNamara and, 45–46, 73; photo of, 74; on the poverty curtain that divides the world, 1, 73; at the "State of the World" forum (1996), 217; World Bank, position in, 46, 72–73

Harrington, Michael: ambivalence between liberal and radical commitments, 54–56; Carter's plans, cautious hopes for, 65; comment on the Brandt Commission, 93; discourse and politics of compared to Ward, 53–54; McNamara, opinion of, 54; NIEO, support for, 62; *The Other America*, 1; on US diplomats' response to Nyerere, 75; on the US opposition to the basic needs approach, 70; *The Vast Majority: A Journey to the World's Poor*, 1–2, 53–55

Hart, Keith, 274n35

Harvey, David, 210

Hasina, Sheikh, 217

Haslemere Declaration, 33

Hatch, John, 209, 214

Hatch, Orrin, 206

Hayter, Teresa, 26

Height, Dorothy, 113, 133

Heritage Foundation, 161–62, 217

Hesburgh, Theodore M., 40, 78

Hewlett Foundation, William and Flora, 165

Hickey, Margaret, 149–50

Hicks, Norman, 72

Honduras, 166

Hong Kong, 91

human development approach, 192–93

Humphrey, Hubert, 23, 110

hunger: Carter's focus on, 79–80, 83–84 (*see also* Carter, Jimmy; Carter administration); mid-1970s focus on, 78–79. *See also* famine

Hunger Project, The, 78

Huntington, Samuel, 28

Hutar, Patricia, 166

IBM, 158

ILO. *See* International Labour Organization

IMF. *See* International Monetary Fund

Immerwahr, Daniel, 239n13

Independent Commission on International Development Issues. *See* Brandt Commission

India: Ford Foundation support for small-scale women's work in, 172; ILO studies acknowledging the exploitation of women in, 172; microcredit in, problems with, 223–24; Self-Employed Women's Association (*see* Self-Employed Women's Association (SEWA)); Working Women's Forum of Madras, 156, 172, 178

Indian National Congress, National Planning Committee, 106

informal economy: development and, 153–55; microcredit and, 211–12 (*see also* microcredit); poor women as entrepreneurs in, 155–60

Institute for Food and Development Policy (Food First), 78

Institute for Policy Studies (IPS): Debt Crisis Network, membership in, 189; the global debt crisis and the IMF's response to it, warnings about, 188; NIEO, support for, 62; protesters at the International Development Conference (1970) from, 27; "South-North" conference in Tanzania (1980), sponsorship of, 188

Institute of Development Studies: founding of, 72; as incubator for development plans, 8; participants for the Columbia conference, consultation on, 23; World Bank, collaboration with, 46

InterAction, 142

Inter-American Development Bank, 183

Inter-American Foundation, 267n79

International Bank for Reconstruction and Development (IBRD). *See* World Bank

International Center for Research on Women, 113–14, 119

International Conference on Microenterprise Development (1988), 183

International Development Association (IDA), 43

International Development Conference (1970), 27

International Development Conference
(1978), 76–77
International Fund for Agricultural
Development (IFAD), 202, 206, 217
International Labour Organization
(ILO): basic needs approach, women
in development and, 124; basic needs
approach to poverty supported by,
55, 70–71, 77 (*see also* basic needs
approach to global poverty); the GAD
variant of WID pursued by, 172–73;
as incubator for development plans,
8; the informal economy, studies of,
153–54; Programme on Rural Women,
123–24, 172; "redistribution from
growth" concept, 47; women's labor
and income in the global South, attention directed to, 107; World Employment Programme (WEP), 37, 154
International Meeting on Cooperation
and Development (1981), 92
International Microcredit Summit (1997),
217–20
International Monetary Fund (IMF): free-
market policies of, GAD's rejection
of, 171; the global debt crisis and, 185;
governing of, call for better representation of the global South in, 89; major
powers' insistence on running the world
economy through, 92; structural adjustment loans/policies of, 6, 186–91, 193;
the "Washington consensus" and, 187
international taxation: Brandt Commission's call for, 90; to fund global economic development, 85–87; revival of
calls for, 230; Tobin tax, 258n99
International Women's Year conference:
confrontations/tensions at, 116–17;
Ford Foundation funding of activists'
travel to, 126; as galvanizing event,
123; World Plan of Action, 117, 123
Interreligious Task Force on US Food
Policy, 78
IPS. *See* Institute for Policy Studies
Isenman, Paul, 72

J. P. Morgan, 158, 166
Jackson, Michael, 141

Jackson, Robert G. A., 22
Jahan, Rounaq, 128
Jahanbani, Sheyda, 239n13
Jain, Devaki, 123
Jamaica, 76
Jaquette, Jane, 114–15, 120
Johnson, Lady Bird: photo of, 24; on
Ward's influence on Lyndon, 23
Johnson, Lyndon: multilateral aid, pref-
erence for, 42; population control
programs, backing of, 103; Ward as an
adviser to, 22–23; War on Poverty, 1, 7,
29–30, 34
Joint Committee on Society, Development
and Peace (SODEPAX), 32–33
Jolly, Richard, 36–37, 47–48, 190–91
Jones, Quincy, 141

Karim, Lamia, 291n14
Kennedy, Edward, 206
Kennedy, John F., 1, 15–16, 19, 22
Kenya: ILO support for developing small
enterprises for women in, 172; infor-
mal sector in, report on, 153; micro-
credit in, limitations of, 215; research
on rural women in, conflict over who
conducts, 119; training of poor women
as entrepreneurs, 156
Kenyan Women's Bureau, 119
King, Martin Luther, Jr., 30
Kirkpatrick, Jeane, 163–64
Kissinger, Henry, 59–60, 64, 112
Kiva, 226
Korea, Republic of (South Korea): credit
cooperative organized in, 195; state-
supported economic growth in, 91
Kragen, Ken, 141
Krauss, Melvyn B., 90–91
Krueger, Anne, 187

LaFeber, Walter, 161
Lal, Priya, 254n68
Lappé, Frances Moore, 78
Leacock, Eleanor, 121
League of Women Voters: Overseas Edu-
cation Fund (*see* Overseas Education
Fund (OEF)); Percy amendment, lob-
bying for, 110–11

Leet, Glen, 158–60
Leet, Mildred, 158–60
Leland, Mickey, 212–13
Letelier, Orlando, 62
liberation theology, 32
life expectancy as indicator of well-being, 8, 68, 192
Lilienthal, David, 290n2
Liljencrantz, Christina, 108
Limits to Growth, The (Club of Rome), 68, 71
literacy as indicator of well-being, 8, 68, 192
Live Aid, 141–42
Long, Clarence, 83
Long, Nira Hardon, 111, 113, 197
Los Angeles Times: cartoon objecting to structural adjustment loans, 191
Lundine, Stan, 204–5

Magdoff, Harry, 27
Malawi, 207
Malaysia, 172, 207
Mali: attempts to replicate the Grameen Bank in, 207; Ford Foundation support for small-scale projects in, 172; women in, NGO projects targeting, 142
Manley, Michael, 58, 76
Marcos, Ferdinand, 58, 92
Marcy, Mildred, 109–10
Marino, Katherine M., 265n58
Marshall Plan, 18, 22
Marxism/Marxists: Amin as, 26; Cockburn as, 223; dependency theory and, 54; Freire and, 134; Magdoff as, 27; Marxist-feminists, 104–5, 120–21, 171–72, 174; *Populorum Progressio* (Paul VI) dismissed as "warmed-over," 31; USAID rejection of, 121; WID supporters included, 11
Mazumdar, Vina, 118, 128
McCain, John, 206
McClelland, David, 101–2
McNamara, Margaret, 125
McNamara, Robert: antipoverty strategy for the World Bank, establishment of, 43–48; antipoverty strategy for the World Bank, reframing as basic needs, 71–72; background of and influences on, 44–46; Brandt Commission, proposal of, 87–88; fertility and economic opportunity for women, connection between, 131; Haq and, 45–46, 73; Harrington's opinion of, 54; New International Economic Order, reaction to, 60; Pearson report, invitation leading to, 19, 87; in photo, 48; structural adjustment program, initiation of, 186–87; Ward as an adviser to, 22; WID, interest in, 125; World Bank relations with the US, 43
McPherson, M. Peter, 161–62, 164, 207
Mennonite Central Committee, 145
Mernissi, Fatima, 118
Mexico: Banco Compartamos as business rather than NGO, investor profits from, 223–24; the debt crisis of 1982, loans with austerity conditions and, 185–86; ILO studies acknowledging the exploitation of women in, 172; Mexico City WID seminar, 116
microcredit: as antipoverty approach, emergence of, 5–6, 183–84, 193–200; contemporary status of, 225–26; critics of/doubts about, 214–16, 219–20, 222–25; the "cycle of poverty" and, 212–13; "discipline" associated with, 211–12, 215; empowerment and noneconomic impacts of, 213–14, 220; Grameen Bank (*see* Grameen Bank); International Microcredit Summit (1997), 217–20; neoliberalism and, 184, 210–11, 216; organizations offering in the mid-1980s, 203; positive images of, 210–14; profit-making model, turn to from NGO model, 223–24; the Southern Development Bancorporation, 208; in the United States, 204–8; for women, 195–200, 208–16
microfinance, 221
MicroStart, 218
Mills, Donald O., 255n71
Minhas, Bagicha S., 255n71

modernization policies/theory: biopolitics and, 102; development programs of the 1950s-1970s, 3–4, 6–7; popularized by Ward, 22; rise and fall in the 1960s, 15–16; trickle-down economics and, rejection of, 36–37, 51; women and, 99–102, 104, 177–78

Moffitt, Michael, 62

Morocco: microcredit repayment crisis in, 224; spending of women with dependents in, 177; spending of young men in, 177

Morris, Cynthia Taft, 38

Moyn, Samuel, 255n71

Moynihan, Daniel Patrick, 59

Moynihan report of 1965, 177

multilateral aid/institutions: United Nations, preference of global South nations for, 42–43 (see also United Nations (UN)); World Bank, preference of the United States for, 43 (see also World Bank)

multinational/transnational corporations: concerns regarding, 27, 50, 54, 56, 59, 61, 71, 84, 89, 91, 118, 121, 229, 230

Museveni, Yoweri, 219

Myrdal, Gunnar: antipoverty discourse, contributions to, 33–34; Boserup and, 105; international tax, advocacy of, 85; Streeten and, 72; untying US foreign aid, campaigning for, 41; world poverty, addressing the challenge of, 2

Nation: review of The Vast Majority: A Journey to the World's Poor (Harrington), 54

National Christian Council of Kenya, 156

National Council of Churches, Coordinating Council for Hunger Concerns, 78

National Council of Jewish Women, 111

National Council of Negro Women (NCNW), 113, 150–51. See also Height, Dorothy

National Federation of Business and Professional Women, 110

National Organization for Women, 108

National Review, 222

National Women's Studies Association, 122

neoliberalism: basic tenets of, 210; microcredit and, 184, 210–11, 216; paler variants of antipoverty and feminist movements accommodated by, 227. See also Reagan, Ronald; Reagan administration

Nerfin, Marc, 68–69

Netherlands, the: Brandt Commission, financial support for, 89; as donor nation, 77; New International Economic Order, endorsement of, 61; Women's World Banking, support of, 198

New Abolitionists, 33

New Directions mandate: codification of antipoverty aims in, 227; congressional action establishing, 2, 38–42, 81; NGOs brought into, 149; Upper Volta project and, 97, 136; WID aligned with, 113; women not mentioned in original legislation for, 108. See also Foreign Assistance Act of 1973

New International Economic Order (NIEO): adoption of by the UN General Assembly, 117; the basic needs approach and, 75–77, 80; Brandt Commission report and, 89–90; the Carter administration and, 64–66, 80; declaration of by the UN, 55–57; declining influence of, 227; development establishment response to, 60–61; endorsements from the Left for, 62; European response to, 61–62; North-South dialogue and, stalemate of, 63–64; racism and political economy as underlying tensions for, 63–64; support for in the global South, 57–58; US government response to, 58–60, 64; women and development (WAD) and, 170, 173

New Internationalist, 33, 62

Newsweek: the North-South split as the new Cold War, 63

New York Times: famine in Ethiopia, public response to, 140; microcredit, praise for, 222; praise for The Vast Majority: A Journey to the World's Poor (Harrington), 54; profits from

Mexican microcredit NGO-turned business, report on, 223–24; skepticism about the Brandt Commission, 87; structural adjustment loans for Mexico, practical implications of, 186; "tying" policy, implications of, 82; women in India devastated by microcredit, story on, 224
"NGOization," 167, 169, 178
NGOs. *See* nongovernmental organizations
Nicaragua, 224
NIEO. *See* New International Economic Order
Niger, 216
Nike, 228
Nixon, Richard: Beijing, visit to, 157; Foreign Assistance Act of 1973, signing of, 111; multilateral aid, preference for, 42; "New Directions" legislation and, 38–39, 41; opposition to foreign aid proposals by, 28–29; public-private collaboration on economic development, promotion of, 144; USAID, poor opinion of, 41
nongovernmental organizations (NGOs): celebrity fundraising for famine relief and, 141–42; the global debt crisis, organization in response to, 189; incorporation as businesses, profits from, 223–24; the informal economy and small enterprise, interest in, 153–60; international agencies and foundations, collaboration with, 169–70; microcredit and (*see* Grameen Bank; microcredit); poor women as entrepreneurs, focus on, 156–60; public-private collaboration, beyond charity and, 144–50; Reaganomics and, 160–69; trends of the late 1970s and 1980s, 142–44; US government assistance to in 1983, 169; women, focus on, 142–44; women in development (WID) and, 149–53, 173–74. *See also* Accion International; CARE; Overseas Development Council (ODC); Overseas Education Fund (OEF); Self-Employed Women's Association (SEWA)

Norris, James, 30–31
North-South: A Program for Survival (Brandt Commission): basic needs and NIEO supported in, 93; broad range of goals of, 89–90; countries in arrears, the debt crisis and, 185; universal taxation, promotion of, 90; women and issues related to women, prominence of, 138
North-South dialogue: Brandt Commission and, 87–90 (*see also* Brandt Commission); as ideological tug of war, 52; shifting center of gravity in the 1970s, 8–9; stalemate in, 63–64. *See also* global South
North-South Roundtable of the Society for International Development, 192
Norway: as donor nation, 77; Grameen Bank, funding support for, 202; SEWA, support for, 197; Women's World Banking, support for, 198
Nyerere, Julius K.: basic needs, supporter of, 75; the IMF and austerity conditions, objections to, 188–89; at the International Meeting on Cooperation and Development (1981), 92; invited to visit the White House, 65; the NIEO, supporter of, 58, 75; photo of, 88; "trade union of the poor" attributed to, 250n12; world poverty, addressing the challenge of, 2

Ocloo, Esther, 197–98
ODC. *See* Overseas Development Council
OEF. *See* Overseas Education Fund
Offner, Amy, 239n13
oil crisis of 1973, 50, 58
Organisation for Economic Co-operation and Development (OECD): Development Assistance Committee, 124; *Voluntary Aid for Development: The Role of Non-Governmental Organisations,* 169–70; women in development, planning meeting to discuss, 107–8
Organization of African Unity, 186
Organization of Petroleum Exporting Countries (OPEC), 58, 77, 91, 185
Osman, Suleiman, 238n8

O'Sullivan, Kevin, 251n27
Overseas Development Council (ODC):
basic needs approach promoted by,
77–78; *Beyond Charity: U.S. Voluntary Aid for a Changing Third World,*
147; "beyond charity" shift promoted
by, 150; bottom-up development, argument for, 37–38; Carter and, 78, 84;
"New Directions" legislation steered
through Congress by, 39; New International Economic Order and, 60–61,
64; nongovernmental organizations
(NGOs), diversity of, 148; nongovernmental organizations (NGOs), promotion of, 147
Overseas Education Fund (OEF): business development model, internal
conflict over, 165–66; CIA, cooperation with, 151; Coalition for Women
in International Development, sponsorship of, 114, 163–64; credit and
business skills for women, appeal for
funding for, 199; criticism of, 153,
167; El Salvador tomato success story,
promotion of, 166–68; renamed OEF
International, 166; USAID funding
for, 149, 151–53, 165–67, 199; WIDTech
Project, 165; women's fish-processing
project in Senegal, funding of, 142
Overseas Private Investment Corporation,
144–45
Owens, Edgar, 39–40, 49
Owens, Sarale, 112
Oxfam, 33, 140, 197

Pakistan, 224
Palmer, Ingrid, 123–24
Papanek, Hanna, 129
Parker, Daniel, 111–12
Partnership for Productivity, 155–56
Partners in Development. See Pearson
report *(Partners in Development)*
Pathmarajah, Appiah, 70
Patterson, Orlando, 76, 255n69
Paul VI, 2, 30–31, 236n3
Payer, Cheryl, 187–88
Peace Corps: CARE and, 145; establish-
ment of, 15; Trickle Up Program,

collaboration with, 158; WID, concerns about cultural imperialism
related to, 131–32; WID, increased
interest in, 164
Pearson, Lester B., 19, 21
Pearson Commission (Commission on
International Development), 19,
87–89
Pearson report *(Partners in Development):* critique from the Columbia
conference, 23–26; critique from
the left, 26–27; the debt crisis and
debt relief as form of aid, 184–85;
formation and popular promotion of,
19–23; increases in foreign assistance
requested in, 90; multilateral aid
endorsed in, 42; women neglected in,
138
Percy, Charles, 110, 112–13, 115, 117, 164
Percy Amendment: divisions within WID
movement regarding, 116–17; enactment
of, background leading to, 108–11;
implementation by USAID, struggle for, 111–15; NGOs and, 149–50,
152; WID, as one foundation for, 170,
227 *(see also* women in development
(WID) movement). *See also* Foreign
Assistance Act of 1973
Philippines, the: attempts to replicate
the Grameen Bank in, 207; focus of
PISCES team on women, 157
Piketty, Thomas, 221, 230
Pinochet, Augusto, 4, 62, 74
Population Bomb, The (Ehrlich), 103
population control movement, 102–4,
130–32
Population Council, 103, 137, 173
Populorum Progressio (Paul VI), 31,
236n3
Portillo, José López, 91
Portman, Natalie, 226
poverty: absolute, McNamara's definition
of, 44; basic needs and, 66–67 *(see also*
basic needs approach to global poverty);
cycle of, 212–13; famine as evidence
of dire, 50; global *(see* global poverty,
campaigns against); Harrington's
description of, 53; internationalizing,

51; market economy as the solution to, faith in, 48–49; microcredit as inadequate to address, 224–25; people living in extreme, 2015 estimate of, 229; recognition of global in the 1970s, 1–2

Prashad, Vijay, 75

Prebisch, Raúl, 57

Presidential Commission on World Hunger, 83–84

private voluntary organizations (PVOs), 145, 162. *See also* nongovernmental organizations (NGOs)

privatization: mandated by the Foreign Assistance Act of 1973, 144–45; "NGOization" and, 167, 169; the Overseas Private Investment Corporation and, 144–45; the Reagan administration and, 143, 162–63

Pronk, Jan, 61

Proshika, 215

Protestant Churches. *See* World Council of Churches (WCC)

Public Law 480, 146

race/racism: avoidance of discussing by development experts, 8; in the population control movement, 103–4; in South Africa, 32; tensions over the NIEO and, 63–64

Reagan, Ronald: election of, 5, 160–61, 227; foreign aid supporting small businesses, support for, 162; free-market advocacy by, 91–92, 292n18; at the International Meeting on Cooperation and Development (1981), 92; the "welfare queen," story of, 177

Reagan administration: "basic human needs" subsumed under "strategic and political interests," 163; battle over foreign aid cuts within the, 161; Clausen, criticism of, 281n11; North-South transfer of resources rejected by, 227; privatization of development and antipoverty efforts, encouragement of, 143; WID goals, endorsement of, 164

redistribution: by "alter-globalization" policies, 229–30; by an international

tax, 85–87, 90, 230; the basic needs approach (*see* basic needs approach to global poverty); of the benefits from growth, 47, 52; limits of by mainstream institutions, 18; the New International Economic Order (*see* New International Economic Order (NIEO))

Redistribution with Growth (World Bank), 47

Regan, Donald T., 92

religion: antipoverty movement/programs, support for, 4, 10, 30–33, 45; Carter, reaching out to religious leaders by, 82; Carter, religious convictions of, 79; contraception opposed by the Catholic Church, 104; discrimination by lenders based on, outlawing of, 198–99; hunger, concerns and actions regarding, 78; the NIEO and, 251n28; Ward as devout Catholic, 22, 45

RESULTS, 206–7, 217

Ritchie, Lionel, 141

Rockefeller Brothers Fund, 198

Rockefeller Foundation: Brookings conference on international taxation, funding of, 86; conference center in Italy, World Bank meeting to discuss antipoverty strategy at, 47; Overseas Development Council (ODC), funding of, 38, 61

Rockefeller Foundation, Winthrop, 208

Rosenberg, Gabriel, 239n13

Rosenstein-Rodan, Paul, 22

Rostow, Walt, 7, 25–26

Rowan, Carl T., 92–93

Roy, Ananya, 181

Ruppe, Loret Miller, 164

Saadawi, Nawal El, 118

Safer, Morley, 207

Sahel, the: Carter's request for famine relief aid for, 79; drought in, 186; famine in, 50, 78, 141

Save the Children, 140, 216

Scali, John, 59

Scott, Gloria, 123, 125

Seers, Dudley, 36–37, 245n59

Seidman, L. William, 59
Self-Employed Women's Association (SEWA): Ford Foundation funding of, 160, 172; founding of, 159–60; as a "good performer" among antipoverty programs, 178; international inspiration, microcredit program as, 196–97; microcredit program of, 196, 203, 208; Women's Cooperative Bank, 196, 198
Sen, Amartya, 192
Sen, Gita, 171
Senegal, 142
Sewell, John W., 174
Shiva, Vandana, 217
Sierra Leone, 133
Simon, William, 59
Singapore: ILO studies acknowledging the exploitation of women in, 172; state-supported economic growth in, 91
Singer, Hans, 37, 76
Singh, Ajit, 76
SKS Microfinance, 224
Smith, Elise Fiber, 142
Snyder, Margaret, 176–77
social business, 222
Society for International Development, 107, 108–9, 191–92
SODEPAX. See Joint Committee on Society, Development and Peace
Sofia (queen of Spain), 217
Somavia, Juan, 255n71
Southern Development Bancorporation, 208
South Korea. See Korea, Republic of (South Korea)
Soviet Union, 77
Speth, James Gustave, 218
Spivak, Gayatri, 158
Sri Lanka, 152
Standing, Guy, 75
State, US Department of, 108–9
Staudt, Kathleen, 114, 122
Stegall, Lael, 164
Steichen, Edward, 30
Stevenson, Adlai, 22–23
Stewart, Frances, 72, 191–92
Stockman, David A., 161
Stoler, Ann Laura, 120

Streeten, Paul: basic needs strategy for the World Bank, creation and promotion of, 72–76; international tax, support for, 85; UNDP's Human Development Report, development of, 192; women as more responsible than men in allocating family income, argument for, 176
Strong, Maurice, 68, 85–86, 258n102
structural adjustment loans, 6, 184–93
Sudan: Ford Foundation support for a small businesses project in, 172; women in, NGO projects targeting, 142
Sussex, University of: Institute of Development Studies (see Institute of Development Studies); negotiations on the NIEO, urging of economists for, 63
Swanirvar, 203
Swaziland: pig-raising project for women funded by USAID in, 151; training of poor women as entrepreneurs, 156; women's need to support themselves, reasons for, 157
Sweden: Dag Hammarskjöld Foundation (see Dag Hammarskjöld Foundation); as donor nation, 77; Grameen Bank, support for, 202; SEWA, support for, 197; women included in development programs, 107; Women's World Banking, support for, 198

Taiwan (Republic of China), 91
Tanzania: project to replicate the Grameen Bank in, 207; USAID, funding accepted from, 75–76. See also Nyerere, Julius K.
taxation, international. See international taxation
Tendler, Judith, 178–79
Thailand, 172
Thant, U, 22
Thatcher, Margaret, 4, 92
Third World First, 33
Third World Forum, 73, 188
Thornton, Thomas, 84
Thorsson, Inga, 107
Tierney, John, 222

Times of India: coverage of the International Microcredit Summit (1997), 219; "Death by Microcredit," 223
Tinbergen, Jan, 71, 85
Tinker, Irene: conflicts between scholarly and applied researchers, recognition of, 120; International Center for Research on Women, establishment of, 113–14; on the lobbying for the Percy amendment, 111; Mexico City seminar facilitated by, 116; at the State Department meeting that helped launch the Percy Amendment, 108–9; at the State Department meeting that helped launch the WID movement, 263n27; women as heads of households, poverty and, 130
Tobin, James, 258n99
Togo, 151
Transnational Institute, 62, 188
Treasury, US Department of: Bradley Plan, rejection of, 190; the "Washington consensus" and, 187
trickle-down economics, rejection of: in the basic needs approach, 66; by development experts, 36–41, 51, 226; emphasis on the informal economy and, 154; by foreign aid advocates, 17; by Haq and the World Bank, 46–47; by the WID movement, 125
Trickle Up Program, 158–60
Trudeau, Pierre, 91

UN Asian and Pacific Centre for Women and Development, 124
UN Economic Commission for Africa: African Training and Research Centre for Women established by, 123; Ford Foundation funding of women's programs of, 126; regional conference on WID sponsored by, 124; women's economic activities, growing interest in, 107; women's program launched in 1971, 112
UN Economic Commission for Latin America (ECLA), 57, 187
United Methodist Church, 198
United Nations Children's Emergency Fund (UNICEF), 190–92
United Nations Conference on the Human Environment, 69
United Nations Conference on Trade and Development (UNCTAD), 42–43, 57, 68
United Nations Development Programme (UNDP): Consultative Group to Assist the Poorest (CGAP), 217; *Guidelines on the Integration of Women in Development* (1977), 123; *Human Development Report*, 192; *Integration of Women in Development: Why, When, How* (Boserup and Liljencrantz), 108; *Rural Women's Participation in Development* (1980), 123; Trickle Up Program, financial backing of, 158; Women's World Banking, support of, 198
United Nations Environment Programme (UNEP), 68–69, 86, 253n56
United Nations Office for Emergency Operations in Africa, 142
United Nations Office of Technical Cooperation, 156
United Nations (UN): *Attack on World Poverty and Unemployment*, 37; automatic contributions for development in the global South, endorsement of, 86; Bangladesh, emergency relief operations in, 200; Carter's speech on basic needs, 79; Commission on Social Development, 107; Commission on the Status of Women, 107; Declaration of the Establishment of a New International Economic Order (1974), 55–56 (*see also* New International Economic Order (NIEO)); "development decade," the 1960s as, 15–16; General Assembly, adoption of NIEO in, 117; General Assembly, shifting balance of power in, 42–43, 56–57; Group of 77 (G-77) formed in, 42, 57; International Women's Year conference (1975), 108, 196–97; "International Year of Microcredit" (2005), proclamation of, 222; Interregional Meeting of Experts on the Integration of Women in Development, 107; NGOs, collaboration with, 169; small-scale urban enterprise

United Nations (UN) (*continued*)
projects pursued by, 155; Sustainable
Development Goals, poverty and, 229;
WCC proposal, endorsement of, 31;
women in development, expanded
commitment to, 123; World Conference on Women (1985), 166, 173–74;
World Food Conference, 78; World
Population Conference (1974), 104
United States: celebrity fundraising in,
141; credit, legislation guaranteeing
access to, 198–99; global debt burden,
legislation addressing, 189–90; hunger
and poverty, walkathons addressing,
34–36; inflation and the "Volcker
shock" of 1979 in, 185; the Mexican
debt bailout by, 186; microcredit in,
207–8; New International Economic
Order, reactions to, 58–60, 64–66;
Peace Corps, WID and, 124 (*see also*
Peace Corps); philanthropic loan
societies in, 195; third world distrust
of, 42; the World Bank and, 43 (*see also*
World Bank); Yunus in, 204–8, 222
United States Agency for International
Development (USAID): basic needs
approach backed by, 80–81, 97; Bureau
for Private Enterprise, 162; "business
development," eclipse of "income generation" by, 164–65; changing priorities
of, 153; Consultative Group to Assist
the Poorest (CGAP), 217; criticism of,
80–81; establishment of, 15; ILO's Basic
Needs Strategy, reservations about,
253n53; impoverished women overseas, bringing sanitation and American
home economics to, 100–101; International Conference on Microenterprise
Development (1988), hosting of, 183;
Micro and Small Enterprise Development Program, 216; microcredit,
limitations of, 214–15; microcredit, psychological gains from, 213; microcredit,
spending on, 216, 226; microcredit legislation, objections to, 207; microcredit
program, focus on women in, 208–9;
Microenterprise Initiative, 216; New
Directions programs, implementation

of, 41–42, 48, 149; New Directions
programs, obstacles to, 50–51; Nixon's
opinion of, 41; nongovernmental
organizations (NGOs), grants for,
149; nongovernmental organizations
(NGOs), the Reagan administration and, 162–70; nongovernmental
organizations (NGOs), working with,
146–49; the OEF and, 165–67; Office
for Private and Voluntary Cooperation,
146; Operation Phoenix, funds funneled to, 29; Percy Amendment, initial
struggle to implement, 111–13; Percy
Amendment, mandate to integrate
women into development projects
from, 149–50; population: funding for
family planning, 103; population: lowering of fertility and economic development, 131; private enterprise approach
to foreign aid, McPherson and, 161–63;
privatization of antipoverty projects,
143–44; Program for Investment in
the Small Capital Enterprise Sector
(PISCES) project, 155–57, 193–94;
SEWA, report on, 196–97; "tying" of
funds spent by, 82; Upper Volta project,
97, 135–37; WID section (*see* USAID
Women in Development (WID)
section); women as key resource in
alleviating food crisis in Africa, report
on, 176; women as preferred allocator
of family income, report stating, 176;
Women's Entrepreneurship Development Program, 203; Women's World
Banking, support for, 198
Upper Volta (Burkina Faso) project, 97,
135–37
Ure, James "Midge," 140–41
USAID. *See* United States Agency for
International Development (USAID)
USAID Women in Development (WID)
section: credit programs for women
in the global South, establishment of,
199; cultural imperialism, response
to charges of, 132–35; establishment
and early years of, 113–16; feminists in
disguise at, 134; the Ford Foundation
and, 128; Goddard as coordinator of,

164; Kenya, tensions over research in, 119; Sierra Leone conference funded by, 133; success stories in congressional testimony, 135–36; suspicions directed at, 120, 122; tensions between scholarly and applied perspectives, 121; Wellesley conference, sponsorship of, 117–19; WID projects of NGOs, funding of, 150–53; "Women-Headed Households: The Ignored Factor in Development Planning" (Buvinic and Youssef), funding of, 130

USA (United Support of Artists) for Africa, 141–42

US foreign aid: basic needs approach, Carter administration support for, 66, 79–81 (*see also* Carter, Jimmy); basic needs approach, Ford administration opposition to, 70; basic needs approach to the grassroots poor, 55 (*see also* basic needs approach to global poverty); bilateral, problems with, 42; dependency theory and leftist attacks on, 27; economic development, hopes for, 3; free-market policies of, GAD's rejection of, 171; global poverty, calls to extend war on poverty to, 29–30; global poverty and, 17–18; implementation of (*see* United States Agency for International Development (USAID)); level of commitment to, 16–17, 21, 50, 77; microcredit as part of, 207–16; modernization theory, foreign aid based on, 3, 6–7, 15–16, 36; multilateral, emerging preference for, 42; Myrdal's critique of, 34; New Directions mandate (*see* New Directions mandate); Nixon proposals and policy, assaults on, 28–29; overview of, 1970s–1980s, 4–6, 9; political, economic, and humanitarian arguments for, 19–21; population control and, 103–4; public opinion regarding, 16–17, 79–80; Reaganomics and, 160–70; self-interest in, 40–41; spending on development assistance in 1963 and 1973, 17; "tying" policy, 20, 34, 41, 82–83; the WID movement and,

98–99, 108–10 (*see also* Percy Amendment; women in development (WID) movement); WID/Percy amendment seen as American imperialism/neocolonialism, 116–22

US International Development Finance Corporation, 144

US National Businesswomen's Committee, 166

Vajrathon, Mallica, 118

Vance, Cyrus, 64–65, 79

Vietnam War, 145

Village Voice: Harrington's impact, 1

Volcker, Paul, 185

"Volcker shock" of 1979, 185

Wachtel, Howard M., 188

Waldheim, Kurt, 92

Wall Street Journal: Bauer piece opposing foreign aid, 28; New International Economic Order, opposition to, 59; *Populorum Progressio*, reaction to, 31

Walmart, 208, 222–23

Walsh, Michaela, 197–99

Ward, Barbara: "An Ecumenical Concern for World Poverty," 30; background information on, 22–23; Brandt Commission, brainchild of, 87; Carter's plans, optimism regarding, 65; changes in development ideas of the early 1970s, outline of, 51–52; Christian initiatives addressing global poverty, support for, 30–33; Cocoyoc symposium, chair of, 68–69; congressional breakfast meeting with, 38; on the deadlock over the new economic order, 64; death of, 92; Harrington, comparison with, 53–54; heckled after a speech, 27; as "influencer," 7; international tax, support for, 85–86; McNamara, as influence on, 45; "new abolitionists," call for, 33; *Only One Earth: The Care and Maintenance of a Small Planet*, 68–69; photo of, 24; *The Rich Nations and the Poor Nations*, 22–23; weekend meeting in 1967 organized by, 18

War on Poverty, 7, 29–30, 34

Washington Post: Carter administration's retreat on development assistance, 82; Haq, description of, 73; Pearson report, editorial on, 21; *Populorum Progressio,* reaction to, 31; Stockman's proposed cuts in foreign aid, report on reaction to, 161; on US standing in the Third World early in the Carter administration, 65

Waters, Maxine, 166

"We Are the World" (Ritchie and Jackson), 141

welfare, microcredit distinguished from, 210–11

Wellesley College WID conference, 117–19, 121

WEP. *See* World Employment Programme

Wolfe, Tom, 4

Wolfensohn, James, 218

women: antipoverty efforts and changing image of in the 1970s and 1980s, 2–3; as entrepreneurs in the informal economy, 155–60, 211–12; the Grameen Bank and, 203; impoverished, alternative perspectives on, 177; as key suppliers of basic needs, 176–78; microcredit and, 195–200, 208–16; modernization and, 99–102, 104; NGO focus on, 142–44; the population control movement and, 102–4. *See also* feminism/feminists; gender

"Women: The Key to Ending Hunger" (Snyder), 176–77

women and development (WAD), 170, 173–74, 176–77

women in development (WID) movement: criticisms of, 131–35, 171; divisions within, 116–22; fish-processing in Senegal, funds for, 142; the Ford Foundation and, 126–29 (*see also* Ford Foundation); launched in the US government, 108–10; mainstream appeal of, 129–31; Mexico City seminar, 116; microcredit, interest in (*see* Grameen Bank; microcredit); nongovernmental organizations (NGOs) and, 149–53 (*see also* nongovernmental organizations

(NGOs)); origin and evolution of, 97–99, 104–8; the Percy Amendment and (*see* Percy Amendment); the Reagan administration and, 163–68; of the 1980s, arguments made by advocates of, 174, 176–77; success stories and impact of, 135–39; the Upper Volta project and, 97, 135–37; Wellesley College conference, 117–19, 121; WID-WAD-GAD chronology of, 170–78; the World Bank and, 125–26; worldwide expansion of, 123–25

Women's World Banking (WWB), 197–99, 203, 208, 216

Woods, George D., 16, 18–19, 22–23

Working Women's Forum of Madras, 156, 172, 178

World Bank: "absolute poverty," call for an end to, 2; American economic interests and, 82–83; antipoverty strategy, limitations of, 48–49, 76; antipoverty strategy, McNamara's establishment of, 43–48; antipoverty strategy, obstacles to, 50–51; antipoverty strategy, revival of, 193; basic needs approach and, 55, 67, 71–75, 77, 138–39 (*see also* basic needs approach to global poverty); Brandt Commission as independent from, 88; campaigns against global poverty, joining, 17; Consultative Group to Assist the Poorest (CGAP), 217; free-market policies of, GAD's rejection of, 171; funding for the Columbia conference from, 23; goal of reducing extreme poverty by 2030, 229; governing of, call for better representation of the global South in, 89; International Conference on Microenterprise Development (1988), hosting of, 183; major powers' insistence on running the world economy through, 92; microcredit promoted by, 217; microfinance industry, size of in 2015, 225–26; New International Economic Order and, 60, 76; NGO Committee, impact of structural adjustment loans addressed by, 189; NGOs, collaboration with, 169; people living in extreme poverty in 2015, estimate of, 229; population control programs, backing of, 103; *Redistribution with Growth*, 47; scrutiny of, 81; small-scale urban enterprise projects pursued by, 155; structural adjustment loans/policies of, 6, 186–93, 227; US dominance of, 43; the "Washington consensus" and, 187; WID and, 125–26, 138–39, 174, 211; Yunus's criticism of, 201. *See also* Haq, Mahbub ul; McNamara, Robert; Streeten, Paul

World Conference on Church and Society (1966), 31

World Council of Churches (WCC), 31–32, 34

World Development: informal sector, special issue on, 155; "What Ever Happened to Poverty Alleviation?" (Tendler), 178; women, special issue on, 174

World Employment Programme (WEP), 37, 154

World Hunger and Moral Obligation, 79

World Hunger Year, 78

World Relief, 216

World Vision, 216

WWB. *See* Women's World Banking

Young, Andrew, 65

Young Women's Christian Association, 111

Youssef, Nadia H., 130

Yudelman, Montague, 125–26, 267n79

Yudelman, Sally Watters, 267n79

Yunus, Muhammad: "discipline" of repaying debts as beneficial to poor women, 211; educational and career background of, 200; entrepreneurial activities of, 221; exchange with Akula at the Clinton Global Initiative, 224; as fundraiser, 202; Germain and, 203; Grameen Bank, establishment of, 202; as "influencer," 7; as international celebrity, 217; at the International Conference on Microenterprise Development (1988), 183; at the International Microcredit Summit (1997), 218–19; microcredit as "business," not welfare, 210; Nobel Peace Prize awarded to, 221–22; non-economic benefits of microcredit, 213–14; politics of, 201–2; rural development project leading to the Grameen Bank Project, 201–2; selling of microcredit and the Grameen Bank by, 204–8; "social business," call for, 222; at the "State of the World" forum (1996), 217; in the United States, 204–8, 222; women, learning to make loans to, 203; women as preferred microcredit borrowers, 209–10; on the World Bank, 201, 217

Zablocki, Clement J., 38

Zambia, 152

Zeidenstein, George, 128

Zeidenstein, Sondra, 128

Zimbabwe, 165

A NOTE ON THE TYPE

———————

THIS BOOK has been composed in Miller, a Scotch Roman typeface designed by Matthew Carter and first released by Font Bureau in 1997. It resembles Monticello, the typeface developed for The Papers of Thomas Jefferson in the 1940s by C. H. Griffith and P. J. Conkwright and reinterpreted in digital form by Carter in 2003.

Pleasant Jefferson ("P. J.") Conkwright (1905–1986) was Typographer at Princeton University Press from 1939 to 1970. He was an acclaimed book designer and AIGA Medalist.